PIONEERS OF FINANCIAL ECONOMICS

To Franck and Franky. Thanks for all the help.
And to TK for being such a gem.

Pioneers of Financial Economics: Volume 1

Contributions Prior to Irving Fisher

Edited by
Geoffrey Poitras

Simon Fraser University, Canada

Edward Elgar
Cheltenham, UK • Northampton, MA, USA

Published by
Edward Elgar Publishing Limited
The Lypiatts
15 Lansdown Road
Cheltenham
Glos GL50 2JA
UK

Edward Elgar Publishing, Inc.
136 West Street
Suite 202
Northampton
Massachusetts 01060
USA

A catalogue record for this book
is available from the British Library

ISBN-13: 978 1 84542 381 0
ISBN-10: 1 84542 381 X

Typeset by Manton Typesetters, Louth, Lincolnshire, UK.

Contents

Figures

Tables

Contributors

Jeff d'Avignon, FINCAD Corporation, 13450 102nd Ave, Suite 1750, Surrey, British Columbia, Canada

Professor Hichem Ben-El-Mechaiekh, Mathematics Department, Brock University, 500 Glenridge Ave, St Catherines, Ontario, Canada

Professor Yuri Biondi, University of St Etienne, IUT – GEA, 28, Av. Léon Jouhaux, F–42023 St Etienne cedex 02, France

Professor José Luís Cardoso, Department of Economics, Institute of Economics and Business Administration, Technical University of Lisbon, Lisbon, Portugal

Professor J.G. van Dillen, (formerly) University of Utrecht, 3508 TC Utrecht, The Netherlands

Professor Robert W. Dimand, Department of Economics, Brock University, 500 Glenridge Ave, St Catharines, Ontario, Canada

Wolfgang Hafner, Economic historian and author, Windisch, Switzerland

Professor Franck Jovanovic, LEO, Department of Economics, University of Orleans, Rue de Blois, BP 6739, 45067 Orleans cedex 2, France

Asha Majithia, New Jersey, USA, asha.nomadlife.org

Professor Antoin E. Murphy, Department of Economics, Trinity College Dublin, Dublin 2, Ireland

Professor Geoffrey Poitras, Faculty of Business, Simon Fraser University, Burnaby, British Columbia, Canada

Professor Alex Preda, Department of Sociology, School of Social and Political Studies, University of Edinburgh, Edinburgh, Scotland, United Kingdom

Professor Edith Dudley Sylla, Department of History, North Carolina State University, 161 Harrelson Hall, Campus Box 8108, Raleigh, NC USA

Professor Heinz Zimmermann, Department of Finance, Wirtschaftswissenschaftliches Zentrum WWZ, Universität Basel, Holbeinstrasse 12, CH-4051 Basel Switzerland

Acknowledgements

The author and publisher wish to thank the following, who have kindly given their permission for the use of copyright material:

Cambridge University Press for allowing publication of a paper building on José Luís Cardoso (2002), '*Confusion de confusiones*: ethics and options on 17th century stock exchange markets', *Financial History Review*, **9**, 109–23.

Duke University Press for allowing publication of a paper that is a much expanded version of Edith Dudley Sylla (2003), 'Business Ethics, Commercial Mathematics and the Origins of Mathematical Probability', *History of Political Economy*, **35**, 309–37.

Société Mathématique de France for allowing publication of the English translation of a paper by Yuri Biondi on Duvillard originally published in 2003 in French in the *Revue d'Histoire des Mathématiques*, **9**, 81–125.

Introduction

Geoffrey Poitras

The origins of financial economics?

A book aiming to identify the 'pioneers' in a subject requires the boundaries of that subject to be defined. Where the subject is financial economics, identifying these boundaries is somewhat elusive. Financial economics is a subject that encompasses disciplines with disparate orientations. In particular, financial economics can be defined as that body of knowledge which lies in the intersection between the subjects of finance and economics. Being a core component of the modern business school curriculum, finance is, seemingly, concerned with practical solutions to problems arising in financial markets. The types of questions to be addressed in finance are: what is a fair price for this security? or, what is the appropriate level of dividend for a corporation to pay out? The more disparate subject of economics has a decidedly greater concern with theoretical solutions. Examples of questions arising in economics include: is this solution Pareto optimal? and, are there multiple equilibria? Economists often perceive financial economics to be a subject where the techniques of economic science are applied to financial topics. The view from finance perceives financial economics to be that area of finance which uses theoretical techniques borrowed from economics. The coverage involved in the different possible specifications is far from identical.

One of the oddities of modern intellectual history is the development of sharp distinctions between closely related subjects. Economics, for example, has a well-developed body of theory that has decided similarities to parts of mathematics, engineering, actuarial science and other subjects.[1] Yet studies of the historical development of economics typically identify only those ideas that relate directly to economic content. Little attention is given to the role that developments in other subjects may have contributed to these ideas. There are numerous examples where advances outside economics that led to progress in modern economics have gone unrecognized. For example, consider the early twentieth-century developments in mathematical statistics that contributed to the emergence of econometrics. Is there any credible source that considers R.A. Fisher or Karl Pearson to be an important figure in the history of economics?

In modern business studies, this predilection to make sharp distinctions between closely related subjects has contributed to the emergence of a number of new disciplines such as management information systems, organizational studies and international business. This emergence of new disciplines has been accompanied by a transformation in the content of traditional business disciplines. In particular, where the subject of finance was once concerned primarily with accounting, legal and institutional content, the subject now focuses on theoretical subjects such as the capital asset pricing model, the efficient markets hypothesis and the Black–Scholes option pricing model (for example, Poitras, 2005, sec. 2.4; Haugen, 1999). Financial statement analysis and securities law have been replaced by mean-variance optimization models and stochastic process theory. In effect, in the contemporary business school curriculum the traditional subject of finance has been transformed into 'modern finance', a subject that can be approximately identified with financial economics.

Examining the content of modern finance, a number of intellectual threads can be found to sustain the subject. These threads include: application of the frequentist interpretation of probability to the valuation of securities; the use of stochastic optimization techniques to model financial decision problems; acceptance of the random walk model of security prices and the associated efficient markets hypothesis; and the adoption of positivism as a philosophical approach to understanding financial phenomena. Much of the content of this volume is concerned with exploring the origins of these topics. However, concentration solely on the early pioneers who contributed to the development of modern finance would tacitly accept the ascendency of this methodological approach to financial economics. To counter this potential bias, early pioneers who contributed to the traditional finance component of financial economics have also been included. This involves examining certain historical figures in early securities markets, such as Isaac Le Maire and John Law.

The search for pioneers of financial economics

The starting point for the history of economic analysis, the beginning of classical economics, is usually identified with Adam Smith (1723–90). The *Wealth of Nations* is justly recognized as the first book to develop a comprehensive and cohesive body of theory that was substantively distinct from other related subjects. Contributors prior to Smith are typically categorized as 'precursors of Adam Smith' or 'pre-Smithian economists' or 'pre-classical economists'. Yet, as demonstrated in Poitras (2000), in key areas of relevance to financial economics, there was an impressive and substantive body of knowledge that had been developed well before Smith. Some of this knowledge, such as the early mercantilist writings on foreign exchange markets, was unjustly discredited by Smith. Other areas, such as the pricing of aleatory contracts, are not examined by Smith. Still other elements of interest to financial economics, such as joint stocks, sinking funds and methods of government financing, receive only cursory coverage in the *Wealth of Nations*.

The roots of financial economics stretch back to antiquity. The valuation of financial transactions, such as determining payment on a loan or distributing profits from a partnership, is so ancient that any search for pioneers would be fruitless. A less ambitious beginning is required. Poitras (2000) uses the late fifteenth century as a starting point for the early history. By this time, elements of financial economics were being widely disseminated among the merchant classes in the commercial arithmetic that formed the core of the reckoning school curriculum. From this point until the appearance of the *Wealth of Nations*, the founding work of classical political economy, financial economics underwent a dramatic transformation. By the latter half of the eighteenth century, sophisticated methods for pricing contingent claims such as life annuities had been developed and applied to the establishment of life insurance and pension funds. Absent a watershed historical figure sufficient to provide a well-defined beginning for financial economics, this book selects the earliest pioneers from the contributors who developed these pricing methods.

The search for 'pioneers of financial economics' contained in this book places the origins of financial economics well outside the conventional boundaries of the history of economic thought. These differences extend to the philosophical foundations underlying the various subjects that have contributed to financial economics. As illustrated in the examination of Jacob Bernoulli (1654–1705) by Edith Sylla in Chapter 1, while the roots of financial economics can be traced to the commercial arithmetic taught in the Renaissance reckoning schools, the identification of pioneers requires more substantive contributions.[2] Before the Enlightenment, many essential problems in financial economics posed ethical and theological, as well as analytical, difficulties. For example, determining the fair price of a sequence of future cash flows involved concepts of interest, which were affected by usury considerations. Other examples involved setting a price for risk or determining fair compensation for a contingent claim, both of which involved the ethics of gambling. All this complicates the task of constructing an early history of financial economics and identifying the pioneers.

Of the possible starting dates, this volume selects the second half of the seventeenth century. While this starting date could be moved back some centuries to facilitate the inclusion of figures such as Fra Luca Pacioli, Nicholas Chuquet, Simon Stevin, Thomas Gresham and Gerard de Malynes, as in Poitras (2000), the latter half of the seventeenth century marks the the emergence of modern notions of probability that form the basis of contingent claims analysis. Following on the development of the concept of expected value by Christian Huygens (1620–99), in 1671 the Dutchman Jan de Witt (1625–72) provided the first actuarially sound solution for the value of a life annuity. In addition to intellectual contributions, the seventeenth century also featured significant institutional developments. In particular, there is the emergence of trading in joint stocks, starting with trading of the shares in the Dutch East India Company in 1602. As reflected in Joseph de la Vega's *Confusion de confusiones* (1688), securities markets had achieved a remarkable level of sophistication by the end of the seventeenth century.

Contents of this volume

The three chapters contained in Part I of this volume deal with the historical and philosophical background for the early history of financial economics. Three seventeenth-century historical figures are featured: Jacob Bernoulli, Isaac Le Maire and Joseph de la Vega. In Chapter 1, Sylla observes of Jacob Bernoulli: 'Like Moses, Bernoulli had seen the promised land – financial economics, in this case – but he did not live to enter it.' Bernoulli's contributions to mathematics and probability theory serve as a useful demarcation point between the intellectual tradition constrained by scholastic and humanistic considerations, and the modern insights generated during the Enlightenment. Sylla admirably examines the roots of probability theory contained in Bernoulli's posthumously published *Ars Conjectandi* (1713), stretching the time-line back to Aristotelean ethics. The foundations for Christiaan Huygens's approach to mathematical expectation are grounded in Renaissance commercial arithmetic and issues of fairness and justice. While Bernoulli was writing around the turn of the eighteenth century, significant earlier contributions to financial economics were unfamiliar to him. In particular, though he was aware of the work of Jan de Witt on life annuity valuation, he was not able to obtain copies of de Witt's contribution. Halley's work on life annuities was unknown to him. As such, Jacob Bernoulli is a more than fitting individual to lay the intellectual foundation for searching out the early pioneers of financial economics.

Chapter 2 examines the institutional origin of trading in common stocks. This trade can be traced to the transactions in shares of the Dutch East India Company (VOC) on the Amsterdam Exchange that began with the founding of the company in 1602. There are two important secondary sources for this early trading: van Dillen (1930), which is written in Dutch and also includes numerous primary documents, such as the text of legal presentations concerning the valuation of VOC shares; and van Dillen (1935), in French, which summarizes much of the material in van Dillen (1930). While providing considerable detail about early stock trading, the discussion in these two sources revolves around the activities of Isaac Le Maire (1559–1624), the first of a long line of stock operators that stretches into modern times. After an introductory overview section, Chapter 2 offers an English translation of van Dillen (1935). In addition to providing details of Le Maire's role in the first stock market manipulation, the chapter also contains a wealth of detail about the workings of early securities markets and the characters that populated them.

By the end of the seventeenth century, stock trading on the Amsterdam Exchange had reached a strikingly modern state of development. Much of what is known about these activities is gleaned from Joseph de la Vega's descriptive insights into the Amsterdam Bourse in the 1680s contained in the *Confusion de confusiones* (1688). Chapter 3 provides a telling examination of this source by José Luís Cardoso. Only Thomas Mortimer and, possibly, Isaac de Pinto in the eighteenth century come close to the standard of descriptive analysis set by de la Vega in *Confusion.* While a careful examination of the primary source fairly indicates that Vega did not fully understand the details of certain transactions that were being conducted, such as arbitrage transactions involving derivative securities, Vega does demonstrate an active appreciation of the trading process, as well as excellent intuition about the impact of specific fundamentals on the value of joint stocks. Cardoso performs the invaluable task of examining the original of this rare source that is only currently available in English in a much-abridged form – with 40 of a total of 391 pages reproduced.

Part II of this volume details the contributions of a select group of important eighteenth-century pioneers of financial economics. While a number of noteworthy pioneers are not included – for example Richard Price (1723–91) and Thomas Mortimer (1730–1810) – the pioneers that are included definitely deserve the distinction. Chapter 4 details the contributions of those pioneers who developed the valuation models for pricing life annuities. After a review of the 1671 contribution of Jan de Witt and an assessment of the connection to the results of Nicholas Bernoulli (1695–1726), the solution for the single life annuity value given by Edmond Halley (1656–1742) is examined. Following Poitras (2000, ch. 6), de Witt deserves recognition for making the seminal contribution of using discounted expected value to price the life annuity. However, the result was developed in a public policy context and was not widely distributed. Halley provides a more rigorous theoretical solution to the valuation problem, as well as solving for annuity prices using an empirically determined life table. Halley also provides an ingenious geometric solution for the value of a joint life annuity for three lives. This chapter also considers the most complete statement of the analytical solution for pricing various types of joint life annuities by Abraham de Moivre (1667–1754) and Thomas Simpson (1710–61). As a pioneer of financial economics, de Moivre was the first to substantively develop important mathematical techniques, such as series solutions, for the pricing of complicated fixed income securities.

Certain pioneers in the early history are important, not so much for a contribution to the theory of financial economics, but, rather, for a contribution to the history of financial markets. One such figure is John Law (1671–1729), the subject of Chapter 5. This chapter is contributed by Antoin E. Murphy, who is not only the leading authority on John Law and the Mississippi scheme, but also on Richard Cantillon (169?–1734), another important figure of the period. Murphy (1986) on Cantillon and Murphy (1997) on John Law are outstanding books that are required reading for all those interested in the history of financial economics. Chapter 5 provides a brief overview of ideas contained in Murphy (1997). While the conventional history of economic thought recognizes John Law for his contributions to monetary economics, Law's importance as a pioneer of financial economics stems from his prime mover status in the Mississippi scheme. Whatever the misguided theories that underpinned the scheme, this event qualifies as one of the most remarkable in recorded financial history. A Scotsman, a fugitive from British justice, was able to assume control over the financial policies of the French government, perpetrating one of the most fantastic 'schemes' of all time. The scheme itself produced a number of financial innovations, including the use of options to facilitate debt management objectives.

Not all the pioneers selected in this volume have the historical stature of Edmond Halley or John Law. Intellectual history is replete with examples of individuals making contributions that were seminal in content but, by and large, did not receive the corresponding recognition and attention. Financial economics is no exception. Based on a translation of Biondi (2003, in French), Chapter 6 examines such an individual, Emmanuel-Etienne Duvillard (1755–1832). Historically, Duvillard's *Recherches sur les rentes* (1787) was concerned with the construction of a sinking fund for the large outstanding amount of life annuities issued by the French government. While Duvillard has received some modern attention, this chapter illustrates that modern sources such as Baumol and Goldfeld (1968) contain considerable confusion about the substance of Duvillard's contributions. As Biondi demonstrates, Duvillard made two pioneering contributions to the development of financial economics: the use of calculus to solve for an optimal lending period; and identification of the modified internal rate of return where variations in the reinvestment rate over time are incorporated into the analysis.

Compared with studies on the contributions to financial economics made during the eighteenth century, relatively little has been written about the nineteenth century. Only recently has it been established that the roots of notions central to modern financial economics – such as the random walk hypothesis and the associated 'science of the stock market' – can be traced to the latter half of the nineteenth century when French writers such as Jules Regnault (1834–94) and Henri Lefèvre (1827–85) extended the positivist program of Auguste Comte (1798–1857) to financial markets. Part III of this volume details these contributions. In Chapter 7, Alex Preda examines the historical and intellectual developments that laid the foundation for the modern theory of efficient markets. Written from the perspective of a sociologist of science, Preda provides a useful examination of the cognitive and cultural background represented by popular efforts to transform financial investing into a science. This involved altering the public perception that financial securities were investments rather than gambling. The distinction between vernacular and academic economics that is used to motivate the discussion is as applicable to modern financial economics as to developments in the nineteenth century, presenting a fascinating area for future research.

In Chapters 8 and 9, Franck Jovanovic provides two path-breaking studies that recognize the seminal contributions to the nineteenth-century 'science of financial investments' made by Henri Lefèvre and Jules Regnault. The remarkable amount of attention given to the 1900 thesis of Louis Bachelier (1870–1946) by modern writers has presented a quandary to historians of financial economics. While Bachelier's thesis has been hailed as path-breaking by modern pundits, the thesis was not as well received at the time it was initially presented. Modern writers have attributed this to Bachelier being too far ahead of his times. These two studies by Jovanovic demonstrate that this judgement is misplaced. Not only did Bachelier borrow the option expiration diagrams used in the thesis from Lefèvre without attribution, but the notion of applying stochastic process theory to price differences to solve for option prices was a central element in Regnault's *Calcul des chances et philosophie de la bourse* (1863). In this light, instead of being a masterpiece of intellectual history that was far ahead of its time, Bachelier's thesis appears to have been justly treated as part of a continuum of contributions.

Part IV of this volume continues with the themes in Part III, moving the time frame into the early twentieth century. Given the remarkable reverence accorded to Louis Bachelier by modern pundits, a volume on pioneers of financial economics prior to Irving Fisher would be woefully incomplete without a detailed and scholarly examination of the work of this pioneer. In Chapter 10, this task is admirably accomplished by the team of Robert W. Dimand and Hichem Ben-El-Mechaiekh. The argument advanced in Chapters 8 and 9 is that, in areas of relevance to financial economics, the modern view of Bachelier as a path-breaking pioneer is misplaced. Bachelier was building on the foundation of scientific financial economics constructed by the likes of Regnault and Lefèvre. While Chapter 10 does lay out the evidence for the modern position supporting the importance of Bachelier, the presentation is even-handed and well reasoned. Numerous modern accolades on Bachelier are provided, recognizing not only contributions to option pricing theory and speculation, but also to the theory of diffusion processes and, in particular, Brownian motion. The history of Bachelier's academic career is critically examined, recognizing the views of, among others, Poincaré, Lévy, Kolmogorov and Keynes. Even if there is debate about Bachelier's pioneering role in financial economics, Chapter 10 demonstrates that Bachelier definitely was a pioneer in the realm of probability theory and stochastic processes. By using these results for the analysis of option prices, Bachelier was also a pioneer in the realm of mathematical finance.

Bachelier rose to current prominence in modern financial economics primarily from the connection to both option pricing theory and the efficient markets hypothesis. Chapter 9 on Regnault brings the 'originality' of Bachelier's contribution to the efficient markets hypothesis into question. In a seminal contribution detailing the fascinating and insightful work on option pricing by Vincenz Bronzin that appeared in 1908, Heinz Zimmermann and Wolfgang Hafner raise serious questions about the claim to primacy for Bachelier in the area of option pricing. As observed in Chapter 10, the 'rediscovery' of Bachelier by Leonard Savage and Paul Samuelson in the mid-1950s was somewhat haphazard. Chapter 11 shows that a more systematic examination of the historical record has revealed Bachelier 'was not the only one who was working successfully on option pricing at the beginning of the twentieth century'. Working in German, it is reasonably certain that Bronzin developed his results on option pricing independently of Bachelier. In addition, based on the analysis in Chapter 11, it appears that Bronzin produced a more rigorous treatment of the subject. While Bachelier produced his doctoral thesis somewhat earlier, a more developed treatment of the subject by a professor and actuary carries considerably more academic weight. Based on the research in Parts III and IV, the modern reverence accorded to Bachelier for his founding role in modern financial economics is debatable.

Notes

1. One interesting study of such distinctions is Ekelund and Hebert (1999), which examines the historical connection between microeconomic theory and engineering. As their title suggests, Ekelund and Hebert are concerned with exploring the mythology surrounding the origins of microeconomics.
2. As was common in this era, a number of different variations of 'Jacob' Bernoulli were used. Jacob is also called Jakob (in German), Jacques (in French) and James (in English). Jacob is the name used on the title page of *Ars Conjectandi*. Jacob was the older brother of John (Johann) Bernoulli (1667–1748), also a prominent mathematician. Three sons of John Bernoulli also achieved prominence: Nicholas (1695–1726), Daniel (1700–82) and John (the younger) (1710–90). John the younger had two sons who were also prominent academics. The Bernoullis – perhaps more correctly called the Bernouillis – were originally of Dutch origin, driven from Holland by the Spanish persecutions, and finally settled at Basel in Switzerland.

References

Baumol, W. and M. Goldfeld (eds) (1968), *Precursors in Mathematical Economics: An Anthology*, ch.10: Duvillard de Durand, J.H.T.: *Recherches sur les rentes, les emprunts et remboursements*, Paris and Geneva, 1787, excerpts from p. 1–22, London: London School of Economics.
Biondi, Y. (2003), '*Les Recherches sur les Rentes* de Duvillard (1787) et *le Taux Interne de Rentabilité*', *Revue d'Histoire des Mathematique*, **9**: 81–103.
Ekelund, R. and R. Hebert (1999), *Secret Origins of Modern Microeconomics: Dupuit and the Engineers*, Chicago: University of Chicago Press.
Haugen, R. (1999), *The New Finance: The Case Against Efficient Markets* (2nd edn), Upper Saddle River, NJ: Prentice-Hall.
Murphy, A. (1986), *Richard Cantillon, Entrepreneur and Economist*, Oxford: Clarendon Press.
Murphy, A. (1997), *John Law, Economic Theorist and Policy-Maker*, Oxford: Clarendon Press.
Poitras, G. (2000), *The Early History of Financial Economics, 1478–1776*, Cheltenham, UK and Northampton, MA, USA: Edward Elgar.
Poitras, G. (2005), *Security Analysis and Investment Strategy*, Oxford: Blackwell.
van Dillen, J. (1930), 'Isaac Le Maire en de handel in actien der Oost-Indische Compagnie', *Economisch-Historisch Jaarboek*: 1–165.
van Dillen, J. (1935), 'Isaac le Maire et le commerce des actions de la Compaigne de Indes Orientales', *Revue d'Histoire Moderne*: 5–21, 121–37.

PART I

THE HISTORICAL AND PHILOSOPHICAL BACKGROUND

1 Commercial arithmetic, theology and the intellectual foundations of Jacob Bernoulli's *Art of Conjecturing*[1]

Edith Dudley Sylla

About the time that he became the Professor of Mathematics at the University of Basel in 1687 Jacob Bernoulli, the oldest of the famous Bernoulli family of mathematicians, conceived the idea of developing a new discipline, in which the sorts of mathematical methods that Christiaan Huygens had applied to games in his *On Reckoning in Games of Chance* (1657) could be applied to civil, moral and economic problems. At the time of his death in 1705, Bernoulli was still working on the manuscript of the book that would be published in 1713, still incomplete, as *The Art of Conjecturing* (*Ars Conjectandi*). At the very end of the book as he left it, Jacob Bernoulli had just finished proving what later came to be called the weak law of large numbers. If Bernoulli had completed his project, the book would have continued to show how the mathematics that Bernoulli had expounded in earlier sections of the book could be applied to the solution of civil, moral and political problems, for instance to the calculation of the value of annuities. For several years before his death, Bernoulli had been writing to Gottfried Wilhelm Leibniz asking him to supply a copy of Jan de Witt's pamphlet in Dutch on life and term annuities, but Leibniz had mislaid the copy previously in his possession. In the middle decades of the eighteenth century, Abraham de Moivre would develop the mathematics of annuities in ways that Bernoulli would certainly have admired and cheered on had he lived to see them. Like Moses, Bernoulli had seen the promised land – financial economics, in this case – but he did not live to enter it.

Ironically, although de Moivre's work was in a sense the fulfillment of a program that Jacob Bernoulli had set in motion, de Moivre established mathematical probability on a conceptual foundation different from that of Jacob Bernoulli and of the earlier writers on games of chance, in particular Christiaan Huygens. De Moivre's foundation led directly to the frequentist interpretation of probability. But the differing conceptual background of Jacob Bernoulli's work (and that of Huygens) is nevertheless of interest because it shows how mathematical probability was first built upon centuries of work in commercial arithmetic, which, via the work of Leonardo Pisano or Fibonacci, transmitted not only algebra but also Islamic business practices and inheritance law. At the same time, Bernoulli's thinking on the law of large numbers was founded in part on his theological training.

This chapter begins by discussing the background of Huygens's *On Reckoning in Games of Chance*, which formed the backbone of Part I of *The Art of Conjecturing* (and of the early sections of Part IV), in commercial arithmetic. Leaving Parts II and III of *The Art of Conjecturing*, which developed the theory of combinations and permutations and applied it to games of chance, to another time, the final part of the chapter examines the theological conceptions to which Bernoulli referred as a conceptual support for his proof of the law of large numbers.

1. The background of Part I in commercial arithmetic

In Christiaan Huygens's *On Reckoning in Games of Chance* (*De Ratiociniis in Ludo Aleae*) and in Jacob Bernoulli's notes on it published in Part I of *The Art of Conjecturing*, expectation is defined in a way that seems 'suspiciously circular' or 'somewhat obscure' from the point of view of modern mathematical probability theory (cf. Daston 1988b, pp. 24–6; Freudenthal 1980; Hald 1990, p. 69). Huygens wrote:

> I use the fundamental principle that a person's lot or expectation to obtain something in a game of luck should be judged to be worth as much as an amount such that, if he had it, he could arrive again at a like lot or expectation contending under equitable conditions. So, for example, if someone hides three similar coins in one hand and seven in the other, without my knowing which hand has which amount, and he offers to let me have the money in whichever hand I choose, then this offer is worth as much to me as if he gave me five coins. This is because, if I had five coins, then I could arrive again at a situation in which I had an equal expectation of getting three or seven coins, contending on equal terms [*aequo lusu*].[2]

Jacob Bernoulli (1713, p. 5) accepted this principle, but tried to make it clearer, saying:

> Here the author of this treatise is explaining the fundamental principle of the whole art ... Since it is very important that this principle be correctly understood, I will try to demonstrate it by reasoning which is more popular than the foregoing and more adapted to common comprehension. I posit only this as an axiom or definition: Anyone may expect, or should be said to expect, just as much as he will obtain without fail [*infallibiliter obtinebit*].

From a modern point of view, this choice of a foundational principle for expectation – and, in Bernoulli's case, for mathematical probability – seems counterintuitive. Where we would expect Huygens and Bernoulli to begin by considering probabilities of chance events, instead they begin with the amount adequate to buy a given position in a game or what a person will obtain without fail.

But how does a player in a game of chance obtain something without fail? If we examine the situations that Huygens and Bernoulli describe, it emerges that the infallibility involved is that of a fair business contract: when the players of a game take a Rawlsian approach to equity or justice and when they assume a veil of ignorance (Rawls 1971, pp. 11–12, 136–7), none of the players knows who will win or lose the game – then they have equal claims to the stake and this is what they will obtain without fail. In Bernoulli's terms, this is contractual or institutional necessity, as opposed to physical or hypothetical necessity:

> Something is necessary if it cannot not exist, now, in the future, or in the past. This necessity may be physical, hypothetical, or contractual. It is physically necessary that fire burn, that a triangle have three angles equal to two right angles, and that a full moon occurring when the moon is at a node be eclipsed. It is hypothetically necessary that something, while it exists or has existed, or while it is assumed to exist or have existed, cannot not exist or not have existed. It is necessary in this sense that Peter, whom I know and posit to be writing, is writing. Finally, there is the contractual or institutional necessity by which a gambler who has thrown a six is said to win necessarily if the players have agreed beforehand that a throw of a six wins. (Bernoulli 1713, p. 212)

It is this contractual or institutional necessity that explains Bernoulli's identification of expectation with what one may obtain without fail. If there were not a market in the sense of other players willing to engage in a fair game, a player could not infallibly arrange to be in the same position.

In following Huygens's path, Jan de Witt, in his *The Value of Life Annuities in Proportion to Redeemable Annuities*, explicitly used fair or equitable contracts to define expectation:

> I presuppose that the real value [*rechte waerdye*] of certain expectations or lots [*expectativen of kanssen*] of objects, of different value, should be estimated by that which we can obtain from as many like expectations or lots [*tot ghelijcke expectativen of kanssen*] dependent on one or several equitable contracts [*by een of meer esgale Contracten*].[3]

In *The Doctrine of Chances*, Abraham de Moivre explained the reasoning behind this approach as follows:

> For supposing that an Event may equally happen to any one of 5 different Persons, and that the Person to whom it happens should in consequence of it obtain the sum of 100 L. it is plain that the right which each of them in particular has upon the Sum expected is ⅕ of 100 L. which right is founded in this, that if the five Persons concerned in the happening of the Event, should agree not to stand the Chance of it, but to divide the Sum expected among themselves, then each of them must have ⅕ of 100 L. for his pretension. Now whether they agree to divide that sum equally among themselves, or rather chuse to stand the Chance of the Event, no one has thereby any advantage or disadvantage, since they are all upon an equal foot, and consequently each person's expectation is worth ⅕ of 100 L. (De Moivre 1756, p.3)

In the preface to his *Of the Laws of Chance, or, A Method of Calculation of the Hazards of Game* – which was more or less an English translation of Huygens's *On Reckoning in Games of Chance* – John Arbuthnot likewise wrote:

> Since Gaming is become a Trade, I think it fit the Adventurers should be upon the Square; and therefore in the Contrivance of Games there ought to be a strict Calculation made use of, that they mayn't put one Part in more probability to gain than another; and likewise, if a Man has a considerable Venture, he ought to be allow'd to withdraw his Money when he pleases, paying according to the Circumstances he is then in: and it were easie in most Games to make Tables, by the inspection of which, a Man might know what he was either to pay or receive, in any Circumstances you can imagin, it being convenient to save part of ones Money, rather than venture the loss of it all. (Arbuthnot 1692, f. A11r)

Thus equity among associates or partners rather than probabilities in the sense of relative frequencies provided the foundation of the earliest mathematical probability theory. This was already true in Cardan's *Book on Games of Chance*: 'The most fundamental principle of all in gambling is simply equal conditions, e.g. of opponents, of bystanders, of money, of situation, of the dice box, and of the die itself. To the extent to which you depart from that equality, if it is in your opponent's favor, you are a fool, and if in your own, your are unjust' (Cardan 1961, p.5). The sense of what was fair or equitable had been worked out in scholastic works on contracts and business partnerships.[4] When the solutions offered to the 'problem of points' evolved from those that took account of what had happened in a game up to the point when it was broken off to those that paid attention, instead, to what might happen in the rest of the game, this can be seen to be the result of thinking about the just or equitable price that a new person willing to buy a player's place in a partially completed game should reasonably be expected to pay.

Thus business ethics helps to explain otherwise perplexing passages in Christiaan Huygens's *On Reckoning in Games of Chance* and in Jacob Bernoulli's *Art of Conjecturing*, the pioneering work of mathematical probability theory. Huygens's mathematics of games treats them using the practical mathematics of business partnerships. At the basis of those partnerships were explicit or implicit contracts that provided security not because of an ability to calculate risks, but rather because of trust that partners would act as promised. Some recent histories of mathematical probability have begun to recognize elements of this conceptual background, both in general and in connection with Jacob Bernoulli in particular. But because the post-de Moivre frequentist interpretation of probability has been dominant, this aspect has sometimes been overlooked and, with it, the background of probability in the Middle Ages.

In the past, historians of financial economics may have skipped over the Middle Ages on the assumption that the Catholic Church's condemnation of usury made modern financial practices sinful or even illegal. What such historians have failed to recognize is that medieval and Renaissance Europe inherited its commercial arithmetic from the Muslims, and while the Muslims also condemned usury, they did not condemn business partnerships in which two or more individuals invested in a company and shared the profits, providing that they also shared the risk of loss. Following the Koran, Islamic law required that there be written contracts between business partners agreeing in advance how profits were to be shared at the end of a temporally limited business contract. Starting with al-Khwarizmi's *Algebra*, Arabic arithmetic and algebra books contained commercial applications, or, even more commonly, applications to inheritances, which were governed by complex laws. When Leonardo Pisano (Fibonacci) studied mathematics in north Africa and came back to Italy to write his *Liber Abaci* (1202), the 'story problems' of Arabic mathematics books were brought *en masse* into the European framework. Whatever the Church may have been saying about the immorality of usury, the sons of European merchants, like the sons of Islamic merchants, learned the mathematics of shared profits in business partnerships alongside the mathematics of mixtures, currency exchange, barter, measurement of volumes and so on. It will be worthwhile to trace these earlier developments in more detail.

1.1 Aristotle's Ethics *and business mathematics*

Aristotle, like Christian and Muslim religious leaders, argued that usury, or demanding that a borrower return more than the principal of a loan, was immoral – particularly when the loan was for consumption and the borrower was poor while the lender was rich. Aristotle had already acknowledged, however, in *Nicomachean Ethics* Book V, ch. 4, 113128–31, the basic principle for equity in business partnerships: 'for in the case also in which the distribution is made from the common funds of a partnership it will be according to the same ratio which the funds put into the business by the partners bear to one another.'

Aristotle's other statements about business ethics in Book V have sometimes confused historians because they use the language of proportionalities in ways that are not easily mapped onto modern mathematical notation. Having defined just distribution as involving geometric proportionality and just recompense as involving absolute amounts to be transferred from the person who received too much to the person who received too little, Aristotle went on to describe justice in exchange, as when a builder of houses exchanges goods with a maker of beds or shoes. He says, for instance (ibid., 1133a5–14):

> Now proportionate return is secured by cross-conjunction. Let A be a builder, B a shoemaker, C a house, D a shoe. The builder, then, must get from the shoemaker the latter's work, and must himself give him in return his own. If, then, there is proportionate equality of goods, and then reciprocal action takes place, the result we mention will be effected. If not, the bargain is not equal, and does not hold; for there is nothing to prevent the work of one being better than that of the other; they must therefore be equated.

The exchange Aristotle seems to have in mind here seems to be one of barter, exchanging shoes directly for houses, but the impractically large number of shoes equivalent to one house would argue for the creation of money to facilitate such exchanges. Aristotle therefore discusses money and then repeats a similar example using a farmer and a shoemaker, where money makes the equation of value possible (ibid., 1133a17–b29):

> For it is not two doctors that associate for exchange, but a doctor and a farmer, or in general people who are different and unequal; but these must be equated. This is why all things that are exchanged must be somehow comparable. It is for this end that money has been introduced, and it becomes in a sense an intermediate; for it measures all things, and therefore the excess and the defect – how many shoes are equal to a house or to a given amount of food ... All goods must therefore be measured by some one thing ... Now this unit is in truth demand ... but money has become by convention a sort of representative of demand ... There will, then, be reciprocity when the terms have been equated so that as farmer is to shoemaker, the amount of the shoemaker's work is to that of the farmer's work for which it exchanges ... Thus they are equals and associates just because this equality can be effected in their case. Let A be a farmer, C food, B a shoemaker, D his product to be equated to C .... .
>
> There must, then, be a unit, and that fixed by agreement (for which reason it is called money); for it is this that makes all things commensurate, since all things are measured by money. Let A be a house, B ten minae, C a bed. A is half of B; if the house if worth five minae or equal to them; the bed, C, is a tenth of B; it is plain, then, how many beds are equal to a house, viz. five. That exchange took place thus before there was money is plain; for it makes no difference whether it is five beds that exchange for a house, or the money value of the five beds.

This discussion is confusing not only because Aristotle keeps switching his example from shoes to food to beds, but also because the mathematics of proportionality, if it is understood as mathematics, is unclear. In medieval commentaries on these passages of the *Ethics*, Aristotle's intention is often represented by a rectangle in which the top two corners are labeled with the two people making the exchange, say the builder and the shoemaker, and the corners below each person are labeled with the product, the house below the builder and shoes below the shoemaker. Then the exchange is represented by the diagonals of the rectangle, with the understanding that the shoes go to the builder and the house to the shoemaker. What is this rectangle supposed to represent? Are the diagonals something like the demand and supply curves of modern economics, where the intersection of the curve represents the exchange price? This is not likely, since the diagram is much older than the medieval attempt to represent what we would call functions by curves, as in Nicole Oresme's configurations of qualities and motions in the second half of the fourteenth century.

A significant problem in understanding what Aristotle intended, if he was thinking in mathematical terms at all, is that in the Greek understanding of proportions or ratios, the two terms of the ratio must be quantities of the same kind, shoes to shoes, houses to houses, or money to money – normally, a Greek mathematician would say that there is no ratio between a builder and a house or between a shoemaker and shoes. And yet medieval commentators on Aristotle often use the operation 'alternando' on the proportionalities that Aristotle sets out here, saying, if A is to B as C is to D, then A is to C as B is to D, or, in notation, if A:B::C:D, then A:C::B:D (Kaye 1998, pp. 58–64). Thomas Aquinas writes:

> let A be one term, for example, two pounds, and B one pound. But let G be one person, for example, Socrates who has worked two days, and D, Plato, who has worked one day. Therefore, as A is to B so G is to D, because a double proportion is found on the one side and the other. Hence, by alternation, as A is to G, so B is to D. (Quoted in Kaye 1998, pp. 59–60)

What is odd about this is that Aquinas is applying an operation that only applies to proportionalities where all four quantities are of the same kind to a 'discontinuous proportionality' in which the quantities on the left, amounts of money, are heterogeneous with the quantities on the right, days of work. It is as if he is dealing only with the numbers 2 and 1 and not with the things in the world that they measure.

1.2 Leonardo Pisano (Fibonacci), Liber Abaci

How mathematicians might actually have made such calculations can be seen from Leonardo Pisano's (or Fibonacci's) *Liber Abaci*, which has a very nice practical example (Fibonaci 2003, pp. 179–80) of how to do the mathematics of barter, in two different ways, where what is known are the price of a certain number of the first type of goods (in this case yards of cloth), the price of a different quantity of a second type of goods (in this case rolls of cotton), and yet a third quantity of yards of cloth that the barterers wish to exchange. The problem is to calculate how many rolls of cotton are equivalent. The full problem shows how the mathematics actually works, including the role of diagonals:

> when you wish to exchange some merchandise for another merchandise, that is barter, you recall the price of each merchandise, which prices must always be in the same currency, and you write down one of the merchandise at the head of a table, and you write the price of the merchandise in the table afterwards towards the left in the same line … . Next in another line below the price of the merchandise you write the price of the other merchandise, and afterwards you write the quantity of the same merchandise. And the merchandise that you will wish to barter for the other merchandise that was first written in the table on the upper line, you then write the quantity of this merchandise that you have below the same merchandise … so that the same merchandise are written below the same merchandise. And therefore five numbers are written; then you multiply the last of them by the number of the price opposite, and that which then results, you strive to multiply by the other opposite number; the product of these numbers you divide by the remaining two numbers, and you will have the desired result.
>
> For example, 20 yards of cloth are worth 3 Pisan pounds and 42 rolls of cotton are similarly worth 5 Pisan pounds; it is sought how many rolls of cotton will be had for 50 yards of cloth. You then write the 20 yards in the table, and afterwards you write the 3 pounds, namely its price, below which you write the 5 pounds; after this 5 you write 42 rolls; next you write the 50 yards below the 20 yards, and you multiply the 50 and the 3 that are diagonally opposite; there will be 150 that you multiply by the 42, as it is diagonally opposite the same three, and that product which results you divide by the remaining numbers, namely by the 20 and the 5, that is by 100; the result is 63, and this is the total number of rolls of cotton that will be had for the 50 yards of cloth.

rolls	Pisan pounds	yards
[63]	3	20
	* *	
*		*
42	5	50

> [Second method of calculation] One indeed proceeds in this way by proportion, the ratio of the first merchandise to the other that is shown to be compounded of two proportions, namely the proportion that the number of the sale of the first merchandise to the number of its price, and the other proportion the proportion that the number of the price of the other merchandise to the number of the sale of its merchandise that is in the problem; I say the proportion of the yards of cloth to the rolls of cotton is compounded with the other proportions which are 20 to 3, and 5 to 42. As 20 is to 3 so is quintuple

> 20 to quintuple 3; I say quintuple because of the 5 that is the price of the aforesaid 42 rolls, that is 100 yards are worth 15 pounds; again as 5 is to 42, so triple 5 is to triple 42; I say triple because of the 3 that is the price of the said 20 yards, that is 15 to 126 rolls of cotton; and because 100 yards are worth 15 pounds, one has 126 rolls; therefore for 100 yards 126 rolls are had; and thus the proportion is compounded of the first merchandise to the second from the two given proportions. and because as 100 is to 126, 50 yards is to the exchange that is had for the rolls; the 50 is multiplied by the 126 that is the 50 by the 3, and by the 42, as we did above, and the product of them is divided by the 100, and the 20 and the 5; the quotient will be 63 rolls which you write above the 42 rolls; it is indeed this proposed proportion that is shown in the rectangular figure, namely the sectors by which Ptolemy taught in the *Almagest* to find the proof of the rectification of the circle, and many other things, and Ametus the Younger put eighteen combinations of it in the book which he composed on proportions.

Thus Fibonacci has here given two ways to solve the problem, one simply by multiplying and dividing numbers without theoretical explanation and the other using the classical approach of compounding proportions, justified by reference to Ptolemy and Ametus filius Josephi. In the second approach, Fibonacci is compounding the ratio of 20 to 3 with the ratio of 5 to 42 by making the denominator of the first ratio equal to the numerator of the second ratio and then taking the first numerator to the second denominator. In other words, he changes the first of the two ratios to the ratio of 100 to 15 (multiplying numerator and denominator by 5) and the second ratio to 15 over 126 (multiplying the numerator and denominator by 3). Then the compound of these two ratios is the ratio of the first numerator to the last denominator, or 100 to 126. This having been done, he has only to solve by the rule of three the relationship: as 100 is to 126, so 50 is to the amount sought, which is thus found to be 63. As a check he does the problem in reverse, starting with 63 rolls of cotton and calculating that they are equal in worth to 50 yards of cloth.

Here the lesson that I want to draw from this example is that it is important to know how merchants actually made their calculations. It looks to me as if the diagonals or diameters that Aristotle talks about in fair exchange are probably the lines drawn between the numbers to be multiplied in calculating the proportional amounts. The examples Aristotle gives are confusingly simple because he mentions only one house, but the method used is probably not that different from that which might have been used by Greek practical calculators in the first case, or theoretical mathematicians in the case of compounding ratios by finding continuous terms.

Fibonacci's *Liber Abaci*, as he says in the introduction, was based on the mathematics he learned from the Muslims in North Africa. The book includes a chapter on the alloying of monies and a chapter on companies and their members. There is no chapter on calculating interest, presumably because the Muslims were opposed to usury. As can be seen from the sample problem given above, the reader is taught how to make calculations by setting numbers out in tables, without words spent on explaining why the numbers should be multiplied and divided in the way directed. When the standard problems for a Muslim merchant were carried over to be taught to the sons of Christian merchants in Europe, Muslim business ethics were implicitly transferred, whether or not anyone paid attention. When Huygens and Bernoulli used equations for games of chance that had the same form as equations for dividing the profits in a business partnership, the notions of equity and moral correctness for business partnerships were implicitly carried over to games. Usury was not relevant.

1.3 European Christian business ethics

As far as early commercial arithmetic and mathematical probability might have contributed to financial economics, then, it is to calculations involving business partners and not to loans at interest that one should first look. But even if one concentrates on what Catholic theologians had to say about business practices, the picture is not as uniformly anti-business as is sometimes assumed. There are a number of recent books and articles that attempt to construct a different narrative of medieval economic ethics.[5] Should we understand that medieval and early modern theologians had a diversity of opinions on business ethics, or would it be more accurate to say that medieval and early modern businessmen found ways to circumvent what their priests might have been telling them (or that they delegated to Jewish bankers the practices forbidden to Christians)? Was commercial arithmetic cut off from business ethics?

Mathematics and science are sometimes treated as morally neutral, so that the mathematician or scientist may explore topics that the moralist would put out of bounds. Thus we find medieval theologian-natural philosophers, wearing their philosophical hats, describing contraceptive and abortifacient herbal preparations, even if, wearing their theological hats, they would argue that abortion is a sin.[6] Is this the reason why we find medieval and early modern works of business mathematics describing how to calculate compound interest even when theologians were arguing that usury, and especially interest upon interest, is a sin?

Or would it be more accurate to argue that, if practical mathematics books were describing how to calculate compound interest – or how to share the profit of a business partnership – someone must have thought that such calculations would be useful in practice? The 1344 manual for confessors, *Memoriale Presbyterorum*, advises:

> Here you should know that usury is exercised by many, both clerics and laymen, every single day, sometimes secretly, sometimes openly. In receiving something beyond the principal, they do not believe that they are sinning and in the penitential forum they do not confess regarding this sin, nor do confessors of today make any inquiry regarding this sin. As for the judicial forum, justice is not done against usurers for this reason, that judges of today, in the execution of justice concerning this sin, are lukewarm and remiss and in no way wish to punish it.[7]

It has often been said that, by its disapproval of usury, the medieval Catholic Church hindered the development of capitalism or at least forced businessmen to resort to subterfuges to justify making a profit on the investment of money. The prohibition of usury is found prominently in the writings of Thomas Aquinas, the most commonly consulted of all medieval theologians, and the general Catholic prohibition is supposed to have been effective at least for some time after Aquinas, perhaps until widespread flaunting of the rules by businessmen (or competition with more permissive Protestants) led some Catholic theologians to loosen their moral strictures.

Many recent historians have relied upon John Noonan's *The Scholastic Analysis of Usury* (1957) as the definitive treatment of the subject. In Noonan's admirably comprehensive organization, the period 1150–1450 saw the classical scholastic theory of usury, while the period 1450–1750 saw criticism and revision of the scholastic theory. De Roover (1967) praised the fifteenth-century sermons of Bernardino da Siena for their pioneering economic thought, but had to admit that the passages in the sermons that he found most impressive were taken nearly verbatim from the thirteenth-century writings of Peter John Olivi, a connection that had remained unknown because – for reasons unconnected with his theory of usury – the Church had condemned Olivi and prohibited the citation of his writings.[8] But Olivi's writings nevertheless remained accessible in Franciscan libraries, where they were read, if not cited by name, and had an influence.[9] Thus there was greater diversity within medieval Catholic opinions on usury than may appear from Noonan's synthesis.

The question of when and where Catholic or Protestant lawyers or theologians began to countenance the taking of interest on loans, against the longstanding condemnation of usury, is a controverted one.[10] For example, in 1933, at the height of the Depression, H.M. Robertson argued in his *Aspects of the Rise of Economic Individualism: A criticism of Max Weber and his school* that Protestantism, or especially Puritanism, should not be made responsible for the rise of the capitalist spirit, since the Jesuits had earlier refused to condemn the pursuit of gain as a principle of Christian conduct. In his *The Economic Morals of the Jesuits. An Answer to Dr. H.M. Robertson*, James Brodrick, S.J., then defended his Jesuit predecessors on the grounds that they were no more lax in their business ethics than the mainstream of Catholic thinking in the Middle Ages. The key to Brodrick's argument was the distinction in medieval thinking about business ethics between 'interest' and 'usury.' Usury, in its core sense, consists in requiring borrowers – often borrowers who under pressure of need have taken consumption loans – to pay back more than they have borrowed. 'Interest' (*interesse*), on the other hand, consists in paying a lender, who would otherwise have used his money as capital in a business enterprise, for the losses he has incurred either because of delay in return of the money borrowed (*damnum emergens*) or because of the profits he has missed (opportunity cost, *lucrum cessans*) because he did not have use of his money.[11] This was indeed a very widespread distinction (cf. McLaughlin 1939, pp. 123, 125–6). While the condemnation of usury argued that money is barren, favorable consideration of interest argued that money is fruitful. In writing on the subject of usury or interest, John Calvin did argue that money may be fruitful, but not a few Catholic theologians and canon lawyers agreed: in the real-world circumstances around them, they could see that investing in business did lead to profits.

A leading advocate of the permissibility of receiving compensation in the form of *interesse* for *damnum emergens* or *lucrum cessans* was Peter John Olivi. In his thirteenth-century consideration of the ethics of loans, Peter John Olivi argued that a borrower could be expected to pay a lender for his loss of the opportunity to earn a profit. The borrower should give the lender the 'probable equivalent' (*probabiliter equivalens*) or preserve him from a probable loss of profit (*a damno probabilis lucrum*) (Kaye 1998, p. 119). Whereas previous authors had been skeptical about the legitimacy of setting a value on such an uncertain equivalent (when there was a possibility that no profit would be made), Olivi argued that a loan on such conditions should be allowed because the borrower and the lender were in equivalent, and hence fair, situations. The receiver of the loan expects to earn more with the money borrowed than he pays to the lender. The lender accepts less in payment for the loan than he thinks he probably could get if he invested the money directly in business, but he has the assurance of a set payment. There will always be some doubt about the exact amounts involved, according to Olivi:

> The judgment of the value of a thing in exchange seldom or never can be made except through conjectural or probable opinion [*coniecturalem seu probabilem opinionem*], and so not precisely, or as if understood and measured by one indivisible point, but rather as corresponding to a latitude, concerning which diverse human heads and judgments will differ in their estimation. And therefore thinking on this includes in itself various degrees, little certainty, and much ambiguity as is the way with opinions. (Kaye 1998, p. 124. I have altered the translation slightly.)

Thus Olivi and others thinking about the business contracts that were already in use in the thirteenth century argued for their fairness not by trying to quantify the risk involved in the businesses, but rather by looking at what usually happens and at the similar uncertainty in the judgment of those entering into the contracts.[12] Fraud must be avoided, in Olivi's view, but people should be allowed to make business agreements that they believe will be to their advantage within the range of varying opinions. What makes such contracts allowable is that the partners enter into them freely, both exercising good judgment (cf. Langholm 1998).

A similar emphasis on fairness or justice entered discussions of the pricing of annuities. What percentage of the amount paid for an annuity should be returned each year and how should this vary with the age of the purchaser in the case of annuities that end with the death of the purchaser? How should these figures change if the annuity will continue until both of two annuitants die? In his *Tractatus de Usuris*, Alexander of Alessandria (1268–1314) argued that for a contract to be permitted the parties to it must intend to share the risks equally. If one party has a significantly better position, the contract is illegal, as would happen if the buyer has a position that is very frequently better, while the seller's position only rarely is better (Kantola 1994, p. 54). The sale of a life annuity will be fair if the price is such that, with care and attention, neither the buyer nor the seller seems to have a notable advantage over the other, taking into account the age and health of the buyer (and hence his life expectancy) and the risks with regard to the benefit the seller can obtain by possessing that amount. If we see men and women 25 years old, Alexander goes on, who buy life annuities for a price such that they will have received back what they paid in less than eight years, then the contract will not be just, because, although it is possible they will die before age 33, it is more probable that they will live longer.[13] Only if the buyer of an annuity were exposed to such great dangers and diseases that it was unclear (*quod non clare videretur*) whether the buyer or the seller would lose significantly, would the contract be fair. Thus buyers and sellers should study their proposed business and they should not commit fraud. Then if the doubt and danger of the two contracting parties are equal, it may follow that the price of the goods exchanged should be less, but the contract will be fair and hence legal.[14] When a life annuity is sold, it is uncertain how long the buyer will live. Because the uncertainty in how long the contract will last depends on nature and not on those making the contract, it is not to be imputed to the intention of one of the parties. It is the intentions of the buyer and seller that determine whether the contract will be allowed (Kantola 1994, p. 54).

In his *Libri decem de justitia et jure* published in 1559, the Spanish Dominican Domingo de Soto argued that games of chance do not violate the law of nature because they are voluntary and involve a sort of pact: I give so that you give, that is I expose my money to a risk and you expose yours in turn. The risk of one is estimated to be equal to the risk of the other. And neither player knows what the outcome will be – the cause of what will happen is known only to God. Thus a game was what came to be called an 'aleatory contract' (on aleatory contracts, see Jacquier 1909–10; Daston 1987).

It was not 'laxity,' then, that led certain theologians to refuse to support a blanket condemnation of those who received or gave interest, but rather parity between the individuals involved, looked at from the perspective of business or economic ethics. This was especially the case if the individuals concerned were understood to be involved in business partnerships or companies. Essentially all scholastic theorists agreed in treating partnerships differently from loans. All the individuals involved in a partnership might be assumed to be in business to earn a legitimate profit. The principle to be applied in deciding whether a given business practice was ethical was that the practice should be fair or equitable. In the simplest case, all of the investors in a company would contribute equal inputs and all would receive an equal share of the profits or losses. But nearly every case was not so simple. Often investors would invest different amounts or for different periods of time. One common partnership (the *commenda*) involved one or more stay-at-home investors (the *stans*) and a traveling merchant or ship captain (the *factor* or *tractator*).[15] Then the ship captain would contribute his labor and expertise and perhaps the use of his ship, rather than capital, so that the inputs of the partners would differ in kind as well as amount. Of course, the partners hoped that the business done on the trip would result in a profit. The contract agreed to before the trip would determine how the capital and profit would be distributed at the end of the enterprise (normally partnerships were assumed to end after the planned voyage rather than continuing indefinitely). In reaching this contract for the division of profits, the partners would take into account who would bear the loss in case of shipwreck or other loss of the partnership's capital. Typically, the stay-at-home investor alone would bear the loss in case of disaster. In recompense, the stay-at-home investor typically received a larger share of any profits.

On the other hand, in the so-called triple or German contract, the stay-at-home investor did not risk his capital and received a guaranteed return, but one less than would normally be expected in a commenda contract (cf. Brodrick 1934, pp. 120–53).[16] A principal early defender of the German contract was Johann Eck in the early sixteenth century, who debated the subject at the universities of Ingolstadt, Bologna and Paris, before being drawn into debate on other subjects with Martin Luther at the start of the Reformation (ibid., pp. 126–7). At Paris, Eck convinced John Major of the correctness of his position. In John Major's commentary on Peter Lombard's *Sentences* printed in 1509, a number of questions elaborate the various grounds on which making a profit might be considered licit or illicit. Concerning distinction 15 of Book IV, John Major discussed 34 questions, of which the twenty-third was whether usury is a sin. In discussing whether a consequential expense or a lost opportunity for profit entitled a lender to a profit that should not be considered usurious, Major writes of probable profit (*lucri verisimilis*) according to judgment of prudent men (*secundum iudicium prudentum*). If, for example, he says, I proposed to travel to Damascus, Syria, and there buy 1000 ducats of silk cloth on which, according to prudent merchants, I might expect to make a profit of 300 ducats, and if, in these circumstances, you asked to borrow my 1000 ducats, how much interest could I ask in return? Not as much as 300 ducats, because if I loan the money to you, I will not have to travel to Damascus, I will not have to pay for lodging for myself and my horse, I will not labor or risk loss, and so forth. So I might ask that 80 or 100 additional ducats be paid. It is very difficult to prove that a loan is usurious, Major says, because the value to be placed on lost profits depends so much on the intent of the lender. If you say that you can make such and such a profit in Scotland, what of the possibility that your ship will sink on the way back to France or that you will be set upon by pirates? Should it be said that a lender deserves less interest in troubled times or in winter because it is more difficult to invest the money profitably then? If one lender deserves interest because he is accustomed to invest his money, while another is not because he leaves his money in a chest, what happens if, halfway through the year when the second has loaned his money he has an unexpected opportunity to buy something that will cost more if he buys it after his loan is repaid?

In sum, whatever theologians and lawyers said about the morality of various business practices, they nevertheless worked out the conceptual framework for business ethics – no matter whether they accepted or rejected a given practice after describing it.[17] And while some historians may try to trace a time-line over which the consensus of theologians changed from condemning usury without exception to accepting extrinsic titles to profit such as *damnum emergens* or *lucrum cessans*, other historians conclude that there was often a diversity of opinion coexisting, not to mention a diversity between theory and practice. And whatever the theologians and lawyers said, from an early date mathematical textbooks explained how to calculate what is owed to business partners in various cases, where the assumption is that profit ought to be distributed in proportion to the capital or labor invested.

1.4 Commercial arithmetic and algebra

Already in the *Algebra* of al-Khwarizmi many of the problems concerned distribution of inheritances according to the applicable law together with the special facts of a case, as, for instance, if, when a man died, one of two sons who would otherwise have inherited equally owed him money, while the man had, at the same time, willed some part of his estate to a non-family member.[18] Thus many inheritances were conditional, depending, for instance, on the order in which the people mentioned in a will died. Mathematicians proposed methods for estimating the value of future inheritances. Problems of dividing the capital or profits of a business partnership fairly when it had to be broken off before the intended end arose because Islamic law required that companies be dissolved if one of the partners died – or at least that they be dissolved if one of the heirs wanted their share as part of their inheritance. This helps explain why the problem of parts played a prominent role in early discussions of games of chance understood as analogous to business partnerships.

A few examples of commercial mathematics problems relevant to the context within which Huygens and Bernoulli approached games will be provided here.[19] In the 1202 *Liber Abaci* of Leonardo Pisano or Fibonacci, there are long series of problems of business partnerships, voyages and so forth. For example, the section on societies begins with the problem: 'Suppose that there are two men who have made a society, of which one paid 18 pounds of some money into the society and the other 25 pounds. And suppose that they have made a profit of 7 pounds. How much of the 7 pounds should each one of them receive?' The succeeding problems increase in difficulty by assuming that the investment of the partners and the profit involves fractions as well as whole numbers and by assuming that the society has three or four members, but the basic principle of distributing the profit in proportion to the investment holds. Nearly every business mathematics book had problems of this sort.[20]

In a later section, Leonardo Pisano then considers 'voyages,' problems that assume that the business conducted between various partners can be segmented into voyages in the course of each of which there is a certain ratio of profit and certain costs. According to the first problem in this section, someone goes to Lucca where he doubles his money and spends 12 denarii; then he goes to Florence and again doubles his money and spends 12 denarii; finally he comes back to Pisa where he doubles his money and spends 12 denarii. It is supposed that at the end he has nothing. What did he begin with? The answer, as Leonardo shows, is 10½ denarii. At Lucca, the merchant doubles his money to 21, but spends 12, leaving him with 9. At Florence he doubles his money to 18, but spends 12, leaving 6. Returning home, he doubles his money to 12 and spends 12, leaving nothing.

Very frequently in the succeeding problems, the voyager ends up with nothing, not a very enticing prospect. A later problem concerns two men who have a society in Constantinople. One takes from the common capital a certain amount and goes to Alexandria to do business, remaining there 5 years and 70 days. There he earns a profit of one-fifth of his capital for each year he is there and spends 25 byzants. The partner who remains at home earns a profit each year of one-seventh of his capital and spends 37 byzants. At the end of the 5 years and 70 days when the partner returns from Alexandria, the partner at home is left with nothing, while the partner returning has as much as the Constantinople partner began with. How much did each partner begin with? In this problem, Leonardo explains, you can assume there are two voyages, one for the partner who travels and one for the partner who stays in Constantinople. He first calculates the financial picture for the man who stays at home. If he had nothing at the end, what did he have 70 days earlier, at the end of the 5 years? This he calculates pro-rating the profit and expenditure assuming that 70 days is seven thirty-sixths of a year, and concludes that at the end of the 5 years the stay-at-home partner had 7 byzants. Calculating back through the 5 years, he first adds the expenses of 37 byzants and then takes seven-eighths of the result to get the capital at the beginning of the year. Doing this five times, which requires an incredibly labored calculation with fractions, gives the result that the partner in Constantinople had at the start fractionally more than 129 byzants.[21] Then the partner who went to Alexandria must end up with this amount. Following the rules for his profits and expenditures over 5 years and 70 days leads to the conclusion that he initially took fractionally more than 206 byzants. Although these problems are notable in the fact that the partners either lose all their capital or come out even, the point to be noted is that the author's attention is on the problems of calculating with fractions, with no attention to particular problems of business ethics, whether a given partnership arrangement is licit or not, and so on. The natural inference is nevertheless that the students learning mathematics from this text might expect to deal with this kind of problem in real life.

In later business mathematics textbooks, not only are there problems of dividing profits according to the various partners' investments, but also problems that take into consideration that one or more of the partners joins the company late or leaves it early. Often the share of a partner in an enterprise was pro-rated by the percentage of the time he was part of the company, irrespective of when, during the course of the business, profits were received or losses incurred. This made sense, since profits received early in an enterprise might later be lost and losses made up before the books were closed at the end of the undertaking. In *Behende und hubsche Rechnung auff allen Kauffmanschaft* (1489), J. Widman includes a problem concerning a society in which several partners join and leave over the course of several weeks. In a complicated calculation, he pays no attention to whether the partners took part in the early weeks of the business or the later ones.

But in certain circumstances the timing of participation in a business was assumed to make a difference. Notably, in his 1494 *Summa de arithmetica, geometria, proportioni et proportionalità*, Distinction 9, Treatise 1 on 'All kinds of companies and their division' (*Compagnie in tutti modi e lor partire*), Luca Pacioli assumed that in such problems it is necessary to look at the pacts and contracts the partners made with each other, whether by faith, by testimony, by writing, or by other instrument (*si deve attendere ali pacti e conventioni che infra loro fanno per fede o per testimonio o per scripto o altro instrumento*). According to these, he says, the profit or loss should be divided. Case 60, for example, poses the following problem. Two people form a company for a year. One puts in 700 florins and the other 500. They agree that at the end of the year they will divide the capital and earnings in half. It happens that, at the end of the tenth month, they dissolve the company and find that the earnings are 200 florins. How should they divide the company (*commo si dovera partire ditta compagnia*) and what should each take? Answer: if the company had lasted 12 months, the second would take 100 florins of capital from the first. How much then should he take for 10 months? If in 12 months he gets 100, then in 10 months he should get ten-twelfths of 100 or 83⅓. So with regard to the capital the first should take 616⅔ and the second 583⅓. Then the profit should be divided, following commercial law (*per le compagnie dritte dicendo*), on the assumption that the first provided 616⅔ in capital and the second 583⅓, and the 200 florin profits should be divided in this ratio. Pacioli thus found that the first should take $102\frac{7}{9}$ of the profit and the second $97\frac{2}{9}$ (Pacioli 1494, p. 156, para. 65).

This case is cited because it shows clearly that Pacioli's calculation assumes that in calculating the distribution of capital and profits when a company ends, it is the previous contract between the partners and commercial law that provide the basis for calculating the desired result. In the example given, which must have seemed to Pacioli's readers to correspond to actual practice, the first partner has agreed to transfer 100 florins of his invested capital to the other during the course of the business. This would amount to the first partner paying the second partner a guaranteed 20 percent return on his investment of 500 florins beyond a half share of any profits. Nothing is said about the morality of this sort of contract, but the obvious implication is that such a contract is a possibility. Neither is anything said about why the company is dissolved before its planned end. Perhaps if one partner had initiated the dissolution against the wishes of the other, he would have been assessed a penalty for early withdrawal (along the lines of *damnum emergens*). For my purposes here, the main point to be made is simply that Pacioli's mathematics assumes that the partners' expectations depend upon the contract that they made initially. In this particular case, the contract stipulates a transfer of capital as well as a division of profits.

In light of this business mathematics background, then, it is hardly surprising that Pacioli solved the division problem for an interrupted game by looking to what had been accomplished of the original agreement up to that point.[22] Niccolo Tartaglia criticized this answer, but gave an alternate one also based on how much more, proportionally, of the contracted number of wins one player had completed than the other (Kendall [1956], 1970, p. 27). For his part, Pacioli said that he had found several different approaches to the problem, but that he was going to give the correct one (Schneider 1985, p. 239).

About the same time as Pacioli, Filippo Calandri, author of a printed arithmetic published at Florence in 1491, in a manuscript work titled *Varie ragioni tratte da vari luogi* and found in MS L.VI.45 of the Biblioteca Communale of Siena, also said that alternative approaches are possible. In problem 12 of Calandri's work, two players who had planned to play until one had won 6 times, break off their game when one has won 4 games and the other 3. How much should each receive? Calandri says: 'There are two methods of determining the ratio of division: one is to determine the ratio by what has been done and the other is to consider what remains to be done' (Toti Rigatelli 1985, p. 231). Whereas Pacioli had preferred the first method, Calandri favors the second. He reasons that since the first player needs 2 to win and the second player needs 3 more, the first should receive, inversely, three-fifths of the deposit, while the second receives two-fifths. Calandri is not sure that this is the correct solution, however, since a game of fortune is involved. In problem 43, Calandri again says that there are two methods of solving a division problem (in this case one for three players) and concludes that it is undetermined which is better (Toti Rigatelli 1985, p. 231).

Ivo Schneider has pointed out that the games discussed by Pacioli and other mathematical authors include chess and other games that are not primarily games of luck. Perhaps this helps explain why mathematicians consider what has been accomplished up until the game is broken off, rather than what might happen afterwards. Schneider argues that what is important in this history is that Pacioli, like the businessmen who formed commenda, thought that there was only one correct solution to the problem, as in the traditional commenda contract, where the ship captain received a set fraction of the earnings after the voyage, whatever might have occurred, whereas, by the sixteenth century, thanks to the commercial revolution, other sorts of business arrangements were possible (Schneider 1985, pp. 239–40). When Jerome Cardan rejected Pacioli's solution to the division problem, his arguments, in Schneider's view, were no more objective than Pacioli's. What seemed fair to Pacioli seemed grossly unfair to Cardan: in a 19-point game, where one player had won 18 and the other 9, Pacioli's method would divide the stake in a ratio of 2 to 1 because one player had won twice as many games as the other up to that point. Cardan argued, to the contrary, that the chances of the player with only 1 more point to go were as much as 20 to 1 better than those of the player with 10 more points to go. Indeed, Cardan's own formula for the division problem gave the ratio 55 to 1 for this case (Schneider 1985, pp. 243–4). Tartaglia, on the other hand, considering the real-world situation, concluded that such a problem was better solved legally than rationally – no matter how it is solved, he said, there will always be grounds for complaint (ibid., p. 244, quoting *La Prima Parte del General Trattato di Numeri et Misure*, Venice 1556, f. 165v).

What should be noticed here is that if the issue is the expectation of a new player buying the place in a game of a person who has been playing up to that point, then, of course, that buyer will only care what his or her future expectations are. In his *Practica Arithmetica* of 1539, after arguing that what has happened up to a certain point in a game does not count, but what still needs to be done to win, Jerome Cardan wrote: 'For the demonstrative reason for this is that if, after the division, the game were begun again, the players would have to stake the same as they received at the time of stopping' (as quoted in Franklin 2001, p. 298). Why should the buyer wish to reward the seller for what he or she has accomplished up to that point? Thus the secondary market for positions in partly completed games might reasonably turn mathematicians to looking at the expectations in the rest of the game rather than at what has gone before. If players on quitting a game part-way through were only intending to divide the stake in a fair way given the rules of the game, they might conceivably look to the history of the game up to that point, but if a new partner is entering and buying the position, the past becomes irrelevant to the just or equitable price to be paid.

Lorraine Daston has suggested that mathematical probability emerged at a time when life in Europe became more predictable, when it became possible to assume that the future on average would be similar to be past (Daston 1988a, pp. 232–5; 1988b, pp. 113, 164, 183–7). In the case of business, one might ask, for instance, when the danger of sending a merchant ship to the East became fairly predictable, so that merchants might consider what percentage of ships were typically attacked by pirates or what percentage encountered storms so severe as to result in the loss of the entire cargo. In the case of selling annuities, one might ask what the average life expectancy might be for individuals who have already achieved a given age. But historians have noticed that when governments first sold annuities as a means of raising government revenue, little or no attention was paid to the age of the person who bought the annuity, so that the expected value of an annuity sold for a given price might vary considerably depending upon whether the annuity was for a young or an old person. They have also noticed that little effort was expended in collecting statistics concerning losses at sea or other shipping disasters.[23] They did not take averages.[24]

In his 1921 book, *Risk, Uncertainty, and Profit*, Frank Knight distinguished 'risk,' where the probabilities of various outcomes are known, from true 'uncertainty,' where what might happen is unpredictable by any known method. The seventeenth-century founders of mathematical probability, such as Jacob Bernoulli, Abraham de Moivre and Pierre Remond de Montmort, all used games of chance as models for calculations of mathematical probability. It has been noticed, however, that of the games for which they calculated probabilities, many were not pure games of chance, but involved skill as well. And in any case, it was not known risks, in Knight's sense, that encouraged mathematicians to calculate probabilities in games or in business partnerships, but rather the implicit or explicit contracts between players or business partners and, further, the existence of markets in which a player or a business investor could sell his position to someone else in case he wanted to withdraw before the anticipated end of the game or business enterprise. The disciplinary context for thinking about these issues was ethics and the relevant characteristic of ethical business practice was equity or justice.

Understanding that it was the contract between business partners or between governments and the purchasers of annuities that underlay business practices, rather than estimates of life expectancies or other actuarial knowledge, helps us to understand the behavior of governments and individuals in the seventeenth and early eighteenth centuries. What one finds are mutual insurance agreements rather than third-party insurance. For instance, at the end of the seventeenth century, we find groups of two thousand or so individuals agreeing that if one of them dies, each of the others will pay a certain amount to the survivors of the deceased. This does not require estimating how many people are likely to die, since there are no set premiums paid in advance to be used for paying survivors a promised amount. On an alternative scheme, set premiums were paid, but then the resulting sum was divided equally between the survivors of all who died in that year, with a smaller amount paid if a larger number died (Poitras 2000, pp. 460–62). In another sort of plan, a number of men joined together to assure that their daughters would have the necessary dowries when the time came – and this, perhaps, before their daughters were even born. What made these contracts legitimate was the parity of knowledge or ignorance among the men.

A different situation arises if individuals desire to create a secondary market for buying and selling contracts of various types. Then the uncertainty cannot be managed simply by the agreement to share costs equally or proportionally, but a value or price must be attached to the ongoing contract, whether for a life annuity or a business partnership. Within a latitude or range of possibilities, the price might be set by negotiation between the buyer and seller, assuming that if a contract is entered into freely by two parties who are equal in their knowledge or ignorance, it must be fair (cf. Langholm 1998). In games, mathematics could be used to estimate a just price for a game position, which the prudent buyer or seller could then use in deciding upon the price to offer or to accept – the individual's conception of a fair price varying depending upon his or her attitude toward risk or chance.

In general, then, the terminology of early works on games of chance reflects their analogy to business partnerships with the added twist of looking forward from any given point in the middle of a game at which one player might sell his position to another (cf. Schneider 1988). When Huygens first wrote *On Calculations in Games of Chance* in Dutch, the word he used for what a player might expect was *kans*, chance, or *kansse*, chances. The Latin word that one would have expected to be correlated with *kans* was *sors*. But when Huygens suggested to van Schooten what words to use in the Latin translation, he proposed the neologism *expectatio*. Van Schooten followed Huygens's suggestions, except that at the beginning of the treatise he used the alternative *sors seu expectatio* – allowing the reader to understand that *expectatio* meant the same thing as *sors* in the usual mercantile use, before going on to use the word *expectatio* on its own. Where van Schooten did not have Huygens's suggestions to follow (Huygens translated only the propositions, not their justifications), he occasionally translated *kans* as *sors*, forgetting to use *expectatio* for this purpose, and Bernoulli, likewise, often used *sors*, when what is referred to is the expectation in the modern sense.[25] In using *sors* for a player's expectation, van Schooten and Bernoulli were identifying a player's lot (*sors*) with an investor's capital investment (also called *sors*) and with his expected receipts from a partnership, something that only makes sense when one is dealing with a zero-sum game. In its original meaning a *sors* was a token upon which the chance in a lottery was supposed to depend. The Romans had used lots or physical tokens to distribute government jobs. From this came the idea of a person's lot in life or fortune. In business contracts, then, the capital a person invested in a partnership or loaned to another person was the *sors* – both what a person paid in and what he could expect back, paying a just price in a fair partnership where, initially, there is assumed to be no net profit. Thus, when people linked a business partner's or a player's investment or stake with his expectations, both called *sors*, they implicitly assumed that they were dealing with non-usurious investments or fair zero-sum games. Thus they assumed that players were gentlemen or women who put up a stake to play a game and who divided the resulting pot of money at the end of the game according to the pre-agreed-upon rules. There was no 'house' or government which skimmed part of the players' wagers off the top. Business partnerships, however, might not have a zero sum, and the partners might make a profit or a loss. In the business mathematics of the day, this difference was dealt with by dividing profits in proportion to the partners' inputs, taking account of the time each partner was involved in the enterprise, the labor expended, the risk assumed, and so forth. As with the problems of inheritance found in al-Khwarizmi, the problems may be designed to correspond to the current legal situation, but when mathematics problems travel from one culture or legal system to another, some confusion about the legal assumptions may arise. It is possible that the mathematics fit the Islamic situation better than the Christian one. It is also possible that in disputes involving international trade, the Christians as well as the Muslims would agree to judgment according to more completely developed Islamic rules.

An idiosyncratic feature of Bernoulli's expressions for probability in Part IV of *The Art of Conjecturing* is that he has probabilities that add up to more than one – something quite unlike the situation in modern probability mathematics. Once one sees the background of his expressions for probability in commercial arithmetic, and, beyond that, in Islamic law, it is no longer surprising that his probabilities add up to more or less than one (see Shafer 1978). In the analogous expressions as they appear in al-Khwarizmi's *Algebra*, it is quite common that the sum of what a decedent owes to his or her various heirs is more than the total of his or her estate – what should be given is expressed proportionally and it is unknown how many heirs will still be alive when a person dies. Similar mathematics problems are found throughout the ancient world, and it is a very normal process to renormalize so that the sum does add up to one or the whole of the estate or payroll.

From a mathematician's point of view, many conceptually disparate problems were seen as analogous because the mathematics involved was the same. In an early publication, Jacob Bernoulli combined a question of usury with the solution to a game problem. In the usury problem, a debtor was supposed to make installment payments on a loan, and the problem was how to allocate the payments made between interest payments and repayments of the principal – affecting the interest due in the next period. In this connection Bernoulli used the word *sors* to mean the principal of the loan. In turning to the game problem, then, he noted that the calculations both of amounts due on an interest-bearing loan (*sors*) and of the ratio of lots (*ratio sortium*) in the game in question involved the summing of infinite series.

As Bernoulli pointed out in *The Art of Conjecturing*, the simplest equation for calculating expectations in games was identical to the equation long used by merchants to calculate the price of a mixture. Commenting on Huygens's Proposition III, which calculates a player's expectation if he has p cases in which he receives a and q cases in which he receives b out of a total $p + q$ cases, Bernoulli noted:

> It is clear from consideration of this calculation that it has great affinity to the arithmetic rule called Of mixtures, according to which things of diverse prices in given quantities are mixed, and the price of the mixture is sought. In fact, the two calculations are clearly the same. Just as the sum of the products of the quantities and prices of the individual ingredients, divided by the total quantity of all the ingredients, gives the required price, which is always intermediate between the highest and lowest prices, so too the sum of the products of the numbers of cases and amount acquired in those cases, divided by the total number of cases, gives the value of the expectation, which likewise is always intermediate between the greatest and least amounts that can be acquired. (Bernoulli 1713, p. 10)

Other mathematicians recognized different analogies to the same law. Leibniz referred to it by the Greek term, *prosthapherisis*, a formula used in astronomy for finding the position of a planet, adding or subtracting the effects of anomalies with regard to the mean motion:

> The foundations they built on involved prosthaphaeresis, i.e. arriving at an arithmetic mean between several equally admissible hypotheses [*suppositions également recevables*]. Our peasants have used this method for a long time, guided by their natural mathematics. For instance, when some inheritance or piece of land is to be sold, they appoint three teams of assessors – these teams are called *Schurzen* in Low Saxon – and each team assesses the commodity in question ... This is the axiom *aequalibus aequalia* – equal hypotheses [*suppositions égales*] must receive equal consideration. (Leibniz 1981, pp. 465–6, translation slightly modified)

Alternately, as Nicolaus Bernoulli pointed out, the mathematics of calculating expectations in games was the same as the mathematics of calculating centers of gravity.

Thus the same mathematical relationships might correspond to very different real-world relationships that nevertheless had the same formal structure. When the history of mathematical probability has been written retrospectively from the modern frequentist perspective, Part I of Jacob Bernoulli's *Art of Conjecturing* has been understood as if he approached games in the modern probabilistic or relative frequency sense. Then Part IV of the work, applying the same mathematics to legal, moral and economic decision making, has been understood as if it were built upon this same frequentist or statistical basis.

As I have argued, however, Part I of *The Art of Conjecturing* and Huygens's work upon which it is based, are founded on the mathematics of equitable business partnerships, not on the mathematics of risk. While the traditional histories of mathematical probability start with Pierre Fermat, Pascal and Huygens because they gave what are from a modern point of view correct frequentist solutions to the problems of division and of expectations in games of chance (and this was the history already given by Pierre Remond de Montmort and de Moivre), the foundation of Huygens's method (and of Bernoulli's method for games, in so far as Bernoulli built upon Huygens's work) was not chance (probability in our terms), but rather *sors* (expectation in our terms) in so far as it was involved in implicit contracts and the just treatment of partners. The importance of justice in partnerships is evident in Huygens's repeated use of such phrases as 'with equitable chance' (*aequa sorte*), 'contesting on equal conditions' (*aequa conditione certans*), and 'equal right' (*aequale jus*).[26] A person's *sors*, lot, or expectation in a gambling game depends fundamentally upon the availability of other people willing to play a fair game. As important as the 'objective' value of a given game position was the willingness of well-informed and free individuals to enter into the game. By restoring this perspective on the work of Huygens and Bernoulli concerning games, it is also restored to its place in the history of financial economics.

2. The theological background of Part IV of *The Art of Conjecturing*

With the understanding that Part I of *The Art of Conjecturing* is based on equity, not frequency, it becomes easier to understand how Bernoulli may have been thinking in Part IV, where he turns to epistemological issues, that is to probability as he understood the word. In the seventeenth century, many of the theologians who judged what were fair and unfair business practices were Jesuits or Calvinists. Standard histories of mathematical probability overprivilege Jansenist critiques of the Jesuits, perhaps because of the role that Blaise Pascal played both in support of the Jansenists and in the development of mathematical probability itself. From the strict perspective of the Jansenists (cf. Taveneaux 1977), the Jesuits were to be condemned for their laxity, often taking the form of so-called 'probabilism,' according to which 'if an educated man considers two opinions to be probable, then, no matter which of the two he follows, he does not sin' (Vitoria 1539, quoted by Brodrick 1934, p. 137). Their critics charged the Jesuits with having adopted probabilism in order to cater to the wealthy businessmen and patrons whose confessions they heard. But as Albert Jonsen and Stephen Toulmin have argued in *The Abuse of Casuistry. A History of Moral Reasoning*, casuistry does not deserve the blanket condemnation it so frequently receives.[27]

Jacob Bernoulli himself included a 'case of conscience' in his intellectual journal or *Meditationes*, asking whether a person whose culture takes it as a sign of respect to remove one's hat should do so when taking part in a sacred ritual in China, given that the Chinese think that keeping one's head covered is a sign of honor. Thus his attitude to casuistry was not that of Pascal's *Provincial Letters*. Moreover, whatever position one took on casuistry, whether 'probabilism' or 'probabiliorism,' the connotations of the word 'probable' up through the late seventeenth century were overwhelmingly epistemic or even ethical and not frequentist, and this is the sense that Bernoulli had in mind. A 'probable profit' was what prudent businessmen thought reasonable. A 'probable opinion' was one that could be reasonably supported and a 'more probable opinion' was one held by more authoritative or respected thinkers. The core meaning of 'probability' was not relative frequency. To determine what a probable profit in a business might be, one consulted experienced businessmen, one did not collect data.

Following his father's wishes, Jacob Bernoulli studied theology and even preached some sermons before deciding that he would rather teach physics and mathematics than serve as a pastor, despite the fact that the pastorate in seventeenth-century Basel was better paid than the professorate. As far as I can tell, Bernoulli's move from theology to mathematics was more a matter of the attraction of mathematics than of a distaste for religion. He seems to have taken his religious training seriously. Even at the end of Bernoulli's life, covenantal theology may help to explain what Bernoulli thought about his law of large numbers. Like a business partner, God might be understood to behave in reliable ways, but, like a gaming partner, God might sometimes 'play dice' with the universe in the sense of including in creation fortuitous or chance events as well as human free will.

At the very end of *The Art of Conjecturing*, Bernoulli makes an enigmatic or perplexing statement in connection with his proof of what came to be called the weak law of large numbers. So he writes:

> Whence at last this remarkable result is seen to follow, that if the observations of all events were continued for the whole of eternity (with the probability finally ending in perfect certainty) then everything in the world would be observed to happen in fixed ratios and with a constant law of alternation. Thus in even the most accidental and fortuitous circumstance we would be bound to acknowledge a certain quasi necessity and, so to speak, fatality. I do not know whether or not Plato already wished to assert this result in his dogma of the universal return of things to their former positions, in which he predicted that after the unrolling of innumerable centuries everything would return to its original state. (Bernoulli 1713, p. 239)

On the surface, this remark might mean simply that, if one considers all of time and counts up the numbers of times various outcomes occur, say that a coin comes up heads or tails, then there will be a fixed ratio between the alternative types of events in question. Of course, it could be said that there is a ratio between any two numbers, so that this conclusion is vacuous. It appears, however, that Bernoulli expected the ratios in question to be expressible in fairly low terms or, at the very least, to be fixed – in his terms, to manifest 'fixed ratios with a constant law of alternation.'

Although Bernoulli said at one point in *The Art of Conjecturing* that he did not wish to enter into theological considerations, there are, nevertheless, echoes of his theological training, which had a large place for the role of God as primary cause of whatever happens in the world. In setting out his views of contingency at the start of Part IV of *The Art of Conjecturing*, Bernoulli wrote:

> The certainty of anything is considered either objectively and in itself or subjectively and in relation to us. Objectively, certainty means nothing else than the truth of the present or future existence of the thing. Subjectively, certainty is the measure of our knowledge concerning this truth.
>
> In themselves and objectively, all things under the sun, which are, were, or will be always have the highest certainty. This is evident concerning past and present things, since by the very fact that they are or were, these things cannot not exist or not have existed. Nor should there be any doubt about future things, which in like manner, even if not by the necessity of some inevitable fate, nevertheless by divine foreknowledge and predetermination, cannot not be in the future. Unless, indeed, whatever will be will occur with certainty, it is not apparent how the praise of the highest Creator's omniscience and omnipotence can prevail. Let others dispute how this certainty of future occurrences may coexist with the contingency and freedom of secondary causes; we do not wish to deal with matters extrinsic to our goal. (Bernoulli 1713, pp. 210–11)

Here Bernoulli alludes to a complex theological doctrine concerning the relation of God as first or remote cause, on the one hand, and secondary or proximate causes, on the other. Historians of mathematics are not normally inclined to probe deeply into the theological context of mathematics, but if we want to understand the conceptual context of Bernoulli's *Art of Conjecturing* it is essential. According to Bernoulli something is necessary if it must always exist and contingent if it may exist only part of the time:

> Something is necessary if it cannot not exist, now, in the future, or in the past … A thing that can not exist, now, in the future, or in the past, is contingent (both free, depending on the will of a rational creature, and fortuitous and by chance depending on chance or fortune). This should be understood with reference to a remote rather than proximate power, for contingency does not always exclude all necessity, even with respect to secondary causes. (Ibid., p. 211)

What we label as necessary or contingent, according to Bernoulli, may have more to do with our knowledge than with reality:

> something can be seen as contingent by one person at one time which may be necessary to another person (or even the same person) at another time, after its causes have become known. So contingency also mainly has reference to our knowledge, insofar as we see no contradiction in something not existing in the present or future, even if, here and now, by the force of a proximate cause unknown to us, it may necessarily exist or occur. (Ibid., pp. 212–13)

If some events seem fortuitous to us because we do not know their causes, nevertheless they may be in fact determined by their proximate causes. On the other hand, for Bernoulli there are outcomes that are really contingent, both outcomes that are the result of human free will and outcomes that are the result of chance.

To understand how Bernoulli could think that this view of contingency and necessity is coherent or consistent, we need to look at the theological background. As Thomas Aquinas explains in his *Summa Theologica* – just to take a treatment of the subject easily available in English – in creation God gives some things necessary causes and some things contingent causes:

> The divine will imposes necessity on some things willed but not on all … It is better therefore to say that this happens on account of the efficacy of the divine will. For when a cause is efficacious to act, the effect follows upon the cause, not only as to the thing done, but also as to its manner of being done or of being. Thus from defect of active power in the seed it may happen that a child is born unlike its father in accidental points that belong to its manner of being. Since then the divine will is perfectly effacicious, it follows not only that things are done, which God wills to be done, but also that they are done in the way that He wills. Now God wills some things to be done necessarily, some contingently, to the right ordering of things, for the building up of the universe … Hence it is not because the proximate causes are contingent that the effects willed by God happen contingently, but because God prepared contingent causes for them, it being His will that they should happen contingently. (Thomas Aquinas 1920, I, Q. 19, art. 8)

In this world view, then, there are in the world really necessary and really contingent things. Aquinas explains this further in answering a question whether angels can know the future:

> I answer that the future can be known in two ways. First, it can be known in its cause. And thus, future events which proceed necessarily from their causes, are known with sure knowledge; as that the sun will rise tomorrow. But events which proceed from their causes in the majority of cases, are not known for certain, but conjecturally; thus the doctor knows beforehand the health of the patient. This manner of knowing future events exists in the angels, and by so much the more than it does in us, as they understand the causes of things both more universally and more perfectly; thus doctors who penetrate more deeply into the causes of an ailment can pronounce a surer verdict on the future issue thereof. But events which proceed from their causes in the minority of cases are quite unknown; such as casual and chance events.
>
> In another way future events are known in themselves. To know the future in this way belongs to God alone; and not merely to know those events which happen of necessity, or in the majority of cases, but even casual and chance events; for God sees all things in His eternity, which, being simple, is present to all time, and embraces all time. And therefore God's one glance is cast over all things which happen in all time as present before Him; and He beholds all things as they are in themselves, as was said before when dealing with God's knowledge. But the mind of an angel, and every created intellect, fall far short of God's eternity; hence the future as it is in itself cannot be known by any created intellect. (Ibid., Q. 57, art. 3)

Thus some events always follow from their causes, some follow in the majority of cases, and some follow rarely. Bernoulli's view of necessity and contingency has similar reasoning in its background.

Moreover, for both Aquinas and Bernoulli, since God is outside of time, God knows everything that will happen in the future, even those things that are contingent and happen rarely. Nevertheless, humans have free will. How is this possible? By the fourteenth century if not earlier, theologians had unpacked the inference 'If God knows that something will occur, it necessarily occurs,' to conclude that the necessity involved in such an inference is, in Bernoulli's terms, 'hypothetical' or, in their terms, not in the consequent but in the consequence. In other words, necessarily if God knows that something will happen, it will happen (the consequence or inference is necessary), but the antecedent (God's knowledge) is not necessary, and so the consequent (that something will happen) is not necessary, but may be contingent, if it depends on human free will or a fortuitous natural process. Because God is eternal and outside of time, it might appear that whatever God knows, he always knows, so it would seem to be necessary in the statistical sense, but it was well established that God has freely chosen, so that what God does as first cause need not be necessary.[28] Thus the future is certain in the sense that God foresees it – it is hypothetically necessary – but it is not therefore physically necessary.

For some, the theology of God's omniscience and omnipotence went further than this. According to the sixteenth-century Jesuit Luis de Molina and his followers, God knows not only everything that ever has or ever will happen; God knows everything that could possibly have happened. This was called God's 'middle knowledge' (see Mahoney 1987, p. 90). From all the possible worlds, God chose to create the best possible world. Gottfried Wilhelm Leibniz famously advocated this view. Elsewhere, I have described some of the mathematical consequences for medieval authors of this doctrine of God's knowledge of everything possible (e.g., Sylla 1998b). Whereas for Aristotle the divisibility of a continuum was potentially infinite, in the sense that no matter how many times a continuum is divided, it can be divided further, for the scholastics God knows all these potential divisions, implying an actual rather than a potential infinity. Thinking along these lines led some medieval thinkers into paradoxes of the infinite (see, e.g., Sylla 1998b, pp. 791–7).

For early mathematical probability theory, the array of all the possible future outcomes of a game of chance – as represented in all the combinations or permutations of the possible outcomes and as represented, for instance, in Pascal's triangle – are structurally similar on a small scale to God's supposed middle knowledge of all possible worlds. Although Bernoulli considers theology extrinsic to his purposes in *The Art of Conjecturing*, his theological training nevertheless affects his thinking. In the theology that he was taught, God foresaw what would happen to human beings if they were left to follow their own free will. Then God sent Christ as a mediator to redeem certain individuals. And finally, God saves those individuals who, with the help of Christ's mediation, deserve eternal life.

Bernoulli was extremely proud of his proof of the weak law of large numbers, that is, of his proof that if you take enough observations there is no limit to the probability that the ratio of results will converge around the *a priori* ratio of cases of the given events. His proof, however, is a conditional one. He assumes an underlying ratio of cases and then shows that, on the assumption of an underlying ratio, the ratio of observed results will tend to converge to this ratio as more and more observations are made (cf. Sylla 1997). As an example to clarify his proof, Bernoulli posits an urn containing three thousand white stones and two thousand black stones. To the objection that real-world problems like disease or the weather would not have such a determinate ratio of underlying cases, Bernoulli replies:

> They object first that the ratio of stones is different from the ratio of diseases or changes in the air: the former have a determinate number, the latter an indeterminate and varying one. I reply to this that both are posited to be equally uncertain and indeterminate with respect to our knowledge. On the other hand, that either is indeterminate in itself and with respect to its nature can no more be conceived by us than it can be conceived that the same thing at the same time is both created and not created by the Author of nature: for whatever God has done, he has, by that very deed, also determined at the same time. (Bernoulli 1713, p. 227)[29]

Thus God's creation is not chaotic or messy, but determinate and lawlike, but it could, even so, involve randomizers like dice or pebbles in an urn, not to mention free will.[30]

Moreover, God not only has foresight and providence: according to what Bernoulli had learned as a part of his theological education, God also makes covenants with human beings. The sort of covenantal theology that lies behind Bernoulli's thinking may be seen, for example, in *The Oeconomy of the Covenants between God and Man*, first published in Latin by Herman Witsius in 1677. With regard to the covenants of God with man, Wittsius speaks of an improper sense in which the Hebrew word '*berith*' in the Bible may mean:

> 1. An immutable ordinance about any thing. In this sense God mentions his covenant of the day, and of the night; that is, that fixed ordinance about the uninterrupted vicissitude of day and night, which is called *chook*, that is, statute limited or fixed, to which nothing ought to be added or taken from it ... 2. A sure and stable promise, though it be not mutual ... 3. It signifies also a precept. (Wittsius 1798, pp. 46–7)

But in its proper sense, Wittsius says, '*berith*' 'signifies a mutual agreement between parties with respect to something' (ibid., p. 48). In this sense there are two covenants between God and man, the covenant of works and the covenant of grace. God's covenants promise happiness in eternal life, prescribe the conditions under which humans acquire a right to this promise, and finally prescribe punishments for those who do not meet the conditions (ibid., p. 52). These covenants, Wittsius says, are in all their parts 'highly equitable' (ibid., p. 55). The similarity between Wittsius's conception of the covenants of God with human beings and moralists' conceptions of equitable business contracts are obvious.

In his journal or research notebook, the *Meditationes*, Jacob Bernoulli included comments on theological topics at least up until 1680 (items concerning theology occur between 1677 and 1680; the earliest item that is clearly connected to the later *Art of Conjecturing*, namely solution of the third problem from Huygens's *On Calculations in Games of Chance*, was entered in 1684/85) (Bernoulli 1975, p. 21).

In a series of connected notes, Bernoulli argues against the proponents of universalism and for particularism in connection with texts from Paul's letter to the Ephesians. What, he asks, is the order of the Divine decrees? The following order seems more natural, according to Bernoulli, and more in accordance with God's justice: first God saw that the human race would fall; next God chose to give a mediator to some, so that they might be redeemed and acquire eternal life. After God had given a mediator to some, God saw that they were redeemed and had a right to eternal life. Therefore God chose them, or in other words God destined them for salvation as their end, and God called them, and gave them faith and sanctification as the means to that end. This order of God's decrees is more justifiable, in Bernoulli's eyes, because Christ as mediator causes the merit of those who are consequently chosen. Otherwise, before Christ mediates for them, those who are still sinners and unredeemed would be chosen by God or destined. In the economy imagined by the universalists, God feels compassion for all sinners, but in the economy of particularists which Bernoulli supports, God's compassion is directed only towards some individuals.

The relation of Bernoulli's entries in his journal to current events is not known, and nobody up to now has taken an interest in Bernoulli's theological ideas that might make it possible to determine whether his ideas are at all original, but doubtless what Bernoulli says in these entries has a relation to the 'Helvetic Consensus Formula' produced by J.H. Heidegger and Francis Turretin in 1675. According to Canon IV of this formula:

> Before the creation of the world, God decreed in Christ Jesus our Lord according to his eternal purpose (Eph 3:11), in which, from the mere good pleasure of his own will, without any prevision of the merit of works or of faith, to the praise of his glorious grace, to elect some out of the human race lying in the same mass or corruption and of common blood, and, therefore, corrupted by sin. He elected a certain and definite number to be led, in time, unto salvation in Christ, their Guarantor and sole Mediator. And on account of his merit, by the mighty power of the regenerating Holy Spirit, he decreed these elect to be effectually called, regenerated and gifted with faith and repentance. So, indeed, God, determining to illustrate his glory, decreed to create man perfect, in the first place, then permit him to fall, and finally pity some of the fallen, and therefore elect those, but leave the rest in the corrupt mass, and finally to give them over to eternal destruction. (Klauber trans. 1990, pp. 105–6)

Elsewhere, the formula argues that there are two covenants between God and human beings, the Covenant of Works and the Covenant of Grace, and, of the latter, different dispensations as in the Old Testament time, the New Testament time, and the end time.

Elsewhere in his *Meditationes*, Bernoulli makes use of the view that God is the first cause of everything that happens, of which there are also secondary causes. Even spirits, like humans, he says, cannot act simply by thinking or wishing: they also have a moving faculty of finite capacity. God must concur with all actions of creatures, but if God does not concur when all the secondary causes of a given effect are in place, then God's nonconcurrence is a miracle. God timelessly knows outcomes that to us are fortuitous or contingent, such as the numbers that appear on the roll of dice. These can even be determined by their proximate causes (there was general agreement that the laws of physics and the conditions of the throw determine what face a die will fall on) and yet be contingent with regard to God.[31] In the special modal logic that applies to thinking about God, God can know eternally how a throw of the dice will turn out, and this outcome can be determined by proximate causes, and yet the outcome need not be necessary. In a sense, all the effort of theologians had expended to explain how God's omnipotence, omniscience and providence could be consistent with human free will had opened the conceptual possibility that non-voluntary events like the throw of a die can be both foreseen by God and fortuitous in the sense of not intended.

Thus in the theology in which Bernoulli was educated in the years 1668–76, the world unfolds as a result of secondary causes with which God concurs except in the case of miracles, such as when he suspends fire from burning. Such miracles do not occur frequently, but are relatively rare. Within the spiritual realm, God has established the oeconomy or dispensation of grace, by which Christ mediates for the sins of the elect, so that they will find salvation. Over long periods of time, the pattern of God's reliable covenant with the elect is manifest. When in his proof of the weak law of large numbers Bernoulli proved that, if there is a pre-existing ratio of cases, the ratio of observed outcomes will come to approximate this *a priori* ratio more and more closely as more and more outcomes are observed, the resulting 'law of alternation' must have resonated with his thinking about God's salvation of the elect.

Abraham de Moivre later argued explicitly that the observation of such laws of alternation proved that an intelligent agent was at work in the world: 'Althou' chance produces Irregularities, still the Odds will be infinitely great, that in the process of Time, those Irregularities will bear no proportion to the recurrency of that Order which naturally results from original design' (De Moivre 1756, p. 251; cf. Daston 1988b, pp. 137–8, 187). This view of God's providence was expressed much earlier by Boethius in *On the Consolation of Philosophy*, quoting from Aristotle's *Physics*:

> If any shall define chance [*casum*] to be an event produced by a confused motion, and without connection of causes, I affirm that there is no such thing, and that chance is only an empty voice that hath beneath it no real signification. For what place can confusion have, since God disposeth all things in due order? ... Aristotle ... in his Books of Nature declared this point briefly and very near the truth ... When ... anything is done for some certain cause, and some other thing happeneth for other reasons than that which was intended, this is called chance [*casus*]; as if one digging his ground with intention to till it, findeth an hidden treasure. This is thought to have fallen thus out by fortune [*fortuito ... accidisse*], but it is not of nothing, for it hath peculiar causes whose unexpected and not foreseen concourse seemeth to have brought forth a chance [*casum*]. For unless the husbandman had digged up his ground, and unless the other had hidden his money in that place, the treasure had not been found. These are therefore the causes of this fortunate accident, which proceedeth from the meeting and concourse of causes, and not from the intention of the doer ... Wherefore, we may define chance thus: That it is an unexpected outcome of concurring causes in those things which are done to some end and purpose. Now the cause why causes so concur and meet so together, is that order proceeding with inevitable connection, which, descending from the fountain of Providence, disposeth all things in their places and times. (Boethius 1962, V. prosa i, 19–58. I have made a slight change in the translation.)

The fortuitous finding of a treasure was not intended by the man who dug in his garden, but nevertheless it 'descends from the fountain of Providence' – not from special providence or miracle, but from 'that order proceeding with inevitable connection.'

God's providence and the 'order proceeding with inevitable connection' could in some cases result from design that involved randomizers like dice or coins. Just before writing about 'the recurrency of that Order which naturally results from original design,' as quoted above, de Moivre gave the example:

> From what has been said, it follows, that Chance very little disturbs the Events which in their natural Institution were designed to happen or fail, according to some determinate Law; for if in order to help our conception, we imagine a round piece of Metal, with two polished opposite faces, differing in nothing but their colour, whereof one may be supposed to be white, and the other black; it is plain that we may say, that this piece may with equal facility exhibit a white or black face, and we may even suppose that it was framed with that particular view of shewing sometimes one face, sometimes the other, and that consequently if it be tossed up Chance shall decide the appearance ... yet the appearances, either one way or the other, will perpetually tend to a proportion of Equality ... What we have said is also applicable to a ratio of Inequality ... . (De Moivre 1756, pp. 250–52; cf. Sylla 1997, p. 89)

In *The Doctrine of Chances*, de Moivre argued that it was possible to distinguish between chance and providence:

> the same Arguments ... may ... be useful in some Cases to establish a due comparison between Chance and Design: We may imagine Chance and Design to be, as it were, in Competition with each other, for the production of some sorts of Events, and may calculate what Probability there is, that those

> Events should be rather owing to one than to the other. To give a familiar Instance of this, Let us suppose that two Packs of Piquet-Cards being sent for, it should be perceived that there is, from Top to Bottom, the same Disposition of the Cards in both Packs; let us likewise suppose that, some doubt arising about this Disposition of the Cards, it should be questioned whether it ought to be attributed to Chance, or to the Maker's Design: In this Case the Doctrine of Combinations decides the Question; since it may be proved by its Rules, that there are the Odds of above 263130830000 Millions of Millions of Millions of Millions to One, that the Cards were designedly set in the Order in which they were found.
>
> From this last Consideration we may learn, in ma[n]y Cases, how to distinguish the Events which are the effect of Chance, from those which are produced by Design: The very Doctrine that finds Chance where it really is, being able to prove by a gradual Increase of Probability, till it arrive at Demonstration, that where Uniformity, Order and Constancy reside, there also reside Choice and Design. (De Moivre 1756, p. v)

If, given an underlying ratio of cases, one can show that the more observations are made the more probable it is that the observed ratio will be close to the underlying ratio, so, conversely:

> if from the numberless Observations we find the Ratio of the Events to converge to a determinate quantity, as to the Ratio of P to Q; then we conclude that this Ratio expresses the determinate Law according to which the Event is to happen. For let that Law be expressed not by the Ratio P : Q, but by some other, as R : S; then would the Ratio of the Events converge to this last, not to the former: which contradicts our Hypothesis. And the like, or greater, Absurdity follows, if we should suppose the Event not to happen according to any Law, but in a manner altogether desultory and uncertain; for then the Events would converge to no fixt Ratio at all. (Ibid., pp. 251–2)

As it is observed that there are fixed laws in the universe, he continues, so it is clear that these laws are evidence of wise, useful and beneficent purposes.

But it was not easy for mathematicians to develop criteria for distinguishing chance results from the effects of design. As late as 1712, John Arbuthnot argued that the stable ratio of births of males and females was an evidence of God's providence, to which Nicholas Bernoulli replied that the stable ratio could be explained simply by chance. In the *Philosophical Transactions*, vol. 27 (1710–12), Arbuthnot argued:

> Among innumerable Footsteps of Divine Providence to be found in the Works of Nature, there is a very remarkable one to be observed in the exact Ballance that is maintained, between the Numbers of Men and Women; for by this means it is provided, that the Species may never fail, nor perish, since every Male may have its Female, and of a proportionable Age. This Equality of Males and Females is not the Effect of Chance but Divine Providence, working for a good End ... (Arbuthnot 1710–12, p. 186)

To demonstrate this, Arbuthnot supposed as a model a die with two sides, male and female. Raising the binomial (M + F) to the power equal to the number of dice or births, Arbuthnot argued that, given the correspondence of the coefficients of the terms of the binomial expansion to the chances of various ratios of male to female, it was very unlikely that the ratios of male to female births observed over many years would occur by chance. In fact, he said, because more males than females are killed by external accidents, 'provident Nature' brings it about that more males than females are born every year in almost a constant proportion. If the chance that more males will be born than women were one-half in any given year, then the chance that more males will be born than females 82 years in a row will be one-half to the 82 power, a tiny number.

Arguing against Arbuthnot in a letter to Montmort of 23 January 1713 (published in Montmort 1713, pp. 388 ff.), Nicholas Bernoulli proposed that if the ease of birthing males to females were in a constant ratio of 18 to 17, it would not be surprising that the observed ratios of births stayed as close to a constant value as they did over many years (translated in Yushkevich 1987, pp. 295–9). Supposing that 14000 children were born in a year, Nicholas calculated that the probability that the number of males born would not differ from 7200 by more than 163 was greater than 43 to 1. Like Jacob in his proof of the law of large numbers and like Arbuthnot, Nicholas based his argument on summing terms of a binomial expansion. This would mean that one could place an even bet that in 82 years the number of years in which the numbers fell outside the limits would not reach 3. In fact, in Arbuthnot's table, the number had fallen outside the limits 11 times, so there was no need to look to providence to explain the stability of the numbers. He concluded:

> Therefore there is no foundation for being surprised that the numbers of children of each sex do not differ more from each other, which is what I wished to prove. I can remember that my dead uncle proved a similar thing in his tract Ars Conjectandi, which is now at the printers in Basel. Namely, if one wants to determine with the help of often repeated trials the number of cases in which some event may or may not occur, then it is possible to increase the number of observations so that in the final analysis the probability that we have found the true ratio between the numbers of cases is larger than any given probability. When this book comes out, we shall see if I have found in these kinds of questions as exact an approximation as he did. (Translated in Yushkevich 1987, p. 299)

In the third edition of *The Doctrine of Chances*, de Moivre reported this exchange between Arbuthnot and Nicholas Bernoulli and sided with Arbuthnot, saying:

> Mr. Nicolas Bernoulli, a very learned and good Man, by not connecting the latter part of our reasoning with the first, was led to discard and even to vilify this Argument from final Causes, so much insisted on by our best Writers; particularly in the Instance of the nearly equal numbers of male and female Births, adduced by that excellent Person the late Dr. Arbuthnot, in Phil. Trans. N° 328 … Dr. Arbuthnot … might have said, as we do still insist, that 'as from the Observations, we can, with Mr. Bernoulli, infer the facilities of production of the two Sexes to be nearly in a Ratio of equality; so from this Ratio once discovered, and manifestly serving to a wise purpose, we conclude the Ratio itself, or if you will the Form of the Die, to be an Effect of Intelligence and Design.' As if we were shewn a number of Dice, each with 18 white and 17 black faces, which is Mr. Bernoulli's supposition, we should not doubt but that those Dice had been made by some Artist; and that their form was not owing to Chance, but was adapted to the particular purpose he had in View. (De Moivre 1756, pp. 252–3)

Some historians of probability have supposed that de Moivre is here suggesting that God must maintain mean statistical values (cf. Hacking 1975, p. 171, referring to Karl Pearson). This is not de Moivre's point. He is supposing, in effect, that God designed whatever in human reproduction is analogous to dice with 18 white and 17 black faces – something about the DNA in our terms. Then Bernoulli's law of large numbers shows that this underlying ratio of cases will manifest itself when there are large numbers involved. Behind statistical regularities, in this view, there are hidden variables, Bernoulli's 'cases,' designed by God.

In contrast to Huygens and Jacob Bernoulli with their emphasis on expectations in partnerships, de Moivre founded his own doctrine of chances on relative frequencies or probabilities in the frequentist sense. He began his *De mensura sortis, seu, de Probabilitate Eventuum in Ludis a Casu Fortuito Pendentibus* with the proposition:

> If p is the number of cases in which some event may happen, and q the number of cases in which it may not-happen, both the events that happen and those that do not have their degrees of probability; if all the cases in which the event may happen or may not-happen occur equally easily, then the probability of happening to the probability of not-happening will be as p to q. (De Moivre 1711, p. 215, my translation.)

Only after establishing this base does de Moivre turn to the game context in which Huygens had operated, saying:

> If two players A and B compete about outcomes, on the grounds that if p cases happen A will have won, but if q cases happen, B will have won; and if a is the sum deposited, the lot or expectation of A will be $\frac{pa}{p+q}$, while the lot or expectation of B will be $\frac{qa}{p+q}$, and therefore if A or B sell their expectations, it will be fair if they receive $\frac{pa}{p+q}$ and $\frac{qa}{p+q}$ respectively for them. (Ibid.)

And similarly, de Moivre goes on, if after the game is agreed upon, the players decide not to play, the premium should be divided according to the same ratios.

In the preface to the first edition of *The Doctrine of Chances* (1718), de Moivre said that when he wrote *De mensura sortis* he had been 'absolutely resolved to reject … the Method of Huygens, … as not seeming to me to be the genuine and natural way of coming at the Solution of Problems of this kind' (de Moivre 1718, p. ii).[32] The first edition of *The Doctrine of Chances* begins with a more general statement corresponding to the opening of *De mensura sortis*: 'The Probability of an Event is greater, or less, according to the number of Chances by which it may Happen, compar'd with the number of all the Chances, by which it may either Happen or Fail' (ibid., p. 1). By the third edition of *The Doctrine of Chances*, de Moivre has added a second proposition: 'Wherefore, if we constitute a Fraction whereof the Numerator be the number of Chances whereby an Event may happen, and the Denominator the number of all the Chances whereby it may either happen or fail, that Fraction will be a proper designation of the Probability of happening' (de Moivre 1756, pp. 1–2). While Bernoulli had probabilities that added to more than 1, de Moivre states on the first page of the first edition, 'Therefore, if the Probability of Happening and Failing are added together, the Sum will always be equal to Unity.' And expectation is the product of the value of the thing to be obtained times the probability of obtaining it (de Moivre 1718, p. 2; 1756, p. 3). The word 'probability,' he explains in the third edition, 'includes a double Idea; first, of the number of Chances whereby an Event may happen; secondly, of the number of Chances whereby it may either happen or fail' (ibid., p. 2).

The thought world of de Moivre's *The Doctrine of Chances*, especially in the later editions, is thus quite different from that of Huygens and Bernoulli as far as expectation and probability are concerned. As de Moivre himself says, he was resolved to reject Huygens's approach to calculations in games of chance. While Huygens based himself on conceptions of fair games, related, as I have argued, to just business contracts, de Moivre bases himself on probability as measured by ratios of chances. Coming so soon after *The Art of Conjecturing*, de Moivre's *The Doctrine of Chances* was immediately recognized by many as the natural approach to mathematical probability. Thus in histories of mathematical probability the origin of mathematical probability in business mathematics has been obscured, and the foundations of Huygens's and Bernoulli's thought in the expectations of business partners has come to seem counterintuitive or even circular. Likewise, since the eighteenth century, the separation between mathematics and theology has become so wide that historians of mathematical probability have not understood the way in which the 'oeconomy of the covenants' between God and human beings lay behind Bernoulli's thinking about the weak law of large numbers. It is at the least very interesting that the same word 'election' is used by Bernoulli for God's choice of those who are to be saved through the mediation of Christ and for the combinations with which any set of possibilities may be chosen:

> Combinations of things are collections [Conjunctiones], such that from a given multitude of things some are removed and joined together, no attention being paid to their order or position … Some call these collections combinations, com3nations, com4nations, etc., all of which are usually described by the single word combinations, even though this word in its stricter sense seems to connote only those collections that join things together two at a time. For this reason, others prefer to use the more general terms complications or complexions. Others more appropriately call them electiones, so that they may also understand the selections of things in which single things are taken by themselves or even in which nothing at all is taken. (Bernoulli 1713, p. 82)

Although in the complexity of everyday life, it may be unclear who is among the elect and who is not, nevertheless in the end – from the point of view of reformed covenant theology in the late seventeenth century – the order of God's providence will be evident. On this point, Jacob Bernoulli and Abraham de Moivre were agreed.

Notes

1. Parts of this chapter, particularly in Section I, are a light revision of Edith Sylla, 'Business Ethics, Commercial Mathematics, and the Origins of Mathematical Probability,' in Margaret Schabas and Neil De Marchi, eds, *Oeconomies in the Age of Newton.* Annual Supplement to Volume 35 *History of Political Economy* (Durham and London: Duke University Press, 2003). Thanks to Duke University Press for permission to republish those parts.
2. Here and elsewhere I use my recent translation in Jacob Bernoulli, *The Art of Conjecturing, together with 'Letter to a Friend on Sets in Court Tennis'* (Baltimore and London: Johns Hopkins University Press, forthcoming 2005). As was common in this era, a number of different variations of 'Jacob' Bernoulli were used. Jacob is also called Jakob (in German), Jacques (in French) and James (in English). Jacob is the name used on the title page of *Ars Conjectandi.*
3. As quoted in Daston 1988b, p. 28. I have modified the translation slightly by comparison to the Dutch in Jacob Bernoulli 1975, p. 329.
4. Cf. Daston 1988b, pp. 18–26; Parmentier 1993, pp. 449–50. Schneider 2000, p. 591, remarks with some surprise that Leibniz in his writings on insurance does not use probability (in the sense of relative frequencies).
5. See, e.g., Baeck 1999, Kantola 1994, Kaye 1998, Langholm 1979, 1992, 1998.
6. Cf. Riddle 1992, p. 139, concerning Albertus Magnus.
7. Cambridge, Corpus Christi College, MS 148, f. 72, as in Haren 2000, p. 164.
8. De Roover 1967, pp. 19, 42; cf. Kaye 1998, pp. 117–18.
9. Cf. de Roover 1967, pp. 40–41, 'As a result the development of capitalism was not hampered as much as the Weber–Tawney school seems to think. Banking was able to thrive by simply shifting the basis of its operations from outright lending to exchange, *et le tour est joué*, as the French say.'
10. See, e.g., Böhm-Bawerk [1890] 2001, Book I, Chapter II, 'The defence of Interest from the Sixteenth Till the Eighteenth Century,' who lists Zwingli, Calvin and the French jurist Dumoulin (Carolus Molinaeus) as being among the first to defend the taking of interest. Later, for the Netherlands, he discusses Claudius Salmasius, in several writings beginning with *De Usuris*, 1638. In England, Henry VIII set a legal maximum interest rate by 1545. According to Böhm-Bawerk, Germany and France were slower to lift the ban on usury than other areas. At the end of the seventeenth century in Germany, Leibniz among others defended usury. In France the prohibition of usury was only lifted in 1789. In Italy no one attacked the church doctrine in theory before the eighteenth century, but the practice was much different.
11. Brodrick 1934, p. 123, 'if a man asked me, in the long past, to lend him £100, and I was really and truly and without pretence going to spend that sum on the sowing of a crop of wheat, which I could be sure would yield me a return of a least 5 per cent., or on repairing a building, which, if left longer, must involve me in 5 per cent. extra expense, then I could quite justly require the borrower to pay me back, not a hundred, but a hundred and five pounds. The two titles arising here on occasion of the loan were called technically *lucrum cessans* and *damnum emergens*, and, after a brief period of discussion and hesitation, nearly everybody, from Pope to peasant,

recognized their validity.' Other titles to additional recompense were (p. 123, fn. 1) 'the *poena conventionalis*, a fine agreed on in the contract, to be imposed for delay in the return of the sum lent, and the *periculum sortis*, meaning the danger to the capital, which could be very real and for which some compensation was reasonable.'

12. In the writing of some later canonists, it was the moral certainty of the outcome considering what usually happens that made the contract legitimate. Cf. McLaughlin 1939, p. 118, citing Henricus Bohic (Venice 1576).
13. Kantola 1994, p. 55, quoting Alexander of Alessandria, *Tractatus de usuris*, pp. 152–3.
14. See Aegidius de Lessinia, *De usuris in communi*, ed. Parmensis 1864, c. 9, as quoted in Kantola 1994, p. 54n.
15. There was a long history of various types of maritime business partnerships in Italy – *commenda, societas maris, collegantia, compagnie* – in which one partner would provide most or all of the capital but stay home and the other would actually sail to the East (and perhaps put up part of the capital), with the agreement that when the ship returned and the cargo was sold, a set percentage of the profits would go to the *stans* (often two-thirds or three-fourths), while the rest would go to the *factor*. See Postan et al., eds, 1963, pp. 48–59.
16. The net outcome of triple contracts was that the investor would receive a fixed interest return (often 5 percent) on his capital (as he might on a usurious loan), but this net outcome was attributed to three separate contracts. The first contract amounted to a partnership in the usual sense, where the stay-at-home investor would receive a relatively large percentage of the profits, but would alone absorb any losses of capital that might occur. Under the terms of the second contract, the stay-at-home investor would agree to accept a smaller percentage of the profits in exchange for the merchant/ship captain agreeing to absorb any loses of capital that might occur and to return at least the investor's entire share of the capital. In effect this amounted to the investor's buying an insurance contract on his capital in exchange for part of his expected profits. Under the terms of the third contract, the investor would agree to accept an even smaller profit than expected, but that return would be guaranteed, thus amounting to a fixed interest rate. If part of the rationale for accepting profits from investment of capital in business partnerships while usury was prohibited was the argument that the investor risked his capital (*periculum sortis*) and therefore deserved some recompense for bearing this risk, the triple contract seemed to undercut this rationale in so far as the return was guaranteed. On the other hand, in the normal contract the stay-at-home investor received a greater share of the profit because he did risk his capital, and so, by symmetry, it could be supposed to make sense that the traveling partner receive more of the profit when he assumed the risk. For the canonists' discussions of such contracts, see McLaughlin 1939, pp. 104–5. Joannes Andreae admitted such contracts in the case of dowries, 'because a special need, the public good, requires that it [a dowry] be kept entire and safe.'
17. Cf. McLaughlin 1939, p. 145. In law there are many individual cases. The theologians tend to systematize the lawyers' cases into types such as *damnum emergens* and *lucrum cessans*.
18. Al-Khwarizmi poses the following problem: 'A man dies, leaving two sons behind him, and bequeathing one-third of his capital to a stranger. He leaves ten dirhems of property and a claim of ten dirhems upon one of the sons. Computation: You call the sum which is taken out of the debt thing ... '
19. For a thorough and thought-provoking exposition of the relevant business mathematics, see the articles by Ivo Schneider listed in the references.
20. Cf. Daston 1988, p. 20, 'the so-called Rule of Fellowship (i.e. distributive proportion) ... specified that the profit of each partner should be proportional to his investment. Every sixteenth-century text on practical arithmetic included a section on the Rule of Fellowship, illustrated with numerous examples and problems. Some also discussed the 'double' Rule of Fellowship, which took into account the duration as well as the amount of the investment.'
21. Leonardo often used unit fractions, as found in Egyptian mathematics, writing 98/100 as 1/100 + 1/50 + 1/5 + 1/4 + 1/2. See Boyer and Merzbach 1991, p. 255.
22. Pacioli is often set aside in discussions of the history of the problem of points because his answer is thought to be false. See F.N. David 1962, p. 37, 'From the probability point of view Luca is interesting for one of his examples in the *Summa*. "*A* and *B* are playing a fair game of *balla*. They agree to continue until one has won six rounds. The game actually stops when *A* has won five and *B* three. How should the stakes be divided?" We would say 7:1, but Pacioli argues 5:3.' David notes that Pacioli based much of the contents of his work on Leonardo Pisano's *Liber Abaci*, but did not find the source of this problem. For the analogy of games and business cf. Schneider 1985, pp. 242–3, 'wie in einer Handelsgesellschaft.'
23. As Daston 1988b, p. 120, comments, partners or insurers rarely looked at frequency of mishaps in determining the risk of the investor bearing the risk: 'While the expertise of a *Toccatore* admittedly increased with experience, insurers evidently did not regard information on the actual frequency of shipwrecks to be relevant in pricing premiums. There exist no records of any attempts to compile such statistics ... Judging from the injunctions of Cleirac and other handbook authors, the sixteenth-century insurer might well have found such a statistical approach impractical, for it presumes stable conditions over a long period.'
24. Cf. Franklin 2001, p. 339, 'To set a premium for an insurance one must, at least unconsciously, have observed a relative frequency. Yet there was no serious numerical study of such things until 1660, despite the apparently obvious commercial advantages. The reasons for this remain obscure. Perhaps a set and a ratio are so simple, and at the same time abstract, that they are easy to overlook ... The absence of averages ... is remarkable. ...

Amazingly, even after Fermat, Pascal, and Huygens invented the mathematical theory of probability, they were apparently quite unaware that the probabilities they had calculated had anything to do with relative frequencies or averages. Pascal explicitly says that what he is calculating is "what is rightly due" and that this can be "little investigated by trial; for the doubtful outcomes of the lot are rightly attributed rather to fortuitous contingency than to natural necessity." ... There is something to be explained, but some mystery remains as to what the true explanation can be.'

25. Already in the opening paragraph Huygens himself had suggested using *sors* where, for consistency sake, he should have used *expectatio*. The question was what a person should pay if he wanted to take over my position in a game. In Dutch he had said, 'my game' (*mijn spel*). Van Schooten indicated his hesitation over Huygens's suggestion to translate this by *sortem meam*, by expanding to read *locum sortemque*.
26. Cf. Grotius, *De jure belli et pacis* 1625, as quoted by Daston 1988b, p. 22, from A.C. Campbell, trans., 1901, p. 147, 'In all contracts, natural justice required there should be an equality of terms.'
27. Jonsen and Toulmin 1988, p. 20, 'the arguments by which Blaise Pascal and his successors have brought the enterprise of casuistry into disrepute contain, in turn, their own fundamental flaw ... '
28. Osler 1991 describes a similar constellation of ideas in the work of Gassendi on ethics.
29. This was an issue that had come up previously in correspondence between Bernoulli and Leibniz. Cf. Sylla 1998a, p. 53.
30. Cf. Daston 1992, p. 42, 'When Bernoulli turns to the theorem which bears his name ... he instead concentrates on revealing the "hidden causes" of the weather or human mortality. These are peculiar sorts of causes, being ... "true ratios," ... Bernoulli likens these ratios to those between black and white pebbles in an urn, and suggests that these ratios "cause" the frequencies of storms, deaths, etc. we actually observe.' Daston argues that Bernoulli is not thinking of 'microscopic mechanisms,' but, in the case of diseases, he writes of the 'human body, that has the germ (*fomitem*) of various changes and diseases within itself as an urn contains pebbles' (Bernoulli 1713, p. 226).
31. Between the two passages from Part IV on necessity and contingency, quoted above, Bernoulli says, p. 212, 'Let me clarify this by examples. It is most certain, given the position, velocity, and distance of a die from the gaming table at the moment when it leaves the hand of the thrower, that the die cannot fall other than the way it actually does fall. Likewise, given the present condition of the atmosphere, given the mass, position, motion, direction, and velocity of the winds, vapors, and clouds, and given the laws of the mechanism according to which all these things act on each other, tomorrow's weather cannot be other than what in fact it will be. Indeed, these effects follow from their own proximate causes no less necessarily than the phenomena of eclipses follow from the motion of the heavenly bodies. Yet it is customary to count only the eclipses as necessary and to count the fall of the die and future weather as contingent. The only reason for this is that those things which, to determine the subsequent effects, are supposed as given, and which indeed are given in nature, are not yet sufficiently known to us. And even if they were, the study of geometry and physics has not been sufficiently perfected to enable us to calculate from these givens their effects, in the way in which eclipses can be computed and predicted once the principles of astronomy are known. Before astronomy was brought to this degree of perfection, eclipses themselves, no less than these other two phenomena, had to be counted among future contingencies.'
32. De Moivre's use of the title *De Ratiociniis in Ludo Aleae* (as found in Bernoulli's *Ars Conjectandi*), rather than the title *De Ratiociniis in Aleae Ludo* (as found in Van Schooten) may indicate that de Moivre read the work as included in Bernoulli rather than in the original.

References

Aegidius de Lessinia, ed. Parmensis (1864), *De usuris in communi*. As in Kantola (1994).

Alexander of Alessandria [d. 1314] (1962), *Tractatus de Usuris*, ed. A.-M. Hamelin, in *Une Traité de morale économique au XIVe siècle*. As in Kantola (1994).

Arbuthnot, John, trans. (1692), *Of the Laws of Chance, or, A Method of Calculation of the Hazards of Game, Plainly demonstrated, and applied to Games at present most in Use, which may be easily extended to the most intricate Cases of Chance imaginable*. London: Printed by Benjamin Motte, and sold by Randall Taylor.

Arbuthnot, John (1710–12), 'An argument for divine providence, taken from the regularity observ'd in the birth of both sexes,' *Philosophical Transactions of the Royal Society of London*, **27**, pp. 186–90.

Baeck, Louis (1999), 'The Legal and Scholastic Roots of Leonardus Lessius's Economic Thought', *Storia del pensièro economico*. Found at http://www.cce.unifi.it/dse/spe/indici/numero37/baeck.htm.

Bernoulli, Jacob (1677–80), *Meditationes*. MS Univ. Bibl. Basel L.I. ac, unpublished transcription. My thanks to Martin Mattmüller for allowing me to see this transcription.

Bernoulli, Jacob [1713] (1968), *Ars Conjectandi*. Basel: Thurneysen Brothers; reprinted Brussels: Culture et Civilisation.

Bernoulli, Jacob (1975), Van der Waerden et al., eds, *Die Werke von Jakob Bernoulli*, Vol. III. Basel: Birkhäuser.

Boethius [*c*. 524] (1962), *The Consolation of Philosophy*, trans. 'I.T.,' revised by H.F. Stewart in *Boethius. The Theological Tractates. The Consolation of Philosophy*, Cambridge, MA: Harvard University Press; London: William Heinemann.

Böhm-Bawerk, Eugen von [1890] (2001), *Capital and Interest: A Critical History of Economical Theory*, trans. William Smart, London and New York: Macmillan. http://www.econonlib.org/library/BohmBawerk/bbCI2.html.
Boyer, Carl, and Uta Merzbach (1991), *A History of Mathematics*, 2nd edn, New York: John Wiley and Sons.
Brodrick, James (1934), *The Economic Morals of the Jesuits. An Answer to Dr. H.M. Robertson*. London: Oxford University Press/Humphrey Milford.
Cardan, Jerome [1663] (1961), *The Book on Games of Chance 'Liber de Ludo Aleae'*, trans. Sydney Henry Gould. New York: Holt, Rinehart and Winston.
Castellani, Maestro Gratia de' [*c*. 1460] (1984), 'Chasi Sopra Chonpagnie,' ed. Marisa Pancanti from MS. Florence, Biblioteca Nazionale, Palatino 573. Quaderni del Centro Studi della Matematica Medioevale 11. Siena: Servizio Editoriale dell'Università di Siena.
Coumet, Ernest (1970), 'La théorie du hasard est-elle née par hasard?' *Annales*, **25**, pp. 574–98.
Daston, Lorraine (1987), 'The Domestication of Risk: Mathematical Probability and Insurance 1650–1830,' in Lorenz Krüger, Lorraine J. Daston and Michael Heidelberger (eds), *The Probabilistic Revolution*, Vol. 1, *Ideas in History*. Cambridge, MA and London: MIT Press, pp. 237–60.
Daston, Lorraine (1988a), 'Fitting Numbers to the World. The Case of Probability Theory,' in *History and Philosophy of Modern Mathematics*, ed. William Aspray and Philip Kitcher. Vol. XI of Minnesota Studies in the Philosophy of Science. Minneapolis: University of Minnesota Press.
Daston, Lorraine (1988b), *Classical Probability in the Enlightenment*. Princeton: Princeton University Press.
Daston, Lorraine (1992), 'The Doctrine of Chances without Chance: Determinism, Mathematical Probability, and Quantification in the Seventeenth Century,' in *The Invention of Physical Science*. eds Mary Jo Nye, Joan Richards and Roger Stuewer, Boston Studies in the Philosophy of Science, vol. 139. Dordrecht, Boston and London: Kluwer, pp. 27–50.
David, F.N. (1962), *Games, Gods, and Gambling. The Origins and history of probability and statistical ideas from the earliest times to the Newtonian era*. London: Charles Driffin & Co. Ltd.
de Moivre, Abraham (1711), 'De mensura sortis, seu, de Probabilitate Eventuum in Ludis a Casu Fortuito Pendentibus,' *Philosophical Transactions of the Royal Society*, **27**, pp. 213–64. Also in *The Philosophical Transactions Abridged From the Year MDCC (Where Mr. Lowthorp ends) To the Year MDCCXX*. ed. Benjamin Motte. London: R. Wilkin, R. Robinson et al., 1721, vol. I, pp. 190–219.
de Moivre, Abraham (1718), *The Doctrine of Chances*.
de Moivre, Abraham (1738), *The Doctrine of Chances*, 2nd edn.
de Moivre, Abraham [1756] (1967), *The Doctrine of Chances*, 3rd edn, London: A. Millar; reprint New York: Chelsea Publishing Company.
de Roover, Raymond (1967), *San Bernardino of Siena and Saint' Antonino of Florence: The Two Great Economic Thinkers of the Middle Ages*. Boston: Baker Library, Harvard Graduate School of Business Administration.
de Witt, Johann [1671] (1975), *Value of Life Annuities in Proportion to Redeemable Annuities*, in Dutch, in Bernoulli (1975).
Domingo de Soto (1559), *Libri decem de justitia et jure*. As in Coumet (1970).
Fibonacci's Liber Abaci (2003), A translation into Modern English of Leonardo Pisano's Book of Calculation, trans. Leonard Sigler. New York, Berlin and Heidelberg: Springer Verlag, 2003.
Franklin, James (2001), *The Science of Conjecture. Evidence and Probability before Pascal*, Baltimore and London: The Johns Hopkins University Press.
Freudenthal, Hans (1980), 'Huygens' Foundations of Probability,' *Historia Mathematica*, **7**, pp. 113–17.
Garber, Daniel and Sandy Zabell (1979), 'On the Emergence of Probability,' *Archive for History of Exact Sciences*, **21**, pp. 33–53.
Gregory of Rimini [*c*. 1350] (1984), *Lectura super Primum et Secundum Sententiarum*, ed. A. Damasus Trapp and Venicio Marcolino, Vol. 3. Berlin and New York: Walter de Gruyter.
Hacking, Ian (1975), *The Emergence of Probability*, Cambridge: Cambridge University Press.
Hacking, Ian (1980), 'From the Emergence of Probability to the Erosion of Determinism,' in *Probabilistic Thinking, Thermodynamcis and the Interaction of History and Philosophy of Science*, J. Hintikka et al. (eds), Vol. 2, pp. 105–23.
Hald, Anders (1990), *A History of Probability and Statistics and their Applications Before 1750*, New York: John Wiley and Sons.
Haren, Michael (2000), *Sin and Society in Fourteenth-Century England. A Study of the Memoriale Presbiterorum*. Oxford: Clarendon Press.
Hauser, Walter (1997), *Die Wurzeln der Wahrscheinlichkeitsrechnung: Die Verbindung von Glücksspieltheorie und Statistischer Praxis vor Laplace. Boethius: Texte und Abhandlungen zur Geschichte der Mathematik und der Naturwissenschaften*, Vol. 37, Stuttgart: Franz Steiner Verlag.
Hintikka, Jaakko, David Gruender and Evandro Agazzi (eds), *Probabilistic Thinking, Thermodynamics and the Interaction of the History and Philosophy of Science. Proceedings of the 1978 Pisa Conference*, Vol. 2, pp. 105–23.
Huygens, Christiaan (1657), *De ratiociniis in ludo aleae*. Included in Bernoulli (1713). Dutch and French, with commentary and appendices, in *Oeuvres Complètes de Christiaan Huygens*, Vol. 14, 1920, pp. 2–179.

Jacquier, E. (1909–10), 'Aléatoires (contrats),' *Dictionnaire de Théologie Catholique*, Vol. 1, col. 695–705.

Jonson, Albert R. and Stephen Toulmin (1988), *The Abuse of Casuistry. A History of Moral Reasoning*. Berkeley, Los Angeles and London: University of California Press.

Kantola, Ilkka (1994), *Probability and Moral Uncertainty in Late Medieval and Early Modern Times*, Helsinki: Luther-Agricola-Society.

Kaye, Joel (1998), *Economy and Nature in the Fourteenth Century. Money, Market Exchange, and the Emergence of Scientific Thought*. Cambridge: Cambridge University Press.

Kelly, John P. (1945), 'Aquinas and Modern Practices of Interest Taking,' *The Aquinas Lecture 1944*, Brisbane: Aquinas Press.

Kendall, M.G. [1956] (1970), 'The Beginnings of a probability calculus,' in E.S. Pearson and M.G. Kendal (eds), *Studies in the History of Statistics and Probability*. London: Griffin.

Keynes, John Maynard (1936), *The General Theory of Employment, Interest, and Money*, London: Macmillan.

Klauber, Martin I., trans. (1990), 'The Formula Consensus Helvetica (1675),' *Trinity Journal*, **11**, pp. 103–23. Found at: http://public.csusm.edu/public/gue…ark/Helvetic_Consensus_Formula.htm.

Langholm, Odd (1979), *Price and Value in the Aristotelian Tradition*, Bergen: Universitetsforlaget.

Langholm, Odd (1992), *Economics in the Medieval Schools*. Leiden: E.J. Brill.

Langholm, Odd (1998), *The Legacy of Scholasticism in Economic Thought. Antecedents of Choice and Power*. Cambridge: Cambridge University Press.

Leibniz, Gottfried Wilhelm (1981), *New Essays on Human Understanding*, trans. and ed. Peter Remnant and Jonathan Bennett. Cambridge: Cambridge University Press.

Leibniz, Gottfried Wilhelm (2000), *Hauptschriften zur Versicherungs- und Finanzmathematik*, ed. Eberhard Knobloch and J.-Matthias Graf von der Schulenburg. Berlin: Akademie Verlag.

Mahoney, John (1987), *The Making of Moral Theology. A Study of the Roman Catholic Tradition*, Oxford: Clarendon Press.

McLaughlin, T.P. (1939), 'The Teaching of the Canonists on Usury (XII, XIII and XIV Centuries,' *Mediaeval Studies*, **1**, pp. 81–147.

Mede, Joseph (1653), 'Problema. An Alea sit Sortitio,' in *Dissertationum Ecclesiasticarum Triga: De Sanctitata Relativa, De Veneratione Sacra. De Sortitione & Alea*. London: Thomas Roycroft et al.

Montmort, Pierre de (1713), *Essai d'analyse sur les jeux de hazard*, 2nd edn, Paris: Jacque Quillau.

Mormando, Franco (1999), *The Preacher's Demons. Bernardino of Siena and the Social Underworld of Early Renaissance Italy*, Chicago and London: University of Chicago Press.

Munro, John (2001), 'The Origins of the Modern Financial Revolution: Responses to Impediments from Church and State in Western Europe, 1200–1600,' Working Paper No. 2. http://www.chass.utoronto.ca/ccipa/wpa.html.

Newton, Isaac [1665?] (1967), 'Loose Annotations on Huygens' De Ratiociniis in Ludo Aleae,' in *The Mathematical Papers of Isaac Newton*, Vol. I, 1664–66, ed. D.T. Whiteside, Cambridge: Cambridge University Press, pp. 58–62.

Noonan, John T (1957), *The Scholastic Analysis of Usury*, Cambridge, MA: Harvard University Press.

Osler, Margaret (1991), 'Fortune, fate, and divination: Gassendi's voluntarist theology and the baptism of Epicureanism,' in eadem, ed., *Atoms, pneuma, and tranquillity. Epicurean and Stoic themes in European Thought*. Cambridge: Cambridge University Press, pp. 155–74.

Pacioli, Luca (1494), *Summa de arithmetica, geometria, proportioni et proportionalità*. Venice: Paganino de Paganini.

Parmentier, Marc (1993), 'Concepts juridique et probabilistes chez Leibniz,' *Revue d'Histoire des Sciences*, **46**.

Peter John Olivi [d. 1298] (1980), *De emptionibus et venditionibus, de usuris, de restitutionibus*, as in Todeschini (1980).

Poitras, Geoffrey (2000), *The Early History of Financial Economics, 1478–1776. From Commercial Arithmetic to Life Annuities and Joint Stocks*. Cheltenham, UK and Northampton, MA, USA: Edward Elgar.

Postan, M.M., E.E. Rich and Edward Miller (1963), *Economic Organization and Policies in the Middle Ages. Cambridge Economic History of Europe*, Vol. 3, Cambridge: Cambridge University Press.

Rawls, John (1971), *A Theory of Justice*, Cambridge, MA: Belknap Press of Harvard University Press.

Riddle, John (1992), *Contraception and Abortion from the Ancient World to the Renaissance*, Cambridge, MA: Harvard University Press.

Robertson, H.M. (1933), *Aspects of the Rise of Economic Individualism: A Criticism of Max Weber and his School*, Cambridge: Cambridge University Press.

Schneider, Ivo (1980a), 'Christiaan Huygens's Contribution to the Development of a Calculus of Probabilities,' *Janus*, **67**, pp. 269–79.

Schneider, Ivo (1980b), 'Why do we find the origin of a calculus of probabilities in the seventeenth century?' in Jaakko Hintikka, David Gruender and Evandro Agazzi (eds), *Probabilistic Thinking, Thermodynamics and the Interaction of the History and Philosophy of Science. Proceedings of the 1978 Pisa Conference*, Vol. 2, Dordrecht and Boston: Kluwer, pp. 3–24.

Schneider, Ivo (1981), 'Leibniz on the Probable,' in Joseph Dauben (ed.), *Mathematical Perspectives*, New York: Academic Press, pp. 201–19.

Schneider, Ivo (1985), 'Luca Pacioli und das Teilungproblem: Hintergrund und Lösungsversuche,' in Menso Folkerts and Uta Lindgren (eds), *Mathemata. Festschrift für Helmuth Gericke*, Stuttgart: Franz Steiner Verlag Wiesbaden GMBH, pp. 237–46.
Schneider, Ivo (1988), 'The market place and games of chance in the fifteenth and sixteenth centuries,' in C. Hay (ed.), *Mathematics from Manuscript to Print*. Oxford: Clarendon Press, pp. 220–35.
Schneider, Ivo (2000), 'Geschichtlicher Hintergrund und wissenschaftliches Umfeld der Schriften,' in Leibniz (2000), pp. 591–623.
Shafer, Glenn (1978), 'Non-additive probabilities in the work of Bernoulli and Lambert,' *Archive for History of Exact Sciences*, **19**, pp. 309–70.
Swetz, Frank (1987), *Capitalism and Arithmetic: The New Math of the 15th C. Including the full text of the Treviso Arithmetic* (trans. D.E. Smith). LaSalle, IL: Open Court.
Sylla, Edith (1990), 'Political, Moral, and Economic Decisions and the Origins of the Mathematical Theory of Probability: The Case of Jacob Bernoulli's The Art of Conjecturing,' in *Acting Under Uncertainty: Multidisciplinary Conceptions*, ed. George von Furstenburg. Boston: Kluwer, pp. 19–44.
Sylla, Edith (1997), 'Jacob Bernoulli on Analysis, Synthesis, and the Law of Large Numbers,' in M. Otte and M. Panza (eds), *Analysis and Synthesis in Mathematics*, Boston: Kluwer, pp. 79–101.
Sylla, Edith (1998a), 'The Emergence of Mathematical Probability from the Perspective of the Leibniz–Jacob Bernoulli Correspondence,' *Perspectives on Science*, **6**, pp. 41–76.
Sylla, Edith (1998b), 'God and the Continuum in the Later Middle Ages: The Relations of Philosophy to Theology, Logic, and Mathematics,' in *Was ist Philosophie im Mittelalter?* Miscellanea Mediaevalia 26. Berlin and New York: Walter de Gruyter.
Thomas Aquinas [1271–72] (1920), *Summa Theologica*, 2nd, rev. edn, literally translated by Fathers of the English Dominican Province. Online edition 2000 by Kevin Knight. http://www.newadvent.org/summa.
Taveneaux, René (1977), *Jansénism et Prêt à Intérêt. Introduction, choix de textes et commentaires.* Paris: J. Vrin.
Ternus, J. (1930), *Zur Vorgeschichte der Moralsysteme von Vitoria bis Medina. Vorschungen zur Christlichen Literatur- und Dogmengeschichte*, 16. Paderborn.
Todeschini, Giacomo (1980), *Un trattato di economia politica francescana: il 'De emptionibus et venditionibus, de usuris, de restitutionibus' di Pietro di Giovanni Olivi*. Studi Storici, Fasc. 125–6. Rome: Istituto Storico Italiano per il Medio Evo.
Toti Rigatelli, Laura (1985), 'Il "Problema delle Parti" in Manoscritti del XIV e XV Secolo,' in Menso Folkerts and Uta Lindgren (eds), *Mathemata. Festschrift für Helmuth Gericke*. Boethius, Vol. 12. Stuttgart: Franz Steiner Verlag Wiesbaden GMBH, pp. 229–36.
Widman, J. (1489), *Behende und hubsche Rechnung auff allen Kauffmanschaft*. Goldsmiths' Library microfilm.
Wittsius, Herman (1798), *The Oeconomy of the Covenants between God and Man*, New York: George Forman.
Yushkevich, A.P. (1987), 'Nicholas Bernoulli and the Publication of James Bernoulli's Ars Conjectandi,' *Theory of Probability and its Applications*, **31** (2), pp. 286–303.

2 Isaac Le Maire and the early trading in Dutch East India Company shares

*J.G. van Dillen, Geoffrey Poitras and Asha Majithia**

The origin of trading in common stocks can be traced to the transactions in shares of the Dutch East India Company (VOC) on the Amsterdam Exchange (e.g. Poitras, 2000, ch. 8). This trade began with the founding of the company in 1602. There are two important secondary sources for this early trading: van Dillen (1930), which is written in Dutch and also includes numerous primary documents, such as the text of legal presentations concerning the valuation of VOC shares; and van Dillen (1935), in French, which summarizes much of the material in van Dillen (1930). Building on the more general overview of Amsterdam exchange trading given, in Dutch, in van Dillen (1927), these two sources focus on Isaac Le Maire, the key figure in the storm of controversy that characterized the early trade in VOC shares. Being produced over 70 years ago, a published reference that translates the sources into English is unavailable. This is an unfortunate omission because, in addition to providing a wealth of information about share trading practices in early seventeenth-century Amsterdam, the events of interest include the first organized attempt to manipulate the share market. As evidenced in De Marchi and Harrison (1994), Barbour (1950) and Wilson (1941), much of what is known about the early trade in shares originates with the work of van Dillen. By providing an accessible English translation of van Dillen (1935), this chapter aims to increase awareness of a range of issues that are of modern interest.

The role of Isaac Le Maire in the early trade in VOC shares is of modern interest for a number of reasons. Perhaps the most significant concerns the actual mechanics of a share price manipulation scheme involving Le Maire. Unlike most manipulations, where forward contracts are used to create a short squeeze resulting in rising prices, the manipulation led by Le Maire involved a series of actions designed to force down the price of shares. Under pressure from the directors of the VOC, the Dutch government acted to eliminate selling of shares for forward delivery that were not owned by the seller at the time of the forward sale. In modern sources, e.g., De Marchi and Harrison (1994), this has been portrayed as a ban on short selling. However, van Dillen (1935) reveals there is considerably more involved. Those involved in the manipulation were speculators making markets in shares. Because there were insufficient shares available for purchase, share traders created contracts that represented claims on shares – often settled with the payment of differences. These were typically forward or 'term' contracts. As a consequence, the market makers were net short the market. The incentive to engage in a 'bear run' follows appropriately.

Another aspect of the manipulation revealed by van Dillen (1935) is the extent of fraud among the participants. Despite being a significant shareholder, Le Maire was removed as a VOC director in 1605 having been found to have embezzled funds from a company-related venture. This was prior to the share price manipulation scheme. In addition, before forming the secret society to trade VOC shares in February 1609, during the period of the manipulation, and after the collapse of the scheme, Le Maire was engaged in attempts to launch a French company to rival the VOC. While being the biggest of the nine players in the secret group, Le Maire was not the only member of the group with unscrupulous motives. In particular, the solvency of the Bouwer brothers was in question. The brothers had sold considerable share positions for the longer term with the expectation of purchasing, at a later date, the positions for delivery at lower prices in the shorter-term market. A fall in prices was necessary for the Bouwers to avoid financial ruin. The adverse upward movement in share prices also brought ruin to a number of the members of the secret society. It seems that the restrictions on short selling (*in blanco* trading) were as much about controlling fraud as about Christian ethics and a negative social attitude toward the 'negative' aspects of speculative short selling.

A final aspect of van Dillen (1935) of modern interest concerns the micro-foundations of early share trading. Van Dillen accurately recognizes that VOC shares had a number of significant differences compared to modern common stocks, describing the VOC as a 'limited company *in training*'. Following Hecksher (1931), the VOC does satisfy the 'capital association of a corporate character' requirement for a joint stock company. Claims against the permanent capital stock of the company provided a forward trading vehicle with more attractive features than wheat and herring, where trading for future delivery was a common practice by the time the VOC was launched. The somewhat demanding requirements associated with actual transfer of VOC shares – involving attendance at the company transfer office and written approval by two directors – gave encouragement to the speculative practice of settlement by payment of differences. In turn, this provided an early foundation for the *rescontre* system for settlement of term sales that became common practice on the Amsterdam exchange by the mid-seventeenth century. The *rescontre* settlement process is described by de la Vega in *Confusion de confusiones* (1688) and was eventually transplanted to England, where it became standard market practice by the mid-eighteenth century.

References

Barbour, V. (1950), *Capitalism in Amsterdam in the 17th Century*, Ann Arbor, MI: University of Michigan Press.

De Marchi, N. and P. Harrison (1994), 'Trading "in the Wind" and with Guile: The Troublesome Matter of the Short Selling of Shares in Seventeenth-Century Holland', in N. De Marchi and M. Morgan (eds), *Higgling: Transactors and their Markets in the History of Economics*, Annual Supplement to *History of Political Economy*, **26**.

Hecksher, E. (1931), *Mercantilism* (2 vols), trans. by M. Shapiro (1935), London: Allen and Unwin.

Poitras, G. (2000), *The Early History of Financial Economics, 1478–1776*, Cheltenham, UK and Northampton, MA, USA: Edward Elgar.

van Dillen, J. (1927), 'Termijnhandel te Amsterdam in de 16de en 17de eeuw', *De Economist*: 503–23.

van Dillen, J. (1930), 'Isaac Le Maire en de handel in actien der Oost-Indische Compagnie', *Economisch-Historisch Jaarboek*: 1–165.

van Dillen, J. (1935), 'Isaac le Maire et le commerce des actions de la Compaigne de Indes Orientales', *Revue d'Histoire Moderne*: 5–21, 121–37.

Wilson, C. (1941), *Anglo-Dutch Commerce and Finance in the Eighteenth Century*; reprinted London: Cambridge University Press (1966).

Appendix

This section contains an English translation ('Isaac Le Maire and the Share Trading of the Dutch East India Company') of the text of J.G. van Dillen (1935), 'Isaac le Maire et le commerce des actions de la Compaigne de Indes Orientales', *Revue d'Histoire Moderne*: 5–21, 121–37.

Part I

Among the many business people from Antwerp who, after the capture of their city by the Duke of Parma, established themselves in Amsterdam around 1585, Isaac Le Maire was one of the best known. He was born in Tournai in 1559.[1] It appears that he lived in Antwerp for quite some time and, just prior to his departure, he married Maria Walraven. Twenty-two children were the result of this union, a detail that serves as more than simply bibliographic, as we will see later.

In Amsterdam, Le Maire practised, with much success, the business knowledge he acquired in Antwerp. Little is known about his first few years in Amsterdam.[2] It wasn't until 1601 that he decided to become a citizen.[3] But legal documents from around 1595 indicate that he was involved in significant business dealings at the time. The fact that many of his brothers had established themselves in foreign business centres no doubt helped facilitate these matters.

Nevertheless, Le Maire's major role begins with the foundation of the Brabantine Company (in 1599). The first Amsterdam company geared towards shipping from the Indian sub-continent was founded in 1594 by Reiner Pauw, Jean Corel, Dirk van Os and others. About 1597, around the time of the return of its first fleet, a rival company was created. Soon enough the first company would come to an agreement with this new company (founded by Vincent van Bronkhorst, Cornelis van Campen and others). The firm, born from the merger of these two companies, which was later named the Expert Company, was probably due to the return of Jack van Neck's fleet of richly loaded ships in 1599, after a quick and fortunate journey. This also formed the motive for Le Maire to create the Brabantine Company. Although only two of the four well-known directors of this company came from the southern Netherlands, namely Le Maire and Jacques de Velaer, it is possible that other Brabantines, such as Louis de la Beeque, were involved in the business.[4] This new company obtained authorization for shipping towards China only, a restriction of little concern to them. Again, a merger appeared to be the answer, but this time the project wasn't effected so easily. The Brabantine Company was founded in August 1599; the merger wasn't achieved until December 1600, and only because of the intervention of the burgomasters. The new United Amsterdam Company, which equipped a total of eight ships within the next year, with Jacques van Heemskerck as commander, was destined to a brief existence. In 1602, this company entered into a larger company, formed from the merger of almost all the Dutch and Zealander companies that existed: the United East India Company (or the byname the Dutch East India Company).

All of the directors of the former United Amsterdam Company obtained administrative functions within the new company. However, a fleet of 14 ships took to the open seas in 1602 under the command of Admiral Wybrant van Warwijck, for the accounts of a combination of directors from different Houses and not for the company. Isaac Le Maire was a part of this combination. Although Le Maire had plenty of zeal and enthusiasm for shipping to India, he spent very little time as a director of the company. At the beginning of the year 1605, he retired, even though he was among the principal shareholders (subscribed in the sum of 60000 florins). His retirement has often been considered voluntary, when in reality things happened in a totally different way.

In his studies of Isaac Le Maire, Bakhuizen van den Brink has already lifted the veil on this issue.[5] He discovered that rumours existed accusing Le Maire of fraudulent activities. According to these rumours, the bailiff of Amsterdam had summoned Le Maire and obtained the right to sentence him by default. But no decisive proof was made available; in vain the bailiff asked the directors for precise information. In the absence of this information, the law of the times, which was very favourable to arbitrators and advantageous to the justice civil servants, allowed the bailiff to sentence him to a fine of 1200 Flemish pounds, to profit himself and the burgomasters.

Unfortunately, the source from which Bakhuizen drew his information is unknown. I had the chance to find confirmation from a source that Bakhuizen certainly did not use, the minutes of the Consistory of the Reformed Church of Amsterdam.[6] On 23 December 1604 the Consistory made the following decision: since unfortunate rumours are spreading around the entire city about Isaac Le Maire, director of the Dutch East India Company, but it is unknown whether these rumours are true, it was decided to communicate with Le Maire. A few weeks later, Pastor Plancius and his predecessor Philips Corneliszoon were put in charge of proceeding with an investigation, an investigation that, it seems, never took place, perhaps because they were waiting for the result of the judicial investigation. But a year and a half later, this issue became current again because of some unfortunate news Le Maire gave his church.[7] At a meeting on 5 July 1605, the Consistory notes that the administrators never pursued an investigation and decided to speak to the 'Majores' (a title often given to directors) for precise information. Again the responsibility of this was put on Plancius and Philips Corneliszoon. On 9 August they released their report; certain directors had told them that Le Maire had definitely committed fraudulent activities and that he had used his son and servant as accomplices; that the company had established his guilt and Le Maire, having confessed his guilt, had been sentenced to a hefty fine and had paid it. After hearing these communications, the Consistory decided to summon Le Maire. He refused to appear in person but consented to receive a delegation from the committee. Once again Plancius and Philips Corneliszoon were put in charge of interrogating Le Maire, this time at his place. Unfortunately the minutes contain little but brief notes on their report. They only state, 'a lot of things explained themselves differently from what was presented by his accusers' and then continue: 'Due to the fact that this is a matter of great importance, the pastors consented to carry on with the investigation.' In reality it doesn't seem as if the investigation took place because the minutes contain no additional references to it.

There exists a document that proves that the accusation relates to the expedition of the 14 ships, under the command of Van Warwijck. This expedition was undertaken, as stated earlier, for the accounts, not of the company but for a handful of directors. In accordance with the custom of the first firms, each of the directors was responsible for some of the arrangements. Le Maire neglected to return, when the accounts were consolidated, the receipts and other documents concerned with his division. Questioned about this neglect, he tried to defend himself, but, based on the events that followed, his explanation was seen as insufficient.

Later on, Le Maire always maintained his innocence. But the extracted minutes mentioned above, along with the communication from Bakhuizen, give the impression that Le Maire was actually guilty of embezzlement, even though the report of Plancius and his predecessor refers to questionable circumstances.

It is clear, now, that Le Maire did not retire of his own accord. On 22 February 1605 he signed a declaration in which he promised, among other things, not to undertake any expeditions around the Cape of Good Hope or by the Strait of Magellan, and also to not participate in any similar expeditions, in any undertakings of others besides himself, either in Holland or in a foreign country.[8] In addition, he was required to hand over all documents in his possession regarding the company to the directors. As a guarantee he committed a sum of 3000 Flemish Pounds, against the accounts of the company and also a few firms he owned in Egmond.

The King of France, Henry IV, had long nurtured the idea of founding an East India Company in his country. The negotiations that started with this in mind, with a few unhappy Dutch merchants, such as Balthasar of Moucheron and Pieter Lyntgens, were not successful.[9] Around the end of 1607, the French minister Jeannin was put in charge of this project. A Brabantine councillor drew attention to Isaac Le Maire. He was eager to accept suggestions made to him. In March 1608, he had, on several occasions, long meetings with the French minister, either at a very late or very early hour, in fear 'of those from Amsterdam', as Bakhuizen would call them. But the uncertainty that existed surrounding the relationship between France and Holland, and negotiations for an armistice with Spain, prevented any definitive agreements.

At the same time, the English explorer Hudson arrived in Amsterdam, around the end of 1608. Seeing that negotiations with the company were as yet unsuccessful, Le Maire tried to persuade him to take a voyage to the extreme north for the service of the King of France.[10] In his letters to the King, Jeannin warmly recommended the project.[11] But as a penalty, the directors, on hearing about this project, got in touch with Hudson. The result of this was that, in April 1609, the *HalveMaen* took to the open seas for the company, in search of a northern passage to India.

Far from being discouraged by this misfortune, Le Maire wrote to Jeannin as early as 25 January 1609 to say that he knew of a captain even more experienced than the Englishman. M. Naber supposes he was referring to Jean Ryp. Henry IV let himself be persuaded by Jeannin, who, apparently, was himself persuaded by Le Maire's enthusiasm, to supply the funds for the expedition. Since it didn't seem that Ryp wanted to take part in this undertaking, they had to settle for Melchior van den Kerckhove, about whom we know only that he was an experienced seaman. Le Maire played an ambiguous enough role: officially, the expedition left under his name, he even obtained a letter of recommendation from Prince Maurice, but the captain received secret instructions, after the possible discovery of a strait, to hoist the French flag and, after the expedition, to stop in a French port. On 5 May, one month after Hudson, Van den Kerckhove took to the open sea, with a ship loaded by Le Maire, from his own account, with merchandise totalling 10 000 florins. Of this expedition all that is known is that the desired result was not achieved.[12]

Before he left for France, in the summer of 1609, Jeannin received a promise from Le Maire that he would come to Paris to start negotiations on the creation of a French East India Company. Le Maire did indeed leave for the capital of France during the month of December. De Jonge has already revealed some details about this visit, details that he found in a letter that François van Aerssen, Minister of the Republic, wrote on 25 December to the General Assembly. Additional correspondence of François van Aerssen with Oldenbarnevelt that I've been able to consult allows me to provide more precise information about this event.[13]

Before 8 December , the minister announced that the question of the creation of an East India Company had re-emerged. Jeannin, who would have been leading this project, also publicly admitted it. On 16 December, Aerssen, in his letter to Oldenbarnevelt, always using the French language, wrote: 'I find that a company for East India is advancing quickly. Girard le Roy, with Isaac Le Maire, both from Amsterdam, are strongly endorsing it; I've been told that the latter is here, staying secretly with Lamet.[14] I still doubt him even though it is true that he promised M. Janin in his letter to leave Amsterdam on 29 November, under the pretext of seeing to his businesses in Antwerp …'. Moucheron and Joris van Spilbergh were also in Paris. They deliberated every day. Aerssen tried in vain to convince the King's advisers that the undertaking would be as disastrous for the French as it had been for the Dutch, particularly because the prices for spices were on the rise in India and decreasing in Europe due to competition. They realized, in part, the truth of this argument; but then they thought of the idea of a United Company of France, England and the Republic. Aerssen responded that this project was unrealizable: 'it is enough that the funding would be too large, with regards to the deposit, but we, with only the original funding, already have more spices than Europe can consume'. A similar project would be more possible in regard to the West Indies, but these men wanted to stick to their original idea; the foundation of a West India Company hardly attracted their attention in the circumstances at the time.

Why did Henry IV hold on to his idea of the creation of an East India Company? Aerssen tells us: 'The King is impressed with this company for the pure profit that he could receive from the sale of spices that, in the same way as salt, could be distributed by his kingdom'. According to Aerssen, the King was making a mistake because the French only demanded nutmeg and cloves and very little pepper!

One of the partners declared that he was willing to sabotage the project, in exchange for sufficient compensation. This was Balthasar de Moucheron. 'Moucheron, who is one of the managers, approached me yesterday and proposed that he has a way to break up the plan, if I would be willing to send a reward with him; I excused myself, with the promise that I would ask you [Oldenbarnevelt] about this, on condition that we would use this opening discreetly and that his role in this affair would be covered up'. A few days later Aerssen wrote that Le Maire was avoiding him and that the negotiations were continuing.

On 25 December, the correspondence takes a positive tone. 'I think I've broken the collar of Isaac Le Maire's plan; as a minimum M. de Sully promised me that within six months, he would stop talking with him and wouldn't allow him to be aided by the King's purse, from which he needs funding.' Around the same time a letter was written in Dutch, addressed to the General Assembly. This letter tells us that Le Maire had finally decided to visit the minister. It is with reason that De Jonge speaks of a dramatic meeting. The cunning businessman started by pretending he didn't know anything, then once Aerssen made it clear that he was up to date with all the events, and that he even knew that Le Maire had worked out an entire plan, Le Maire decided to confess. He tried to justify his actions by reminding Aerssen about his large family and of the wrong that other directors had done to him. And, whereas in the past he had always assured Jeannin that, born in Tournai, he had always felt like a Frenchman, he showed himself in front of Aerssen like a good Dutchman, who would never undertake anything without the consent of the State.[15]

However, Aerssen had claimed victory too soon. Even if he had been, as stated by De Jonge, the most perspicacious diplomat of his time, his influence wasn't as unlimited as seemed. He had taken the declarations of the French too seriously. On 29 December he was obliged to admit his ignorance to Oldenbarnevelt: 'Le Maire, who had to leave, renewed his pursuit with the encouragement of M. Jeannin, who took him to see the King this morning, whom he spoke to about the advantages of this commerce for more than half and hour. He argues strongly that he had told you the subject of his voyage and that you had approved it. I did not believe that he discovered that you had real funds; I learned of that later.' It should be noted that in a previous letter Aerssen had said that Le Maire claimed the approval of Oldenbarnevelt.

At last, on 5 January 1610, Aerssen could say that the dangerous man had left: '[He] carried [letters] from the King for his discharge and must return as first in command and undertake the direction of this company, M. les Etat consulted with him. We will spend this year preparing; M. de Sully told me that they are not as far on as they think, that one year is as far as resolution of this matter is concerned. M. Janin said as much; but it is he who is in charge of the direction of all this and of the way Le Maire is treated. I do not have anything else, I had done what you asked of me when I advised you of what was happening … .' The tone of the letters had definitely changed. Even though, ten days earlier, he had again announced with an air of triumph that he had struck a fatal blow for the plans for the project, he was forced to recognize that the matter was progressing.[16] He consoled himself with the idea that he had done as much as he could.

During this time, rumours about what was going on in Paris had reached Amsterdam. The directors had addressed the burgomasters with a petition in which they maintained that the company was compelled to take on excessive expenses for the wars against Spain and Portugal and that therefore their shares were selling at an extremely low price. It would be very unfair if others could profit from the sacrifices made by the company by going to look for spices in ill-equipped ships with low overhead. After receiving this petition the burgomasters quickly persuaded the General Assembly, in a letter in January 1610, to do anything within their power to prevent the creation of a French East India Company.[17]

This illustrates well that, in fact, there was reason to worry. Le Maire probably didn't find his welcome by the Stock Exchange too joyous. On 1 May he gave his cousin, Alexandre Le Maire, full permission to transfer stock in his name. His name disappeared from Aerssen's letters. The assassination of Henry IV (14 May 1610) was a cruel blow to Le Maire. Following this event, the opportunity to create a French East India Company disappeared for quite some time.

In the early companies, the names of shareholders were unknown to anyone except the administrator to whom they made their payments. One could sell or pass on a stock and the company would hardly notice.[18]

At the Dutch East India Company (founded in 1602) things happened differently. The shareholders were inscribed in the books of the houses of the company, where the money was deposited. At first, it was decided that payments would be made in three allotments but in reality they were completed in 12, with the last one being in 1606.[19] When a shareholder sold their 'stock', a word that came into use much later, it had to be transferred to the name of the purchaser in the presence of two directors. Also the seller had to present himself in person at the office of the relevant division.

It is with reason that the Dutch East India Company is considered as one of the first models of a limited company. However, its structure differed a great deal, especially in the beginning, from those institutions that we designate today with this title. It was really a limited company *in training*. One of the points of difference is that shares of the company didn't have a set, round nominal value; they had various values. Next, the shareholder had almost no rights. With the exception of the General Meeting, the shareholder had no influence over the choice of directors. At first it was thought that the State houses of the different respective provinces appointed the directors, and very quickly, at least in the province of Holland, the burgomasters of cities where the houses were established seized on this idea. Only in 1623, to comply with the wishes of unhappy shareholders, were they allowed to present a list of nominees, a right that was purely theoretical!

Did the company issue securities? Many authors are inclined to give an affirmative response to this question. Sayous is of the mind that we can consider the receipts given to shareholders when payment was made as a security. Van Brackel is in agreement with him, and considered the existence of securities as a necessary condition for the development of share trading.[20]

This opinion was decisively refuted by M. Smith.[21] Negotiable securities never existed. When van Brackel speaks of a 'paper' trade of the company, he presents matters in a very modern way. If securities really did exist, the transfer and complicated formalities that are linked to them would be superfluous. The matter could have been considered resolved, if it hadn't been for the arrival of F.W. Stapel.[22] He recognized that sellable securities didn't exist but, nevertheless, believed he could prove that shareholders received a supporting document. He declared this with satisfaction, having discovered that, after the last payment, the provisional receipts were exchanged for a general receipt. He found proof of this fact in a resolution passed on 28 August 1606, when it was decided that shareholders who had paid the last of the 12 payments would be given a general receipt for the entire sum they had invested into the company and that the provisional receipts would lose their value. In my opinion, he didn't prove anything except that a specific distinction was made between general and provisional receipts. Also he forgot that the shareholders had the right to sell parts of their shares, at a considerable price, a right that they used quite often. The general receipt could never serve as proof that one held a share of a specific value. It only proved that the named person was absolved of their payment obligations; in other words it was nothing but a simple receipt.

Stapel was even more mistaken, in my opinion, when he maintained that the new buyers also received a security. Here's what he wrote on the subject: 'The process for transferring a share has been explained on several occasions: the new shareholder received a document signed by the seller and two directors. This document was proof of their shareholding. The note of transfer played the same role for the subsequent buyers as the general receipt did for the primary shareholder.'

This way of presenting things is not correct. The author seemed to have read the pages of Smith that he refers to only very superficially. The transfer form that he speaks of, signed by the seller and two directors, was never given to the buyer, but was, in contrast, carefully preserved by the company.[23] The Transfer Books, of which an entire series has been preserved in the National Archives, were essentially made up of completed forms. One could ask if the transfer certificate could have been duplicated and if the buyer could have received this copy; but no indication of this has ever been found. In the many legal documents that exist, there is no mention of such use.[24] Also it should be noted that a transfer certificate differs from a security, since the share named in the certificate could be resold. All that I have just stated permits, in my opinion, only the following conclusion to be drawn: the company never issued securities. The shareholders identified themselves exclusively by the books of the company, namely the great book of shareholders and the books of transfer.

The only 'paper' received, from time to time, by those who bought and sold shares was an agreement of sale. It is doubtful that similar agreements were drawn up for cash dealings, but it was the law when the deals were a matter of a term sale. Towards 1629, models for term sales were available everywhere; a white space allowed for the inscription of the name of the company.[25] It must be noted that these were not legal documents but were for private use.

The absence of securities didn't, however, prevent the development of an extensive stock trade. The centre of this trade was the Amsterdam Stock Exchange. With a few exceptions, it was mainly the shares of the House of Amsterdam that traded regularly. This fact was explained with the requirement imposed on the dealers to present themselves in person at the time of transfer, which obviously made it difficult for residents of Amsterdam to partake in trading stock from other houses.

The demand for securities, with a view to their investment alone, can never in itself create active trading. This is achieved only with speculation, that is by the operations of those who buy and sell in order to profit from price differences. In the trade of wheat, very important in Amsterdam for a long time, speculation was far from uncommon. So it is not surprising that the first transactions entered into at the Amsterdam Stock Exchange were part of the same schemes.

The 'shares' of former companies had also been sold, but up to now no information has been found to document stock market transactions about them. It is with the creation of the Dutch East India Company that the first modern company appears. Its capital was divided into a large number of shares: those of the House of Amsterdam alone were worth 3687415 fl; divided between 1201 subscribers. Some of the capital was fixed but there were a good number of shareholders ready to sell a part of their total share if it was profitable for them. The unequal value of each share was obviously a significant obstacle to steady trade. But a large number of important shareholders, among them Isaac Le Maire, who had invested 60000 fl., could, in subdividing their assets, offer shares at a fixed, round value. It is well known that, in the second half of the seventeenth century, all share trades were made with a nominal value of 500 Flemish pounds, that is 3000 florins. Documents prove that, a few years after the creation of the company, the Exchange preferred shares of this value; but shares of different values, always round, were also sold.

In documents, shares valid for ten years are always referred to. That meant that every ten years there was a projected closing of the accounts: the shareholders had to retake possession of their deposited sum, augmented by their portion of the profits. Afterwards a new ten-year subscription needed to be opened. Moreover, the grant certificate contained a clause stating that shareholders would receive a first dividend as soon as the bank recovered 5 per cent from the sale of cargo upon return. Mansvelt remarked that at the time of the creation of the company there apparently wasn't the slightest idea about the needs of a continuing company.[26] The first dividend wasn't paid until 1610; moreover, in 1612 the State excused the company from clearing the accounts and returning the deposits to the shareholders. This decision was motivated by the argument that the shareholders who wanted to could use the Stock Exchange to realize their returns.

Alongside the ten-year shares, the Exchange also sold shares in the 14 ships. I've already alluded to the fact that in 1602, 14 ships took to the open sea, for the accounts of a combination of directors and their shareholders. The management of this enterprise was separate from that of the company. These shareholders, who received their dividends well before those of the company, received a total of 265 per cent. Many authors wrongly considered this sum as a dividend; the initial capital deposited was obviously included in this figure.

At the beginning, a share with all the rights attached to it was considered an indivisible whole. That is, not only the right to future dividends was sold but also the dividends already paid, where the latter were included in the purchase price. A report from 1613 shows that the purchaser could fold back the purchase price by the value of the dividends already received, unless the share was already selling at a 'remaining' price. This explains the expression 'remaining shares' that we often see later. As the first dividend of the ten-year shares wasn't paid until 1610, this last complication had little impact on trading activities before then.

The shares sold not only for cash but also on term. This wasn't anything new in Amsterdam, since term sales had been the custom for trade in wheat and herring. It goes without saying that only term sales could serve speculative goals. Those who term sell don't need to have the merchandise in possession at the time of sale. This is why the 'white' sale of shares doesn't seem to be disappearing.

A few years after the foundation of the company, a large number of shares were bought and sold on term. This gave rise to complicated mutual obligations. It was clear that the settlement of the positions was occurring without the unwinding purse of the Exchange and that only the difference was being paid out in cash. The word 'rescontre' refers to this sort of trade. On this point, it would be tempting to talk about the term market, but fixed terms of liquidation were not yet in use.[27]

Part II

For several days following the 1602 subscription, and even before the payment, East India Company shares increased to 14–15 per cent above par. Then interest became weaker and the trading rate remained unchanged for several years at 103 per cent and 105 per cent. However, when good news arrived from the Indies – the occupation of the islands of Amboine and Timor and especially when the vessels from the Steven Verhagen fleet returned richly loaded in 1605 – the trading rate rose to 140 per cent. Over the course of the following year, optimism was bound. At the news – which turned out later to be false – of the taking of *Malaque*, the shares even climbed to above 200 per cent. But in 1607 bad news arrived, and the trading rate fell to 158–160 per cent. In the two following years, the decline continued, so that in January 1610 the trading rate was quoted very low at 126 per cent at the time and at 131 per cent after a one-year term. At that time, there was once again a sudden turnaround. The news coming out of the East Indies improves; the vessels return richly loaded. The directors agree on a 75 per cent mace dividend, with a dividend of 50 per cent in pepper and yet another of 7½ per cent in silver to follow yet again in the autumn. It goes without saying that the trading rate then increased considerably.

It was especially in the spring of the year 1609 that the decline in the trading rate of the shares was the steepest. The directors believed that this phenomenon was due, not to natural causes, but to the intrigues of a group of decline speculators. They saw in this particular situation the hand of Isaac Le Maire, whose negotiations with Hudson and with the King of France had not remained secret.

This is why – probably in the summer of the year 1609 – they addressed a petition to the General Assembly. They say that there is a conspiracy, a 'dirty scheme'. The conspirators continuously sell large share portions which include a long term of one to five years for amounts which exceed what they own by several thousand florins.[28] At the time of delivery, they weigh down the trading rates by spreading unfavourable rumours. With much trickery, they sell for reduced amounts 'shares often purchased by their own accomplices' and at the same time they purchase large amounts at very low prices. This is to the disadvantage of a large number of shareholders, in particular widows and orphans, who let themselves be persuaded by the false rumours into getting rid of their shares. In addition, the agitators have sold such large parts that they will soon no longer be able to deliver. The directors even believe that 'the general enemy has its accomplices among the important sellers'.[29] This is why they are asking the States to render impossible the blank sale of shares by decreeing that from now on the entry into the books will have to take place no later than one month following the sale.

This petition did not remain unanswered. 'Several businessmen' presented a request of their own in which they declared that the decrease in the trading rates was in no way caused by 'dirty schemes'; it came about as a result of natural causes. Did the company not have a whole gamut of difficulties: the loss of the islands of Tenerate and Timor, the siege without success of Malaque, and the sinking of several vessels?

Mr De Jonge had already used the two documents mentioned above and it was he who published them. However, I found a paper which, given the handwriting, was probably from the hand of Isaac Le Maire himself and which was most likely written in August 1609.[30] There is no indication to whom this document is addressed; it may have been intended for Oldenbarnevelt, whom Le Maire knew, to inform him personally.

The author begins by listing the vessels which sank. He evaluates the loss at no less than 1 500 000 florins. Four vessels have just docked, but one of them, the *Ter Gouw*, still belongs to the 14 vessels. Of the other three, the *Ter Veer*, the *Ceylan* and the *Bantam*, part of the freight is destined for the consortium which equipped the 14 vessels. Based on this, the total value of the merchandise going to the company is less than fl.1 800 000. The vessels are bringing a quantity of mace equal to the value of fl. 800 000, which, however, will not be able to be sold for five years because there is still a large quantity of mace in stock in the stores and even more is expected. The proportion that will be able to be sold annually should be estimated at most at 10 per cent and it should be taken into account that the quality tends to diminish.

Before the arrival of the vessels, the shares were being sold at 123–124 per cent cash and 134 per cent at a year; then they increased to 150 per cent at a year; but as soon as it was discovered that a part of the merchandise was intended for the group of 14 vessels, it reduced once again to 132 per cent cash and 142 per cent at a year, a price which exceeds the real value. The directors were irritated by the fact that the trading rate remained so low. They would have liked to see it increase to 180 per cent and even 200 per cent 'as the shares have done in the past'. This is why they accused those 'constantly busy buying and selling shares' of trickery. Two years before, when the shares were trading at 180–200 per cent, many people with no business knowledge purchased shares 'as soon as they saw that some directors were purchasing them as well, because the directors knew the right time'.

There was no reason to say that the decrease would be harmful to widows and orphans. As a general rule, those people kept the shares they had. If some of them were selling, 'this was a service to other widows and orphans who, not knowing how to place their money, purchased new shares with the Company'.

The author believes that the directors were motivated by greed, for several of them purchased 'large portions of shares at a very high price'. They knew that several of their colleagues were more reasonable and even sold part of what they owned. For some time, we find repeated several times the point made in discussions in the Assembly of the Seventeen – and again at the Assembly of 1 September in Middelburg – the question of knowing if the directors still own the required amount of shares. 'The president must question them specifically regarding this.' This proves that people were realizing the dangerous situation the company was in.

The States of Holland consulted with the Court of Holland and the Superior Court regarding the administrators' request. It was about this consultation that the share merchants addressed the Court in January 1610. In this petition, they listed again the losses suffered by the company, which they valued this time at a million florins. They noted also that the large mace reserves piled up in the stores would not be able to be sold within the first few years. In effect, without authorization, the directors took considerable amounts of money as deposits, for which they had to pay 8 per cent in interest. It is therefore 'clear as day that the share merchants are not the cause for the decrease, but that it can be found in the Company's actual situation'. One would even be justified in saying that the current price was still too high. It was in fact the trade of shares which was maintaining the price. The authors see proof of this in the fact that the shares from the Rotterdam, Delft, Hoom and Ekhuiz Chambers usually are traded at 3–5 per cent less than those from the Amsterdam and Zealand Chambers, because there one does not know business or '*rescontre*'. The term sale has always been allowed: 'often herring was sold using term sales before it was even caught, wheat and other merchandise, before it was grown or before it was received'. Up until now the sellers have settled their obligations; several of the buyers, on the other hand, among whom one finds several directors, went bankrupt. The petition requesting the forbidding of share trading is, in their opinion, related to individual interests: several directors bought, through term sales, shares for a large sum of money, and these people are already announcing 'loudly' that they are certain that the sellers will be unable to deliver them, 'adding to this the threat of kicking them out of the city if they do not follow through on their obligations'. The petitioners then insist strongly on the maintenance of the freedom of trade. If this freedom is reduced, it is quite likely that the trade of shares will move, as it is already no longer taking place in Amsterdam and Middleburg, but it also occurs in Hamburg, in Frankfurt, in Cologne, in Rouen and elsewhere.

As a supplement, they added to this petition a sort of report which was to show clearly the bad situation the company was in. It is very interesting that, among the liability positions, there is, besides the capital, a sum amounting to 26 per cent of the capital. We remember that the trading rate for the shares was at the time 126 per cent cash.

Just like Le Maire's paper, the two petitions on the part of the merchants show a wealth of knowledge, both of the commerce in the Indies and of the interior business of the company. It is not far-fetched to speculate that Le Maire had his part in the writing of these documents. One might ask: how did Le Maire get his hands on such precise data regarding the company? I believe the solution to the problem lies in the fact that the head accountant for the company was also an enemy of the directors. This person was a certain Barent Lampe, cited by the Minister of France as being among those who were ready to support Henry IV's enterprise.

The petitions were without success. On 27 February 1610, an ordinance was promulgated banning the blank [*in blanco*] sale of shares. This is therefore an absolute ban on selling shares that one does not own. The shares sold must be transferred no later than a month following the sale. The intention was not, however, to make term sales impossible. But the proclamation specified that, when it was decided to defer the payment until a later date, the seller would keep, regardless of the transfer, 'mortgage rights' over the shares sold. There is one point, however, where the directors were not able to impose their will: they had wanted the obligation to transfer no later than a month following the sale to be applied to current contracts as well. But the proclamation does not speak of such a decision, which would have caused great difficulties for blank sellers.

The documents mentioned above leave no doubt as to the fact that 'decline speculation' and blank sales existed on the Amsterdam Stock Exchange in 1609. But should one conclude that there existed a real bear speculators *organization,* a 'dirty scheme', as the directors say? A happy discovery made in the legal archives enables me to prove that the accusation was well founded. On 11 February 1609, Isaac Le Maire and eight other merchants founded a society which had as its goal to trade East India Company shares at their common expense. Their collaboration was to last several months, until April at the latest. Reinier Lems[31] was appointed accountant. The goal was as much to buy as to sell shares. The associates were to meet two or three times a week. The one put in charge of buying or selling something for the society was to give account of his dealings at the next meeting. It is not certain whether they operated with a fixed capital. But it is mentioned that Le Maire had four-fifteenths' interest in the business. He was followed by Hans Bouwer with two-fifteenths, with most of the others only interested for one-fifteenth. The society is listed under the name 'the big company'. One would therefore be tempted to conclude that there also existed a 'small company' of the same type, but until now no trace of one has been found.

Unfortunately the founding act has never been found. What I have just said was revealed through several acts dated 1610 and 1612, relating to dissension between the associates regarding the way the business was run. One of these acts states that on 28 March 1610, which is to say one month after the promulgation of the proclamation, the associates made the decision in one of their meetings 'never again to sell to profit their company, but to "*resconter*" only the parties who are yet to receive with the parties who have yet to deliver'. This passage is important because there is already mention of liquidation, which would later become one of the essential elements of the term market. The term '*resconter*' is also found in one of the petitions from the share merchants.

Le Maire's company was without a doubt a secret organization. The business was always done in the name of one of the associates. One of them, named Steven Gerritsen, lived in Dordrecht. The accountant Reinier Lems, who was sometimes given the title of 'director', bought and sold in his own name. The term sale was still being done using a private agreement. A notary public was only contacted if one of the two parties did not fulfil his obligations. I published a great number of the legal notices in the *Annals of Economic History* ('Isaac Le Maire en de handel in actien der Oost-Indische Compagnie', *Economisch-Historisch Jaarboek 1930*: 1–165).

The term sales are often rather long, sometimes of several months, almost always of two or three years. In his paper, Le Maire says that the shares were again at 180–200 per cent in 1607, whereas in the summer of 1609 they were only at 132 per cent cash and 142 per cent with a one-year term. The second petition by the merchants lists a trading rate of 126 per cent cash for January 1610. The legal acts confirm that this information is correct. In the spring of the year 1607 people are selling with a three-year term with 112 per cent in advance, which means it is at a trading rate of 212 per cent; in September people are only selling at 183 per cent with a three-year term. In spring 1609, trading rates are quoted as being at 155–6 per cent at two years; in August the trading rate is of 140 per cent at one year; in October, 144 per cent at two years; in December, 133 per cent at six months. These data are very incomplete, but at least they give a good idea of the considerable decline in the trading rates, although one might expect to see an even stronger decline. De Jonge was of the opinion that the shares were below par, but this is incorrect. The word 'advance' obviously means the profits.[32] Is it in fact possible that, from the year 1608 to the year 1610, the shares were above par? In 1612, the ten years of the first application would be finished and then shareholders would be able to take back their money if they wished to do so. People had become a little less optimistic with regard to the profits, but no one was thinking of the possibility of a loss of a part of the capital.

However, in 1610, the trading rate increased considerably once again; in July and in August it was at 152 per cent and 156 per cent and in spring 1611 it even reached 200 per cent.[33] This increase is related, on one hand, to the favourable news coming from the Indies and, on the other, to the announcement of the distribution of the dividends to the shareholders. In all likelihood, the decision made in April 1610 by the directors to distribute 75 per cent in mace can mainly be explained by the hope they had of stopping the decline of the trading rates.[34] The company had very little money available but had much merchandise, which was impossible to sell at a reasonable price. In the autumn the shareholders received yet again 50 per cent in pepper at the same time as 7½ per cent in silver.[35] In 1612 there followed the distribution of 30 per cent in nutmeg. The right to receive merchandise they could not sell was obviously a doubtful advantage for the shareholders. Also, most of them did not seem to have exercised this right. Several years later, the spice market had much improved. The company was then able, little by little, to sell its stocks. To the shareholders who did not accept the distribution of merchandise, the same percentage, 162½ per cent, was distributed in silver over several terms during the years of 1612 to 1620.[36]

During the year 1610, the contributors to the decline found themselves in very big difficulties. The shares purchased with a one-year term had expired and, following the increase in the trading rates, they were forced to buy them at a higher price. But they were also burdened with regard to the contracts that had not yet expired. For, in the trading of shares, it was a rule that the shares be sold, including dividends. The buyers were having the sellers warned, using a legal act, that they would have to take delivery of the mace and the pepper to profit the buyer and that, if this didn't happen, they would themselves subtract the dividend already distributed in silver from the purchase price at the time of delivery. In addition, the buyers usually required the sellers to prove that they actually were in possession of the shares sold. Le Maire and the other contributors to the decline declared with good reason that nothing forced them to do this. Despite this, Le Maire declared that he was registered in the company's book for an amount higher than 87 000 florins. The other contributors to the decline, who apparently did not hold an interest representing a big sum of money, were smart enough to remain silent.

When the contributors to the decline saw that the game was lost, they tried to liquidate the then current contracts. Instead of delivering the shares, people were content most often to pay the surplus, the difference between trading rates, which had to be settled later.

In the months of April and May 1610, several of the contributors to the decline declared bankruptcy, including Hans Bouwer, Harmen Rosenerans, Reinier Lems and Jacques Damman.[37] Soon the situation became even more difficult when it surfaced that Hans Bouwer and his brother Jasper were convicted of fraud: they had transferred shares for a total value which was well above the amount of their interest in the company.[38] The fact that this was possible despite all the required formalities was due to their complicity with the accountant from the Barent Lampe Company, whom I mentioned above was working with Le Maire. In accordance with the practice, two directors assisted with each transfer; however, since they had total confidence in their accountant, they neglected to check if the person completing the transfer really held interest in the company in the amount being transferred.

Despite the irrefutable proof of fraud, those who had been registered in the company's books in this manner claimed to be recognized as shareholders, which the company refused to do. A long trial, whose outcome we do not know, was born from this dispute.

One of the documents relating to the trial contains the following testimony, given by the directors, regarding the Bouwer brothers. In their opinion the purchasers should have avoided any relationship with people whom they knew intended to pillage the prosperity of the company, and whose meanness was proven in, among other things, their behaviour when they were in Amsterdam at the Doelen with several others of their associates and several vessels returning from the Indies were in great difficulty near the island of Texel following a storm: they drank a toast while singing 'The vessels have sunk, the crew was saved, let's drink to that!'[39]

The purchasers (say the directors) let themselves be seduced by the hope of making a profit, thanks to the difference in trading rates, even though they should have known about the doubtfulness of the Bouwer brothers' solvency. In particular, the fact that the latter were acting out of desperation made it certain that, if the price of the shares did not decline considerably (either by accident or because of trickery), they were ruined. 'For having sold for purchase [*sic*] numerous long-term shares, they had as their goal to bring down the trading rates – by buying large portions of shares at modest prices – and thus to buy, before the expiration date at a lower price, the shares already sold, which would enable them to make a considerable profit'.[40]

Hans Bouwer was not only a brave speculator, he was also an impostor who, in a very clever way, led the purchasers to believe that they had come into possession of the shares by legal means.[41] All of this does not give us a very high opinion of the people who were Le Maire's associates in the 'big company'.

It would seem that the losses the 'big company' suffered were not too great; one of the acts gives an approximate figure of fl. 45 000. But the personal losses seem to have been worse, with several bankruptcies following, including that of Reinier Lems, who was the accountant for the 'big company' but had never actually become one of the associates.

Thus we can conclude that in 1609 there existed on the Amsterdam Stock Exchange a 'dirty scheme' led by Le Maire.[42] The sentences defining the 'big company's' goal seem quite innocent; but, when one considers them in relation to the rest, one must note that the company had as its goal to cause the decline by artificial means. Everything leads to the belief that the manner in which the directors presented matters was overall correct. The associates did in fact sell as *in blanco* large portions of shares. The fact that they tried to lower the trading rates by spreading worrying rumours is also no doubt true. Nevertheless, it is certain that they negotiated share trades among themselves. This also confirms the complaint from the administrators, who accused them of having negotiated small portions of share trades among themselves in order to reduce the trading rate and thus to be able to buy at an advantageous price.

However, for their part, Le Maire and his friends are probably right when they say that it is the fate of the company which decides the increases and decreases. If, around 1609, there was any reason to worry, the speculators seem to have exaggerated. They were basing their claim, it is true, on a factor they could not mention in their request, which was the hope of success of the negotiations of Le Maire with Henri IV! Ludwig Samuel exaggerates, however, when he says that 'the speculators claimed to know much more about business than the directors of the East India Company'.[43] If it is true that the directors exaggerated the influence the speculation had on the trading rates, it is certain on the other hand that the speculators can, using well-thought-out manipulations, have an influence for some time on the trading rate. In addition, in the trading of shares, the 'big company' can be considered as the prototype of a well-organized association aiming at decline.

Most of the members of the 'big company' probably had no other goal than to make a nice profit. However, Le Maire had something else in mind. Following the failure of his negotiations with Hudson, he had, as I mentioned above, suggested to the Minister of France to send out another experienced explorer, a suggestion which was met with enthusiasm and which strengthened the project to found a French Company of the East Indies. In his paper addressed to Oldenbarnevelt dated 24 January 1609, Le Maire fought with numerous arguments the directors' request asking for an extension of the concessions on the deltas which remained to be discovered; the company had wanted to take on too much and was thus unable to dispense its true functions; instead of broadening them, its grants should have instead been reduced; next to it, there needed to be room for other companies.[44] Just when Le Maire was taking care of this opening of the way for the foundation of a competing company, the 'big company' was doing its work! One can't help but think that, in contributing to the decline of the shares, Le Maire wanted to confirm the assertions that the company was being badly administrated.

His projects failed. Henry IV's death removed for a long time the possibility of founding a French company. Van den Kerckhove's voyage brought no results. In 1610, the company's shares increased instead of declining.

In the spring of the year 1611, Le Maire leaves Amsterdam to settle permanently in Egmond. There is only one document stating that he is no longer able to settle his delivery obligations; but nowhere does it mention anything about bankruptcy. He seems to still hold some assets but he can't have access to them. He still holds an interest in the company in the amount of 3000 Flemish pounds (fl. 18 000) but based on the 22 February 1605 contract, the directors refuse to transfer them. He is also disallowed the distribution of what is his of the products from the eight and fourteen vessels. The directors bring up at length a lawsuit against him.[45] In March 1613, Le Maire asks the business community to take appropriate action so that the differences can be resolved by arbiters, but they let him know, through Reinier Pauw, that they can do nothing for him and that they 'do not wish to establish any relationship with him'. The anonymous author of the letter communicating the refusal to him – probably his brother, Pastor Johannes Le Maire – attributes the unfavourable results to the influence of the directors whom everyone tries to flatter. These are 'mean and enraged' people who are very unfair to Le Maire. The author even claims that they increased the share trading rates 'by sinister and dishonest means'!

If you believe the request, Le Maire had lost over fl. 1 500 000 in 28 years. But despite all the losses and all the disappointments, he does not lose hope. In 1614, with a few notables from Hoom, he founds the 'Australische Company' (Southern Company), which equips two vessels the following year. One of the two captains of this expedition is his son, Jacques Le Maire.

During this expedition, a new delta is discovered and given the name of Le Maire, and he was thus saved from being forgotten. But no sooner had the vessels arrived in the Indies than they were confiscated by the governor general Jan Picterszoon Coen, who acted upon orders from the directors. During the return trip, Jacques Le Maire dies. When the vessels return in 1619, Le Maire goes in person to the meeting of the States General to share the important discovery. Bakhuizen rightly notes that, after so many afflictions and disappointments, this day must have been for Le Maire a day of triumph. He must have also felt some satisfaction from finding out that the trial regarding the confiscation of the vessels had been won by the Australische Company.

As can be concluded from several legal acts, during the years 1619 and 1620, Le Maire once again made efforts to obtain the payment of the amount he believed to be his. This was still the 3000 Flemish pounds representing his interest in the company and his share in the profits from the Van Heemskerck and Van Warwijck expeditions. He had even been deprived of the 162½ per cent dividend.

Le Maire constantly bothers the directors with legal notices. In order to settle his previous commitments, he must still deliver shares and, for this reason, requests free access to his portion.

The directors are not very obliging. Referring back to the contract of 1605, they continue to refuse free access by Le Maire to his portion. They agree to pay him the dividends that are owed him from the three different companies, on the condition that he commit in writing not to undertake anything, either in Holland or abroad, that would be contrary to the interests of the company. He therefore still seems to be considered a dangerous man!

Le Maire refuses to accept these conditions. The 3000 Flemish pounds representing his interest in the company, he had sold several years ago. He refuses to sign the declaration as it is submitted by the directors, which would be contrary to the Charter granted to the company, even though he is prepared to promise not to do anything. He adds that he has in fact never violated this concession. Basically, he is stating that he is ready to reveal to the directors 'several secrets on trade in the East Indies, which could be useful'. He believes that the differences must be decided by arbiters.

Le Maire wrote these papers with much skill. A few times he takes on a threatening tone: he could reveal some things which would be very disagreeable and compromising for the directors. The company is powerful, but one knows 'that a mouse can very well tease an elephant'. However, his threats have as little effect as his promises. He then tries to get at his enemies through feelings: he is getting old, he is tormented by alcohol, his finances are in very bad shape, and he has under his responsibility an 'excessive number of children'. But his call to 'Christian charity' is also without success. The directors remain in haughty silence.

It is only following renewed efforts from the notary, van Banchern, with the East India Company that Le Maire finally receives a response: an absolute refusal. The directors claim they had nothing to do with the Van Heemskerck and Van Warwijck expeditions. As for his 3000 Flemish pound share and the dividend, they refer not only to the 1605 contract but also to the fact that these amounts have already been seized by Le Maire's creditors. Nor do they forget to remind him of the embezzlement and of the 'sinister' trickery schemed against the company. Even the intervention by Prince Maurice does not make them more acceptable. The suggestion of arbitration is declined, but the directors claim to be prepared to resume the 1611 trial.

Le Maire stands firm and finally addresses the Assembly of the Seventeen with a detailed paper. He even claims to be ready to make a solemn promise not to undertake anything that would be contrary to the company's interests, which is therefore more or less the declaration he had at first refused to make. But the highest-placed college of the company does not seem to have been favourable to him. No one knows if Le Maire ever received any dividends, but it is certain that he was never able to avail himself of the 3000 pounds.

A few years after this futile feud, in 1624, Isaac Le Maire dies at the age of 65 years. A strange epitaph was carved into the headstone at his grave, which is located in village church of Egmond-Binnen. 'Here lies Isaac Le Maire, merchant, who, during his activities over all the parts of the world, by the grace of God, knew so much abundance that in thirty years he lost (save his honour) more than 150,000 florins. Died as a good Christian on September 20, 1624'.[46]

Referring to the request of 1613 in which Le Maire claims to have lost, over 28 years, 1 600 000 florins, Bakhuizen demonstrated that in the epitaph a zero is missing in the number and that it should have been a million and a half. The epitaph is still strange because it shows to what extent Le Maire and his family wanted to show that his honour had remained intact. It is hard to judge whether or not this was the case. Isaac Le Maire is an interesting figure, not only from an economic, but also from a psychological, point of view. He was certainly not a vulgar rogue, but it is difficult to see him as an innocent victim of the directors' meanness as he liked to show himself to be. Though the embezzlement accusation at the time of the equipping of the 14 vessels may have been a bit exaggerated, it did not seem to be without foundation. Later, also, his actions and his words are ambiguous and suspect to a high degree. However, it is impossible to take away from Le Maire the honour of having been one of the most active and energetic merchants in the days of a budding international trade in Amsterdam.

Notes

* This chapter provides an English translation of van Dillen (1935), originally written in French and translated by Asha Majithia, with an introductory section and assistance by Geoffrey Poitras.

1. A document from 21 October 1599 states that Le Maire was 40 years old (Noordkerk, Handvesten van Amsterdam).
2. A treasury bill according to which on 26 December 1586, Isack de la Mer lent the sum of 75 fl. to the treasury shows that Le Maire was in Amsterdam towards the end of 1586.
3. It is incorrect for Bakhuizen to state that he was never a citizen: cf. Civil State B, f. 230v: Isaack la Meer of Antwerp, businessman, took his oath of citizenship on 19 February 1601.

4. This man, whose name can also be written as de le Beeque or del Beecke, found himself among the first directors of the House of Amsterdam of the Dutch East India Company, whereas he was not among the directors of the former company. Later on he was among the adversaries of Isaac Le Maire.
5. Bakuizen's study first appeared in *Gids* in 1869 and was later inserted in *Studien en Schelsen*. It can also be found in *Historisch Leesboek* from 1906, edited by Professor Brugmans of Nijhoff.
6. Archives of the Reformed Church of Amsterdam. *Minutes of the Consistory*, vol. III.
7. It was learned that Isaac Le Maire had promised his daughter to a young man from Antwerp and that she would settle in that city, which would have caused a scandal. The Pastors Hallius and Middlegeest would have admonished him about this.
8. This declaration can be found in *Pieter van Dam's Beschryvinge van de Oost-Indische Compagnie* (Pieter van Dam's *Description of the East India Company*), ed. by F.W. Stapel, vol. I, p. 227, *Bijks Geschiedkundige Publicatien*, series, no. 63.
9. Both Bakhuizen and De Jonge saw Lyntgens as a successful businessman but Dr Yzerman showed that at the time of his meetings with Henry IV his finances were in a deplorable state.
10. See, along with the articles by Bakhuizen already cited: J.K.J. de Jonge, 'De opkomst van het Neederlandsch gezag in Oost-Indie' ('The rise of the Dutch authority in East India'); also H.G. Murphy, *Henry Hudson in Holland*, re-edited by Nijhoff in 1909; and Honourable S.P. Naber, *Henri Hudson's reize onder Nederlandsche vlag, Ouvrage de la Societe Linscholoen*, vol. XIX.
11. There is a good edition of this correspondence of Jeannin by M. Petitot, Paris, 1822.
12. Hessel Gerritszoon speaks in passing of 'an unfortunate voyage of Kerchhoven for Isaac Lameir': cf. Honourable S.P. Naber, *Henri Hudson's reize*, p. 24.
13. National Archives at The Hague, 618.
14. In 1601, and again in 1604, Le Roy took a voyage to India for the Zealand Company. He tried to create at Rouen a company for navigation to the Indian sub-continent: see M. Weber, *La Compagnie Française des Indes*.
15. He presented himself as being fond of France, being a native of Tournai where the residents all have the fleur-de-lis in their hearts. Three of his brothers, settled in Spain, Portugal and Italy, had to take part in the project. See *Negociations du president Jeannin*, ed. Petitot, vol. III, p. 280.
16. Since De Jonge didn't know anything apart from the letter from 25 December, he overestimated the success of Aerssen.
17. National Archives, General Assembly Suite 62.
18. See my article in *Tijdschreift voor Geschiedenis* 1930, vol. IV, entitled 'Nieuwe gegevens belraffende de Amsterdamsche Compagnieen van Verre' ('New information regarding faraway Amsterdam companies').
19. Cf. F.W. Stapel, *Economisch-historisch Jaarboek*, vol. XIII, p. 240.
20. S. van Brackel, *De Hollandsche Handelscompagnieen der seventiende eeuw* (*The Dutch Trading Companies of the Seventeenth Century*).
21. M.F. Smith, *Tijdaffaires in effecten aan de Amsterdamsche beurs* (*Trading for Time in Financial Securities on the Amsterdam Stock Exchange*), p. 35.
22. F.W Stapel, 'Aandeelbewijzen der Oost-Indische Compagnie' ('Share scripts of the East India Company'). *Economisch-historisch Jaarboek*, vol. XIII, p. 240.
23. Smith, *Tijdaffaires*, p. 32.
24. In the shareholder inventory of the company there is no mention of transfer certificates. Only once did I find, in similar inventories, a general receipt.
25. The East or West India Company.
26. W.M.F. Mansvelt, *Rechisvorm en geldelijk beheer bij de Oost-Indische Compagnie* (*Legal Structure and Financial Administration of the East India Company*).
27. I've spoken before of the term market in an article in *The Economist*, 1927. All things considered, I felt it was better to avoid this expression.
28. Notarized stock was never written with a term of greater than three years.
29. This accusation was probably not true. Nothing seemed to have come from it.
30. The vessels named in this paper arrived at the beginning of August. It was another question for the next Assembly of the Seventeen in September. The record is published in *Economisch-historisch Jaarboek*, Vol. XVI.
31. Reinier Lems was originally from Anvers.
32. A sale of 31 0/0 of 'advance' signifies a trade of 131 0/0. This is what M. De Jonge did not understand.
33. These trades were of stocks where the dividend had not yet been distributed.
34. Already by 1609, 30 0/0 was offered to the shareholders, not as a dividend, but to buy them.
35. The shareholders could not receive payment unless they also accepted pepper!
36. Cf., *Pieter van Dam's Beschryvighe*, vol. I, p. 434.
37. The contributors were composed not only of members of the company, but also of many other people. Jacques Damman, of Anvers, married, in 1607, one of Isaac Le Maire's daughters.
38. *Pieter van Dam's Beschryvighe*, vol. I, p. 149. Hannen Rosencransm, Jacques van de Geer and Corelis van Forest were convicted of the same fraud, but for a considerably lower amount. The total equalled 39000 florins.

39. Place of recreation for the nobility.
40. This quote was borrowed from a collection of pieces of a lawsuit, relating specifically to competition between the 'Magellaansche Compagnie' and the East India Company: Library of the Municipal Archives of Amsterdam.
41. Hans Bouwer was once part of the India Company. He took part in the voyage of De Houtman as second officer or candidate of the navy, while it had been the expedition of Jacob van Neck as first officer. Cf. M. De Jonge, 'De opkomst', II, p. 188 and 204.
42. The events of 1609 didn't take place at the stock exchange built by Hendril de Keyser, as M. Bakuizen believed. This didn't open until 1611. Before the opening of this exchange people gathered at the *Nieuwe Brug* (new bridge) or, when the weather was bad, in the *Oude Kerk* (Old Church).
43. Ludwig Samuel, *Die Ejjeklenspekulation im 17 und 18. Jahrunderl. Ein Beitrag zur Borsengeschichle* (*Stock speculation in the 17th and 18th centuries. History of Stock Exchanges*), Berlin, 1923.
44. This exposé was published by De Jonge, 'De opkomst', III, p. 364.
45. The records of Amsterdam from this time were only partly conserved, so that one finds nothing more about this lawsuit brought in front of the aldermen of Amsterdam.
46. A second epitaph revealed that his wife Maria Walraven, mother of 22 children, had already died in 1621.

3 Joseph de la Vega and the *Confusion de confusiones*[1]

José Luís Cardoso

This chapter provides a broad picture of the financial operations taking place on the Amsterdam Stock Exchange at the end of the seventeenth century, examining the relevance of the description offered in a pioneering book by Joseph de la Vega (1688). This book is usually acclaimed as the first attempt to describe trading in modern financial securities: stocks, options and forward contracts. It is the purpose of the present contribution to testify to the historical consistency of that claim.

Sections 1 and 2 give a general outline of both the historical background in which Joseph de la Vega wrote his book and the ethical issues he was intending to address. The following sections 3 and 4 analyse and discuss the importance of Vega's book, both in the form of a detailed description of options and futures markets and as an appraisal of decision-making processes in a context of risk and uncertainty. In section 5 a final appraisal of Joseph de la Vega's endeavour is presented.

1. Iberian Jews in Amsterdam

The author of the work analysed in this chapter was a member of the Jewish community of Iberian, and predominantly Portuguese, origin, who since the end of the sixteenth century had been stimulating commercial activities in Amsterdam.[2] It was the greater repression imposed by the Inquisition which had caused several families of Jewish or New Christian merchants to move away from both Portugal and Spain. The intimidating effects of the public rituals of the *autos-da-fé*, the compulsory confiscation of their property and capital and the terrible social discrimination to which they were subjected represented more than enough justification for their flight.

Although there is no definitive documentary evidence of Joseph de la Vega's precise nationality – so that equal credence can be lent to the claims of his various biographers that he was born in Portugal, Spain or even Holland[3] – the most plausible hypothesis would seem to be that he was born in Spain, in the province of Cordoba, in 1650, and that in the following year he travelled with his parents to Antwerp and then on to Amsterdam, where his family were to settle on a permanent basis.

In the second half of the seventeenth century, Amsterdam was the main financial centre in a fairly sizeable world economy. The secret of this supremacy was explained by the Dutch productive strength and efficiency, especially in the textile industry and shipbuilding, by the multiple relations that its commercial companies enjoyed with the sea ports of Asia, Africa and America, and by the credibility of its banks and the relative stability of the financial and foreign exchange dealings that were carried out there.[4] The prices of the products traded in the Amsterdam Exchange were taken as the reference prices for the main European markets.

The building of the Amsterdam Stock Exchange in 1631 allowed for the rapid spread of trading, investment and speculation, not only in commodities from different geographical origins, but particularly in the shares of the Dutch West India Company and the Dutch East India Company, which could only be traded on the Amsterdam Stock Exchange. These companies were responsible for the organization and leadership of world commerce and their crucial role was to ensure the complete satisfaction of a steadily growing demand for consumer goods in European markets. It was therefore natural that the then prevailing spirit of speculation – of which the *tulipomania* of 1634 to 1637 is perhaps the most notable example – should begin to affect the behaviour of investors seeking to buy into the stock of the Dutch India Companies.[5]

Among all the various private economic agents operating on the Amsterdam Stock Exchange, the Portuguese Jews had carved out for themselves a truly proverbial reputation. The close contacts and extensive connections that they had with the main European commercial markets afforded them a certain amount of control over the information networks that were of crucial importance for ensuring the success of their dealings.[6]

It was in such an atmosphere that Joseph de la Vega grew up. In fact, it was this same atmosphere that he sought to describe in the book that he published in 1688 under the suggestive title of *Confusion de confusiones*, and which has traditionally been acclaimed as the first systematic treatise on the workings of the stock market.

Joseph de la Vega's book has enjoyed various re-editions,[7] which have given rise to a series of interesting prefaces and studies on the historical importance of this work, especially in relation to the testimony that he has bequeathed about the daily activities of the Amsterdam Stock Exchange. The most complete of all these studies is that by H. Kellenbenz (1957), who, besides providing an overall introduction to the author and the role played by the Portuguese Jewish community in speculative activities in Amsterdam, attempts to rewrite Joseph de la Vega's experiences by transforming his recondite language into a modernized classification of the main stock-exchange practices described. Jonathan Israel (1990) based his description and analysis of the 1688 crash in the Amsterdam Stock Exchange on historical evidence provided in Joseph de la Vega's book published in that year. Neil de Marchi and Paul Harrison (1994, 60–63) used the same book as a means of exemplifying the moral dilemmas experienced by anyone wishing to justify or condemn the legitimacy of the activities of short selling and trading in the wind. Antoin Murphy (1997, 42) underlined the contemporary importance of the treatment given in *Confusion de confusiones* to the questions of the uncertainty and expectations associated with the speculative business of buying and selling shares.

Joseph de la Vega is frequently mentioned as being a pioneer in describing the workings of the options and futures markets, although the actual references made are frequently little more than a sign of erudition used to punctuate a reflection on the current working of these types of markets (cf. Merton 1992). One of his greatest modern admirers believes that 'Three centuries later, however, *Confusion de confusiones* exudes universality as it describes trading gambits that have never gone out of fashion [... and] leaves a distinct impression that any innovation in the trading of securities during the last three hundred years has been of an incidental nature' (Fridson 1996, 7–8). Though there are reasons to support this strong claim – as we will see in section 3 below – it has to be carefully addressed and argued.

2. Ethical concerns and moral judgements

One of the most attractive features of Joseph de la Vega's book is to be found in its design. The author presents us with a series of four dialogues involving three different characters: a philosopher, a merchant and a shareholder. The last spends most of his time explaining to his interlocutors the procedures, secrets and stratagems used in business and speculation on the Amsterdam Stock Exchange.

Using a fairly common seventeenth-century stylistic device, Joseph de la Vega organizes the dialogues in such a way that the text becomes more interesting to read and more pedagogical in tone, given that his mission was, in addition to 'whiling away his own moments of idleness', that of 'describing a business that is the most real and the most useful known throughout Europe today' and 'painting with the brush of truth the stratagems by means of which such business is conducted' (1688, 7).

At the beginning of the first dialogue, the shareholder hears the following queries being put by the philosopher and merchant:

> *Philosopher*: And what business is this [shares], which although I have frequently heard speak thereof, I do not understand, nor have I ever attempted to do so, nor have I even found any book that speaks of this business in an understandable fashion?
> *Merchant*: That is also my request, because the brokerage fees, shipments and costs of sending bills of exchange are so wearisome that I should wish to apply myself to this new task, to see if I may acquire a fortune and, even at the risk of loss, free myself from my current exertions.' (1688, 17)

Being interested in capturing the attention of his listeners and readers, the shareholder answers these questions at the beginning of the work with unbridled optimism, even seeming to conceal one of the features that later on will prove to be decisive to an understanding of the workings of the financial markets that he describes, namely the question of risk and uncertainty:

> The best and most agreeable aspect of all this is that you can become rich without risk and without exposing your capital to the storms of the market place, and that without the costs of agents, disbursements, warehouses, transport charges, cashiers, bankruptcies or other unforeseen accidents, you can be on the verge of attaining opulence. (Ibid., 17–18)

The four parts or dialogues into which the book is divided are intended to provide the text with a structure in which two distinct levels of analysis are intermingled. First, there is the technical and descriptive level of the activities of the stock market, which are the author's main concern. Second, there is the level of ethical reflection as to the legitimacy of the behaviour of the various agents involved in this special type of financial market. In order to establish a connection between these two levels of analysis, Joseph de la Vega resorts to rhetorical devices and linguistic embellishments in which the use and abuse of metaphors and erudite analogies invite the reader to remember examples from the Bible, as well as to consider details of Greek and Roman history and their respective mythologies. This immense compositional padding sometimes makes the text very cumbersome and difficult to read.[8] But there is no doubt that it plays an important role in helping us to understand the book's overall coherence.

I shall give more details about the technical level of the book in the next section. However, it is important, right from the outset, to note that Joseph de la Vega covers such a wide range of subjects that his book has become an essential reference work in the history of stock markets and even of the financial operations conducted nowadays. Among such subjects, attention should be drawn to the description of the different types of participants in stock-market activities, the characterization of the options markets, the explanation of fluctuations in share prices, and the analysis of the behaviour of shareholders, brokers, gamblers and speculators. It goes without saying that one should not expect, from the reading of *Confusion de confusiones*, a perfect and sound description of what is going on in financial markets today; nor could one read the author's comments and recommendations as a pertinent guide to financial investments in present times.

As to the the discussion of ethical issues, it is possible to detect a central thread that gives the dialogues between the three characters the sense of a particular plot that is being recounted with a beginning, middle and end.

At first, there is the doubt and fear shown by both the merchant and the philosopher, who permanently question the honesty and honour that are lost through less scrupulous business. In the philosopher's most elaborate words:

> What I find most disturbing is that there should be someone who entrusts his entire fortune to these gluttons, because I have always understood from books that he who attempts to embrace too much does not keephold of anything, and even the old adage says that he who wants everything loses everything (27). … What does it matter that they gain money, if they equally gain infamy? I do not call ignominy progress, nor do I seek to increase what is already quite disgraceful. What does it avail a man not to risk his riches, if he loses his soul? (31)

Gradually enlightened by the shareholder, although they are never totally convinced of the merits of gambling on the stock market, the merchant and philosopher cannot resist the temptation of attempting a brief incursion into the business that the shareholder has not ceased to exalt. Yet the results could not have been worse. After declaring their intention to purchase shares at the nominal price of 586, they reached the conclusion that the market value of these shares was no more than 64. Faced with such shame and humiliation, their solution was to conceal the bad business that they had done because, in the words of the philosopher, 'although it may cost me my wealth and my life, I set greater store by honour than I do by my life and riches' (160). The philosopher was right to confess later on that he had learned that 'not only is the road to virtue difficult, but the road to vice is even more difficult to tread' (353).

In the aftermath of this episode, recounted at the beginning of the third dialogue, the shareholder is no longer able to restrain his feeling of impotence at not being capable of successfully transmitting his teachings. But the disgrace of the merchant and philosopher is shared in the end by the shareholder himself, who confesses, at the beginning of the fourth and final dialogue, to his losses and failures on the Amsterdam Stock Exchange. Such a confession may be interpreted as an autobiographical reference by Joseph de la Vega, who reveals, through the shareholder's literary discourse, the *confusiones* in which he himself had become involved in this same year of 1688, when the shares of the East India Company fell far more than had been expected.

In this way, the direct discourse of the merchant and philosopher provides an ethical counterpoint through their critical assessment of financial activities that had been reduced to the level of a simple game. Consequently, Joseph de la Vega identifies with the attitude of the philosopher in formulating the following question: 'How else could a philosopher expect to feel amongst shareholders, if not as a sheep amongst wolves, a hare amongst hounds?' (286). Certainly, he also sees his ideas expressed in the wry formula adopted by the merchant:

> For my own part, I thank you for the instruction that you have given me. I esteem business but I detest gambling. It is quite possible that I may become a shareholder through business; but I am quite sure that I shall never become a shareholder through gambling. If I have already lost one eye with shares, this is all the more reason not to become totally blind, so that I may at least retain one eye with which to cry over the loss of the other. (381–3)

And he also identifies with the most elaborate statement made by the philosopher:

> I consider it much better not to be a shareholder than to be one, and to deliberately cease to be one than to have been one. I am speaking of the shareholder who gambles, not the shareholder who does business; because all that I consider to be true in the latter, I know to be false in the former. (385–6)

The fact of the matter is that the shareholder himself emerges from the dialogues with a sense of defeat. The crisis that broke out on the Amsterdam Stock Exchange in mid-1688 caught Joseph de la Vega in the final phase of writing his book and helped him to compose the ethical message that was, after all, to become the moral of his story: 'This year was a *year of confusion* for so many unfortunate wretches who unanimously declared that the present misfortune was a labyrinth of labyrinths, a horror of horrors, a CONFUSION OF CONFUSIONS. I suspend this discourse because agonies begin to disturb my spirit' (380).

3. Options and forward markets

In the final statements made by the merchant and philosopher, a clear distinction is drawn between two types of shareholders, namely 'shareholders who do business' and 'shareholders who gamble'. This is a subject to which Joseph de la Vega devotes a certain amount of attention at the beginning of the book and which represents one of the main justifications for its technical and analytical contents. Those who trade in the share market are characterized as follows:

> For a better understanding of this astounding fact, it should be noted that there are three classes of people involved in this business, some acting as *princes*, others as *merchants*, and finally those who are *gamblers*.
>
> The former live as the princes of revenue; every year they enjoy the dividends from the shares that have either been left to them by their ancestors, or have been purchased with their own stock. They are little concerned that these shares are worth more or less, through gambling or through news [and rumours], for, as their intention is not to sell them but to reap the fruits thereof, their only interest is that they should be worth a great deal for their own imaginary enjoyment, considering (as is in fact the case) that were they to sell them, they might indeed obtain a high price.
>
> The second class consists of the merchants who either buy a share (of 500 pounds), causing it to be transferred to their account (since they are of the opinion that it will be worth more, depending upon the proceeds that are expected from India, or the peace that is achieved in Europe) and selling it again when it has increased in value; or else they buy this same share with cash, and, fearing the effects of novelties or changes, sell it again immediately for delivery at a later date (when normally more money will be given for it), contenting themselves with the interest that accrues to them from their original outlay …
>
> The third class of gamblers … buy one or twenty shares (which quantity is generally referred to as a Regiment), and upon arriving at the twentieth day of the month (being the date upon which they are due to receive them) can choose only one of three means for their settlement: either they sell them for what they are worth, thereby making a loss or profit on what they cost; or they pledge them into the hands of those that may offer four-fifths of their value (which is done by the wealthiest traders without the least harm to their reputation); or they cause them to be transferred to their own account, paying for them at the bank, which can be done only by the most powerful. (22–4)

Two fundamental points should be noted in this careful distinction. First, the author distinguishes between two main types of shareholders: the *princes* and *merchants* presented as long- and medium-term investors who wish to enjoy a steady profit from their shares and who are implicitly interested in continuing to maintain and administer them without paying much attention to short-term fluctuations; and the *gamblers* or short-term speculators who, despite the risks involved in this operation, seek to profit from the fluctuations in the prices at which the shares are traded on the stock market.[9] The activities of the so-called gamblers seem to contradict the rational behaviour of maximizing individual utility, since investors are thus forced to operate in a climate of much greater instability and uncertainty. This may, however, be the most tempting way of making substantial gains on the stock market, because of the high rate of return that they can provide.[10] In this respect, as well in all references to calculations concerning price fluctuations, it should be pointed out that Vega's use of data and figures does not allow a rigorous historical reconstruction of gains and losses in the stock-exchange market. His main concern was not to provide a rigorous, systematic account of financial operations ruled by numbers, but rather to outline a broad picture of those operations and activities that could change the lives and fortunes of the agents willing to play the game and run the risks.

The second aspect is related to the treatment that Joseph de la Vega gives to the problem of the time lag between the buying and selling of shares, which in turn leads us to another of the more interesting questions dealt with in his book: the making of contracts involving financial assets, operations that nowadays would be classified as options and futures markets.

It is useful to remember that, although isolated examples of such markets were known to have existed throughout the nineteenth century in both Europe and the USA, and even though it is always possible to retrospectively reconstruct situations that have acquired the status of pioneering experiments, the first options market expressly organized for the trading of these financial products was the Chicago Board Options Exchange (CBOE) in 1973, a fact which underlines the genuinely innovative nature of the description provided by Joseph de la Vega.

Let us now take a look at what the author had to say about the options market.

> As regards OPSIES, these are premiums or quantities that are paid in order to safeguard shares or to make a profit. They are like sails that ensure happy progress in calm weather and anchors that provide safety during storms.
>
> The price of shares is currently 580. It seems to me that, because of the great proceeds that are expected from India, the consequent increase in the Company's business, the reputation of its goods, the dividends that are promised and peace in Europe, this price will rise much higher than it is now. I, however, decide not to buy shares, for I fear that should these predictions prove false, I might suffer a loss or meet with an embarrassment. I therefore turn to those who tell me that they will take these Opsies and ask them how much they want in return for the obligation to deliver 600 for each share at a later date. I agree upon the premium, transfer this sum immediately to the bank and I know that I cannot lose more than that which I have spent, so that I gain the entire amount by which the shares exceed 600. And should they fall in price, I shall not be at all troubled, nor worried as to my honour, nor disturbed as to my peace of mind: if, on the shares reaching more or less 600, I change my mind and conclude that not everything is as splendid as I had predicted, then I may sell them without any danger, because every amount by which they fall represents a profit. And as the person who received the money is obliged to deliver the shares to me at the agreed price, even though they may have risen above this, I cannot suffer any loss other than the Opsie nor lament any penalty other than the premium …
>
> The Flemish call this business OPSIE, deriving from the Latin word *Optio Optionis*, which signifies *choice*, because the giver has the choice of either requesting or delivering the share to the receiver … This correctly illustrates the etymology of the term, for the payer of the premium wishes to choose that which he deems more appropriate, and if he makes an error he can always decide not to choose that which he wishes. (47–9)

This lengthy quotation[11] perfectly illustrates the characteristics of an options market in the way in which it is defined in current terms.[12] Joseph de la Vega explains how these contracts confer the possibility of exercising a right (option) to buy an asset on a previously specified date, at a previously agreed price, through the payment of a fee (premium) at the time when the contract is agreed upon.

It is this right of choice or option that establishes the difference between the options market and the forward market, which does not involve the payment of an initial fee and which binds the parties to the contract to complete the operation of buying and selling within the time specified for this purpose. In his book, Joseph de la Vega also analyses the case of the forward contracts, namely when he attributes to shareholders the possibility of operating in the share market through the 'sale [of shares] at a later date, in the month specified, on the twentieth and twenty-fifth days of which shares must be delivered and their gains paid' (227), describing in great detail the forms by which these shares must be registered and the administrative and bureaucratic procedures that are essential for verifying the agreements made, explaining them one by one.

In addition to dealings which involve options and forward contracts, Joseph de la Vega also describes simpler operations involving direct transfer and cash payment (226), which would probably have been amongst the most frequent operations on the Amsterdam Stock Exchange.

4. Individual behaviour, risk and expectations

Joseph de la Vega helps us to form a clearer understanding of the different types of financial dealings, with the technical exactness appropriate to the historical context in which he lived. Regardless of the particular merit, it should be stressed that his lively accounts also recreate the atmosphere and gestures used in the agitated daily life of the stock exchange, as can be seen from the following colourful description:

> The way in which dealings are carried out is as ridiculous as the game itself. In the Levant, agreements are reached by a nod of the head, yet here agreements are made through the slapping and beating of hands. But how painful this can be! Because, although many aspire to hear the clapping that would accompany victory, they are just as likely to feel the cruel slap in the face of fate …
>
> One dealer opens the palm of his hand and another slaps it, thereby releasing a share for sale at such and such a price. Another slap of the hand offers another price for it, and then it is offered once more to the first bidder with another slap of the hand, so that the second dealer can once again offer more. The palms are coloured with the marks of their beating (I believe that this is due to the shame that the most respected people feel in having to do deals by beating their hands). Then this slapping of hands is followed by shouting, the shouting gives way to insults, which in turn are followed by quarrels, until the deal is completed in such a way that one can only conclude that it has been made through quarrels, insults, shouting, and the beating and slapping of hands. (207–9)

The stock exchange therefore becomes a space where many different agents meet, each of whom has a different motivation, although they all share the frenetic sociability of business and gambling and the compulsive atmosphere of high-pressure dealing.[13] The princes of revenue and the merchants, distinguished by their greater nobility of character, tended to keep themselves at a distance from this great commotion and appointed special agents – the so-called brokers – to do their business for them. But, on occasions, the merchants themselves might also become directly involved in the dealings, and Joseph de la Vega shows an extraordinary perspicacity in listing the material and psychological motives that could justify such behaviour: not wishing to pay brokerage fees, the vanity of wishing to be seen in the company of the brokers and gamblers, the desire to know more about the mechanics of the actual operations or else to better control the stratagems inherent in this kind of market (cf. 222–3).

This question of the stratagems, ploys and tricks used by shareholders, gamblers and brokers is one of the areas in which Joseph de la Vega was able to reveal his extremely detailed knowledge of the internal workings of the Amsterdam Stock Exchange. The secrecy maintained in acts of buying and selling, the careful management of the time-scales for different deals, the spread of news and rumours with the aim of influencing or manipulating the thoughts and minds of the other people involved, the systematic gathering of information about economic and financial matters through international networks are all common procedures that are analysed by the author (293–313). This importance given to information and to its different sources, types and levels, is a clear sign of innovation and modernity in dealing with issues related to the study of human behaviour in financial markets.

Joseph de la Vega carefully assesses the important role played by brokers as intermediaries in the transactions that were carried out or in the fulfilment of orders for buying and selling. And he is in fact amazed by the great elegance and skill with which they performed their duties:

> A most interesting feature is to be noted when a disinterested broker has a large order and seeks to carry it out as prudently and consummately as possible. For, if he is endeavouring to buy, all his efforts are directed towards studying how best to add some shares to his stake ...; when alternating selling with buying, and in order to disguise his intentions, he will sometimes offer shares and sometimes make bids for them too, so that he can dispose of them exactly as he wishes ... he fences with such grace and dexterity, wielding his sword with such admirable refinement, that it is a pity that there is not a victory for each thrust and a trophy awarded for each wound inflicted. (318)

He does not, however, forget to mention that one of the main stimuli for the way in which the stock market worked was to be found in the ambitions of those brokers who endeavoured to act for their own benefit and who used their privileged position to obtain additional profits and 'accumulate wealth'. Joseph de la Vega does not condemn this type of activity. Instead, he seeks to fit it into an overall vision of the reward that is due to whoever takes such risks, as can be clearly seen from his own words:

> Those who devote themselves voluntarily to this business, since they consider themselves endowed with sufficient means or courage to emerge unscathed from the blows and with the necessary confidence to withstand the reverses, experience an even more glorious triumph ... but they will nonetheless confess that it is always risky, always frightening, always horrible. (255)

The risk involved in operations conducted on the Amsterdam Stock Exchange is a recurrent theme throughout Joseph de la Vega's book. In fact, the analysis that he makes of options and forward contracts is in keeping with the basic idea that this is a process that involves both the management and transfer of risk and is of interest to all parties. In this way, the role of the gamblers and speculators who are walking the tightrope of risk tends to be legitimized through the implicit acceptance of the fact that they are in some way helping to keep the market working efficiently.

In turn, the risk involved in financial operations is explained by Joseph de la Vega as being the result of the instability and uncertainty that is naturally produced by the evolution of real economic activity. He makes this idea a little clearer by showing that, although the variation in the prices of shares in the East India Company partly depended on the role played by the gamblers and speculators, it was also influenced by a wide variety of factors that intervened in the formation of the prices of the goods sold by the Company. Joseph de la Vega summarized this idea quite succinctly: 'Please note that there are three reasons why shares rise, and three more to explain why they fall: the state of India, the mood of Europe and the gambling of shareholders' (66). This reference to the 'state of India' represents the author's attempt to underline the importance of the network of international contacts in obtaining first-hand information about cargoes, about the quality and quantity of goods in transit to Europe and about the company's success or failure in oriental markets. In other words, the most important consideration was to have as accurate a knowledge as possible of those factors that directly influenced the formation of the price of goods, whether these were supply-side factors, involving the prediction of the actual supplies that would be made over a certain period, or demand-side factors, involving the anticipation of purchasing patterns.

The 'mood of Europe' directs our attentions towards the political and diplomatic context of the time and to the possibility that a climate of latent war might have produced an adverse environment for the normal conduct of business. The commercial rivalry between Holland and England did not prevent these two maritime powers from becoming major partners in a strategic grand alliance against the hegemonic pretensions of Louis XIV's France. But it goes without saying that such partnership could suddenly break down. The Amsterdam Stock Exchange could not remain unaffected by the political news referring to the imminence of a fresh outbreak of military conflict in Europe.[14]

Finally, 'the gambling of shareholders' is the internal factor that, as far as Joseph de la Vega was concerned, could explain the fluctuations in stock-market prices. However, the greater or lesser readiness of the gamblers to take risks, and the unexpected results of their speculative transactions, were also dictated by the way in which they assessed the possibility of obtaining profits from short- and medium-term financial operations.

The two first reasons show Vega's extreme concern with the political environment and its influence on the way that expectations were formed among those who were most directly involved in the stock market. They demonstrate the relevance of a complex network extremely busy in collecting, transfering, manipulating and spreading information, news and rumours.[15] The way in which investors and speculators calculated the profit that they might make in the future depended on the extent of their confidence in the present, according to the news available, or in other words 'the state of India' and 'the mood of Europe'. It was the experience of the present that served to either eliminate or exacerbate the instability and uncertainty of the future.[16]

5. Virtue and vice in the 'world comedy'

Joseph de la Vega shows a certain ambiguity in his treatment of the activities of gamblers and speculators. On the one hand, there does not seem to be any hint of malice, irony or pejorative intention in the terms that he uses to describe their behaviour or to define the guidelines for their activity. In fact there is a clear suggestion of a certain sympathy when he establishes the following guideline for gambling on the stock market: 'For those who wish to grow rich through this business, both patience and money are necessary, for as there is so little stability in prices and even less justification for rumours …, it is necessary for them to wait if they are to prevail, and, if they have enough money to wait, then they will win' (74–5).

It should, however, be noted that in the dialogues between the philosopher and the merchant there is a certain critical tension that Joseph de la Vega manipulates into an ethical concern that society might be disturbed by less noble practices in the desire to satisfy individual interests. Gambling on the stock market therefore represented a condensed example of vice and virtue, a script that illustrated the plural nature of the comedy of life.

> Yet, of all those comedies that men perform, and in which they play such different roles in the magnificent theatre of the world, there is no comedy that resembles the one enacted by shareholders, who excel in such inimitable fashion in their entrances and exits, their concealments, masking, disputes, challenges, trickery, nonsense and commitments, in putting out the lights, in refining their deceptions, betrayals, artifices and tragedies. (156)

Seen from an overall viewpoint, *Confusion de confusiones* is a work whose main aim was not completely achieved. It was probably thought of originally as a manual for the use of those trading on the stock exchange. But the author's own lack of success as a shareholder in the Amsterdam Stock Exchange prevented the pedagogical and persuasive contents of the work from ever achieving complete coherence. Nevertheless, there should be no dispute about the main purpose of Joseph de la Vega when writing his book: to demonstrate that, though the inner or potential risks and dangers of financial operations, the dealings at the stock exchange market were worth pursuing.

It is difficult to assess the precise impact that the book had upon the community of Jews and New Christians of Spanish and Portuguese origin resident at that time in Amsterdam, and to whom it was dedicated. Therefore it was written in Spanish, which was the everyday language of communication within this community. The book was certainly issued in a small print run[17] and it quickly disappeared into oblivion. The scant attention that has been paid to this book by historians of economic and financial thought has only served to strengthen the belief that it is a fairly forgotten work. However, that there should be no doubts as to the pioneering nature of his understanding of some of the features involved in the organization and working of financial markets, and that, in spite of the somewhat primitive nature of his analysis, there is good reason for comparing some of his findings, more than three centuries ago, with the reality of present-day financial markets. Modern investors will hardly find practical, down-to-earth hints in the pages of *Confusion de confusions*. But they will definitely learn how similar financial operations were addressed and conceived, aiming at an open recognition of their good impact on society.

Notes

1. This chapter is based on J.L. Cardoso, '*Confusion de confusiones*: ethics and options in seventeenth-century stock exchange markets', *Financial History Review*, 2002, **9**(1), 109–23. Reprinted with the permission of Cambridge University Press.
2. At the end of the seventeenth century, the Jewish–Portuguese community living in Amsterdam numbered roughly three thousand (cf. Teensma 1991).
3. Cf. Amzalak (1925), Anes (1986) and Torrente Fortuño (1980). The last study brings together all the declarations that are known to have been made about the author's nationality.
4. The analysis of the Dutch advantages in the world economy through the sequence production–distribution–finance was particularly emphasized by Immanuel Wallerstein (1980, 36–71). His thesis became conventional wisdom as an explanation of the Dutch hegemony during the Golden Age. Jonathan Israel, who has also stressed the wide-ranging and multi-faceted nature of Dutch world-trade primacy, carried out a similar interpretation. Its originality can be found 'in new forms of productive efficiency and technological innovations, combined with new techniques of stockpiling commodities, buying ahead, and speculative trading' (Israel 1989, 415).
5. For a clear summary of the role played by the Amsterdam market in this period, see Braudel (1979, II, 80–86); and Parker (1974, 551–60). The high volume of trading on the stock exchange was mainly the result of the buying and selling of the stock of the Dutch East India Company, which had been set up in 1602. In order to understand the exact scale of such dealings, it should be noted that the initial nominal value of this company's shares (which was 500 Flemish pounds) had increased by roughly 600 per cent by 1688, i.e. by the date when Joseph de la Vega first started to write his book.
6. It is not the purpose of this chapter to discuss the economic role played by the Portuguese Jewish Community (the Portuguese Nation) in Amsterdam. A detailed survey of this subject based on archive documents was first presented by Bloom (1937). Further historical evidence was provided by Israel (1983) and especially by Vlessing

(1995), who has studied the financial records and regulations of the taxes paid by the Portuguese Jewish merchants to their community. In this study it is shown that the high level of their net profits – particularly those obtained in the sugar trade – 'indicate that they must have attracted more business activities to the city than the East India Company' (Vlessing 1995, 243). For a presentation of both the social and cultural environment of the Portuguese community in Amsterdam and the problems concerning their identity and organization, see Bodian (1997).

7. Cf. Vega (1688) [1919], [1939], [1957] and [1997]. The English translation [1957] includes a relevant selection of 40 pages, out of a total of 391. It has been recently reprinted in Fridson (1996). Rather disturbingly, the English translator has made a number of substantial changes in the style of writing that sometimes affect the actual content of the book, presumably in his desire to make the text more readable to a contemporary public. Even more lamentable were the stylistic changes introduced in the Spanish re-edition [1997], which deprived the reader of any contact with the original source. For this reason, all the quotations made in this chapter from *Confusion de confusiones* have been translated from the original version (facsimile reprint included in Vega 1688 [1939]).
8. It should be said that Joseph de la Vega also produced a number of other works of a literary nature that did not, however, earn him a great reputation as a writer. He cultivated his own style of funeral orations, moral discourses and courtly dalliances. A list of his panegyrical and literary writings can be found in Amzalak (1925).
9. Regarding the significance of this distinction in the light of the legal framework for modern public limited companies, see Garrigues (1971, 57–63).
10. It should be emphasized that when Joseph de la Vega is presenting the different types of speculators there is by no means any attempt to condemn the activities of gamblers by considering the supposed irrational nature of their behaviour. On the contrary, their attitudes served perfectly to demonstrate that there could be a rational explanation for those who impose strict deadlines to their daily investments.
11. In other sections of his book, Joseph de la Vega refers specifically to the different workings of this type of market, as, for example, on pp. 157–9; 228–32; 298.
12. Cf. the definition provided by Merton (1992): 'A "European-type call (put) option" is a security that gives its owner the right to buy (sell) a specified quantity of a financial or real asset at a specified price, the "exercise price", on a specified date, the "expiration date". An American-type option provides that its owner can exercise the option on or before the expiration date. If an option is not exercised on or before the expiration date, it expires and becomes worthless.

    Options and forward or future contracts are fundamentally different securities. Both provide for the purchase (or sale) of the underlying asset at a future date. A long position in a forward contract obliges its holder to make an unconditional purchase of the asset at the forward price. In contrast, the holder of a call option can choose whether or not to purchase the asset at the exercise price. Thus, a forward contract can have a negative value whereas an option contract never can' (90).
13. This point has been discussed by Simon Schama (1991, 348–50) who has also seen in other contemporary sources signs of the indignation of certain circles of the magistracy as well as the Church against the practices and rituals of the financial agents in the stock market.
14. A full demonstration of the role played by political events in the functioning of financial markets is given by Jonathan Israel (1990) when he studies the role of the Amsterdam business community preparing for the invasion of England by William of Orange in 1688 and its impact in the crash of that same year in the Amsterdam stock exchange. Israel concludes that 'political news was more likely than business news to transform the business scene as a whole' (1990, 414).
15. The impact of this information exchange network has been considered as one of the innovative features explaining the success of Dutch economy in the seventeenth century (cf. Smith 1984).
16. I do not intend that this reference should be read as a kind of anticipation of the interpretation that Keynes (1936) was to make regarding the state of long-term expectations. But it is inevitable that, once the necessary historical distances have been safeguarded, Joseph de la Vega's book should reveal some of the ingredients that were to make Chapter 12 of the *General Theory* so famous.
17. Torrente Fortuño (1980, 277) refers to the existence of only five copies of this book in University and national libraries throughout the world.

References

Amzalak, Moses B. (1925), 'Joseph de la Vega e o seu livro *Confusion de confusiones*' ('Joseph de la Vega and his book *Confusion de confusiones*'), *Revista do Instituto Superior de Comércio de Lisboa*, 47–53.

Anes, Gonzalo (1986), Introduction to Vega 1688 [1997].

Bloom, Herbert I. (1937), *The Economic Activities of the Jews of Amsterdam in the Seventeenth and Eighteenth Centuries*, reprint, Port Washington, NY: Kennicat Press, 1969.

Bodian, Miriam (1997), *Hebrews of the Portuguese Nation. Conversos and Community in Early Modern Amsterdam*, Bloomington: Indiana University Press.

Braudel, Fernand (1979), *Civilisation Matérielle, Économie et Capitalisme. Tome 2: Les Jeux de l'Échange* (*Civilization and Capitalism, 15th–18th Century. Volume 2: The Wheels of Commerce*), Paris: Librairie Armand Collin.

De Marchi, Neil and Paul Harrison (1994), 'Trading "in the Wind" and with Guile: the troublesome matter of the short selling of shares in seventeenth-century Holland', in Neil De Marchi and Mary Morgan (eds) (1994), *Higgling: Transactors and their Markets in the History of Economics*, Annual supplement to *HOPE*, Vol. 26, Durham and London: Duke University Press, pp. 47–65.

Fridson, Martin S. (ed.) (1996), *Extraordinary Popular Delusions and the Madness of Crowds* (by Charles Mackay) and *Confusion de confusiones* (by Joseph de la Vega), New York: John Wiley & Sons.

Garber, Peter M. (2000), *Famous First Bubbles. The Fundamentals of Early Manias*, Cambridge, MA: The MIT Press.

Garrigues, Joaquin (1971), *Hacia un Nuevo Derecho Mercantil* (*Towards a New Commercial Law*), Madrid: Editorial Tecnos.

Israel, Jonathan I. (1983), 'The economic contribution of Dutch Sephardi Jewry to Holland's Golden Age, 1595–1713', *Tijdschrift voor Geschiedenis*, Vol. 96, 505–35.

Israel, Jonathan I. (1989), *Dutch Primacy in World Trade, 1585–1740*, Oxford: Clarendon Press.

Israel, Jonathan I. (1990), 'The Amsterdam Stock Exchange and the English Revolution of 1688', *Tijdschrift voor Geschiedenis*, Vol. 103, 412–40.

Kellenbenz, Hermann (1957), Introduction to Vega 1688 [1957].

Keynes, John M. (1936), *The General Theory of Employment, Interest and Money*, London: Macmillan.

Merton, Robert (1992), 'Options', in Peter Newman, Murray Milgate and John Eatwell (eds) (1992), *The New Palgrave. A Dictionary of Money and Finance*, London: Macmillan, Vol. III, pp. 90–92.

Murphy, Antoin (1997), *John Law. Economic Theorist and Policy-Maker*, Oxford: Clarendon Press.

Parker, Geoffrey (1974), 'The Emergence of Modern Finance in Europe, 1500–1730', in Carlo M. Cipolla (ed.), *The Fontana Economic History of Europe. The Sixteenth and Seventeenth Centuries*, Glasgow: Collins/Fontana Books.

Schama, Simon (1991), *The Embarrassment of Riches. An Interpretation of Dutch Culture in the Golden Age*, London: Fontana Press.

Smith, Woodruff D. (1984), 'The function of commercial centers in the modernization of European capitalism: Amsterdam as an information exchange economy in the seventeenth century', *Journal of Economic History*, Vol. XLIV (4): 985–1005.

Teensma, Benjamin N. (1991), 'Os judeus portugueses em Amsterdão' ('The Portuguese Jews in Amsterdam'), in J. Everaert and E. Stols (eds), *Flandres e Portugal. Na confluência de duas culturas* (*Flanders and Portugal. The Convergence of Two Cultural Traditions*), Lisboa: Inapa, pp. 275–87.

Torrente Fortuño, José António (1980), *La Bolsa en Jose de la Vega* (*The Stock Exchange Market in Joseph de la Vega's Work*), Madrid: Colegio de Agentes de Cambio y Bolsa de Madrid.

Vega, Joseph de la (1688), *Confusion de Confusiones. Dialogos curiosos entre um filósofo agudo, um mercader discreto e un accionista erudito, descriviendo el negocio de las acciones, su origen, su etimologia, su realidade, su juego y su enredo* (*Confusion of Confusions. Curious Dialogues between an Acute Philosopher, a Prudent Merchant and a Learned Shareholder, depicting the Stocks Business and its Origins, Etymology, Reality, Gambling and Plot*). Amsterdam.

Vega, Joseph de la (1688) [1919], *Die Verwirrung der Verwirrungen. Vier Dialogue über die Börse in Amsterdam*, German translation by Dr Otto Pringsheim, Breslau: Druck und Verlag H. Fleischman.

Vega, Joseph de la (1688) [1939], *Confusion de confusiones*, reprint of the Spanish edition, with a modern translation into Dutch by G.J. Geers, edited by M.F.J. Smith, The Hague: Martinus Nijhoff.

Vega, Joseph de la (1688) [1957], *Confusion de confusiones*, portions descriptive of the Amsterdam Stock Exchange, selected and translated by Hermann Kellenbenz, Boston: Baker Library.

Vega, Joseph de la (1688) [1997], *Confusion de confusiones*. New Spanish edition with an introduction by Gonzalo Anes. Madrid: Bolsa de Madrid.

Vlessing, Odette (1995), 'The Portuguese-Jewish Mercantile Community in Seventeenth-Century Amsterdam', in C. Lesger and L. Noordegraaf (eds), *Entrepreneurs and Entrepreneurship in Early Modern Times. Merchants and Industrialists Within the Orbit of the Dutch Staple Market*, The Hague: Drukkerij Smits B.V., pp. 223–43.

Wallerstein, Immanuel (1980), *The Modern World-System II. Mercantilism and the Consolidation of the European World-Economy, 1600–1750*, London: Academic Press.

PART II

EIGHTEENTH-CENTURY CONTRIBUTIONS

4 Life annuity valuation: from de Witt and Halley to de Moivre and Simpson

Geoffrey Poitras

The roots of financial economics stretch back to antiquity. The valuation of financial transactions, such as determining payment on a loan or distributing profits from a partnership, is so ancient that any search for pioneers would be fruitless. A less ambitious beginning is required. A common thread connecting various elements of modern financial economics, such as asset pricing theory, financial risk management and contingent claims valuation, is the application of notions from probability theory to the valuation and management of financial securities and to the analysis of financial market equilibrium, for example, Rubinstein (2005). As discussed by Sylla (2006), the intellectual revolution associated with the Enlightenment marks the emergence of the modern frequentist interpretation of probability. Some of the earliest practical applications of this probability theory were concerned with a problem in financial economics: the valuation of life annuities. Not only were these securities important in state and municipal finance in France, England and Holland; in an era pre-dating actuarially sound pension plans and life insurance the life annuity performed an essential social function. As such, those that first applied the frequentist concept of probability to the valuation of life annuities deserve special recognition as 'pioneers of financial economics'. Within this group of pioneers that includes Jan de Witt and Nicholas Bernoulli, the contributions of Edmond Halley (1656–1742) and Abraham de Moivre (1667–1754) are outstanding.

While detailed modern summaries of the early contributions to life annuity valuation are available in Pearson (1978), Alter and Riley (1986), Hald (1990) and Poitras (2000), there is little direct examination of the primary sources. The essence of the solutions in the contributions is converted to the modern context, leaving in the background the original methods and arguments used to determine the solutions. As a consequence, Halley's novel geometric analysis of the joint life annuity for three lives or de Moivre's application of 'fluxions' to determine a life annuity valuation formula go unrecognized. With this in mind, the primary objective of this chapter is to demonstrate how this work on life annuity valuation contributed to 'the genesis of ideas and the evolution of methods' (de Roover 1969, p. 358) within financial economics. In the following, section 1 provides a historical overview of the development of life contingent contracts. Section 2 examines the contributions to life annuity valuation in the seventeenth and early eighteenth centuries, focusing on the insights of Jan de Witt (1625–72) and Nicholas Bernoulli (1695–1726). Section 3 details the analysis of the single life annuity contained in Halley (1693). Section 4 discusses the de Moivre solution procedure for the single life annuity valuation formula. Section 5 gives specific consideration to the various solutions proposed to valuing the joint life annuity. In addition to Halley's geometric approach used to assess the joint life annuity, the evolution of de Moivre's solution to the valuation of joint life annuities is discussed, together with advances to the available solutions made by Thomas Simpson (1710–61).

1. Development of life contingent contracts[1]

An aleatory contract has a payoff that depends on a random outcome, for example, Daston (1988). Examples of such contracts arise in the early history of insurance where, say, a contract would be made to protect against the loss of a cargo at sea. In a sense, any security that is not riskless is aleatory, but this stretches the notion in a direction that is not too helpful. In the early history of financial economics, it is aleatory contracts with outcomes dependent on life contingencies which are by far the most significant. Not only were such contracts socially important before the development of modern pension plans and life insurance schemes; life contingent contracts also provide the first instance of significant analytical solutions to aleatory security pricing problems. In providing contingent claims pricing formulas for the range of life annuity contracts that were traded in the late seventeenth and early eighteenth centuries, intellectual giants of that era, such as Edmond Halley and Abraham de Moivre, laid the foundations for modern financial economics.

The origins of life annuities can be traced to ancient times. Socially determined rules of inheritance usually meant a sizeable portion of the family estate would be left to a predetermined individual, often the first-born son. Bequests such as usufructs, maintenances and life incomes were common methods of making provisions for family members and others not directly entitled to inheritances.[2] One element of the Falcidian law (*Lex Falcidia*) of ancient Rome – law 68 of the Justinian Code effective from 40 BC – was that the rightful heir(s) to an estate was entitled to not less than one quarter of the property left by a testator, the so-called 'Falcidian fourth' (Bernoulli 1709, ch. 5). This created a judicial quandary requiring any other legacies to be valued and, if the total value of those other legacies exceeded three-quarters of the value of the total estate, these bequests had to be reduced proportionately. The Falcidian fourth created a legitimate valuation problem for jurists because many types of bequests did not have observable market values. Because there was not a developed market for life annuities, this was the case for bequests of life incomes. Some method was required to convert bequests of life incomes to a form that could be valued for legal purposes.

In Roman law, a legal solution for valuing bequests with a life contingent component was introduced by the jurist Ulpian (Domitianus Ulpianus, ?–229), who devised a table for the conversion of life annuities to annuities certain, a security for which there was a known method of valuation. Ulpian's conversion table is given by Hald (1990, p. 117); see Table 4.1.

Table 4.1 Ulpian's conversion table

Age of annuitant in years

0–19	20–24	25–29	30–34	35–39	40 … 49	50–54	55–59	60–
30	28	25	22	20	19 … 10	9	7	5

Comparable term to maturity of an annuity certain in years

While the stated connection between age and the pricing of life annuities is a fundamental insight of Ulpian's table, this interpretation of the table may be too generous. For example, Greenwood (1940, p. 246) and Hendricks (1852–53, p. 224) both maintain that Ulpian took no account of interest in the calculations, so the reference to 'annuities certain' is misleading.

Nicholas Bernoulli (1709, p. 27) observes that, in practice, the use of Ulpian's table produced valuations that were often determined by taking the annual value of the legacy, and multiplying this value by the term to maturity of the annuity certain to get the associated legacy value. For example, if the individual was 24 years old and was receiving a life income of £10 per year, then the legacy value according to Ulpian's table would be £280. Bernoulli correctly identifies the method of multiplying the table value by the size of the payment as faulty due to the omission of the value of interest. Bernoulli (1709, p. 41) observes that at the conventional 5 per cent compound interest the value of the legacy would be only £148.93.

While it is tempting to attribute a valuation aspect to Ulpian's table, there appears to be little more in the table than an early attempt to estimate life expectancy. Even this interpretation is generous. For example, the use of a 30-year life expectancy for the 0–19 group ignores the significantly higher mortality in the early years of life in ancient Rome. In addition, as Bernoulli (1709, p. 40) discusses, various authors have observed the obvious inconsistency in the table associated with a person of, say, 24 being given a longer life expectancy (24 + 28) than a person of, say, 26 (26 + 25), despite the 26–year-old having already lived longer. Similarly, the possibility of individuals living beyond 65 is not admitted, though it is known that there were septuagenarians and octogenarians in Roman times. Ultimately, the table was useful for the purpose for which it was designed: to ensure that the legal inheritance rights specified in the Falcidian law were protected. The biases associated with practical application of the table typically result in an overvaluation of the life contingent bequests, thereby ensuring that at least one-quarter of the estate passes to the rightful heir.

Ulpian's table was concerned with life incomes, maintenances and the like, which are not quite the same as life annuities which are traded securities with defined cash flow patterns dependent on life contingencies. The life annuity evolved from the *census*, which was a form of investment dating at least to feudal times. The English word annuity is an approximate translation, but annuity does not make the appropriate connection to the source of the *census* return being derived from a 'fruitful good' (Noonan 1957, p. 155). In Roman law, the *census* was not used, though different types of annuities were available. The various forms of *census* contracts formed a basis for the emergence of government debt issues. The types of securities employed were annuities certain (fixed-term annuities), perpetual annuities and life annuities to fund, first, municipal and, eventually, national borrowing.

Census contracts were initially designed, in feudal times, as a type of barter arrangement, present goods for future goods. The contract appears to have originated in continental Europe, eventually facilitating the evolution of a market for long-term debt (for example, Tracy 1985, pp. 7–8). The conventional *census* contract gradually took the form of a modern annuity where cash was received by the seller of the annuity in exchange for an agreement to make a stream of annual payments over time. By the end of the fifteenth century, the nobility, the Church, the state and the landed gentry were all involved as sellers of *census*. Many different variations of *census* were offered: a life *census* in which payments were made over the life of a buyer, or their designee; a perpetual *census*, which had no fixed maturity date; and a temporary or term *census* that ran for a fixed number of years, similar to a mortgage. A *census* could have conditions that permitted it to be redeemable at the option of either the buyer or seller. Noonan (1957) estimates that credit raised using *census* arrangements may have exceeded that raised through *societas* (business partnerships).

A major impetus to the development of securities markets was provided by the various 'financial revolutions' in government finance. These revolutions started at different times, in different countries, beginning with the Italian city states and, somewhat later, extending to the cities in northern France and Flanders. The key feature of these revolutions was the transition of government debt from the status of a short-term loan to an individual, debt as an obligation of the sovereign, to a long-term loan to a political entity independent of the ruler. The revolutions in government finance transformed government debt operations from the realm of individual borrowing, which was typically short term and secured by assets, to long-term borrowings which were secured by specific funding sources and were, to varying degrees, independent of the creditworthiness of the monarch.

The earliest forms of 'public debt', issued by Italian city states and the northern European cities and municipalities, were either forced loans on wealthy citizens, for example, the *prestiti* in Venice, or were *rentes* backed by specific revenue sources of the sovereign or town government. Northern European towns favoured annuities or *rentes* secured by urban taxes. As early as 1260, such issues of *rentes héritables* and *rentes viagères* (life annuities) appeared in the French cities of Calais and Douai, spreading to the Low Countries and German towns such as Cologne (Tracy 1985, p. 13). Between 1275 and 1290 the city of Ghent in Flanders issued *lijfrenten* or life annuities followed by issues of *erfrenten* or redeemable *rentes*. There was a form of guarantee by the sovereign associated with some of these municipal issues, for example, the Court of Flanders 'undertook to see that the city lived up to its promises'. Municipalities, particularly in Holland, Flanders and Brabant, continued to issue life and redeemable annuities leading to increasingly larger stocks of public debt and, ultimately, to repayment difficulties for some towns by the sixteenth century.

The transition from municipal to national public debt issues was gradual. Though claims could be made for certain German territories, Dutch provinces or the Spanish monarchies, Hamilton (1947) traces the beginnings of national public debt to sixteenth-century France. For some centuries before, the French had a tradition of the monarch selling long-term *rentes*, supported by the income from royal properties. These sales were often made at deep discounts to royal officials and could not be considered 'public debt' but, rather, were obligations of the sovereign. Hamilton (1947, p. 119) marks 1522 as a turning point. Though sovereigns had recognized the importance of the debt market in financing state military ventures for some time, the emergence of the public debt gave the debt market a new status as an instrument of state power.

Despite this claim to first-mover status by the French, there were numerous difficulties with the administration of the French public debt. Large increases in outstanding principal to sustain various military adventures led to periods of suspended interest payments and forced reduction of a portion of the outstanding principal. By the beginning of the eighteenth century, French national finances were in a sorry condition. The Dutch were decidedly more successful in developing their public debt. The Dutch provincial governments pioneered various innovations in public debt issues during the sixteenth century, including the development of a 'free market' for provincial *renten* issued in Holland (Tracy 1985, ch. IV). The English were relative latecomers in developing public debt issues, with the beginnings of English public debt starting only with the reign of William and Mary in 1688. However, by the mid-eighteenth century the English had assumed front-runner status and the system of English public debt had become a model for European governments.

In the late seventeenth and early eighteenth centuries, actuarially sound analytical solutions were proposed to the problem of valuing life annuities. Arguably, these analytical solutions represent the most important theoretical contributions to the early history of financial economics. The intellectual preliminaries required to sustain these contributions start around the latter part of the sixteenth century in Holland where important university mathematicians, such as Simon Stevin, were drawn to solving practical fixed-income valuation problems, complementing the work of the commercial algorists; see, for example, Poitras (2000, ch. 4); Hawawini and Vora (1980). Even though the development of discounting and compounding techniques was important for determining the return from partnerships and valuing commonly traded term annuities such as mortgages and lease–purchase transactions, these techniques were not sufficient to value life annuities and other types of securities involving life contingent claims. Such problems were important because, in the absence of pension funds and life insurance, life annuities performed an essential social function.

The life annuity usually was a contract between three parties, the subscriber who provided the initial capital, the shareholder who was entitled to receive the annuity payments and the nominee on whose life the payout was contingent; see, for example, Weir (1989). Different variations were possible. For example, one person could be subscriber, shareholder and nominee; a parent could be a subscriber and designate a child as the nominee with the shareholder status passing from parent to child as an inheritance; or joint life annuities could be specified where more than one nominee was designated and payments continued until both nominees died. Similarly, payments on a reversionary annuity (reversion) would be paid to nominee x after the death of nominee y and would continue until the death of x. If x died before y, then no payments would be made. Reversions could also have joint features. For example, x could be both parents and y could be their children.[3] The life annuity was further complicated by the need to establish proof of survival for the nominee before each annuity payment date. While it was technically possible to resell most life annuity contracts to third parties, the difficulties associated with verifying the survival and probability of survival for the nominee made resale difficult. Oddly enough, until the nineteenth century, market practice usually involved governments selling life annuities without taking accurate consideration of the age of the nominee.

Though there were larger and less frequent issues of life annuities by the emerging nation states starting in the seventeenth century, the typical government issuers of life annuities were municipalities, with prices varying widely from town to town depending on prevailing local interest rates and pricing conventions. Annuity prices were quoted in '*years' purchase*', which is the price of the annuity divided by the annual annuity payment. For a perpetual annuity, years' purchase is the inverse of the annual yield to maturity. Nicholas Bernoulli (1709, pp. 27–8) provides numerous historical examples of single life annuities selling for 6 to 12 years' purchase, without allowance being made for the age of nominee. Reference is also made to the valuation of dowries at 10 years' purchase. De Witt quotes a 1671 price for a single life annuity in Amsterdam of 14 years' purchase with a 4 per cent interest rate and no allowance for age of nominee; this is compared with a price of 25 years' purchase for a redeemable annuity, effectively a perpetual annuity with an embedded option for the borrower to redeem at the purchase price. Houtzager (1950) quotes a sixteenth- and early seventeenth-century Dutch pricing convention of 1.5 to 2 times the years' purchase for a redeemable annuity to determine the price for single life annuities, i.e., the years' purchase of a life annuity equaled the years' purchase for a redeemable annuity divided by 1.5 to 2. The inefficiency of the practice of selling life annuities without reference to the age of the nominee did not escape the notice of those responsible for government finance. However, solving the problem of determining a correct price was not easy. The first sound solution to this difficult analytical problem was proposed by Jan de Witt.[4]

2. Valuation of life annuities by de Witt and Nicholas Bernoulli

Jan de Witt was not a professional mathematician. He was born into a burgher–regent family and attended university at Leiden as a student of jurisprudence, where he lived in the house of Frans van Schooten. While he was formally a professor of jurisprudence, van Schooten was also deeply involved in mathematical studies. Van Schooten encouraged Christian Huygens, Jan Hudde and de Witt in their mathematical studies and published their efforts as appendices to two of his mathematical books. De Witt's contribution on the dynamics of conic sections was written around 1650 and published as an appendix to van Schooten's 1659 exposition of Cartesian mathematics, *Geometria a Renato Des Cartes*. From the perspective of the history of mathematics, de Witt's contribution is an interesting and insightful exposition on the subject but 'marks no great advance' (Coolidge 1990, p. 127).

Around 1650, de Witt began his career in Dutch politics as the pensionary of Dordrecht. In 1653, at the age of 28, he became the grand pensionary or prime minister of Holland. During his term as grand pensionary, de Witt was confronted with the need to raise funds to support Dutch military activities, first in the Anglo-Dutch war of 1665–67 and later in anticipation of an invasion by France which, ultimately, came in 1672. Life annuities had for many years been a common method of municipal and state finance in Holland and de Witt also proposed that life annuity financing be used to support the war effort. However, de Witt was not satisfied that the convention of selling of life annuities at a fixed price, without reference to the age of the annuitant, was a sound practice. Instead he proposed a method of calculating the price of life annuities which would vary with age. Poitras (2000) considers this remarkable contribution to be the start of modern contingent claims analysis.

More precisely, aided by contributions from Huygens in probability and Hudde in mortality statistics, in *Value of Life Annuities in Proportion to Redeemable Annuities* (1671, in Dutch) de Witt provided the first substantive analytical solution to the difficult problem of valuing a life annuity.[5] Unlike the numerous variations of fixed-term annuity problems which had been solved in various commercial arithmetics, the life annuity valuation required the weighting of the relevant future cash flows by the probability of survival for the designated nominee. De Witt's approach, which is somewhat computationally cumbersome but analytically insightful, was to compute the value of a life annuity by applying the concept of mathematical expectation advanced by Huygens in 1657.

De Witt's approach involved making theoretical assumptions about the distribution of the number of deaths. To provide empirical support for his calculations, he gave supplementary empirical evidence derived from the register at The Hague for life annuitants of Holland and West Friesland for which he calculated the average present values of life annuities for different age classes, based on the actual payments made on the annuities. This crude empirical analysis was buttressed by the considerably more detailed empirical work of Hudde on the mortality statistics of life annuitants from the Amsterdam register for 1586–90. For the next century, the development of pricing formula for life annuities is intimately related to progress in the study of life contingency tables, a subject which is central to the development of modern demographics and actuarial science.

The solution to the problem of pricing life annuities given by de Witt uses an age interval between 3 and 80. Hence, de Witt is considering the value of a life annuity written on the life of a three-year-old nominee. Adjusting the solution to price life annuities for older nominees at different ages is straightforward, involving a reduction in the number of terms being summed and an adjustment of the divisor. As the practice up to his time was to sell life annuities at the same price, regardless of the age of the nominee, it was conventional to select younger nominees from healthy families. Based on Hudde's data for 1586–90 Amsterdam life annuity nominees, approximately 50 per cent were under 10 years of age, and 80 per cent under 20 (Alter and Riley, 1986, p. 33). Throughout the following annuities will be assumed to make a payment of 1 unit of currency (florin, dollars, etc.) each period. Instead of assuming a uniform distribution where death at each age would be equally likely, De Witt divided the interval between 3 and 80 into four subperiods: (3,53), (53,63), (63,73) and (73,80). Within each subperiod, an equal chance of mortality is assigned. The number of chances assigned to each subgroup is 1, 2/3, 1/2, 1/3. The chance of living beyond 80 is assumed to be zero. While de Witt corresponded with Hudde about mortality data he was collecting and tabulating for the 1586–89 Amsterdam annuitants, these probabilities were assumed and not directly derived from a life table.

From these assumptions, de Witt constructs a distribution for the number of deaths and calculates the life annuity price as the expectation of the relevant annuity present values. In doing this, he explicitly recognizes that life annuities were paid in semi-annual instalments, requiring time to be measured in half-years and for survivors to be living at the end of the half-year in order to receive the payment. The 77-year period translates into 154 half-years. Using a discount rate of 4 per cent per annum, de Witt uses his assumed chances of mortality in any half year to calculate a weighted average of the present values for the certain annuities associated with each half year. The resulting value is the expected present value of the life annuity, which is the recommended price at which the annuity should be sold.

Algebraically, de Witt's technique can be illustrated by defining A_n to be the present value of an annuity certain with a 4 per cent annual rate to be paid at the end of the half-year n:

$$A_n = \sum_{t=1}^{n} \frac{1}{(1+r)^t} = \frac{1}{r} - \frac{1}{r(1+r)^n} \quad \text{where} \quad (1+r) = \sqrt{1.04}$$

To evaluate the expected present value of the life annuity, de Witt performs the calculation:

$$E[A_n] = \frac{\sum_{n=1}^{99} A_n + \frac{2}{3}\sum_{n=100}^{119} A_n + \frac{1}{2}\sum_{n=120}^{139} A_n + \frac{1}{3}\sum_{n=140}^{153} A_n}{128}$$

Interpretation of the sums is aided by observing that individuals must be alive at the end of the half-year to qualify for annuity payments. For example, dying in the first half-year means that no payments will be received. The divisor of 128 is calculated by determining the total number of chances as:

$$(1001 + (20)\frac{2}{3} + (20)\frac{1}{2} + (14)\frac{1}{3} = 128$$

where the number in parentheses is the number of half-years in each subgroup. De Witt's solution can be compared to the less realistic case where the distribution of deaths is assumed to be uniform:

$$E[A_n] = \frac{\sum_{n=1}^{153} A_n}{154} = \frac{1}{154}(0) + \frac{1}{154}\frac{1}{1+r} + \frac{1}{154}\sum_{t=1}^{2}\frac{1}{(1+r)^t} + \ldots + \frac{1}{154}\sum_{t=1}^{153}\frac{1}{(1+r)^n} + 0$$

By assigning less weight to the largest cash flows, de Witt's calculated expected value of 16.0016 florins for annual payments of 1 florin differs from the expected value of 17.22 florins calculated using a uniform distribution.[6]

Though there is evidence that de Witt's solution to the life annuity valuation problem was known by the intellectual community outside Holland, it does not appear that the results were widely disseminated. For example, Sylla (Chapter 1, p. xx) observes that 'For several years before his death, Bernoulli had been writing to Gottfried Wilhelm Leibniz asking him to supply a copy of Jan de Witt's pamphlet in Dutch on life and term annuities, but Leibniz had mislaid the copy previously in his possession.' Though Nicholas Bernoulli (1709, p. 34) does not specifically identify de Witt's contribution, an explicit reference is made to the issue of life annuities that de Witt (1671) was involved in pricing. In addition, the solution to the life annuity valuation given by Bernoulli (1709, p. 33) uses a similar approach to that of de Witt, albeit with a different life table and an easier solution methodology.

Before stating the solution to the life annuity valuation, Bernoulli (1709) first explores the possibility of solving the value of a life annuity by using an annuity certain with a term to maturity equal to the expected duration of life from a given starting age x. The difference of such a solution from an $E[A_n]$ valuation was recognized by de Witt, but the point was still of enough interest that Bernoulli (1709) calculated the relevant values for individuals with ages from 6 to 76 (by decades). At 5 per cent compound interest, the values given by Bernoulli are shown in Table 4.2.

Table 4.2 Life annuity values (Bernoulli, 1709)

Age of annuitant in years

Newborn	6	16	26	36	46	56	66	76
18.2/11.8	20.8/12.7	20.3/12.6	19.4/12.2	17.5/11.5	15/10.4	11.7/8.7	8.3/6.3	5/4.3

Life expectancy in years/value of the annuity certain in years' purchase

Having done these calculations, Bernoulli states: 'I notice that the value of (life annuity) incomes is not correctly calculated by supposing that the return will last as many years as someone is supposed probably to live.' This is followed by a derivation of life annuity values that is in the spirit of that given by de Witt. The values determined by Bernoulli are shown in Table 4.3.

Table 4.3 Life annuity values, revised (Bernoulli, 1709)

Age of annuitant in years

Newborn	6	16	26	36	46	56	66	76
9.420	10.600	10.593	10.576	10.164	9.457	8.148	6.545	4.558

Value of the life annuity

Though the valuation method provided by Bernoulli appears decidedly simpler than that of de Witt, the only substantive differences between the solution methods are the use of: annual instead of semi-annual payments; seven age groups instead of four; and a maximum life span of 86 instead of 80.

Bernoulli provides the following description of his solution procedure:

> For the sake of brevity we will demonstrate with a single example for a youth of sixteen years. From Chapter 2 [of *De Usu*] it was established that there are 15 chances that a youth of 16 years will die in the first decade, 9 for the second decade, 6 for the third, 4 for the fourth, 3 for the fifth, 2 for the sixth and 1 for the seventh; if he should die in the first decade, the just premium is 4.558 (which is the arithmetic mean of the first ten numbers in this Table [of the value of annuities certain for each year]) ...; if he should die in the second decade the premium is 10.519 ... therefore by our general rule the value of this return is:

$$= \frac{15*4.558 + 9*10.519 + 6*14.179 + 4*16.427 + 3*17.806 + 2*18.653 + 1*19.173}{40}$$

$$= \frac{423.720}{40} = 10.593$$

Bernoulli reduces the number of direct calculations done by de Witt by averaging the A_n by decade. For example, the value of 4.558 for the first decade is the arithmetic average of A_1 to A_{10}. However, because the life probabilities are the same across the averaging period there is no substantive difference with de Witt's method. Bernoulli's approach does make the bias introduced by this simplification more apparent, as illustrated by a comparison of the values for 66- and 76-year-olds for the annuity certain using the duration of life and for the life annuity.

3. The contribution of Edmond Halley

It is difficult to assess the impact of de Witt's contribution on the practice of pricing life annuities. Based on his recommendation, in 1672 the city of Amsterdam began offering life annuities with prices dependent on the age of the nominee. However, this practice did not become widespread and by 1694, when Edmond Halley (1656–1742) published his influential paper 'An Estimate of the Degrees of Mortality of Mankind, drawn from the curious Tables of the Births and Funerals at the City of Breslaw; with an Attempt to ascertain the Price of Annuities upon Lives', the English government was still selling life annuities at seven years' purchase, independent of age. Halley's paper is remarkable in providing substantive contributions to both demography and to financial economics. The importance of this paper reinforces the intellectual stature of an individual who is recognized in modern times primarily for his contributions to astronomy. Yet, despite this importance, Bernoulli (1709) makes no reference to Halley's solution for a life annuity, reflecting the speed at which research contributions spread in this era.

The Breslau data used in the preparation of Halley's 'Estimate' were much better suited to construction of a life table than the bills of mortality. Thanks to Leibnitz, the data set came to the attention of the Royal Society, and Halley, the editor of the Society's journal, was selected to analyze the data. From the end of the sixteenth century, Breslau, a city in Silesia, had maintained a register of births and deaths, classified according to sex and age. For the purposes of constructing a precise life table, only the population size is missing. The paper is primarily concerned with constructing Halley's life table and uses the valuation of life annuities as an illustration of applying the information in the life table. In the process, Halley presents a more general and, arguably, more correct approach than de Witt to the valuation of a life annuity. While this paper was Halley's primary effort in demographics, he did make another contribution to financial economics detailing the use of logarithms in solving present value problems; see, for example, Poitras (2000, p. 155).

General details of Halley's life are available in numerous sources, such as Pearson (1978), Ronan (1978), Poitras (2000, ch. 6). Unfortunately, there is so much in the life of Edmond Halley that a conventional historiography quickly becomes overwhelming; the process of sifting out important details becomes unmanageable. For example, Halley had an important relationship with Sir Isaac Newton. Some of the connections between Halley and Newton were immediate, such as Halley being instrumental in getting the *Principia* published: 'There is little doubt that we owe its publication to the good offices of Halley' (Pearson 1978, p. 86). This aid came in financial support for publication from both the Royal Society and Halley, as well as 'important editorial aid' (Ronan 1978, p. 68) in preparing the manuscript. Newton was a reluctant author, if only because he was not fully satisfied with the results that were being published.

Halley is best known for his work on the periodicity of comet orbits. The naming of Halley's comet was a posthumous recognition for his theoretical and empirical work on a particular bright comet which exhibited a periodicity of 75 years. Though Halley's observations were well known to astronomers, 'it was not until the 1682 comet reappeared as predicted in 1758 that the whole intellectual world of western Europe took notice. By then Halley had been dead fifteen years; but his hope that posterity would acknowledge that this return 'was first predicted by an Englishman' was not misplaced, and the object was named "Halley's comet"' (Ronan 1978, p. 69). This recognition was a fitting tribute for someone who had contributed to so many fields, from astronomy and mathematics to history and philology.

As was the fashion at the time, Halley's presentation of the life annuity pricing problem was done by presenting mathematical concepts in a verbal format. Halley (1693, pp. 602–3) provides the following solution for the life annuity valuation:

> Use V. On this depend the Valuation of Annuities upon Lives; for it is plane that the Purchaser ought to pay for only such a part of the value of the Annuity, as he has Chances that he is living; and this ought to be computed yearly, and the Sum of those yearly Values being added together, will amount to the value of the Annuity for the Life of the Person proposed. Now the present value of Money payable after a term of years, at any given rate of Interest, either may be had from Tables already computed; or almost as compendiously, by the Table of Logarithms: for the Arithmetical Complement of the Logarithm of Unity and its yearly Interest (that is, of 1,06 for Six per Cent. being 9,974694.) being multiplied by the number of years proposed, gives the present value of One Pound payable after the end of so many years. Then, by the foregoing Proposition, it will be as the number of Persons living after that term of years, to the number dead; so are the Odds that any one Person is Alive or Dead. And by consequence, as the Sum of both or the number of Persons living of the Age first proposed, to the number remaining after so many years, (both given by the Table) so the present value of the yearly Sum payable after the term proposed, to the Sum which ought to be paid for the Chance the person has to enjoy such an Annuity after so many Years. And this being repeated for every year of the person's Life, the Sum of all the present Values of those Chances is the true Value of the Annuity. This will without doubt appear to be a soft laborious Calculation, but it being one of the principal Uses of this Speculation, and having found some Compendia for the Work, I took the pains to compute the following Table, being the short Result of a not ordinary number of Arithmetical Operations; It shews the Value of Annuities for every Fifth Year of Age, to the Seventieth, as follows:

Age	Years' Purchase	Age	Yrs' P.	Age	Yrs' P.
1	10	25	12,27	50	9,21
5	13,40	30	11,72	55	8,51
10	13,44	35	11,12	60	7,60
15	13,33	40	10,57	65	6,54
20	12,78	45	9,91	70	5,32

With this in mind, it is possible to reexpress Halley's formula in a more modern mathematical form by observing that the total number of annuities sold on a life starting at year x, ℓ_x, equals the sum of $d_x + d_{x+1} + \ldots + d_{w-1}$ where d_i is the number of annuities which terminate in period i due to the death of annuitant nominees in that year and that $d_i = 0$ for $x \geq w$. Taking ℓ_{x+t} to be the number of nominees, starting in year x surviving in period $x + t$, it follows that: $d_{x+t} = \ell_{x+t} - \ell_{x+t+1}$ and that the probability of death in any given year j is (d_{x+j}/ℓ_x). Starting with the expected value formulation used by de Witt and Bernoulli, the connection to Halley's pricing formula for a life annuity follows:

$$E[A_n] = \frac{1}{\ell_x}\sum_{m=1}^{w-x-1} A_m d_{x+m} = \frac{1}{\ell_x}\sum_{m=1}^{w-x-1} d_{x+m}\sum_{t=1}^{n}\frac{1}{(1+r)^t} = \frac{1}{\ell_x}\sum_{t=1}^{n}\sum_{m=1}^{w-x-1} d_{x+m}\frac{1}{(1+r)^t}$$

$$= \frac{1}{\ell_x}\sum_{m=1}^{w-x-1} \ell_{x+m}\frac{1}{(1+r)^m}$$

The last step in the derivation (which gives Halley's formulation) comes from progressively collecting terms associated with $(1+r)^{-t}$. For example, the $(1+r)^{-1}$ term will appear in each annuity and will, as a result, have coefficients which are the sum of $d_{x+1}, d_{x+2}, \ldots d_{w-1}$. Recalling the definition of d in terms of ℓ, this sum returns ℓ_{x+1}. In symbolic form, this is the single life annuity pricing formula presented by Halley (1693).

4. De Moivre's approximation for the single life annuity

In assessing Halley's contribution to the history of financial economics, it is natural immediately to mention Abraham de Moivre (1667–1754), an expatriate Frenchman transplanted to London following the Repeal of the Edict of Nantes. Halley and de Moivre were first acquainted in 1692 and in 1695 de Moivre's first paper contributed to the Royal Society was presented by Halley. Unlike Halley, who touched only briefly on the pricing of securities, de Moivre spent much of his productive life studying the practical problem of pricing life annuities. By the time de Moivre undertook his work on life annuities, the basic groundwork had been laid. However, Halley and others recognized that the brute force approach to calculating tables for valuing life annuities would require 'a not ordinary number of Arithmetical operations'. Halley attempted to develop simplifying mathematical procedures, 'to find a Theorem that might be more concise than the Rules there laid down, but in vain'.

In the early history of security analysis de Moivre can be recognized for fundamental contributions involving the application of applied probability theory to the valuation of life annuities. This work laid the theoretical foundation for Richard Price (1723–91), James Dodson (*c.* 1710–57) and others to develop the actuarially sound principles required to implement modern life insurance. The immediate incentive for de Moivre was to value the various aleatory contracts which became increasingly popular as the eighteenth century progressed. Being (together with Laplace) one of two giants of probability theory in the eighteenth century (Pearson 1978, p. 146), de Moivre was singularly well suited to the task of developing the foundations of insurance mathematics. It is one of the quirks of intellectual history that de Moivre's most significant contributions, which lay primarily in the area of probability theory and applied mathematics, contributed little to his personal comfort while his contributions to security analysis and valuation managed to help de Moivre maintain body and soul.

De Moivre began his close friendships with Newton and Halley around the same time in the early 1690s. The timing of the 1693 publication of Halley's 'Estimate' and his subsequent presentation of de Moivre's first paper to the Royal Society in 1695 make it possible, though not likely, that de Moivre played some role in the inclusion of the life annuity valuation problem in the 'Estimate'. It is more likely that any enlightened interaction between the two on the subject of applying Halley's life table to the important problem of life annuities influenced de Moivre to examine this subject more closely. In any event, de Moivre's primary contribution to pricing life annuities did not appear until much later in the *Annuities upon Lives* (1725) with a second edition (1743) which has an improved exposition and correction for some errors identified by Thomas Simpson. Also important is the 1738 edition and 1756 edition of his *The Doctrine of Chances*. The 1738 edition contains much of the material from the 1725 edition of *Annuities* with some additional topics being discussed, such as temporary life assurances and a valuation for successive lives. The 1756 edition contains a section titled 'A Treatise of Annuities on Lives' together with discussion of the life tables of Halley, Kersseboom, Simpson and Deparcieux.

In *Annuities*, de Moivre examined a wide variety of the life annuities available in the early eighteenth century: single life annuities, joint annuities (annuities written on several lives), reversionary annuities, and annuities on successive lives. His general approach to these valuation problems involves two steps: first, to develop a general valuation formula for each type of annuity based on Halley's approach; and, second, to produce an approximation to the general formula suitable for calculating prices without the considerable efforts involved in evaluating the more exact formula. In order to implement most of the approximations, de Moivre developed a mathematical formulation of the information contained in the life table using: arithmetically declining life probabilities; geometrically declining life probabilities; or a piecewise linear approximation to the sequence of life probabilities. The selection of a particular assumption depended on the analytical usefulness for the type of problem being solved.

De Moivre provided an important simplification for the value of a single life annuity under the assumption that the 'Probabilities of Life … decrease in Arithmetic Progression' or, in other words, are uniformly distributed starting at year x up to some terminal year w, $n = w - x$. Generalizing the uniformly distributed case, de Moivre's result is derived by observing that for the uniform case:

$$E[A_n] = \frac{n-1}{n}\frac{1}{1+r} + \frac{n-2}{n}\frac{1}{(1+r)^2} + \ldots + \frac{n-(n-1)}{n}\frac{1}{(1+r)^{n-1}} + \frac{n-n}{n}\frac{1}{(1+r)^n}$$

$$= \sum_{t=1}^{n} \frac{1}{(1+r)^t}\left(1 - \frac{t}{n}\right) = \sum_{t=1}^{n} \frac{1}{(1+r)^t} - \sum_{t=1}^{n} \frac{t}{n(1+r)^t}$$

From this point, in the first edition of *Annuities upon Lives* de Moivre provides an obscure reference to a general result for series from the *Doctrine of Chances* that is used to determine the solution. In later editions, a more tedious demonstration depending on the relationship between the properties of logarithms, 'fluents' and 'fluxions' is given. A more modern derivation is provided in Poitras (2000, p. 213) where it is observed that:

$$\sum_{t=1}^{n} \frac{t}{n(1+r)^t} = \frac{1+r}{n} \sum_{t=1}^{n} \frac{t}{(1+r)^{t+1}} = -\frac{1+r}{n} \frac{dA_n}{d(1+r)}$$

It follows that:

$$E[A_n] = \left[A_n + \frac{1+r}{n} \frac{dA_n}{d(1+r)} \right] = \frac{A_n}{n} \left[n + \frac{1+r}{A_n} \frac{dA_n}{d(1+r)} \right]$$

The last term contains the familiar Macaulay duration for the annuity applicable to the longest life.

Substituting the relevant expressions back into $E[A_n]$ and evaluating the derivative gives:

$$E[A_n] = \left[A_n + \frac{1+r}{n} \frac{dA_n}{d(1+r)} \right] = \left(\frac{1}{r} - \frac{1}{r(1+r)^n} \right) + \frac{1+r}{n} \left[\frac{n}{r(1+r)^{n+1}} + \frac{1}{r^2(1+r)^n} - \frac{1}{r^2} \right]$$

$$= \frac{1}{r} - \frac{1+r}{n} \left[\frac{1}{r} \left\{ \frac{1}{r} - \frac{1}{r(1+r)^n} \right\} \right] = \frac{1}{r} \left\{ 1 - \frac{1+r}{n} A_n \right\}$$

The final right-hand-side expression is de Moivre's approximation to the value of a single life annuity. If only for the computational savings provided, this formula is a considerable advance. From the tedious calculation of a long weighted sum, with weights extracted from the not completely accurate life tables available at his time, de Moivre provides a calculation which could be done in a matter of seconds with the aid of an appropriate table for annuities certain. While the derivation provided is not the same as de Moivre's (see Hald 1990, pp. 521–2), the connection to the familiar notion of Macaulay duration is instructive for modern readers. Similar to the improvement of the duration measure provided by the introduction of convexity, the accuracy of de Moivre's formula can be improved by considering higher order derivative terms (Pearson 1978, pp. 150–52). In this case, the higher-order terms improve on the inaccuracy associated with the initial assumption of uniformly distributed death rates.

5. Solutions for the joint life annuity value

Though more difficult to value, joint life annuities – where the annuity payment continues until all nominees have died – have a history as long as the single life annuity. Joint annuities featuring a husband and wife or a father and his sons as nominees were common. Considerable variation in the relationship between the prices of joint and single life annuities has been observed. Bernoulli (1709, pp. 26–7) reviews a number of historical instances for joint life annuity valuations, including a case where, on scholastic grounds, the pricing convention was for single and joint life annuities to be sold at the same price. Referencing du Moulin, Bernoulli observes: 'If the rent should be purchased on the lifetime of two in its entirety, a considerably more ample premium ... must be constituted.' For individuals of comparable age and health, 12 years' purchase is recommended by du Moulin for an annuity on two lives compared to 10 years' purchase for a single life. Daston (1988, p. 121) observes that, starting in 1402, Amsterdam sold municipal annuities at regular intervals typically 'charging flat rates of 9 1/11 percent for annuities on two heads and 11 13/17 percent for one, regardless of age'. The 1704 life annuity issued by the English government charged 9 years' purchase for a single life, 11 years' purchase on two lives, 12 years' purchase on three lives and 15 years' purchase on a 99-year annuity certain.

While the development of theoretical solutions for the value of joint life annuities parallels that for single lives, the details do differ. In the *Value of Life Annuities* (1671), Jan de Witt only examines the solution for single lives. Based on correspondence during 1671 between Hudde and de Witt reported in Hendricks (1852–3), it appears that a solution for the joint life annuity was also actively discussed and attempts at appropriate calculations executed. As the joint life solution was decidedly more complex than for a single life, after a number of false starts the solution settled on an ingenious method involving the use of a binomial expansion to specify a weighted average of (Hendricks 1852–3, p. 109):

> 8 young lives (that number being given in order to avoid here too great a complication) and who are found to have lived as follows – the first to have become defunct 7 full years from the well-established date at which ... has been bought ... a life annuity; the second life 15 years; the third 24 years; the fourth 33 years; the fifth 41 years; the sixth 50 years; the seventh 59 years; the eighth 68 years.

Using an equally weighted average of the annuity certain values for each of the life spans, de Witt determines a single life annuity value (with 1 florin annual payment) of 17.22 florins. Solutions for joint life annuities for two, three, four up to eight lives are to be determined by using a weighted average with weights determined as binomial coefficients (Table 4.4).

Table 4.4 Joint life annuity values using a weighted average (de Witt, 1671)

Years from purchase to death of nominee

7	15	24	33	41	50	59	68
	1	2	3	4	5	6	7
		1	3	6	10	15	21
			1	4	10	20	35
				1	5	15	35
					1	6	21
						1	7
							1

Weights

To apply these coefficients, de Witt gives worked examples for two, three and four lives. For the two-life annuity case de Witt gives the weighted average as

> the value of a life annuity upon 2 lives ... is rightly and precisely equal to the value of a life annuity upon one life of a class of 28 lives, of which one life has lived 15 complete years; 2 each 24 years; 3 each 33 years; 4 each 41 years; 5 each 50 years; 6 each 59 years; and 7 each 68 years.

The solution of 20.76 florins (for a 1 florin annual payment) is determined by using a weighted average with 28 total chances. From the table the three-life case would have 56 total chances and values of 1 for 24 years, 3 for 33 years, 6 for 41 years, 10 for 50 years, 15 for 59 years and 21 for 68 years. Solutions for a joint life annuity on four, five, six and seven lives follow appropriately with the value for eight lives being equal to the annuity certain value for 68 years (23.26 florins). While not directly stated in the correspondence, based on the maximum 80-year life span used in *The Value of Life Annuities*, the underlying assumption is that the lives involved are initially all 12 years old. For simplicity, de Witt uses only eight lives in calculating the solutions. However, reference is made to Hudde using calculations with 80 lives which would make for more complicated calculations but would avoid the degenerate solution given by de Witt for eight lives.

Though the correspondence between de Witt and Hudde only examined the uniformly distributed case, it is not difficult to see that the binomial coefficients in the weighted average could be adjusted to reflect the theoretical life table used in *The Value of Annuities*. However, being available only in correspondence that was not uncovered until Hendricks (1853) in the middle of the nineteenth century, this ingenious method of solving the joint life annuity faded into history, leaving the more cumbersome and computationally intensive approach proposed by Halley to influence the development of solutions for the joint life annuity value. While recommending the usefulness of logarithms for 'facilitating the Computation of the Value of two, three, or more Lives', Halley does not provide completely worked solutions for any joint life annuity values. Though the proximate reason given by Halley is that the Breslau life table was not based on 'the Experience of a very great Number of Years', de Moivre (1725, p. ii) recognizes that

> even admitting such as Table could be obtained as might be grounded on the Experience of a very great Number of Years, still the Method of applying it to the Valuation of several Lives would be extremely laborious, considering the vast Number of Operations that would be requisite to combine every Year of each Life with every Year of all the other Lives.

What Halley does provide is a novel geometric analysis of the solution method for determining the individual terms in the sum that determines the joint life annuity for two and three lives. That Halley spent considerable time and effort on the solution to the joint life annuity value is apparent in Halley (1693), where fewer than two pages are dedicated to single life annuities with about four and one-half pages to joint life annuities, concentrating almost exclusively on the valuation for two and three lives.

While being computationally demanding, the approach to joint annuity valuation proposed by Halley does have the desirable feature of allowing for nominee lives that are unequal. Halley (1693, p. 604) verbally describes the brute force method for solving the joint life annuity on two lives:

> for the number of Chances of each single Life, found in the [Breslau life] Table, being multiplied together, become the chances of Two Lives. And after any certain Term of Years, the Product of the two remaining Sums is the Chances that both Persons are living. The Product of the two Differences, being the numbers of the Dead of both Ages, are the Chances that both the Persons are dead. And the two Products of the remaining Sums of one Age multiplied by those dead of the other, shew the Chances that there are that each Party survives the other: Whence is derived the Rule to estimate the Value of the Remainder of one Life after another. Now as the Product of Two Numbers in the Table for the Two Ages proposed, is to the difference between that Product and the Product of the two numbers of Persons

deceased in any space of time, so is the value of a Sum of Money to be paid after so much time, to the value thereof under the Contingency of Mortality. And as the aforesaid Product of the two Numbers answering to the Ages proposed, to the Product of the Deceased of one Age multiplied by those remaining alive of the other; So the Value of a Sum of Money to be paid after any time proposed, to the value of the Chances that the one Party has that he survives the other whose number of Deceased you made use of, in the second Term of the Proposition.

This explanation is followed by a numerical illustration of the relevant calculations for one term in the sum. Recognizing the difficulty involved in understanding the various calculations, Halley then provides a geometric justification for these calculations (see Figure 4.1).

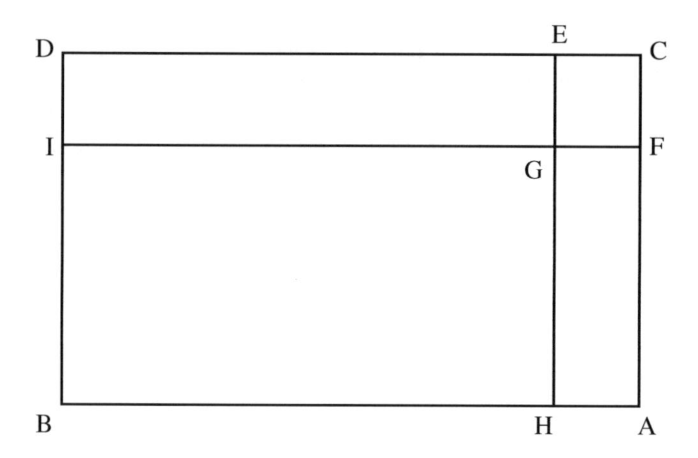

Figure 4.1 Halley's method for calculating a joint annuity on two lives

The whole area of ABCD ($= \ell_x \ell_y$) is the total number of chances for two lives at $t = 0$. The area of the inner rectangle HGIB ($= \ell_{x+m} \ell_{y+m}$) is the total number of chances that both are alive at $t = m$. The two side rectangles IDGE ($= \ell_x (\ell_y - \ell_{y+m})$) and HAFG ($= \ell_y (\ell_x - \ell_{x+m})$) are the chances that one nominee is alive while the other is dead, leaving the upper rectangle EGFC to be the chances that both nominees have died. Subtracting the ratio of EGFC to ABCD from one determines the weight applicable to the discounted cash flow associated with $(1 / (1 + r))^m$.

Formally, because no allowance is made for the portion of joint annuity payments that would be made when there are no chances that the eldest nominee will be alive, this geometric argument only fully covers the situation where the two nominees have equal ages.[7] Given this, Halley extends the geometric analysis for a joint life annuity on two lives to three lives (see Figure 4.2).

For Halley (1693, p. 606), the discussion for the two-dimension case 'is the Key to the Case of Three Lives'. By extending to analysis to three dimensions, it is apparent that the fraction of total volume associated with the volume where all three nominees are dead is associated with the cube KLMNOPAI. Unlike the two-dimensional case, Halley does not provide numerical calculations. It is apparent that the calculations involved are too numerous and tedious to warrant a complete resolution. Having laid this rough foundation, Halley never returned to publish efforts on this subject, leaving the next series of developments to Abraham de Moivre.

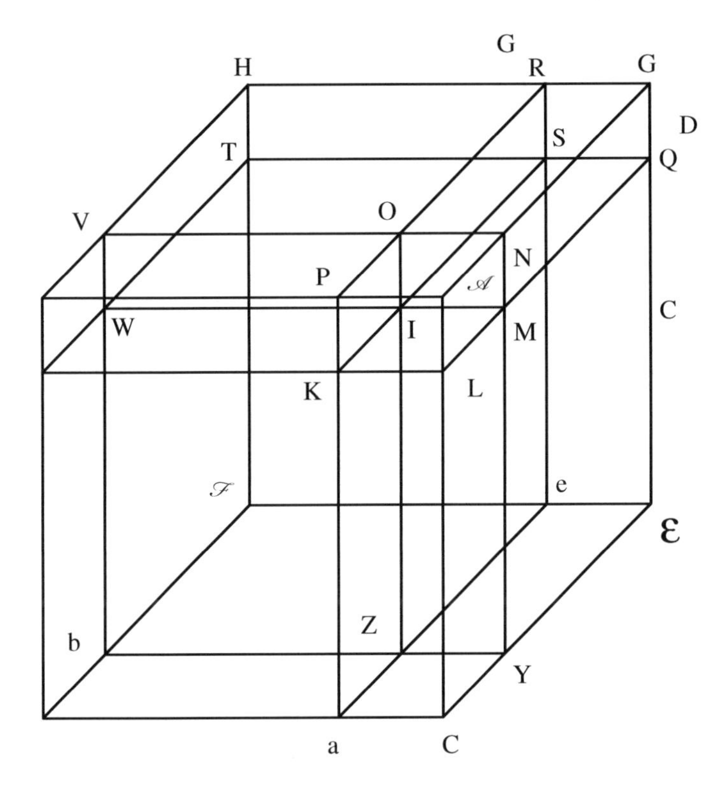

Figure 4.2 Halley's method for calculating a joint annuity on three lives

De Moivre provided numerous approximations relevant for joint life annuities using different theoretical assumptions about the life table. Some of de Moivre's approximations were more successful than others, and Simpson expended considerable effort showing that direct calculation making use of actual life tables was substantially better for pricing the joint life annuity (Hald 1990, p. 532). Starting with de Moivre and continuing with Simpson, a direct approach to the price of a joint life annuity, $E[A_{mn}]$, for two lives was employed. This approach involved the price of two single life annuities $E[A_n]$ and $E[A_m]$ and an annuity for joint life continuance which makes payments only when both nominees are alive $E[{}_mA_n]$. Given that the pricing problem for single life annuities was solved, the joint life annuity problem involved solving for $E[{}_mA_n]$.

The de Moivre approach to solving a joint life annuity written on two lives involved the relationship:

$$E[A_{mn}] = E[A_n] + E[A_m] - E[{}_m A_n]$$

This result follows from observing that the probability of having survival of at least one of the two lives at time t is $1 - (1 - Prob[x,t])(1 - Prob[y,t]) = Prob[x,t] + Prob[y,t] - Prob[x,t]Prob[y,t]$, where $Prob[x,t]$ is the probability of x (y) surviving at time t which can be related to ℓ_{x+t}/ℓ_x in the $E[A_n]$ formula given previously. Multiplying by $(1 + r)^{-t}$ and summing gives the required result, which holds for any life table. From this point de Moivre used two approaches to solve for approximations to $E[_m A_n]$. The approach initially used in the first edition of *Annuities upon Lives* (1925) takes $Prob[\cdot]$ to be geometrically declining. More precisely, having already provided a simple solution for the single life annuity values, using geometrically declining life probabilities de Moivre is able to show that the value of the joint continuance is

$$E[_m A_n] = \frac{E[A_n] + E[A_m](1+r)}{(E[A_n]+1)(E[A_m]+1) - (E[A_n]E[A_m](1+r))}$$

While this approach leads to a less complicated result for $E[A_{mn}]$, later in the first edition de Moivre provides a more complicated, but presumably more exact, result for $E[A_{mn}]$ using arithmetically declining life probabilities. A numerical example for two lives aged 40 and 50 is provided and, with $r = 5$ per cent, the value of $E[_m A_n]$ for the arithmetically and geometrically declining cases are solved as 14.53 and 14.55 years' purchase, respectively.

Compared to Halley's obscure and incomplete effort, the simplicity of de Moivre's solution for the joint life annuity on two lives is impressive. The extension to three lives follows appropriately:

$$E[A_{mnq}] = E[A_n] + E[A_m] + E[A_q] - E[_m A_n] - E[_q A_n] - E[_m A_q] + E[_{mn} A_q]$$

where $E[A_{mnq}]$ is the value of the joint life annuity on (the longest of) three lives and $E[_{mn} A_q]$ is the value of an annuity paid when all three nominees are alive. Having already provided approximations to solve all but one term, using geometrically declining life probabilities de Moivre gives the result:

$$E[_{mn} A_q] = \frac{(E[A_n] + E[A_m] + E[A_q])(1+r)}{(E[A_m]+1)(E[A_n]+1) - (E[A_q]+1) - (E[_{mnq} A](1+r)^2)}$$

While no results or calculations are given for the three-life joint annuity using arithmetically declining life probabilities, de Moivre does provide the solution methodology for 'finding the Values of as many *joint* Lives as may be assigned'. The simplification provided by assuming that the nominees' lives are equal, and the use of the binomial expansion to solve the coefficients in this case, is also recognized.

A detailed examination of de Moivre's contributions to joint life annuity valuation would be incomplete without considering *The Doctrine of Annuities and Reversions* (1742, 2nd edn 1775) by Thomas Simpson. As evidenced in preface of the 1743 edition of *Annuities on Lives*, the contents of *The Doctrine* (1742) incensed de Moivre. Without identifying Simpson by name, de Moivre makes the following observations that were clearly directed at Simpson: 'he mutilates my Propositions, obscures what is clear, makes a Shew of new Rules, and works by mine, in short confounds in his usual way, every thing with a croud of useless Symbols'. This attack by de Moivre compelled Simpson to include in future printings of *The Doctrine* an additional 'Appendix containing some remarks on Mr. Demoivre's book … with answers to some personal and malignant misrepresentations, in the preface thereof'. In this appendix, Simpson claims:

> It is not my design to expatiate on the unseemliness of this gentleman's usage, not to gratify a passion, which insinuations so gross must naturally excite in a mind that looks with contempt on such unfair

proceedings; but only to offer a few particulars to the consideration of the public, with no other view than to clear myself from a charge so highly injurious, and do justice to the foregoing work.

In the appendix, Simpson makes a strong case for the credibility of his contributions that is difficult to deny. In addition, it is likely that the results and comments in *The Doctrine* led de Moivre to make some substantive changes to the 1743 edition, and later versions, of *Annuities on Lives*.

At the time *The Doctrine* (1742) appeared, Thomas Simpson was still in the early stages of an academic career that was to produce a number of seminal advances, primarily in mathematics, earning the eponym Simpson's Rule for a method of approximating an integral using a sequence of quadratic polynomials.[8] His appointment as the head of mathematics at the Royal Military Academy at Woolwich – a position that provided Simpson with sufficient security to pursue academic interests – was not to occur until 1743. Being the son of a weaver with little formal education, Simpson had for some years made a living as an itinerant lecturer teaching in the London coffee houses. Around this time, certain coffee houses functioned as 'penny universities' that provided cheap education, charging an entrance fee of one penny to customers who drank coffee and listened to lectures on topics specific to that coffee house; see for example, Poitras (2000, pp. 293–7). Popular topics were art, business, law and mathematics. It is well known that de Moivre was a fixture at Slaughter's Coffee House in St Martin's Lane during this period.

In support of his activities at the penny universities and continuing at Woolwich, Simpson started producing a successful string of textbooks beginning with a text on the theory of fluxions (*A New Treatise of Fluxions*) in 1737. His next book, *The Nature and Laws of Chance* (1740), bears a strong similarity to de Moivre's *Doctrine of Chances* (1718, 2nd edn 1738). In both *The Nature and Laws of Chance* and *The Doctrine*, Simpson makes a grateful reference to de Moivre in the preface but no references in the body of the text despite obvious similarities in the content. De Moivre's incensed reaction to *The Doctrine* can be viewed as a response to Simpson's continuing plagiarism, though this is not the only possible interpretation. A precise explanation requires information that is unavailable. The seemingly damning evidence that Simpson was also accused of plagiarism by a number of others can, initially, be attributed to a desire to build a reputation required to sustain his livelihood and, over time, to a lack of sympathy for formal academic procedure. Even after his appointment at Woolwich and election to the Royal Society (in 1745), Simpson continued to be accused of plagiarism, though not by persons of the academic stature of de Moivre.[9]

Given that much of the seminal work on joint (and single) life annuities had been accomplished by de Moivre, assessment of Simpson's contributions has a significant subjective element. Hald (1990, p. 511) identifies three important new contributions: '(1) a life table based on the London bills of mortality; (2) tables of values of single- and joint-life annuities for nominees of the same age based on this life table; and (3) rules for calculating joint life-annuities for different ages from the tabulated joint-life annuities'. This assessment would appear to be based largely on the content of *The Doctrine* and ignores the practical content of *A Supplement to the Doctrine of Annuities and Reversions* (1752, 2nd edn 1971) which appears as Part VI of *Select Exercises for young Proficients in the Mathematicks*. Judging from Richard Price's references to Simpson, de Moivre and Halley in the seminal *Observations on Reversionary Payments* (1772) – one of the outstanding intellectual achievements of the eighteenth century – it was the practical content of Simpson's numerous worked problems and examples that had the most relative impact. While recognizing the importance of de Moivre's approximations, Price dedicates Essay II of *Observations* to the unacceptable errors that assuming geometrically declining life probabilities has on the calculated values for joint life annuities on two and three lives.

Even casual reading of *The Doctrine* reveals the close connection to *Annuities on Lives*. The presentations are similar and various results are, more or less, the same. This said, Simpson does not mimic de Moivre's analytical approximation agenda. The results are adapted to practical ends. To see the implications of this, consider the solution for the joint life annuity on two unequal lives given in terms of two equal lives provided by Simpson:

$$E[A_{mn}] = E[A_{nn}] + \frac{\frac{1}{2} E[A_{nn}](E[A_{mn}] + E[A_{nn}])}{E[A_{mm}]} \quad \text{where } m < n$$

This solution, which does not appear in *Annuities on Lives* (1725), reduces the unmanageable practical problem of preparing tables for the value of joint annuities on two unequal lives to be solved using a manageable table for joint annuity values on two equal lives, a table that Simpson provides. On balance, Simpson's contributions to life annuity valuation are sufficient to warrant closing this discussion of the pioneering contributions to life annuity valuation with his work. Building on the initial efforts of James Dodson, Richard Price was about to pioneer a new route for the subject of life contingency valuation by refocusing intellectual efforts on the core subjects of actuarial science: insurance and pensions. But the story of these pioneers will have to wait for another time.

Notes

1. This section and section 2 are based on Poitras (2000, ch. 6) and Poitras (2005, sec. 2.1).
2. A usufruct is the right of temporary possession, use or enjoyment of the advantages of property belonging to another, so far as may be had without causing damage or prejudice to the property.
3. Reversions and other types of life contingent claims such as copyholds and advowsons could arise in situations other than a formal life annuity contract. For example, reversions could arise in marriage settlements and wills and be of interest for legal reasons of establishing an estate value.
4. It was common at this time for a number of spelling variants to be used, all of which can be considered correct. The spelling Jan de Witt is found in Hald (1990), Coolidge (1990) and Pearson (1978). Hald also gives the variant Johan de Witt while Pearson reports John de Witt. Heywood (1985) uses Johannes de Wit while Hendricks (1852–53) uses John de Wit. In the *Valuation*, the author is listed as 'J. de Wit'.
5. Karl Pearson, who had strong views on a number of individuals involved in the history of statistics, depreciates de Witt's work by claiming: 'the data are uncertain and the method of computation is fallacious' (Pearson 1978, p. 100). This is at variance with Hald (1990), Alter and Riley (1986) and others. Pearson (1978, p. 702) also appears to have been unaware of Hudde's contribution, 'I was unaware that (Hudde) had contributed to the theory of probability.'
6. Not long after he had submitted his *Value of Life Annuities* to the States General, de Witt's life came to a tragic end. The invasion of the Dutch Republic by France in 1672 led to a public panic which precipitated de Witt's forced resignation and his replacement by the Stadholder William III. However, the demand for public retribution for the grand pensionary's perceived failings did not end with his resignation. Later in 1672, de Witt was set upon by a mob and shot, publicly hanged and his body then violated.
7. Hald (1990, p. 140) provides a helpful exposition of the geometric argument for two lives but does not recognize this point.
8. It is likely that Simpson's Rule was not originated by Simpson but, rather, by Newton, a point that was acknowledged by Simpson. However, Ypma (1995) demonstrates that the Newton–Raphson technique for solving non-linear equations is most appropriately credited to Simpson.
9. Sources on Simpson's life are limited, the most detailed being Clarke (1929). Pearson (1978, p. 166) has a discussion of other sources sympathetic to Simpson that rely on Hutton's 1792 introduction to the second edition of Simpson's *Select Exercises*. In his typical flourishing style Karl Pearson observes: 'to me he is a distinctly unpleas-

ant and truculent writer of cheap textbooks, not a great mathematician like de Moivre'. Pearson (1978, pp. 176–85) takes great pains to document this view.

References

Alter, G. and J. Riley (1986), 'How to Bet on Lives: A Guide to Life Contingency Contracts in Early Modern Europe', in P. Uselding (ed.), *Research in Economic History*, **10**: 1–53.

Bernoulli, N. (1709), *De Usu Artis Conjectandi in Jure* (translation by R. Pulskamp) from cerebro.xu.edu/math/Sources/NBernoulli/deusu.html.

Clarke, F. (1929), *Thomas Simpson and His Times*, New York: Columbia University Press.

Coolidge, J.L. (1990), *The Mathematics of Great Amateurs* (2nd edn), Oxford: Clarendon Press.

Daston (1988), *Classical Probability in the Enlightenment*, Princeton, NJ: Princeton University Press.

de Moivre, A. (1725), *Annuities upon Lives; or, The Valuation of Annuities upon any Number of Lives; and also, of Reversions. To which is added, An Appendix concerning the Expectations of Life, and Probabilities of Survivorship*, London: Fayram, Motte and Pearson; with a 2nd edn appearing in 1743, printed by London: Woodfall; 3rd edn 1750; and 4th edn 1752.

——— (1756a), *The Doctrine of Chances* (3rd edn), London: A. Millar; reprinted by New York: Chelsea Pub. Co. (1967).

——— (1756b), *A Treatise of Annuities on Lives* (2nd edn), London: A. Millar; included as an Appendix to *The Doctrine of Chances*, reprinted by New York: Chelsea Pub. Co. (1967).

de Roover, R. (1969), 'Gerald Malynes as an Economic Writer', *History of Political Economy* (Fall): 336–58.

de Witt, J. (1671), *Value of Life Annuities in Proportion to Redeemable Annuities*, originally published in Dutch with the English translation in Hendricks (1852–3), pp. 232–49.

Greenwood, M. (1940), 'A Statistical Mare's Nest', *Journal of the Royal Historical Society*, **103**: 246–8.

Hald, A. (1990), *A History of Probability and Statistics and Their Applications before 1750*, New York: Wiley.

Halley, E. (1693), 'An Estimate of the Degrees of Mortality of Mankind, drawn from the curious Tables of the Births and Funerals at the city of Breslaw; with an Attempt to ascertain the Price of Annuities upon Lives', originally published in *Philosophical Transactions*: 596–610 and 654–6; reprinted in Heywood (1985).

Hamilton, E. (1947), 'Origin and Growth of the National Debt in Western Europe', *American Economic Review* (May): 118–30.

Hawawini, G. and A. Vora (eds) (1980), *On the History of Interest Approximations*, New York: Arno Press.

Hendricks, F. (1852–53), 'Contributions of the History of Insurance and the Theory of Life Contingencies', *The Assurance Magazine*, **2** (1852): 121–50, 222–58; **3** (1853), 93–120.

Heywood, G. (1985), 'Edmond Halley: Astronomer and Actuary', *Journal of the Institute of Actuaries*, **112**: 279–301.

Houtzager, D. (1950), *Life Annuities and Sinking Funds in the Netherlands before 1672*, Schiedam: Hav-Bank.

Noonan, J. (1957), *The Scholastic Analysis of Usury*, Cambridge, MA: Harvard University Press

Pearson, E.S. (ed.) (1978), *The History of Statistics in the 17th and 18th Centuries, Lectures by Karl Pearson*, London: Charles Griffen.

Poitras, G. (2000), *The Early History of Financial Economics 1478–1776*, Cheltenham, UK and Northampton, MA, USA: Edward Elgar.

Poitras, G. (2005), *Security Analysis and Investment Strategy*, Oxford: Blackwell Publishing.

Ronan, C. (1978), 'Edmond Halley', in C. Gillespie (ed.), *Dictionary of Scientific Biography*, vol. 6, New York: Scribner, pp. 67–72.

Rubinstein, M. (2005), 'Great Moments in Financial Economics, IV: The Fundamental Theorem Parts I and II', *Journal of Investment Mangement* (forthcoming).

Simpson, T. (1742), *The Doctrine of Annuities and Reversions, Deduced from General and Evident Principles with Useful Tables, shewing the Values of Single and Joint Lives, etc. at different Rates of Interest*, London: Nourse (2nd edn 1775).

Sylla, E. (2006), 'Commercial arithmetic, theology and the intellectual foundations of Jacob Bernoulli's *Art of Conjecturing*', Chapter 1 in this volume.

Tracy, J. (1985), *A Financial Revolution in the Hapsburg Netherlands*, Los Angeles: University of California Press.

Weir, D. (1989), 'Tontines, Public Finance and Revolution in France and England, 1688–1789', *Journal of Economic History*, **49** (March): 95–124.

Ypma, T. (1995), 'Historical Development of the Newton–Raphson Method', *SIAM Review*, **37**: 531–51.

5 John Law: financial innovator

Antoin E. Murphy

When John Law converted to Catholicism, a necessary change for him to become the effective Prime Minister of France (Contrôleur Général des Finances) in January 1720, one wag commented that he would have no difficulty with the doctrine of transubstantiation as he had already achieved a similar feat in transubstantiating the French monetary system from specie to paper money. John Law, the counter alchemist, was a man of change, of metamorphosis, of transformation. He changed his profile from that of a rake to a serious monetary projector, he converted from Protestantism to Catholicism, and he altered his nationality to become a Frenchman.

Central to Law's desire for change was his belief that the financial architecture of his time needed to be dramatically restructured. This restructuring involved a financial revolution. The very foundations of the French financial system were embedded in metallic money, foundations which he believed blocked the development of the economy. From an early stage – he had started writing on economic issues by 1704 – he identified the possibility of substituting paper money and bank credit for metallic money. By 1720 he had achieved this dream in that France had become specie-less. This was a dramatic financial revolution causing Nicolas Du Tot, the under-treasurer of the Royal Bank, to later remark that posterity would scarcely believe that this had happened. Changing one's religion and one's nationality was not atypical of eighteenth-century life. The 'Glorious Revolution' in England and the Revocation of the Edict of Nantes in France by Louis XIV were major factors in causing the interchange of religions and nationalities. However, the transformation of the financial architecture of a major economy away from gold and silver to paper money was a change of a very different order of magnitude. The achievement of this, albeit for a brief period in 1719–20, presaged the future global monetary system that would not be reached until the USA broke the last formal links with the gold standard in 1971. This chapter asks how someone with such a chequered background as that of John Law could have produced this financial revolution in Europe's most powerful economic nation, France. How could a Scotsman with the reputation of a rake and a gambler who had been convicted for murdering a man in a duel come to such prominence and have his ideas accepted in France?

Financial revolutions are a product of ideas and circumstances. The ideas emerge during periods when the existing orthodoxy is under pressure because of historical circumstances that cause people to have doubts about the efficiency and/or relevance of the current system. At these two levels of ideas and circumstances it may be seen how Law was able to initiate his programme for change in France. To do so he needed to challenge the existing theoretical orthodoxy through his economic writings. But he also needed to find the historical circumstances propitious to the acceptance of these ideas. In this chapter it will be argued that circumstances in the form of Law's Scottish banking background were an important catalyst for sparking his interest in monetary theory. It will then be shown how he was able to produce a range of cogently argued ideas in 1704 and 1705 through *John Law's Essay on a Land Bank* (1994) and *Money and Trade* (1705). In these works he contended that it was not necessary to base the monetary system on an intrinsically valuable metallic money and that a bank-based system could be used to increase economic activity. These ideas constituted the template for his views on monetary policy. But then, after his ideas were rejected by the English authorities and the Scottish Parliament, it seemed that he was just a prophet speaking in an arid desert. No one appeared to want his ideas to be implemented as policy. It took another ten years for circumstances to intervene, and, when they did, Law was ready. It will be argued that the circumstances took the form of Louis XIV's legacy of a bankrupted French economy. The need to restructure the financial system and to punish the perceived profiteers provided Law with the opportunity to present his ideas. The monetary and financial crises that the French Crown faced led to Law implementing his system. The Chamber of Justice, introduced to punish the profiteers, led to the silencing of Law's potential critics for a critical two-year period, allowing him to the put the system in place. In the final section the inherent tensions created by the system are analysed.

Scottish circumstances

Law's Scottish milieu was a catalyst in encouraging this change of mentality that imbued his career. Born in Edinburgh, in 1671, he was the son of an Edinburgh goldsmith. Whilst first appearances could have created the impression that the goldsmiths were the custodians of gold and silver, a more detailed analysis of their operations shows that they were actually moving away from such a role to becoming embryonic bankers by lending out part of the money deposited with them to borrowers. Furthermore, banking ideas were very much in the air in Scotland. A Scottish projector, William Paterson, had been instrumental in establishing the Bank of England in 1694. A year later Scotland's first joint-stock bank, the Bank of Scotland, was established. This was followed by the establishment of two further joint-stock banks, the Royal Bank of Scotland in 1727 and the British Linen Company in 1746. Thus, by the middle of the eighteenth century Scotland had produced three publicly quoted joint-stock banks as against one, the Bank of England, south of the border.

As the son of a Scottish goldsmith, Law was able to activate his incipient banking gene once he had sown his 'wild oats' in London in the 1690s and escaped from jail while awaiting the death sentence for having killed Edmund Wilson in a duel in Bloomsbury Square. London at this time was a centre of change, at both the political and financial levels. The change in monarchical dynasties that had led to the replacement of the Catholic James II by the Protestant William of Orange also produced a far stronger Parliamentary system built on the Lockean principles of government by consent of the people. New ideas were in the air. Banking and financial ideas were imported from the King's old country, Holland. The 'Glorious Revolution' saw the quick introduction of the Bank of England – a far more daring innovation than the Bank of Amsterdam. There was a spurt of small company flotations and contemporary pamphlets abounded in new ideas on how to change the financial system. Chief among the latter was the idea to launch land banks. The inspiration for this had earlier been developed in the 1650s by William Potter. In the 1690s the establishment of the Bank of England prompted a wide range of projectors to propose that land banks, with land constituting the collateral for the banknotes they issued, would be far more suitable financial institutions than the Bank of England – see Horsefield (1960). So from this perspective Law was not offering an original proposal when he successively suggested to the English (1704), Scottish (1705) and French (1706) governments his recommendations to establish a land-based bank. The revolutionary element in his proposals was his method of formulating the economic theory behind his proposals. Law rose like a new fish in the pool of land bank projectors using a language and terminology that was so modern that it distanced him from his competitors.

Law's economic theories

In the 'Essay on a Land Bank', published recently as *John Law's Essay on a Land Bank* (Law 1994), that he sent to Lord Godolphin in 1704, Law first introduced the term 'demand' into the economics lexicon.[1] More importantly, he was able to show how the interaction of supply (quantity) and demand influence price. Then, building on the concept of demand, he coined the term the demand for money. This enabled him to discuss the determination of the overall price level in a supply and demand for money framework. Law showed how, if the money supply was increased out of line with the demand for money, prices would rise. His analysis of inflation in this supply and demand for money framework may be regarded as very modern some 250 years before Friedman (1956) reinterpreted the quantity theory of money in such a way.

There were many other major monetary features in this work, particularly Law's definition of money. He defined money as follows: 'Money is used as the measure by which goods are valued, as the value by which goods are exchanged and in which contracts are made payable' (1994: 55). Law's insistence that money was the value by which goods were exchanged represented a massive break with the existing orthodoxy that defined money as the value for which goods were exchanged. Law's replacement of the preposition 'for' with 'by' showed that he believed that money did not need to be intrinsically valuable. By decoupling money from intrinsic value he produced an alternative conceptualization to the metallist view of money. This decoupling involved a significant liberation in that instead of waiting for the supply of money to be changed by the vagaries of metallic discoveries, it was possible to have a flexible money supply through the development of the banking system. If money was in short supply, the policy maker could arrange for the issue of more banknotes/bank credit to meet the shortage. Here Law believed that it was vital for the policy maker to have this type of power because he believed that money drove economic activity. If there was unemployment and underutilization of resources, money could and should be used to expand economic activity.

While Law emphasized the inflation problem in the *Essay* and discussed it in *Money and Trade*, the main focus of the latter work was the link between money and output. The title of the work *Money and Trade* showed Law's concern for their interrelationship. Trade may be interpreted as a synonym for output. Law wished to show that there was a direct relationship between money and trade (output), with the causality running from money to trade. Scotland, and later France, he believed, were suffering from significant unemployment and underutilization of resources. He identified the cause for this arising from a shortage of money in both economies. To show the beneficial effects of increasing the supply of money, Law elaborated the basic elements of the circular flow of income, a theory which his rival Richard Cantillon would later develop in the *Essai sur la nature du commerce en général* (1755), and, which would be put, still later, into diagrammatic format by François Quesnay in the *Tableau Economique*.

Law's conceptualization of the macroeconomic system in a circular flow of income process was activated by his concern to show the primary role of monetary forces in the system. He regarded money as an essential ingredient in both exchange and production. He maintained that economies were excessively reliant on the vagaries of the metallic monetary system and he wished to remove this reliance on metallic money and replace it with a credit-creating paper money system. Furthermore, his concept of money did not stop with banknotes. From his earliest writings Law had put forward the view that there were other financial instruments, besides banknotes, that could be used as money. He had seen dealings in the coffee houses of Exchange

Alley where the shares of the East India Company and the Bank of England had been used as money. Though these shares did not have a constant value through time, they had a known value at the time of the transaction and could therefore be used as media of exchange to pay for commodities and assets:

> Money to be qualified for exchanging goods and for payments need not be certain in its value. If it have the other qualities it will be received in payments and goods will be exchanged by it ... If money was proposed, that, because of the uncertainty of its value, was not qualified to be the measure by which goods are valued, nor to be the value in which contracts are taken payable, yet, it might be qualified to exchange goods by and to make payments in which are the great uses of money. (1994: 63)

Law was interested in the media of exchange qualities of financial instruments and as early as 1704 was prepared to categorize the shares of the Bank of England and the East India Company as media of exchange money. The inclusion of shares is important. This visualization of a broad range of financial instruments that could be used as media of exchange ranging from gold and silver to banknotes, to bills of exchange, to shares of the Bank and the large trading companies later led him to consider the shares of the Mississippi Company as a type of money and furthermore, as will be shown below, to monetize these shares at a guaranteed price of 9000 livres per share in the spring of 1720.

Law's financial policies

Law understood that it was necessary not only to develop a monetary theory, but also to outline the financial architecture in which such theory could be activated. He would draft part of this financial architecture from institutions that were already in place. Though many aspects of Law's monetary theory were highly original, the financial template that he drafted, when given the opportunity in France, relied, in its initial stages, on the British models of the Bank of England and the trading companies – the East India Company, the Royal African Company and the South Sea Company. Law was not back to reinventing the wheel. The Bank of England had shown how it was possible to create a mutuality of interests between the government and the financial community. In return for the government providing banking privileges to the Bank, the latter institution agreed to lend money to the government at advantageous interest rates. In this way the Bank obtained its monopoly banking privilege and, in return for this favour, assisted the government with the management of the debt. Furthermore, given its monopoly banking powers, the Bank had sizeable opportunities to grow its business and to expand credit. As its business grew, so also would its share price.

The British trading companies were constituted along similar lines. They acquired monopoly trading concessions in return for loans to the government. The successful exploitation of the trading concessions pushed up their share prices and improved the marketability of their shares. Because of this marketability, Law, as shown above, regarded their shares as another type of money; see *John Law's Essay on a Land Bank* (1994).

So, before Law implemented his system in France, many of the financial elements that he would use were already in operation in Great Britain. The Bank of England was a credit-creating financial institution capable of expanding the money supply and assisting the government in its debt management operations. The trading companies had been able to acquire monopoly trading privileges in return for lending money to the government. The shares of the Bank and the trading companies were highly marketable in the coffee houses of Exchange Alley such as Jonathan's and Garraway's, the prototype of the emerging London stock exchange.

Having failed to interest either the British government in 1704, or the Scottish Parliament in 1705, Law was forced to turn his attention to France. The Act of Union between England and Scotland meant that he could no longer hide from British justice in Scotland and he was forced to move to the continent. Over the next decade Law spent his time profitably, making a fortune at the gaming tables of Europe through his sophisticated use of probability theory when gambling. Furthermore, he wrote numerous papers on monetary issues which he sent to Victor Amadeus, duke of Savoy, and Louis XIV and his ministers. For ten years there was no positive response from these monarchs but then, on the death of Louis XIV in August 1715, opportunity struck for Law.

French circumstances and the Chamber of Justice

Financial revolutions require more than economic theories. They require circumstances that provide a receptive audience for them. France in 1715–16 was such a country. Louis XIV's death in 1715 produced an interregnum allowing Philippe, duc d'Orléans, to come to power during the minority of the future Louis XV. Law, who had earlier returned to France in 1714 with a considerable sum of money that he had won at various European gaming tables, had already made contact with Orléans and impressed him with his ability to win consistently at gambling games such as faro. Law was a man of money, someone who used his mathematical skills in gambling to increase his fortune. But he was also someone who had ideas on how to produce a transformation of the French financial system. Notwithstanding Orléans's friendship there was a problem in that the financial system was controlled by the financiers. This grouping privately farmed out the tax system and lent money to the Crown. The surplus profits that they made from tax farming enabled then to be significant lenders at high interest rates to the Crown. The excessive expenditure of the bellicose Louis XIV during his long reign had imposed excessive demands on the French exchequer. The reduced revenue returns generated through tax farming and the high interest rates paid on state loans produced a climate hostile to the financiers. Widely regarded as 'bloodsuckers' (*les sangsues*), the financiers periodically faced hostile public reaction, particularly during changes of regime. All could be blamed on the financiers. Hostility was adroitly directed against them and in this climate the establishment of a Chamber of Justice (*chambre de justice*) was a natural outcome. The Chamber of Justice, established in March 1716, was a tribunal of 30 magistrates to examine the fortunes made by the financiers and to sentence them if they were found to be guilty of misappropriation of public funds. An Almanach[2] for 1717 provided a colourful depiction of the activities of the Chamber of Justice with the magistrates attired in black in the background facing richly dressed financiers who are described as 'public thiefs' (*voleurs publics*). In the foreground there is a wine press squeezing money from the financiers. In the corner foreground there is an account of some of the punishments of the Chamber. On 28 May 1716, Antoine Dubout, the director of the army's meat provisioning, was banished and fined 50 000 livres for selling bad meat to the troops. Jacques le Normand, 'directeur de plusieurs traitez et affaires pour le Roy tresorier payeur des gages et augmentation de gages des Corps et Communautez' was sentenced to the galleys and fined 100 000 livres. On 12 August 1716, a Madame de la Forge, described as 'the princess of dealing in Royal notes', was banished and subjected to a fine of 100 000 livres for usurious trade. On 14 October J. Penot, a tax administrator in the town of Guerre, was sentenced to death and had all his property confiscated. The death sentence was commuted and, unlike some of the earlier Chambers of Justice, no one was executed.

The Chamber presented the image of fire and fury directed at the financiers, but, in reality, it was a type of window-dressing to appease the public in creating the impression that it constituted a bloodletting (*une saignée*) of the bloodsucking financiers. Most of the major financiers were able to escape the apparent public wrath of the Chamber and negotiate behind closed doors for the payment of lower fines than those levied on them. Of the 220 million livres in fines levied by the Chamber, the duc de Noailles, the President of the Council of Finance, estimated in April 1717 that only 50 million livres had been collected.

Writing on the economic situation that he witnessed in France in 1715–16, Law maintained that France faced two crises. The first, the monetary crisis, was due to the acute shortage of money. The second, the financial crisis, was due to the excessive burden of the Crown's indebtedness. Both needed to be addressed, and, when given the opportunity, Law attempted to produce solutions for them. Initially, between 1716 and 1718, he did so by copying the Bank of England and the British trading company models. Then, in 1719–20 his system gained its own momentum and started to differ markedly from the British models. Law, as will be shown, centralized all the French trading companies, the tax system, the mint, the tobacco farm etc. under one giant conglomerate, the Mississippi Company. He then merged this company with the Royal Bank. The success of Law's operations forced the British to start copying his system, a process that gave rise to the South Sea Bubble of 1720. However, in order to do this he needed to have historical circumstances on his side. Fortunately for him, these circumstances presented themselves in the form of the Chamber of Justice.

The Chamber of Justice produced two highly favourable outcomes for John Law. First, the activities of the Chamber forced the financiers to keep their heads down and adopt a low public profile. This meant that they could not be vocal in their opposition to Law when he started to introduce elements of his system. Their enforced silence provided Law with a golden opportunity to present his ideas aimed at addressing both the monetary crisis and the financial crisis without meeting any real opposition from them. The adoption of Law's ideas instigated the dismantling of the established financial system and the removal of the financiers from their central role in it. The activities of the Chamber of Justice in suppressing the financiers between 1716 and 1719 thereby gave Law both the opportunity and the time to implement his plans without their vocal opposition.

The second beneficial outcome of the Chamber of Justice for John Law was that it forced the financier, Antoine Crozat, to abandon his plans for the development of French Louisiana. The fine of 6.6 million livres levied on him by the Chamber obliged him to give up his trading rights over the French colony of Louisiana as part payment of the fine. Crozat's ceding of these trading rights presented Law with the ideal opportunity to launch the second part of his plan aimed at addressing the second crisis, the financial crisis. In August 1717, Law was given permission to launch the Company of the West (Compagnie d'Occident). It had two major objectives. The first was the development of the trading concession of French Louisiana, a land mass stretching from Canada to the Gulf of Mexico, bounded by the British in the Carolinas and by the Spanish in Texas. French Louisiana, as distinct from the eponymous present-day state, covered almost half the land mass of the USA (excluding Alaska). The trading concession to such a vast territory constituted massive potential collateral for the Company. The second objective was the use of the Company to reduce the burden of the Crown's debt. This was met by the stipulation that the first issue of shares in the Company could only be acquired through the transfer of short-term government debt instruments, the *billets d'état*, to the Company. The Company, in return for the Louisiana trading concession, agreed to accept a lower interest payment from the government on the *billets d'état*. This had two advantages for the government: reducing the interest cost on the short-term debt and taking the overhang of this short-term debt out of the financial market. A contemporary French administrator wrote at the time:

> The Company that it is proposed to form, under the name of the Company of the West, has like the English South Sea Company two objects – that of trade and that of retiring a considerable quantity of billets d'état and replacing them with shares, the credit of which it is hoped will be better sustained than those of the billets d'état.[3]

So at this stage Law was closely following the British models. His General Bank was in very many respects modelled on the Bank of England and the new Company of the West had many parallels with trading companies such as the South Sea Company.

However, Law would soon distance his Company from its British counterpart through his expansionist policies for the Company. Initially, these possibilities did not appear to be all that great. In 1717, on its establishment, the Company was permitted to issue 2 000 000 shares with a nominal issue price of 500 livres per share. However, as the *billets d'état* were standing at a very significant discount of 68 to 72 per cent, the real cost of acquiring shares worked out between 140 and 160 livres per share for the initial subscribers.

For nearly two years the progress of the Company was very moderate. This was due to an initial lack of public enthusiasm for the shares and may also have been because Law was busy expanding the business of the General Bank which he de-listed and converted into the Royal Bank in December 1718. Furthermore, by an *arrêt* of July 8, 1719, it was stipulated that the Royal Bank's banknotes would no longer be guaranteed in terms of 'écus de banque', which had been the case for those notes issued by the former General Bank. By this measure all the banknotes issued by the General Bank were withdrawn from circulation and presumably converted into banknotes of the Royal Bank which had no metallic content guarantee to their value. This decoupling of the link between the banknotes and a stipulated value of silver meant that there was no guaranteed conversion rate for banknotes into silver, a development consistent with Law's idea that money should not be intrinsically valuable. This move also gave the Bank *carte blanche* to issue banknotes as it wished. Additional to these monetary developments the banknotes were made legal tender and tax payments had to be made using them.

By May 1719 Law needed to generate some momentum in the Company of the West, whose shares were still at a discount, that is, below their nominal issue price of 500 livres per share. The first action he took was to merge two trading companies, the Company of the East Indies and the China Company, with the Company of the West. The newly merged group was named the Company of the Indies (Compagnie des Indes). Another trading company, the Company of Africa, was taken over on 4 June 1719. These operations required financing, for both the Company of the East Indies and the China Company were heavily in debt. Additionally, fresh funds were required to re-equip existing ships and build up a new fleet to exploit the colonial trade which, as a result of the merger, was now almost completely under the control of the Company of the Indies.

To finance such ventures the Company proposed on 15 May a second issue of shares, known as the *filles* (daughters) consisting of 50 000 shares at 550 livres per share, the nominal value of the share remaining at 500 livres. The shares were kept so to speak in the family in that the shares were issued as a rights issue stipulating that purchasers needed to be holders of four *mères* in order to acquire one *fille*. This measure reinforced the value of the *mères* and ensured that the shares remained within the group of the first subscribers, which included the Regent and his circle. To encourage their uptake soft payment terms were offered. Subscribers paid 50 livres in a down payment and then faced 20 monthly payments of 25 livres. Unlike the first issue, which had been totally subscribed in *billets d'état*, all payments were to be made in cash. On making the first payment subscribers were given a certificate authenticating their purchase of the share. As each future payment was made the certificate would be stamped to this effect. Cochrane (2001) has suggested that because of this payment procedure the certificates effectively acted as options, with transactors having the option to discard purchasing the share by not making future payments.

Two months later, on 26 July, Law tapped the market again, issuing 50 000 shares at a price of 1000 livres per share payable in 20 monthly instalments of 50 livres. These shares were known as the *petites filles* (grand-daughters). Again this was a rights issue aimed at keeping the shares closely held among the first subscribers because each purchaser had to have four *mères* and one *fille* in order to purchase a *petite fille*. Again they could also have been regarded as options in that subscribers could decide to abandon purchasing the shares at any stage during the prescribed payment schedule.

By August 1719 Law had made four share issues. The first involved the General Bank, whose shares had been bought back from the original shareholders before its transformation into the Royal Bank in December 1718. The other three share issues involved the Company of the West, later called the Company of the Indies, which will now be referred to as the Mississippi Company. In all the Company had issued 200 000 *mères*, 50 000 *filles* and 50 000 *petites filles*, a grand total of 300 000 shares. These share issues had been used to acquire 100 million livres of *billets d'état*, to purchase capital assets for the trading companies, and to acquire the rights to the Mint. Thus Law could contend that he had mopped up a large part of the floating debt and in the process pushed the remaining *billets d'état* back to par, that he had injected much-needed funds into the trading companies, and that he had added an important revenue-earning source, the Mint, to the Company. At the same time the Royal Bank had expanded the money supply, a process which had produced further reductions in the interest rate.

While some extolled the great progress that Law had made, the problem of debt management was still dominating his thought:

> the deepest wounds of the State were still not cured and it was necessary to apply even stronger remedies. What had been seen up to this point was more a preparation for the cure rather than a radical cure …[4]

What did this radical cure involve? I believe that the author of the above was referring to Law's attempt, starting in August, to tackle the problem of France's national debt. This was to move the system up several gears.

On Saturday, 26 August 1719, Law produced his master plan, which was unveiled by the *arrêt* of August 27. He proposed that the Company would lend 1.2 billion livres at an interest rate of 3 per cent to the King – this sum was later raised to 1.5 billion by an *arrêt* of 12 October 1719. This money would be used to repay the long-term state debts, the annuities (*rentes*), the remaining short-term floating debt (*billets d'état*), the cost of offices (*charges*) that had been or would be suppressed, and the shares of the United Tax Farms that had been taken over by the Company. There were two main elements in Law's proposals. First, the Company was given the right to borrow the 1.2 billion livres by creating *actions rentières* or *contrats de constitution de rentes* (annuities) bearing an interest rate of 3 per cent. Second, the lease of the tax farms which had been granted to a company headed by Aymard Lambert, a straw man for the Pâris brothers, for six years on 29 August 1718, was to be annulled and given to Law's Company for a period of nine years. In this way Law blocked the use of the United Tax Farms as a potential competitor to the Mississippi Company, taking over the joint-stock company that the Pâris brothers had created to manage it.

By these two measures Law proposed 'the radical cure' for the French economy. He had transformed the Company from a trading company to a trading-cum-financial conglomerate, controlling the State's finances, most notably tax collection and debt management. Nicolas Du Tot said of this measure:

> This was a project which was big, elegant, and advantageous to the King and the people: but its principals were diametrically contrary to those of the old financial administration, so that its implementation was bound to encounter opposition ...[5]

Though the *arrêt* of 27 August indicated that *actions rentières* or *contrats de constitution de rentes* would be used for the takeover of the debt and the acquisition of the tax farms, it quickly became clear that Law did not intend resorting to such financial instruments. Law promptly announced that shares, rather than annuities or debentures, would be used to purchase the debt. Edgar Faure (1977) classified the decision to take over the debt with annuities as the 'wise plan' (*le plan sage*) and then criticized Law's apparent change of mind to use shares for the acquisition of the debt as the 'mad plan' (*le plan fou*). Velde (2003) has recently sided with Faure's interpretation on this issue. This, I believe, is to misunderstand Law. According to the 27 August *arrêt*, the financial instruments to be used in taking over the debt were to be *contrats de constitution de rentes* and/or *actions rentières*. *Contrats de constitution de rentes* were the traditional type of annuities and it is difficult to envisage Law using annuities as financial instruments because of his consistent criticisms of them. It is more difficult to define *actions rentières*. They may have been a type of debenture, although I feel that the term may have been loosely drafted and that the underlying meaning was to be *actions* i.e. shares. However, despite the imprecision of the 27 August *arrêt*, Law, in my opinion, would not have resorted to using annuities or debentures. He had been, as shown above, deeply impressed by the way in which the Bank of England and the British trading companies had been able to take over government debt by the issue of shares. He had already shown the possibilities of shares for debt conversion operations through both the General Bank and the *mères* issue by the Company of the West in 1717/18. Why would he suddenly go back on such an approach and just convert long-term government debt into further long-term government debt, albeit at a lower rate of interest? Rightly or wrongly, Law believed in the power of shares as a new financial vehicle for these conversion operations. The first legislative text relevant to these operations was the *arrêt* of 27 August. This text, as has been shown, specifically mentioned 'actions rentières au porteur, ou des contrats de constitution à trois pour cent' (section IV). Four days later the language of section IV of the 27 August *arrêt* was qualified by the *arrêt* of 31 August. This 'Arrest du Conseil d'Estat du Roy qui ordonne le remboursement de toutes les rentes ...' offered debt holders the choice of either shares or annuities ('soit des actions soit des contracts de constitution de rente').[6] This choice of either shares or annuities as the financial instruments clears up some of the earlier ambiguities of the 27 August *arrêt* as it becomes clearer from this latter *arrêt* of 31 August that shares were to be offered to debt holders. The possibility of using annuities was quickly abandoned over the next few weeks. On 13 September 1719 there was a new issue of 100 000 shares which were created at a price of 5000 livres a share. Within two weeks, on 26 September, a further issue of another 100 000 shares at the same price was made. The text of the latter *arrêt* specifically points out that the public wanted to use the proceeds of the repayment of their annuities and offices to purchase shares. Quite clearly shares were now the envisaged financial instruments for the debt conversion and there was no further mention of some new type of annuities being offered as an alternative to shares. A further issue of 100,000 shares at the same price was authorized on 2 October. There was also a smaller issue of just 24 000 shares on 4 October, though this latter issue was never actually sold to the public. Thus within a three-week period the Company issued 324 000 shares, of which 300 000 were sold to the public at 5000 livres a share, amounting in all to 1.5 billion livres when fully paid up. Purchasers of the September/October *soumissions*, the *cinq-cents* as they were called, had only to put up 500 livres to acquire their rights to the shares and then to repay the rest in nine monthly instalments.

Movements in the share price indicated that the time was appropriate to use shares for the debt conversion. Using Du Tot and Giraudeau[7] as sources, a sharp rise in the share price during August may be observed. On 1 August the original shares, the *mères*, which, as has been shown, could have been bought for between 160 and 180 livres in 1717, stood at 2750. By 30 August they had risen to 4100 and by 4 September they were at 5000 livres, with the *filles* and *petites filles* rising *pari-passu*. The debt holders, recognizing the prospect of a capital gain, were quite happy to transfer their debt into shares rather than bonds. Their difficulty in fact became one of converting quickly enough into the shares of the Company as the price rose very sharply during September. To activate further interest in the new issues, Law provided further soft instalment payment terms giving subscribers nine months to complete the payment for the shares. Such instalment payment terms were one of Law's favourite marketing ploys to increase the marketability of the shares to the general populace. Even when the approaching monthly payment dates caused problems for investors, and perhaps more importantly for the price of shares, Law softened the repayment terms by changing them from monthly to quarterly repayments. Small down payments and an ever increasing demand for shares pushed the price of fully paid up shares to over 9000 livres in the autumn of 1719. On 2 December the share price peaked at 10 025 for the year.

These monetary and debt management innovations in France, initially modelled in part on the Bank of England and the East India Company, were perceived to be so successful that the British, belatedly, attempted to copy part of them with the South Sea Company in 1720. Britain followed the debt management approach, but did not produce a new paper money system – the Bank of England was already well established, issuing a partially backed paper money and resisted the attempts of the South Sea Company to take it over. In Britain there was a further development in that the debt management initiative of the South Sea Company spawned a wide range of new issues by fledgling 'bubble' companies, some with serious objectives such as insurance and others the creation of confidence tricksters.

In France there were no bubble companies. The Mississippi Company/Royal Bank reigned supreme. News coming through from France in the first weeks of January 1720 would have greatly encouraged the directors of the South Sea Company, for as the New Year passed the Mississippi-dominated stock market boom gathered further momentum and went to a new high in the second week of January. This second week produced one of the most intense bouts of speculative buying during the system, when there was a huge upsurge in demand to purchase newly created options, called *les primes*. Law, in an effort to destroy the private derivatives markets that had been set up in Mississippi shares, proposed a scheme whereby subscribers, by paying 1000 livres, would have an option to purchase Mississippi shares at a guaranteed price of 10000 livres over the next six months. Some members of the public, believing that the share price would move even higher, sold their old shares to purchase the *primes*. By selling a share for 10000 livres it was possible to acquire ten *primes* worth 10000 livres each when all the future payments would be made on them. In the early days of the issue of these *primes* they sold at a premium and the quantity sold indicates that it was in this second week of January that the Mississippi share price peaked. Ironically, Law's attempt to dampen the future price of the Mississippi shares led to the most intensive bout of speculation in them through these sizeable sales of the *primes*. According to Law, 300 million livres of *primes* were sold to the public, indicating a commitment by transactors to contemplate purchasing another 300000 shares!

The inherent tensions of the system

While the activities of the second week of January appeared to indicate that all was well with the system in that confidence in it had never been so high, it had an artificial element because Law had started to use the Royal Bank to provide banknotes to underpin the share price. As Law, from as far back as 1704 in the 'Essay on a Land Bank', had regarded shares as another type of money, he could have argued that his policy of using the banknote issue to purchase shares was consistent with his wide definition of the money supply. However, his policy of using the banknote issue to push up the share price and later to guarantee the share price at 9000 livres ultimately meant that he created a financial circuit that was out of line with the real economy. His realization of this in the early spring of 1720 led to an attempt to provide a deflation of the financial circuit. However, his efforts to do so in February were overruled and then, when forced to take corrective action in May 1720, it was too late.

Nicolas Du Tot was the under-treasurer of the Royal Bank for most of 1720. *De facto*, because of the laziness of the treasurer Etienne Bourgeois, he was effectively the treasurer for most of the time. His detailed analysis of the system (Du Tot 2000), published recently, provides a fascinating insight into the tensions created by Law's policy of using the Royal Bank's note issue to support the Mississippi Company's share price. Du Tot showed that Law did this from as early as 6 October 1719, when the Company provided money to those shareholders who needed it by purchasing their old shares at 5000 livres each.[8] Du Tot explained that this strategy was implemented to ensure that the share price did not fall and expressed surprise that the Company, at the very time that it was issuing 300000 new shares, was also buying back its own shares. His wry comment on this was 'A merchant who buys and sells at the same price does not gain the public's confidence.'[9]

The share support operation was extended to the provision of soft loans to existing shareholders. Du Tot explained that one of the reasons for the success of the Company in the closing months of 1719 was its policy of lending 2500 livres per share at an interest rate of 2 per cent to shareholders.[10] Soft loans of this nature enabled shareholders to leverage up their holdings of new shares by making down payments of 500 livres. It is quite clear from Du Tot's account that Law was using the Bank – expanding the banknote issue – to provide loans to shareholders who wished to acquire more of the Company's shares.

He noted later that Law attempted to dampen the rise in the price of shares when they pushed towards 10000 livres in November 1719 by selling 30 million livres of shares in one single week.[11] However, this sale of shares did not push the price down.

The share support operation became a more important element of the Company's strategy in 1720. At the AGM of the Company on 30 December 1719, two agencies (*les bureaux d'achat et de vente*) were established, one to purchase shares and the other to sell them. Du Tot expressed considerable reservations about the wisdom of the Company purchasing its own shares, though he admitted that the sale of shares by the Company might be regarded as useful in that it reduced the quantity of banknotes in circulation – 'this was the good aspect of this operation'.[12]

Between 30 December 1719, when the *bureau*x were established, and 22 February 1720, the Company purchased 800 million livres of its shares. Taking an average price for the stock during this period as 9300 livres, Du Tot estimated that this involved the *bureaux d'achat et de vente* purchasing around 85 000 shares.[13] These statistics show that the *bureaux* had been extensively used to purchase the Company's shares in order to maintain the share price at a high level. As a result, the printing presses of the Royal Bank had started to work overtime.

By late February Law's realization that the banknote issue was moving out of control through the share support operation resulted in a decision to close the *bureaux d'achat et de vente*. On 22 February a further general meeting of the Mississippi Company's shareholders gave rise to an *arrêt* the next day, the 'Arrest du Conseil d'Estat du Roy concernant la Banque & la Compagnie des Indes' unifying the Royal Bank and the Company. One of the articles of this *arrêt* stipulated the closure of the *bureaux d'achat et de vente*. Thus, at the very moment that the Royal Bank's operations were formally merged with those of the Company, the previous policy of share price support was abandoned. It was reasoned that it was undesirable for it to go on providing support for the share price and so the *bureaux* were shut down and the shares were left to find their own price in a free market. Consistent with this new policy, article ii decreed that there was to be no further issue of banknotes unless authorized by *arrêts* of the Council rendered as a result of the deliberations of a general meeting of the Company. It appeared that Law had recognized the error in over-expanding the money supply in order to support the Company's shares and that a new policy of retrenchment was required. From then on the Company's shares were no longer to be supported artificially and the money supply no longer expanded. But Law's retrenchment policy had an extremely short life.

Within less than a fortnight the 22 February measures had been repealed by the *arrêt* of 5 March. There were a number of key elements in this *arrêt*. Article ii fixed the price of shares of the Company at 9000 livres per share and article v created a *bureau de conversions* which would, from March 20, convert shares into banknotes and vice versa at the price of 9000 livres. Thus the earlier policy of allowing the price to be determined by market forces was reversed. The *bureau de conversions* was just another name for the *bureaux d'achat et de vente*. More significantly, Law, by providing a guaranteed price of 9000 livres per share, had monetized the shares of the Mississippi Company.

Du Tot expressed considerable surprise at this change in policy, reminding readers of the extent to which it was contrary to earlier decisions that had been taken by Law:

> It was truly astonishing that the System's creator took this approach. More than anyone he should have been aware of the danger of buying shares and that the excessive increase in banknotes generated by such purchases would necessarily weaken its credit and create alarm everywhere. Had he not forgotten that he was in some ways responsible in that he had made them [the banknotes] the state's money and that they were not the same as shares, subscriptions and options whose prices were determined by public opinion? Had he not remembered the specific stipulation that he had inserted in article 2 of the February 22 deliberation and of the arrêt of the 24th [of February] that there would be no fur-

> ther increases in banknotes except by decisions made at the Company's AGM and in article XI of the same deliberation that there would be no more agencies for buying and selling shares, etc?[14]

Du Tot explained that Law could have greatly reduced the banknote issue by obliging share subscribers to pay their outstanding commitments in banknotes. The dilemma Law faced was that banknotes were universally held, whereas shares, even though possessing a greater value (the valuation of shares – excluding the 80000 held by the Bank – was 4.9 billion livres as against 1.1 billion of banknotes in circulation), were only held by a small section of the population.

It is clear from Du Tot's analysis he believed that a decision had been taken to sacrifice the banknote in an attempt to preserve shares. He had decided 'to maintain the shares and sacrifice the banknotes'.[15] Du Tot was clearly against this policy because it implied that the printing presses of the Royal Bank would be used to support the share price at 9000 livres.

There was a further measure in the 5 March *arrêt* which was in Du Tot's opinion fatal to the system. It was article ix which stated that paper money was invariable to domestic exchange rate changes of specie relative to the unit of account. Put another way, paper money would not to be changed, *pari passu* with silver and gold, when there were devaluations or revaluations of these coins. Du Tot described this part of the 5 March *arrêt* as 'the mortal blow' to the system. He maintained that Law had been forced, against his judgement, to acquiesce in this measure. A powerless Law, he maintained, was forced to act like an army general obliged to miss an occasion to rout his enemies because of the secret and confidential orders not to attack.[16]

The 5 March measures created a disproportionate gap between the value of paper money and specie. First of all they created a situation in which the banknote issue would go out of control when the public sold shares for banknotes. Second, article ix of the 5 March *arrêt* declared that 'the banknote was a money which was not subject to any variation'. Combining this with the 11 March arrêt stipulating the progressive reduction in value and eventual demonetization of specie, it effectively meant that value of specie would decline progressively relative to the banknotes. Law's 1723 comments suggest that he was aware of this problem from March onwards. His argument was based on his value theory. As early as 1704 and 1705, in his *Essay on a Land Bank* (1994) and *Money and Trade* (1705), he had argued that value was determined by supply and demand. Du Tot contended that his value theory principles had not changed in 1720:

> His principles are that the value of everything changes according to quantity and demand. Thus he was unable to promise that the banknotes would be invariable, this was to promise an impossibility.[17]

Was this retrospective wisdom, or, did Law effectively lose the first of his battles to dampen down the system in late March 1720? If the latter hypothesis is correct, and it is the story advanced by Law and Du Tot,[18] then the start of the collapse of the system may be dated to early March rather than late May 1720.

According to both Law and Du Tot, the Scotsman wished to dampen down the System in March 1720 by introducing the measures that he later attempted to introduce on 21 May. Du Tot's account stressed that the situation would never have arisen if 'the state had been less indebted than it was at the start of the regency'. Law had been forced to attack not just the monetary crisis but also the financial crisis created by the overhang of the Crown's debt. It was necessary to expand credit 'to open the doors to abundance'.[19]

The situation was developing to crisis proportions because of the monetization of the shares of the Mississippi Company. Ever fastidious in compiling the monetary statistics, Du Tot showed how the banknote issue, which stood at 1 billion livres at the end of 1719, expanded by close to 1.7 billion livres to a total of 2.7 billion in May 1720. Not all of these new banknotes were in circulation and in some cases they were issued to replace previous issues that had been burned.

Law attempted to remedy the oversupply of banknotes and shares through the famous *arrêt* of 21 May 1720 stipulating that banknotes would be reduced on a monthly basis to half their value by December 1720 while shares would be reduced on a similar monthly phased basis by four ninths to 5000 livres. These were the measures that he had wished to introduce in March but was prevented from so doing by the Regent's circle. The shock to public confidence created by this *arrêt*, even though it was hastily repealed, left Law in a weakened situation. Law was sacked as Contrôleur Général des Finances and briefly placed under house arrest. Though he was quickly reinstated to continue to manage the Company's fortunes, he never really recovered from these events and was ultimately forced to flee from France in December 1720. He was replaced by his enemies the financiers, the Pâris brothers, who returned the financial system to its former *modus operandi* with the financiers at the centre of power. Law's career as a financial innovator had come to an end. Intriguingly, the Regent wanted to invite him back to France in 1723 to have an another attempt at restructuring the French financial system. Law's former secretary Jean-François Melon was sent to London to offer this invitation to Law. The latter was enthusiastic about returning to France but, unfortunately for him, the Regent died and the new Regent, the duke of Bourbon, by now a friend of the financiers, the Pâris brothers, was hostile to Law's return. Law spent his final years in Venice, dying there in 1729.

Conclusion

Law's monetary theory developed into a policy aimed at solving France's financial and monetary crises. It appeared to work for a brief period in 1719 and the first half of 1720. He appeared to solve the monetary crisis by substituting banknotes for specie. To address the financial crisis he converted France's state debt into equity of the Mississippi Company. Both policies were deemed initially to be highly successful – so much so that Law was made Prime Minister of France and the British authorities, imitating Law, decided to use the South Sea Company to convert government debt into equity.

So Law had both the ideas and the opportunities to implement a financial revolution. For a brief period he had introduced one, but it was not to last. Why did he fail? At a political level, sustaining his financial revolution was always going to prove difficult once the financiers, bereft of their control of the finances, regrouped and waited for an opportunity, like that of 21 May 1720, to attack Law. Du Tot, a man at the centre of the Royal Bank's operations, continually criticized the financiers for their opposition to Law. At an economic level Law made the mistake of too closely linking the activities of the Royal Bank with those of the Company. He had already won two important battles in substituting banknotes for silver and shares for government debt. These were highly significant achievements in such a short space of time. But then he used the printing presses of the Royal Bank to sustain the Company's share price at an artificially high level. Belatedly, he realized that he had over-expanded excessively the financial circuit of banknotes and shares relative to the real capacity of the economy. Perhaps if he had been able to introduce the 21 May measures at an earlier stage in late February 1720 he might have been successful in dampening the excessive optimism in the system. The Regent's reluctance to allow him to do so meant that the attempted resuscitation came too late in May.

One also suspects that Law had a failing in that whenever a problem arose he used his considerable improvisation skills to buttress the system rather than asking whether such improvisation was covering up a deeper issue. For example, in January 1720 when some pressures started to emerge with the public attempting to cash in their gains by purchasing specie and bullion, Law counterattacked by prohibiting the use of specie for all but very small transactions and by criminalizing the holding of specie and bullion above a stipulated amount. To further increase the attractiveness of banknotes he produced a demonetization of gold and a phased devaluation of silver. These were attempts to keep transactors within the financial circuit trading shares for banknotes and vice versa but preventing them from moving outside this circuit. If Law had analysed why there was this desire to leave the circuit, instead of designing ways to keep transactors within it, he would have realized that there was a fundamental flaw in his system, namely an overissue of paper money in the form of banknotes and monetized shares. That realization would have provided an early warning of the need to deflate the system. Instead, his improvisations diverted his attention from the main issue to be addressed.

Notes

1. For a discussion of this see Murphy (1997, pp. 57–8).
2. *Almanach pour l'année MDCXVII – Les Ordres du Roy executez par sa Chambre de Justice pour punir le vice, abolir l'usure et faire regner l'abondance et la paix dans ces états* (Private collection).
3. Paris, Archives des Affaires Etrangères, M&D, Amérique, I, fo. 317r.
4. Law (1934), vol. iii, pp. 343–4.
5. Du Tot (2000).
6. Section XI of the arrêt of 31 August 1719 is quite specific in offering debt holders a choice between shares or annuities: 'Veut & entend sa Majesté que conformément à l'article IV, de l'Arrest du 27 Aoust, toutes personnes puissant acquerir à leur choix sur ladite Compagnie des Indes, soit des actions, soit des contracts de constitution de rente; sur lesquels contracts toutes hypotheques, privileges & saisies tiendront comme sur les contracts de constitution de rente sur la ville.'
7. Du Tot, op. cit.; Giraudeau, Paris, Bibliothèque de l'Arsenal, 'Variations exactes de tous les effets en papier, qui ont eu cours sur la place de Paris, a commancer au mois d'Aout 1719 jusques au dernier mars 1721'.
8. Du Tot (2000), op. cit., p. 302.
9. Ibid., p. 231.
10. Ibid., p. 252.
11. Ibid., pp. 250 and 252.
12. Ibid., p. 304
13. Ibid., p. 347
14. Ibid., p. 372, emphasis by Du Tot; see also Du Tot (1935), vol. i, p. 243.
15. Ibid., p. 374.
16. Ibid., p. 427.
17. Law (1934), vol. iii, p. 219.
18. See Du Tot (2000), p. 422.
19. Ibid., p. 418.

Bibliography

Cantillon, Richard (1755), *Essai sur la nature du commerce en general*, London (Paris).

Cochrane, John H. (2001), review of 'Famous First Bubbles' by Peter M. Garber, *Journal of Political Economy*, **109** (October), 1150–54.

Du Tot, Nicolas (1935), *Réflexions politiques sur les finances et le commerce*, ed. Paul Harsin, Paris: Librairie E. Droz.

Du Tot, Nicolas (2000), *Histoire du systême de John Law (1716–1720)*, Paris: INED.

Faure, Edgar (1977), *La Banqueroute de Law*, Paris: Gallimard.

Friedman, Milton (1956), 'The quantity theory of money – a restatement', in M. Friedman (ed.), *Studies in the Quantity Theory of Money*, Chicago: University of Chicago Press.

Horsefield, J. Keith (1960), *British Monetary Experiments 1650–1710*, Cambridge, MA: Harvard University Press.
Law, John (1704 [1994]), *John Law's Essay on a Land Bank*, ed. Antoin E. Murphy, Dublin: Aeon Publishing.
Law, John (1934), *Oeuvres complètes*, ed. Paul Harsin, Paris: Sirey.
Law, John (1705), *Money and Trade Considered*, Edinburgh.
Murphy, Antoin E. (1986), *Richard Cantillon: Entrepreneur and Economist*, Oxford: OUP.
Murphy, Antoin E. (1997), *John Law Economic Theorist and Policy-Maker*, Oxford: OUP.
Velde, François (2003), 'Government equity and money: John Law's system in 1720 France', Working Paper, Federal Reserve Bank of Chicago, December.

6 Duvillard's *Recherches sur les rentes* (1787) and the modified internal rate of return: a comparative analysis

Yuri Biondi, translated by Jeff d'Avignon and Geoffrey Poitras

The Man of Forty Ecus: This appears to me impracticable and impossible.
The Geometrician: You have very great reason, and this impossibility is a geometrical demonstration that there is a basic vice of reasoning in our new ministers.

(Voltaire, *The Man of Forty Ecus*)[1]

1. General introduction

Emmanuel-Etienne Duvillard of Durand is best known as one of the first authors of mortality tables. It is for these tables that historians of demography have studied his work, in particular the mortality table in *Analysis and tables of the influence of smallpox at each age and that which a preventative such as a vaccine can have on the population and its and longevity* (Duvillard 1806).[2] The 'critical fortune' of Duvillard is thus essentially bound to his mortality tables. In 1807, Dr Odier wrote a greatly favorable account in the *British Library*. By 1830, however, other specialists were strongly critical and this damaged the reputation of the author.[3] J. and M. Dupâquier (1985) state that Duvillard published the mortality tables in connection with his quarrel with the management of the first Bureau of Statistics in France, of which he was an assistant director between August 1805 and 1 September 1812.[4] As highlighted by Jonckheere (1965), these tables rested on the compilation of very disparate statistics: several French parishes of the *ancien régime* and, especially, those for the town of Geneva from the years 1770–83. Duvillard's goal was by no means to propose a representative table of French mortality; rather he wanted to put an end to the quarrel about smallpox transmission of 45 years earlier between Daniel Bernoulli and D'Alembert, which had been decided in favour of the former.[5]

In his 1806 work, Duvillard mainly seeks to express the law of mortality using a simple equation, assumping a stationary population. Moreover, the work itself was only the tenth chapter of an unpublished work, 'Travail sur une Caisse nationale d'epargnes' (Work on a National Saving Plan), presented to the Academy of Sciences in the 22 germinal year IV (11 April 1796). The author explains:[6]

> *Numerical* work is not the essential part of the work that I last had the honor to present to the Institute. If there is any merit in this work, it consists, in the first place, in having imagined that there are necessary relations, independent of the actual empirical observations, between the various elements of a *regular* population. Secondly, in having discovered & demonstrated these *analytically* in all their extent and to have found a *criterion* to gauge, according to empirical observation, if a population is or is not in a regular state, and to decide on the time period when it approached this state most closely, in order to be able, by putting these facts into application, to deduce the law of mortality and population.

This quotation, as well as the studies of Bardet (1977), Baumol and Goldfeld [1968], Crépel (1990), Israël (1991, 1993) and Thuillier (1997), ably demonstrates that Duvillard's first interest was not limited to empirical demography. He was also interested in insurance, as well as actuarial and financial calculations, using demographic statistics in the analysis of life annuities and life insurance, and applying abstract methods of a quantitative and geometrical nature. These are precisely the methods that we will study in examining his previous: *Recherches sur les rentes, les emprunts et les remboursements* (*Researches on annuities, loans and refunding*), published in 1787.

Studies on Duvillard's work give scant biographical or historical information on the 1787 publication. Duvillard himself spoke little on the period of his life during which he conceived and wrote this work. Born in Geneva into a French family of Protestant origin, he settled in Paris in January 1775 to work at the office of the General Comptroller of Finances. Having returned to his native city after Turgot's retirement, he prepared the manuscript of his book, and it was for its approval by the Academy of Sciences that he returned to Paris in August 1786, carrying a letter from Charles Bonnet à Bailly (see Appendix III in Biondi 2003). Almost nothing is known of the life of Duvillard during his stay in Geneva between 1776 and 1786. He obtained a doctorate there on 8 March 1777 and married Marguerite Christine Rouvière on 20 October 1782 (Stelling-Michaud 1972). He undoubtedly played a part, in one way or another, in the innumerable banking and speculative activities involving life annuities which took place in this city. In 1784, he advertised for funding to support a publication project leading to a class on mathematical applications in trade and industry (Thuillier 1997, pp. 135–6). It was while preparing this publication that he conceived the idea of a maximum, which constitutes the core of his *Recherches sur les rentes* (Duvillard 1787, p. 22, note 8), published in Paris and Geneva in 1787 'under granted privilege from the Paris Royal Academy of Sciences'. As highlighted by G. Thuillier (1997, pp. 1, 125) Duvillard established a connection with Condorcet, who, with Cousin, had written the Academy's report. Having brought his family, he settled permanently in Paris where he pursued his career.

Duvillard's *Recherches sur les rentes* centers on the life annuities issued by the French government and the difficulties of their repayment. Many experts discussed this problem and tried to find solutions that were more or less equitable.[7] To summarize, his own general idea consisted of finding an equivalent value for a life annuity using a discounting method aimed at bringing all the cash flows to the same point in time, and incorporating the probabilities of death provided by mortality tables.[8] The French author of reference on such matters at the time was Antoine Deparcieux. The subject fits within the evolution of studies on loans and financial investments, as in the activities of insurance, originating with the early tables on discounting that appeared in the sixteenth century.

A new attitude of facing risk, rents and probabilities emerged into the great debate on usury.[9] During the thirteenth century, Thomist masters did not condemn risky gain as such. Instead they distinguished allowable industrious return, either for one's own labor or for risk-sharing companies (*ratio capitalis*, or investing reason), from speculative loans without labour or sharing (*ratio usurae*, or usury reason), justifying this distinction with the Aristotelian idea of the intrinsic *sterility of money*.

Still in a framework of ethics and theology, the late Scholastics (especially in Spain) sought to contend the claims made against expanding commercial and financial practices. They came to justify certain practices, formerly considered as usury, by presenting them within a framework of an equitable proportion between risk and return, which could thus transform prohibited gambling speculations into compensation for risk. At the beginning of the seventeenth century, Grotius (Huig van Groot) turned to this argument in order to exculpate bankers of a charge of usury. As early as the middle of the seventeenth century, several scholars tried to develop questions concerning compound interest issuing from the field of probability. On the epistemological level, this debate is part of the evolution of the theory of discounting future cash flows. Retrospectively, Parker (1968) makes a connection with three modern subjects: actuarial science, engineering science and, finally, economics, to which we can add 'engineering economics' or applied economics.[10] As Daston (1988, p. 112) observes, these early scholars invented a new abstract method to tackle the question of risk, studied until then by theologians and lawyers, by proposing 'scientifically' founded general rules for determining its price.

Created in England a little after the middle of the seventeenth century, in particular by Graunt and Petty, and quite quickly diffused on the Continent, initially in Holland by the brothers Huyghens, Hudde and de Witt, then everywhere in Europe, political arithmetic further developed this new framework for discounting and constituted a significant stage in the development of economic science. Moreover, it was at this time that mortality tables were first constructed by Edmond Halley. This new science then became diversified, particularly in relation to the great probabilistic scientists of eighteenth century, such as the Bernoullis, de Moivre, Condorcet and Laplace. Several traditions have at times ignored or opposed them, but have always remained more or less connected to the analysis of life annuities. In France, then, the work undertaken by scientific theorists such as Deparcieux and Buffon, and then Condorcet and Laplace, was more concerned with public investigations until the end of the century. The debates were also marked by the bitter discussions between D'Alembert and Daniel Bernoulli on the probabilistic quantitative analysis related to the transmission of smallpox. In England, on the contrary, it is the more 'private' analysis of life annuity prices which draws the attention of authors such as de Moivre, Simpson, Price and Morgan.

Through his early contact with the Turgot ministry (1774–76), Duvillard found himself somewhat in the 'French tradition'. This is confirmed by his highly mathematical style as well as by the fact that he submitted his 1786 work to the Paris Academy of Sciences. We now know that in spite of the relations maintained by Price with encyclopedists such as Morellet, Turgot and Condorcet, the French and English traditions in political arithmetic did not have the intellectual foundations that might have been assumed before making a closer investigation (Martin 2003; Hampsher-Monk 2005). It is, therefore, unlikely that Duvillard drew inspiration from the ideas (although remarkable) of Richard Price.

In any case, in the eighteenth century, the evolution of ideas, as well as the newest economic and financial practices at the core of the Industrial Revolution, changed the philosophical and epistemological developments described above, which resulted from the opposition to the medieval prohibition of usury. Certain authors, such as Norton Wise (1995) and Ted Porter (1995), associate this proposition with the emergence of a 'quantifying spirit of capitalism', which establishes in theory and practice an ideal of quantification and, consequently, the habit of relying on numbers ('trust in numbers'). Moreover, since the beginning of the twentieth century, there have been, arising from the debates between M. Weber, G. Simmel and W. Sombart, many studies pointing in this direction and devoted to the emergence, evolution and forms of the capitalist spirit. Duvillard's contribution, studied and approved by Condorcet, Cousin and Vasco, falls within this general movement. It demonstrates a definite modernity, in particular in its use of maximization and in his analysis based on a sequence of financial cash flows.

This chapter analyzes the financial analysis of Duvillard as well as his 'economic views' by situating them in their historical context and by comparing them with the recent analytical framework.[11] In section 2, we will demonstrate the exactness of his financial analysis (already highlighted by G.B. Vasco in his report of 1787 for the *Biblioteca Oltermontana*). Duvillard develops, using mathematical methods that combine analytical calculations and graphical representations, an original financial technique, analogous to the current internal rate of return, which he applies to the evaluation of life annuities. Beyond acknowledging the analytical similarity between the formulas of Duvillard and today's internal rate of return, the question of interpreting this analytical device remains open. Section 3 is devoted to the author's economic views, in particular to his account of discounting methods. Today's usual reference points, such as inter-temporal preferences and the logic of discounted cash flows, can be thus understood by a comparative perspective.

2. Duvillard's analysis

2.1 The subject of Duvillard's work

Duvillard begins his *Recherches* with the following:

> I show in particular, in the work which I present to the public, that a mathematician experienced with these matters, working under the command of the Minister of Finance, could have been able, on many occasions, to allow the State to borrow the same amount that it borrowed in the past, while letting it save many millions, without at all decreasing the attraction offered to the lenders, nor their real advantage. (Duvillard 1787, Author's Preface)

Then he introduces the topic by giving some definitions. First, regarding loans refunded with annuities certain:

> If we do not want to refund capital in lump sums which include the interest, we can initially refund the quantity a, then the quantity b, then successively the quantities $d, e, f, g,\ldots,u$, until the entire debt is extinguished.
>
> Such an unspecified capital has to be refunded with the annual interest i for 1, & this will make $1 + i = q$.
>
> For the first year we will owe $c{\cdot}i$ for the interest; & if we pay a, what will be as principal will be $a - c{\cdot}i$; therefore, the balance of outstanding capital owed will be $c - (a - c{\cdot}i)$ *or* $c{\cdot}q - a$. (Ibid., p. 1)

Duvillard wishes to analyze, therefore, a refunding profile based on what the author calls the annuities $a, b, d,\ldots, u$. If the number of annuities is fixed from the beginning, and if they are all equal, we can always imagine that a fraction of each annuity is devoted to pay the interest and the remaining fraction devoted to pay back the capital. These fixed coupon annuities are then a mode of refunding the capital that remains either by constant fractions (thus a straight-line depreciation for each year) or by a lump sum at maturity (thus a single repayment at the end of the fixed period). This can be seen in Table 6.1.

Duvillard explains this repayment method in a more general way:

> And in general, at the end of t years, the remaining amount owing is [in capital account] $cq^t - (aq^{t-1} + bq^{t-2} + dq^{t-3} + eq^{t-4} + \ldots + u)$. I suppose here a compounded interest rate. ... As well as supposing that the discount rate is compounded and taken as it should be, the quantities $a, b, d, e,$ & c can be such that the debt is reduced to zero, that is, we will suppose that $cq^t - (aq^{t-1} + bq^{t-2} + \ldots + u) = 0$. (Ibid., pp. 1, 2, 3)

Duvillard also adds that the quantities *a, b, d, etc.* can be equal, increasing or decreasing according to all kinds of laws. He goes on to tackle the particular case where the quantities are

Table 6.1 Repayment methods

Payment (in capital account)	Periods 1	2	3	4	5	total
Constant for each year	20.00	20.00	20.00	20.00	20.00	100.00
Fraction of the annuity	18.10	19.00	19.95	20.95	22.00	100.00
Repayment in a lump sum	0	0	0	0	100.00	100.00

equal and annual, consisting of fixed coupon (that is, constant) annuities. Duvillard's repayment equation then becomes:

$$cq^t - a(q^{t-1} + q^{t-2} + q^{t-3} + \ldots + q^0) = 0 \tag{1a}$$

with:

$$m = c(1 + i)^t = cq^t = [a(q^t - 1)]/i \tag{1b}$$

This specification consists of the value discounted to the year t of the initial borrowed capital, or of the 'amount m of all these perceived annual installments, at the time where we cease to receive payments'[12] (ibid., p. 20). We will call this the 'future value', in keeping with modern terminology.

Starting from this formula, the author applies his method to the refunding of life annuities; it is undoubtedly for this reason he considers time t as variable in the rest of his analysis. This passage from a fixed time to a variable time brings his analytical framework closer to what today is referred to as a series of cash flows resulting from investment in capital account from an initial sunk expenditure (subsections 3.2 and 3.3).

In this way, Duvillard tries to advance towards his practical objective: to find remedies for the financial crisis of the French state caused in part by the very high interest payments being made on life annuities.[13] Having established this basic formula, Duvillard examines this type of annuity and identifies in particular what it brings to its owners (the so-called 'natural rate') and the price they pay to buy it:

> If life annuities were not calculated only with an ordinary interest rate, it would not suffice to bring in as many Lenders as the Borrower desires. From this result the necessity is to increase the natural rate to the owner without increasing its price. (Ibid., p. 13)

Within his analytical framework, indeed, Duvillard does not link the calculated profitability of the investment with its current market price. This point of view leads him to develop his own economic analysis free from any reference to today's concept of a 'financial market' that ought to align the supply price with the cost for the buyer of the security, at least in equilibrium (see subsections 2.5 and 3.3).

Duvillard's framework consists of a borrower, i.e. the State's Treasury, borrowing above the ordinary interest rate. The author does not define precisely the meaning of this ordinary level; it does not represent a legal rate, but rather the usual level that is generally accepted without specific reference to the economic sector or the kind of financial investment. In fact, it was common in the eighteenth century and still in the nineteenth century to regard as ordinary a rate around 5 percent, as Duvillard seems to do throughout his work.

He thus defines the 'apparent rate from the annuity' r, i.e. the relationship between the annuity received each year and the initial invested start-up capital, by $r = a/c > i$, where i is the ordinary rate.[14] This r consists of the rate of a perpetual annuity with constant terms, a common way at the time to evaluate investments that is still used today, especially in real-estate investments.[15]

Duvillard distinguishes three classes of people likely to buy these 'enhanced' annuities:

1. Those able to accumulate, through compound interest, only a fraction of the annuity.
2. The professional investors, such as bankers and all those who enjoy assured credit (ibid., p. 15), who must make payment on borrowed funds and cannot accumulate the entire annuity either.
3. Finally, 'the capitalists who seek the highest return for their funds' [ibid., p. 17] and accumulate these annuities and the resulting interest.

Although he is interested in those who accumulate only a fraction of their annuity and also in those who spend it all (no accumulation, therefore no reinvestment is possible), he pays particular attention to the third class of lenders, whom he calls capitalists, 'since it seems possible for them to accumulate their annuities in such a trade with an interest so extremely below the one that the borrower can support that they can raise their profits as high as the promised sacrifices of the borrower seem to promise'[16] (ibid.). Thus he summarizes the practical purpose of this work: to show that the lender could not exploit the borrower in this repayment operation.

The analytical framework is that of a sinking fund investment, which produces positive annual inflows that the lender can reinvest only at the current rate (that is, where the interest rate i is used) lower than the return on the investment itself (in this case, the interest rate r for which the annuity is established).

As previously observed, Duvillard (ibid., p. 54) proposes using constant annuities as a benchmark for analyzing life annuities where the number of annuities (according to the meaning this term had in the eighteenth century) was not fixed in advance; indeed, the concept of annuities (with the number of periods fixed in advance) slips, for the author, towards the current concept of a cash flow having a constant amount for each year, paid during an unspecified number of periods and thus variable according to time. This idea can be confirmed by the fact that the author further examines the case where the annuities are of variable amounts.

In conclusion, therefore, there are two assumptions, explicitly considered by Duvillard, that represent the keystones of his analysis:

- the initial investment must be into a sinking fund;
- the lender reinvests the received annual annuity payment (from the sinking fund) at a interest rate lower than the rate r of the original annuity.

2.2 *The 'internal rate of return' in Duvillard's formulation*

> Indeed, how can one find at which interest rate [compounded] one invests money, when one places it in a sinking fund with a certain annuity, paid only for a certain specified time period? (Duvillard 1787, p. 20)

Duvillard establishes two criteria relevant for his analysis, for the case where time is still given. First he looks for the future amount m, the previously mentioned 'future value', following from the accumulated annuities in the sinking fund. Second,

> We will then seek to find the interest rate [compounded] at which the original capital should have been invested to reach this above mentioned amount m for the duration t of the annuity a, which will be found using the following formula:[17]

$$y = -1 + \sqrt[t]{(m/c)} \tag{2}$$

Having determined these two values, the future value of the accumulated annual annuities m and the compound interest rate y, the solution will be completed:

> & we will be able to say that the investment in the annuity, as it was mentioned, is equivalent to a simple investment, during the duration of the supposed annuity [t], at the rate [compounded] that we just determined [y]. (Ibid., p. 20)

Starting from this method, Duvillard built his formulas and developed his analysis, in particular making the number of time periods variable.

Here Duvillard determines what is called in modern terminology the internal rate of return (*IRR*) of a given investment, even if he frames it in a different perspective.[18] As in contemporary financial analysis, Duvillard considers the compound interest rate for an equivalent investment deposit. Analyzing the formula which defines y: $m = c(1 + y)^t$, Substitution from (1b) gives:

$$c\,(1 + y)^t = (a\,(q^t - 1))/i = a(q^{t-1} + q^{t-2} + \ldots + q^0) \tag{1c}$$

On the left side, we find the future value of the original capital invested at the 'internal rate of return' y, the rate at which Duvillard computed the future value. In this way, the author arrives at the same result as in the modern method. We will see how Duvillard calculated the *IRR* as it has been adopted nowadays, even if he based his analysis on the future value. To understand the reason behind this equivalence, let the usual internal rate of return be computed as the rate which neutralizes the net present value (*NPV*), that is, for a series $a_0, \ldots, a_t$, at the rate ρ:

$$NPV_\rho = a_0/(1 + \rho)^0 + a_1/(1 + \rho)^1 + \ldots + a_t/(1 + \rho)^t,$$

where, for simplicity, $a_0 < 0$ (the initial investment), $a_1, \ldots, at \geq 0$ and $\rho > 0$. In the case of annuities (that is with $a_1 = \ldots = a_t$ and $a_0 = -c$):

$$NPV_\rho = -c + a(1/(1 + \rho) + 1/(1 + \rho)^2 + \ldots + 1/(1 + \rho)^t)$$

The 'internal rate of return' (*IRR*) is then defined as the value of the rate ρ for which NPV_ρ is equal to zero, that is, in this last formula:

$$c = a(1/(1 + IRR) + \ldots + 1/(1 + IRR)^t) \tag{3}$$

Thus, there is an elementary mathematical relation between the *NPV* and the net future value (*NFV*) usually defined as:

$$NFV_\rho = (1 + \rho)^t \, NPV_\rho \quad \text{given that } -1 < \rho < \infty \tag{4}$$

We can find *IRR* either from the equation $NPV_\rho = 0$ or from $NFV_\rho = 0$, the two methods being equivalent. Starting from net future value (*NFV*), thus, equation (3) will become (taking $\rho = IRR$):

$$c((1 + IRR)^t) = a[(1 + IRR)^{t-1} + ((1 + IRR)^{t-2}) + \ldots + 1] \tag{5}$$

In this relationship, the right side represents a reinvestment of funds at rate *IRR* during time *t* (which is given).

Duvillard (ibid., p. 18) had, of course, emphasized that, if the reinvestment of the right side of (5) and the investment rate of the left side are equal, the internal rate of return *y*, which he defines, is also equal to the two above-mentioned values (=*IRR*). Nevertheless, he developed his analysis on the explicit assumption that the annual replacements of the right side are being made at an interest rate *i* lower than the investment rate *r* of the capital *c* (related to the annuity *a*, since $r = a/c$).

In this case, with $q = 1 + i$, the following definition for modified internal rate of return (*MIRR*) is determined starting from equation (5):

$$c(1+MIRR)^t = a\sum_{j=1}^{t}(1+i)^{t-j} = a(q^{t-1} + q^{t-2} + \ldots + q^0). \tag{6}$$

In other words, the modified internal rate of return *MIRR* is defined as the rate for which the future value of the investment of the initial capital at the rate *MIRR* and the future value of the installments' replacement at the rate *i* are equal. We can easily verify the identity of this formulation with Duvillard's equation (1c), since the right side of (6) is equal to the right side of (1c).

We will thus call from now on *DIRR* the 'modified' internal rate of return such as defined by Duvillard. It consists of a special case of today's *MIRR*.[19]

2.3 *Duvillard's 'maximum' in the modified internal rate of return*

The true purpose of Duvillard's analysis was not only the construction of this financial measure *y*, or *DIRR*, but rather the analysis of a maximum, which he finds in the evolution of *y* over time. Compared to contemporary analysis, this point implies a significant difference that will be examined in section 3 (see in particular subsection 3.2).

> A curious & significant result presents itself, which initially seems as a paradox, & which will be taken for nonsense by any person who will not be able or will not want to follow attentively my reasoning. This paradox, is that there is a maximum here; that is, a certain annuity duration such that the required interest rate is higher than with any other, so that increasing or decreasing the annuity's duration, fixed as such, will decrease the required interest rate. (Ibid., p. 20)

To find this 'maximum' (optimal lending period, rate and value), Duvillard (ibid., p. 22) formulates the following question:

> We ask: which is the interest rate *y* for *1* which we have set up as our investment, from which we will receive an annuity *a* on *1,* that we will replace by measure of *i* on *1*, as we reach time *t*?

The answer is obviously contained in the formula (1b), with $c = 1$:

$$(1+y)^t = \frac{a(q^t - 1)}{i} \tag{7}$$

where $y = DIRR$, i = the current rate, $a = r$ = interest rate of the annuity (for $c = 1$). The author thus establishes a function $y(t)$ which he solves for a and i that will maximize y^* at the time t^*.[20] He employs a method that we can call geometric, but he also begins with an intuitive explanation for the existence of such a maximum: there is a certain time where 'the annuities and their accumulating compounded interest' will be equal to the initial capital (ibid., p. 20).[21] At this time, the modified internal rate of return, that defined by *DIRR*, is zero; after this point, the *DIRR* continues to increase and soon it will become larger than the ordinary interest i applicable to the annuities.

As Duvillard explains, it is for this reason there will be a maximum; since the left term in (7), initially smaller, will increase according to a rate bigger than the rate i which the amount of the annuity (right term) yields. There will necessarily be:

> One time where the annual increase (of the original capital) is equal to double the increase (by the ordinary interest and the constant annual installment which will be paid) that is received from the amount of the annuities. (Ibid., p. 21)

Beyond this point, the *DIRR* always will be included between the rate to which one reinvests the annual installments i and the rate r (which is greater than i by definition). Therefore, there is a maximum for the *DIRR* with respect to the time that Duvillard calculates by differentiating equation (7).[22] He suggests several ways of obtaining this maximum value, including an interesting method of recursion.[23] This consists of choosing an unspecified value for t, provided that the value for y which will result from it be positive; we can then substitute the value for $Q = y + 1$ determined by computing the equation given by Duvillard; so we bring this result equal to t and reintroduce it into the initial equation, and this process will continue until the time the maximum gain from the annuity is determined.

Presenting his scientific research in a letter to the Academy of Sciences, in May 1813, Duvillard regards this recursive method as novel:

> Thus, for example, in my *Recherches sur les rentes*, on page 23, I had to solve for the value of r from the exponential equation … Even though I gave it in various forms, the Lagrange theorem could never give me this value in a convergent series. I was obliged to seek a new method. I have developed this method in the text. It was considered as skillful and clever by the commissioners [Condorcet and Cousin] charged with the examination of this work. I could have easily generalised it if the nature of my principal purpose had allowed it.[24]

Both Lagrange and Legendre demonstrated interest in the mathematical techniques used by Duvillard (Thuiller 1997, p. 238):[25] 'He thus let this part of mixed Mathematics contribute to the progress that modern Geometricians have made with the Analysis.' Duvillard further built several tables with the corresponding values for the optimal time, the *DIRR* and the future value.[26]

In conclusion, we demonstrate the existence of a maximum y^* by studying the function $y(t)$ and its first derivative, using the assumptions made by Duvillard. Let us return to Duvillard's equation (7) in which c is not equal to 1; we can write it in the following way, with a, i, c being given:

$$y(t) = -1 + \sqrt[t]{\frac{a(q^t - 1)}{ci}} = -1 + \sqrt[t]{\frac{a}{c}}\sqrt[t]{\frac{q^t - 1}{i}} = -1 + \sqrt[t]{\frac{a}{c}}\sqrt[t]{q^{t-1} + q^{t-2} + \ldots + q^0}$$

Duvillard begins by calculating t while supposing $y(t)$ to be equal to zero, which he reports in the annexed table to his work; note that this case is close to the modern idea of a 'pay-back' modified by discounting the cash flows.[27] For Duvillard:

$$t = \frac{\log(a + i) - \log(a)}{\log(1 + i)}$$

and so $y(t) = 0$. He points out that

$$\lim_{t \to +0} y(t) = -1^+ \text{ and } \lim_{t \to +\infty} y(t) = i^+.$$

We can write the first derivative in the following form, by using the formula for deriving compound functions:

$$y'(t) = \left(-\frac{1}{t^2} \log \frac{a(q^t - 1)}{ci} + \frac{q^t \log q}{t(q^t - 1)} \right) \exp\left(\frac{1}{t} \log \frac{a(q^t - 1)}{ci} \right).$$

When we study the derivative $y'(t)$, we check that for t sufficiently small, it is close to the second factor; for t sufficiently large, it is close to the first factor, as soon as the second tends towards $q = 1 + i$ we can show the existence of the solution for the derivative equal to zero.[28]

2.4 *Increasing and decreasing annuites; life annuities*

Although the focus in this work is on constant annuities, Duvillard does not forget to deal, at least briefly, with more general cases. For example, he mentions the case of a series of annuities in arithmetic progression; it is the case of annuities which decrease by a constant quantity (which is a percentage of the annuity a); he calculates the *DIRR* and the time associated with his maximum. He finds that, in this case, under certain conditions, there will always be a maximum (ibid., pp. 39–40).

In the case of the regularly increasing annuities, if the rate r of the annuity is larger than the rate of reinvestment i, there be always a maximum and, if the increase is itself variable, there could be more than one (ibid., p. 41).

He also examines several methods of reimbursements for life annuities, with random draws and premiums on reimbursements, or by amortization in arithmetic or geometrical progression. He provides the rate y and the time of the maximum for these cases (ibid., pp. 42–54).

Furthermore, Duvillard compares two annuities with different amounts, each payable until their different maximum times and with the same rate of re-employment for the proceeds. Such a comparison is not possible with the *IRR* as it is used today.[29] In fact, with the *DIRR* (or the *MIRR*) the comparison can be done so long as we choose the longest duration as the reference and imagine the earnings from the shorter annuity to be invested at the rate of re-employment i until the end of the longest duration. This is also the assumption used by Duvillard (ibid., p. 29):

Moreover, it is easy to see that it is not necessary to hesitate over the choice between two different annuities, each payable until the time of their maximum; even though the time T during which one will pay the smallest annuity a, being larger than that t, during which we would pay the larger annuity A; since we compare these two products

$$q^{\frac{t \cdot q^t}{q^t - 1}} \cdot q^{T-t} \;\&\; q^{\frac{T \cdot q^T}{q^T - 1}}$$

Duvillard's result consists in always choosing the largest annuity A, if it is paid until the time of its maximum. He underlines, moreover, that times of the maxima relative to the rates of 6 to 12 percent are included within the limits of human of life, the ordinary rate being 4 to 6 percent. Lastly, he makes the following remarks:

In general, the higher is the interest rate at which one will place the annuity [i], the more distant will be the term of the maximum; & on the contrary, the larger the annuity will be [hence a higher r], the interest rate of accumulation [i] remaining the same, the shorter the term of its maximum will be, & the accumulated amount smaller. (Ibid., p. 29)

2.5 Consequences and applications

The true purpose of Duvillard's analysis is, as mentioned earlier, the study of life annuities. The Geneva scientist applies to them the logic just presented (ibid., p. 54ff.) in order to criticize their issue by the State's Treasury. The most remarkable consequence of this maximum is, in his opinion, that the advantage of the lender is not always increasing over time, 'though the burden of the borrower' (ibid.) becomes even larger.

Even if the author barely refers to the political and financial context of his time, one should not forget the financial crisis of the *ancien régime* with all its political and social implications. It is known that Duvillard, as an employee of the Ministry of Finance, took part in the decisions to repurchase the life annuities during the Revolution. The calculations for these very delicate repurchases were based on his analysis of these public loans (Crépel 1990). In spite of his efforts, he never really achieved influence over the final decisions, as he explains in the following text:

I showed that it was enough to reimburse without reducing the received capital when the rate of the life annuity exceeded that which was naturally owed; and reconciling as much as it was possible, the interest of the State and justice due to the holder, providing service to all, I provided ways to liquidate this Debt …

… I have directed this operation scientifically until the moment where another legislative assembly will change this mode of liquidation and reduce to a third the Capital of the National Debt.[30] We can feel certain that I was not consulted on this last operation.[31]

Duvillard finally finds that there is, in these life annuities with a higher rate than the current level, a 'money unemployment' (*chômage d'argent*).[32] As he sees it, the monarch should borrow only to invest in some advantageous business, such as in commerce, agriculture or manufactures that can be regarded as paying the debts allocated to this business. He must thus borrow:

to gain returns from this commerce or manufacture at higher interest than he is engaged to pay. Thus the subjects of a monarch face the commitments from borrowing that he makes, & he only borrows in such a way to not deprive the funds that industry values with an interest rate much higher than the

> interest from which he borrows, & to service, in this manner, the capital of others to the profit of the nation. (Ibid., pp. 85–6)

Elsewhere, he is even more explicit:

> This capital, if reversed in circulation, would have been used to service different loans and different purchases; it would have been employed to build houses, clear lands, refresh neglected lands, to better harvest the country fields, to better direct the fruitfulness of the ground towards the most useful plants for mankind, to increase the number of manufactures, to extend the businesses etc., etc., and all that would have been operated by sums which did not exist before, or which had no value. (Duvillard, quoted in Thuillier 1997, p. 231)

Duvillard (1787) is very critical of life annuities. He alludes to the bankers who negotiate to buy them at a much lower price than their actual value:

> Everyone can easily verify these calculations. If we find them correct, we will conclude that if several people made a great fortune, while being interested in the annuities of the used form, that is because they purchase them at a price much lower than their true value, wherever they negotiated them. But the true lenders are those which always keep the annuities, & it is their benefit which is the focus here; however this benefit is extremely small compared to that which we would have initially believed. (Ibid., pp. 68–9)

It would be appropriate then, for example, for the borrower to remove these annuities as soon as they reach their maximum, provided that he lets the holders re-lend to him on the same conditions. The lenders will have at the end of the period a much greater sum, and the borrower will pay them the same amount as for the previous annuities, but after having received new funds (ibid., p. 34). As Duvillard argues, 'It is thus not necessary to ask here who loses when both profit, as someone asked me' (p. 85). There is here a reference to the difficulties Duvillard had in making his analysis understandable: 'I was astonished by the ease with which Mr. de Calonne seized the reason of these results [from his *Recherches*] which appeared to others as paradoxes' (Duvillard, quoted by Thuillier 1997, p. 1).

The author devotes several paragraphs to developing solutions aimed at avoiding as much as possible excessive expenditure by the state.[33] Ultimately, all these methods use the analytical results from the *DIRR* analysis. According to Duvillard, the simplest consists in transforming the previous annuities into new compound interest annuities fixed at the level of the *DIRR*, either for the maximum or during an indefinite time period.[34] The borrower will thus make a great saving on the interest paid.

Another method is based on the substitution of life annuities with several annuities equal or larger, for a shorter time. For example, a succession of 104 annual annuities of 9 percent can become two loans of 52 annuities each, or better still three loans of approximately 34 years. In this case, successive loans of new funds are made. We could nevertheless borrow with the matured successive annuities. Duvillard (ibid., p. 102) demonstrates a general solution for this last case. He points out that without being able to reinvest an annuity at the same interest rate as the one supported by the borrower, lenders must prefer to the single loan a succession of successive loans over a fixed length of time (ibid., pp. 105–6), since the total amount of accumulation would indeed be higher in the case of successive loans. In this case, nevertheless, the debtor does not always have advantages, and Duvillard further develops his method to find the right conditions, while also taking into account the timing of the maturities. For this, he assumes an interest rate j which the borrower is supposed to gain on the borrowed amounts (ibid., p. 107).

2.6 Replying to the critics

In their collected studies devoted to the 'precursors of mathematical economics', Baumol and Goldfeld situate the contribution of Duvillard's *Recherches* as follows:

> This book was by no means the earliest writing on actuarial mathematics but it does provide a contribution in its use of the differential calculus to calculate an optimal lending period. Professor Robertson describes Bernoulli, Paolo Frisi and Buquoy as the three earliest users of the differential calculus in economic analysis.[35] But Duvillard de Durand anticipates the relevant writings of the latter by more than a quarter of a century. (Baumol and Goldfeld 1968, p. 151)

They offer sufficient information to explain the author's analysis of a maximum, through extracts translated into English, while formulating a brief critique, which proves to be inaccurate.[36] On the basis of formula (2), Baumol and Goldfeld (1968, p. 151) claim that:

> the [right-hand] side of the equation is the present value of a sequence of repayments, a, on a debt of one unit of currency, say one dollar, lent at a rate of interest i. On the [left-hand] side y is a sort of lender's 'internal rate of return' which is to be maximized.

Their analysis is based on an assumed identity between the two interest rates y and i, that is, between the *DIRR* and the current market rate, which they claim to attribute to the author himself:

> But a little consideration suggests that if the rate of interest is i, then y must equal the given interest rate, i, and there is nothing to be maximized. This also follows directly from the author's own equation …
>
> $$\frac{a(q^t - 1)}{i} = cq^t = c(1+i)^t \quad \text{[see (1b)]}$$
>
> where c is the amount of money lent so that in the present case $c = 1$. Moreover, with t variable and all other entries in the equation taken to be fixed (as the author assumes in his differentiation) it should be clear that a maximum present value (rather than internal rate of return) would be obtained by lender with $t = \infty$!

Baumol and Goldfeld did not really try to repeat Duvillard's analysis, as shown by the following misunderstandings:

- They call *present value* a formula which obviously represents the future value of the series of the annuities in question, expressly defined by Duvillard himself (see our equation (1b) and the quotation above).
- They claim that the internal rate of return y must necessarily be equal to the current interest rate i, probably because they use the logic of the modern construction of the *IRR* from the formulation $NPV = 0$, i.e. from the point of view of the borrower.[37]

Duvillard himself had underlined expressly that, if the rate of the annuity r and the current interest rate i were equal, there would be nothing to maximize, since y, i and r are equal by definition. The French author nevertheless bases his analysis on the explicit assumption that r

is larger than *i* and takes the point of view of the lender who accumulates and reinvests the annuities.

From a thorough reading of the work, we, on the contrary, tried to show (see subsections 2.2–2.5) the connection of Duvillard's analysis with the *modified internal rate of return*, that is with the analysis of the internal rate of return within a framework characterized by several return and interest rates, while taking into account the elementary relation (4) between the present value and the future value. Moreover, the debate surrounding the net present value (*NPV*) and of *IRR*, during the 1950s, tackled this specific question.[38]

Within this framework concerned with the assumption of reinvestment, there is no difficulty, technical or theoretical, in using the *DIRR* to compare two projects having two different durations (see subsection 2.5), contrary to what Baumol and Goldfeld (1968, p. 152) claim. Finally, Duvillard's words, already quoted, seem relevant here: '[it is a] curious & significant result, which initially seems as a paradox, & which will be taken for nonsense by any person who will not be able or will not want to attentively follow my reasoning'.

3. Duvillard's economic views

Duvillard did not, as far as we know, tackle the subject of political economy. However, he did seek to extend and develop the 'social mathematics' of Condorcet, as demonstrated by Thuillier (1997), Israël (1991) and Crépel (1990). Here, we will investigate Duvillard's views on financial economics. Although a complete analysis of such would go beyond the framework of this chapter, we nevertheless want to approach two topics that seem particularly interesting: the approach based on multiple discounting methods and the relation between capital and interest.

3.1 Multiple discounting methods and their impact on the maximum

Although modern financial mathematics textbooks still quote the formulas for commercial and arithmetic discounting, both based on simple interest, contemporary economic theory emphasizes a logical and epistemological basis for using only compound discounting. In the eighteenth century, on the other hand, Duvillard seems to have had a much harder time defending and justifying what he calls the 'good' way of discounting, with respect to the customs and practices of his time.[39]

Having exposed the subject of his *Recherches*, Duvillard makes the following comment:

> I suppose here that the interest is compounded; because any person who puts forward capital, either in his own business, or in that of others, adds at least, at the end of each year, the interest on this capital, & then makes the capital grow with it added. I will therefore suppose that the discounting is compounded and applied appropriately. (Duvillard 1787, p. 2)

Nevertheless, at the end of this same paragraph, he adds the following note, related to discounting methods analyzed further down, where he further explains 'appropriate discounting':

> I say appropriate, since I recognize that there are four different ways to discount, that are necessary to use in turn for certain cases. Indeed, one asks what is the value for *y* of an amount *m*, payable at time *t*, the former for money being *i*?
>
> 1st. If discounting is done using the method employed by commercial traders for short times, which involves calculating the initial discount at simple interest, we have $y = m\,(1 - i\,t)$; this method means, for example, that the payouts really cost more provision to the trader committing them than commercial paper, though the percent rate is the same; [this method] further reduces to zero even the greatest

amounts payable at the end of time $t = 1/i$ (=20 years if the interest rate is 5 percent); & it can deceive some people when time is shorter.

2nd. If the initial discount is calculated using compound interest, we have a $y = m(1 - i)^t$; or to say it better, this formula shows to which sum m the capital y will grow to at the end of time t, when we will have used this capital, discounted year after year by sums corresponding to its successive values, & that according to the method used.

3rd. If we take the discount using the outside method, compounding the interest in the appropriate way, we have:

$$y = \frac{m}{(1+i)^t}.$$

4th. If, in this third method, simple interest is used, we have

$$y = \frac{m}{1+it} = \frac{m}{i(1/i+i)^t}.$$

(Ibid., p. 2, note 1)

According to Duvillard, there are four methods of discounting, different according to whether they rest on a simple or compound interest and whether they are taken from 'outside' or 'within' the amount, as shown in Table 6.2.

Table 6.2 Four methods of discounting according to Duvillard

Interest	Simple	Compound
Discount taken from inside	1	2
Discount taken from outside	4	3

It is the two 'outside' methods that concern us more, because of their potential complementarity with modern economic analysis. Duvillard indeed develops two discounting methods from 'outside', that is, using continuous time: discounting with compound interest and with simple interest. If we take a sum m equal to 100 and a discount rate i equal to 5 percent, then we can compare the four methods in Table 6.2.

In Duvillard's time, commercial relations and practices relied on other arrangements, such as the first and second method (which he calls 'discount from within'). It is then the case of a linear calculation in discrete time. In other words, we calculate, each year, the difference between the capital in question and the relative interest for each period (see Table 6.3).

Table 6.3 Comparison of the four discounting methods

M=100, i = 5%	1	1	1	1
1st	95.000	90.000	85.000	75.000
2nd	95.000	90.250	81.451	77.378
3rd	95.238	90.703	82.270	78.353
4th	95.238	90.909	83.333	80.000

Duvillard prefers the third method, which is compound interest from outside, for technical as well as theoretical reasons. He justifies it by the assumption that accumulation of interest proceeds with the same profitability as the initial capital. Even if he considers it as the 'appropriate' discounting method, he obviously does not believe this assumption to be valid in all cases if the reinvestment rate considered is different.[40] The author takes care, throughout his work, to make all his calculations in the following three cases: for the third formula, for the fourth formula and without any reinvestment (in the *DIRR*, the usual rate i then being zero).

Duvillard does not seem isolated from his time. His mentor, Condorcet, was interested in the same subjects and we can recognize the same inherent logic. In an undated manuscript which he did not publish, Condorcet presents the 'outside' discounting method with compound interest:

> In the calculation made above we took the ordinary method to evaluate the interest on the loans. This method consists of discounting the amounts that need to be paid at different times back to the single time … when the borrowing was made, and to evaluate these amounts by calculating what the value of a 100 amount payable in, for example, one year is if the interest on the loan is 8 percent, for example, 100*100/108; if it is 7 percent then the calculation is, 100*100/107. (Condorcet 1994, p. 593)[41]

However, Condorcet notes:

> But, in my opinion, this manner appears to be defective, since it consists of assuming that if I must pay in one year 100 pounds for example I only have to lend 100*(100/108) per year at 8 percent; in other words, I am entitled to give [to] the one to whom I owe 100 pounds in one year 100(100/108) in the present time. (Ibid.)

He adheres here to the same logic as Duvillard; to justify the discounting, he assumes a reinvestment at the discount rate, which allows the equivalent calculation between the present and future times. Condorcet, indeed, suggests that the borrower ('I') re-lends to himself the money borrowed in order to repay himself the money borrowed, or it will be the lender himself who will do it. Here is his conclusion:

> This discounting method is therefore exact only when we can refund the annuities on the account of the borrowing, or when the return on the former loan does not diverge from the current interest. It should therefore, at least for all the cases where the proceeds will not be specified on the return of the loan, be letting the current interest enter. [Ibid., p. 594)

Therefore, Condorcet does not agree with discounting in all cases by the return on the loan, without an equivalent replacement available; hence the reference to the level of the current interest rate. In particular, he explains that it is preferable to discount using the current interest rate of the country instead of the return on the loan: this reasoning is again based on the same framework as Duvillard.

3.2 Who really invented the 'internal rate of return'? Duvillard's contribution in a comparative perspective

Since informed readers can recognize the contemporary *MIRR* in the remarkable analysis developed by Duvillard, they may also go as far as recognizing the identity of the method to grasp both the underlying perspective and the interpretation to give to this analytical device.

For Duvillard, the two theoretical and analytical keystones are the idea of the maximum (subsection 2.3) and the various discounting methods (subsection 3.1); these do not relate just to note 1 of the *Recherches*, but can also be connected to the crucial idea of the reinvestment of the inflowing repayments (subsection 3.3).

Duvillard (1787, pp. 37–8) takes care to develop his optimizing analysis in the cases of compound interest, simple interest and even of no interest. He approaches, thus, every case of reinvestment, therefore all types of lenders, not only those who each year reinvest the annuity as well as the interest on proceeds accumulated, but also those who 'accumulate the interest without investing it at no interest' or 'those who spend this interest'.

Contemporary techniques for evaluating investments based on discounting logic, such as the *MIRR*, find their justification in the Marginalist Revolution.[42] In his work *Eléments d'économie pure*, which frames his 'scientific theory of capitalization', Léon Walras (1900, pp. 250–51) refers to the devices developed by actuarial science and the ancient notion of the *denier*. Moreover, we know of the considerable influence exerted by this French economist on Irving Fisher, usually credited with the introduction of discounting into the American economic literature of the time.

Since the end of the nineteenth century, several economists have extended this logic to fields other than the analysis of annuities and loans: Marshall, Böhm-Bawerk, Wicksell and, just after them, Fisher, developed in their works a perspective that integrates discounting as the present value of future financial cash flows, conceived in an impersonal way, and giving it a new epistemological and theoretical status in economics.[43] This change relates to different ways of understanding the relationship between capital and interest, and between credit and capital. We know the mess of theoretical quarrels on these issues, with scholars looking at discounting from at least the following three different perspectives: the optimal evaluation of industrial productive investments, financial efficiency compared with the current market rate, and the notion of a subjective rate for inter-temporal preferences.

At the same time, engineers were starting to use discounting in the evaluation of investments, especially in the railroad industry. Nevertheless, according to Jones and Smith (1982, pp. 104–5), although the importance of discounting logic increased during the interwar period, cost evaluation (costing) still seems to be the key point at this time, at least in the applied American literature, and few efforts were devoted to the development of the discounting-related techniques.

On their part, economists seem to highlight the productive and material aspects of capital as related to some technical constraints, undoubtedly since the focus on production costs, inherited from the classical approach, was maintained as benchmark for long-term markets' equilibria.[44] According to Solomon (1987), we had to wait for the end of the Second World War, in particular the 1950s and 1960s, for the development of a body of coherent doctrine in this field, more precisely the optimal employment of funds devoted to investments in capital account.[45] At the same time, in the USA initially and then in Europe, the logic of discounting continued to spread throughout corporate practices, in principle at least.[46]

If we want to go beyond recognizing a simple shift of the intellectual benchmarks between the eras, the idea of the maximum developed by Duvillard can suggest to the modern reader: (a) an unorthodox economic perspective on the relationship between capital, time and discounting; (b) a renewed formulation of the maximum, which would regard it as an endogenous optimal duration for the investment in question.[47]

The discounting technique makes it possible to take time into account in corporate decision making; it is, in particular, possible to consider interest as a 'price for time' and to compute this price among other costs and revenues of those investment projects that have to be assessed and ranked.

As also claimed by Fama (1996, p. 427), the *measures* of this price pose problems of a technical as well as a logical nature, as soon as it is a question of situating the present decision in the context of future development and, more generally, of the future of the firm itself. As we can see in Appendix I and in Biondi (forthcoming), contemporary authors still question the 'reinvestment problem' and the related reference rate; Duvillard suggests to them not to reduce this analysis to a linear preference for the present (point a), provided simply by a negative exponential weight on the future states (the assumption of compound interest). We can, on the contrary, consider these measurements as the search for a synthetic value to compare investments, in order to obtain a simple quantity that we can substitute for the quantities given without misunderstanding our overall vision of the situation. The analysis carried out on the general series of cash flows lies in the search for a weighted mean of the series in question. It is necessary to establish the weights according to the requirements under consideration by the actual decision maker(s).[48] Following Duvillard's insight, it would then be the case for a generalized discounted value with two discounting rates, one for investment outflows (y) and the other for reinvestment inflows (i):[49]

$$\sum_{t=1}^{n} f(1+i;1+y;t;a_t)\cdot a_t$$

or, in the continuous case:

$$\int_{1}^{n} f(y;i;t;a_t)\cdot a_t dt$$

The assumptions of a single discount rate and that of the simple or compound discount rate are expressed by a function $f(y;\ i;\ t;\ a)$ which takes into account the relation between capital and time under consideration by the decision maker, generally regarded as independent of the values of $a(t)$.[50]

Thus we reach the idea of the maximum that is at the heart of the *Recherches*. The relevant theoretical context seems to be that of jointly financed projects, where several different agents take part in the same investment (point b). Although every real situation moves away from the world of perfect and complete markets (PCM), we could sometimes regard this as one sort of approximate idealization. But, as Hirshleifer (1987, p. 994) explains, the concept of wealth or discounted value is defined without ambiguity only within this framework of PCM. Only in this case we can define investment decision criteria independently of subjective preferences while taking into account risks and beliefs.

In all the other cases, Hirshleifer (1987) suggests a unanimity rule for investment choice under jointly financed projects, a rule which establishes, in particular, a conventional discount rate to employ in computing the present value even with incomplete or imperfect markets. Duvillard's framework also deviates from the idealized world of PCM, since it explicitly supposes two different interest rates for the investment and the reinvestment, in an economic analysis that is far from efficient financial market logic (subsection 3.3).

Within this context, perhaps a more realistic one, the maximum proposed by Duvillard may provide the decision maker(s) with an optimal duration for financing, linked to the investment's profitability, which we can apply, for example, to the endogenous completion of a concession, whereas the contractual and institutional framework regulating contracts removes it from the world of PCM by fixing, through long-term agreements, tariffs, quantities produced, further decisions to be taken, etc. In this respect, it would be interesting to generalize Duvillard's maximum to any series of cash flows and to verify the conditions for existence.[51]

3.3 The relation between capital funds and interest flows

In Duvillard's analysis, we can see emerging what strangely resembles the modern notion of 'capital as a sinking fund', which also evokes the work of the Revd Richard Price, in England, known for his theories on debt amortization based on applying compound interest.[52] Thiveaud (1994, p. 5) explains this logical and epistemological change, as follows:

> Between simple interest and compound interest, a passage between a discontinuous time and a continuous time operates, making the distinction between capital and its interest price vanish. Compound interest brings a more sophisticated credit system than simple interest, transforming the definitions of the deposit and the agent.

Duvillard seems to consider the initial expenditure as much of the annuity as cash flows, at least from an analytical and quantitative viewpoint.[53] As we saw earlier, annuities, life as well as constant, confuse the capital installments and the payment of interest.

In a report written in 1790 and further modified in year XI (1800), Duvillard briefly approaches the origin of his 'theory of the interest on money':[54]

> Calculation [by social mathematics] can only be immediately applied to one thing at a time, and its uses would be very limited, if men had not been led by the necessity of establishing a common measure of valuing more than one thing. But the existence of this common measurement makes it possible to make comparison between things, and to subject them to calculation in spite of their natural differences from which we make abstraction.
>
> The value of a thing can not be the same as if we consider it as actually and absolutely available, compared to if it was only available for a time and after that time it must cease being that thing for the same individual, compared to what it will grow to at a certain time.
>
> These various considerations apply to all the things for which we cannot draw a service without deteriorating them, or whose alterations can be evaluated. On this ground the theory of what we call the interest on money can be established. (Duvillard, quoted by Thuillier 1997, p. 149).

In this, Duvillard establishes a relation between the availability of a thing in time, its effective use and its value. As for Condorcet, 'the theory of amounts suitable for proportional increases with time … contain that of the interest on money'[55] (Duvillard, quoted in ibid., p. 151). In continuing this text, he affirms, once again, the existence of his maximum, which is the most remarkable result of his *Recherches*, in particular in the case of a loan. From this point of view, interest can no longer simply be the price of capital, to echo Thiveaud (1994) quoted above, but it becomes a consequence of the use of the funds themselves.[56] In the logic of Duvillard, as well as that of Condorcet and Vasco, the discount requires a specific justification, which they found in the idea of the actual reinvestment of the received funds, thus allowing the equivalence between present and future times.

Often, in the *Recherches*, the author imagines the funds borrowed as destined to give profits:

> I have supposed here that the borrower could put forward the 3 8/99; because I suppose that any borrower, whatever he is, only takes capital to make profits; such, for example, borrows on the 5 to put forward on the 10, & could by consequence be paying the 6. It is true that one could imagine that a

borrower only made a loan to pay a debt; but then he would do a bad deal for himself & the lenders, & he wouldn't find credit ... (Duvillard 1787, p. 85)

In this context, each loan (or refunding) is regarded as giving rise to an investment at a given rate, the discount being possible and justified only if this investment (reinvestment) exists; it is likely that Duvillard (1787, pp. 70–71) grounds his analysis on the fundamentally different positions taken by the borrowers, who really hold funds, and by the lenders, who only receive annual refunds throughout the loan in question, a difference which leads him to develop his theory of optimal duration.

On the one hand, Duvillard introduces the idea of sinking fund capital, but on the other, he considers that all types of debts must have a lucrative goal; one can thus regard these debts as 'paying the loans with the funds devoted to this lucrative goal' (Duvillard 1787, pp. 85–6). It is also necessary to note that Duvillard strongly distinguishes the activity of trading by bankers from productive debts with a lucrative goal; he thus does not seem to consider the role of banks in credit making as a source of financing for productive activities.

His analysis of compound interest on capital invested in sinking funds does not accept the contemporaneous idea of 'time value of money', in which discounting is based on the concept of the opportunity cost of money.[57] The modern concept considers investment as an arbitrage between the present and the future; agents do not feel the same attraction for an immediate satisfaction compared to a satisfaction which is to come; the discount rate then constitutes a measure of the intensity of present preference (time preference) which exists independently of the notion of interest rate.[58]

Duvillard imagines, on the contrary, that the notion of interest rate consists of an actual and systematic reinvestment of capital and its interest rate. The four methods of discounting, taken into account throughout *Recherches* (see subsection 3.1), correspond indeed to several cases of reinvestment, in the case of accumulation that is complete (compound interest), or partial (simple interest), or without any accumulation (no interest drawn for reinvestment).

In his review of Duvillard (1787), Vasco (1787) also concludes that the true 'lost profit' (*lucrum cessans*) or the 'added loss' (*damnum emergens*) is the justification for applying accrued (or compounded) interest to monetary investments; by consequence this analysis is useless for somebody who dissipates his capital and proceeds without making them bear fruit.

If we want to situate Duvillard among 'pioneers of financial economics', we can view him as the first to apply an optimizing method from the viewpoint of the individual agent, by formalizing it using differential calculus. Even though D. Bernoulli and P. Frisi had already applied differential calculus, the first did not use it to optimize, and the second was limited to calculating a 'social' optimum.[59] Duvillard analyzes this optimum from an individual viewpoint, one might say microeconomic today, and draws some valid consequences for the public welfare in general, and for the state in particular. He associates with the *DIRR* the possibility of an exact reconciliation between the burden of the borrower and the benefits of the lenders, calculated 'by an economic order to be established in the timing of the repayments'[60] (Duvillard 1787, p. 119).[61]

However, we cannot completely agree with Baumol and Goldfeld (1968, p. 152) that 'Duvillard of Durand did show noteworthy ingenuity in his approach and may perhaps be considered the father of the (rather unfortunate) internal-rate-of-return measure for the desirability of an investment.' According to his analytical and theoretical framework, Duvillard aims to distinguish the apparent interest rate for the lender, the actual return calculated and the current interest rate of the market. Duvillard does not consider the *DIRR* as 'the expected rate of return', in today's sense of 'expectated'; nor it is like a measurement of desirability, but like the real profitability of the loan for the lender. We observe this in his work as well as in his 'memories'.[62] As observed by Vasco (1787), Duvillard (1787) bases his analysis on the future value of the series of proceeds refunded and is also concerned with the context in which the evaluation is made:

> I suppose here that the annuities are clear of all costs & free from reserves; that there is no default; that they are made up on a well selected basis; that the annual increase in the *numeraire* will not appreciably weaken the value of the annuities in time to come; & that the bankers provide them at the purchase price. (Ibid., p. 66, note 18).

The *DIRR* is not a measurement of the desirability of the investment, which the author finds expressed at his time, even if in a misleading way, by the apparent rate of the annuity r (=a/c).

> However, 1st, I already showed that, even in the case of constant annuities, far from the profits from interest of the lenders increasing with the rate which the borrower supports, when the annuities are higher & of long duration; these profits of interest decrease after a certain time. But 2nd this disproportion between the (apparent) return of the loan, & the (actual) return of the lenders, will diminish as they could accumulate at a higher interest, & completely disappeared if they can be accumulated at the return of the loan. Thus it is generally shown that in the life annuities involving a large return & of long duration, the borrower has pure loss of a burden of interests from which nobody benefits; that, by consequence, this form of refunding is flawed & that it would wish, for the interest of everyone, that one can modify it in such a way that they did no more have the double disadvantage I mentioned above. (Ibid., pp. 69–70)

In his review of Duvillard (1787), Vasco (1787 p. 722) also harshly criticizes the speculators who would like to gain a rate higher than the current level without accepting the related risks and thus losses. He then accepts the analysis of Duvillard about the true profitability of the placement for speculators.

Finally, if Duvillard undoubtedly has recourse to the virtues of quantitative economic analysis, he does not seem to relate them to the logic of market adjustments, because otherwise:

- he would have proposed, as did Price (1772), some arbitration on the actual market prices of the annuities (much below the value known as real);[63]
- he would have noticed that we ought to find the same interest rate for the loan as for the debt (Fisher's separation principle) within the framework of 'complete and perfect markets', i.e., of one unique 'capital market'.

In the practice of the time, the capital and the debt are not yet, as in the modern theory of financial economics, completely equivalent from a financial perspective. By his analysis, and its mathematical method, Duvillard takes a step towards these current financial theories, but he remains at an intermediate level of abstraction, preserving a concern with realism related to the context and the practices of his time.

4. Summary and conclusion

In spite of his contributions to various fields, such as demography, social mathematics, and finally to the insurance and financial economics, the work of Duvillard has been largely neglected.

According to the recent studies by Thuillier (1997), Israël (1991) and Crépel (1900), this brilliant 'geometrician' was a closely related to Condorcet and was one of the passionate promoters of the application of quantitative analysis to political and moral sciences. In this chapter, we have discussed the economic contribution of the author, whom we can see as a pioneer of modern financial economics, as much for the invention of the *DIRR* as for the application of differential calculus. Duvillard pioneered optimization from the viewpoint of the individual agent, further drawing valid implications for public welfare and the state's financial policies.

However, the shift between times, intellectual frameworks, ways of viewing and of writing, suggests a comparative perspective. The economic views of the author led him to develop the logic of optimization and economic analysis without framing them in the logic of one unique, efficient financial market. This approach is certainly distinct from the contemporary approach, but it allows Duvillard to invent an original optimizing technique able to suggest valuable financial policies for the difficult financial conditions of his time.

Who actually invented the modified internal rate of return (*MIRR*)? The answer suggests some intriguing issues in a comparative perspective. Although Duvillard made his analysis a long time ago, it still provides valuable insights on the relationship between *MIRR* and time. He emphasizes a connection that the recent debate has neglected. Even though Baldwin (1959) fully develops the generalized approach and discusses the critical relationship between the double rate of reference and the project's economic life in real time, he does not derive from them the optimal rate. Bernhard (1979) actually finds it, but he did not analyze its implications, limiting himself to a short, odd criticism of the related generalization.

The differences between the present and the past are obvious and significant, but recent theoretical debate renews such old ideas as 'replacement rate' and 'reinvestment problem'. In this context, Duvillard would find its own 'reversed modernity' (Biondi forthcoming). He used not only two discount rates of reference, but also many discounting methods. Indeed, Duvillard's analysis may suggest to the modern reader both (a) an open, realist understanding of time and discounting, and (b) a reformulation of his optimal rate, which we can still understand as the endogenous optimal duration of the investment project.

The modern framework for investment evaluation criteria (point a) aims to enhance corporate decision making. It is especially concerned with ranking different investment projects by means of synthetic scores such as *IRR* or *NPV*. Discounting allows for financial timing in these scores.

According to Fama (1996, p. 427), nevertheless, it is hard to account for the financial valuation of time, since this valuation is related to future states and conditions of the firm: 'A fundamental open question nevertheless remains. Given the massive uncertainties inherent in all aspects of project valuation, does a [compound] discounting rule produce [reliable] value estimates …? … The [usual affirmative] conclusion is based more on faith than evidence.' In this perspective, the contemporaneous approach is still concerned with issues like 'reinvestment rate' and 'reinvestment problem' (see Appendix I), especially if the idealized world of perfect and complete markets is in question. The usual assumption of a unique discount rate implies a strong preference for the present, calculated by charging future cash flows with an exponentially increasing weight (compound interest discounting). But, as Duvillard early suggested, different discounting methods provide different sequences of weights. The statistical notion of mean would fit better, indeed, with generalizing the relationship between time and decision making. Compound or simple discounting become two special methods of weighting cash flows into synthetic scores to rank investment opportunities.[64]

In this perspective, the optimal rate discovered by Duvillard (point b) may relate to joint-financed projects undertaken by agreement from different investors under conditions other than perfect and complete markets. In this context, as Hirshleifer (1987, p. 994a) states, a further possibility exists of a conventional rule within the firm, agreed by all the investors (unanimity). This rule may declare a conventional discounting rate that should be employed in calculating discounted value. If the technique developed by Duvillard were applied as rule, it would provide investors with an endogenous economic term for capital investments by means of his internal optimal value.

Appendix I The second birth of the modified internal rate of return

Although they had already been considered by the marginalist revolutionaries as early as the end of the nineteenth century, investment evaluation techniques based on discounting only acquired a central role in a coherent framework of reference and analysis in the 1950s and 1960s (Solomon 1987).

We are facing here a frequent paradox in the history of economic thought: when a logic such as discounting becomes dominant, at least from a theoretical viewpoint, difficulties of a technical and theoretical nature are highlighted, at least in certain cases, especially since, in this case, its mathematical design was deepened and improved. This debate thus raised certain epistemological questions and gave rise, on the one hand, to a financial measure that is the analogue of the *DIRR* invented by Duvillard, and, on the other, old-fashioned ideas such as the reinvestment problem and the reference rate. Questions arise especially in the case of what these authors call the 'pump project'. This case implies the following series of cash flows, initially presented in Lorie and Savage (1955; see Solomon, 1956, p. 128):

Period	Cash flows from the investment during the period
t_0	–$1 600
t_1	+10 000
t_2	–10 000

The second degree equation (4), $NPV_{irr} = 0$, which defines the *IRR*, gives then two results: *IRR* = 0.25 or *IRR* = 4, i.e. the internal rate of return is 25 percent or 400 percent. Thus Lorie and Savage (1955, p. 161) conclude that:

> The [internal] rate-of-return criterion [*IRR*] for judging the acceptability of investment proposals, as it has been presented in published works, is then ambiguous and anomalous. This is in contrast to the clarity and uniform accuracy of the decisions indicated by the principle proposed earlier, which relates to the present value of an investment at the cost of capital [*NPV*] rather than to a comparison between the cost of capital and the rate of return. (Also quoted by Teichroew et al., 1965b)

In this kind of project, Hirshleifer (1958, p. 349bf.) also confirms the validity of the *NPV*, but he nevertheless agrees to generalize the *IRR* to the *MIRR*.[65] Furthermore, the analysis carried out by Teichroew et al. (1965b, p. 161) leads us to question the usual preference, so widespread in academic circles, for the *NPV* (DPV in the quotation below) over the *IRR*:

The present value of project E [pump project] as a function of rate *i* … reaches a maximum of $900 for i = 100 % and then decreases. … *DPV* = 0 for *i* = 25 % and 400 %. Under the Discounted Present Value (*DPV*) rule the project would be acceptable (i.e., P(*i*) ≥ 0) if the rate is greater than or equal to 25 % but less than or equal to 400 %.

The present value [of project E] is negative for rates less than 25 % or greater than 400 %; e.g., P(.10) = $ –760. Consequently this project would be rejected by firms with ρ < .25 and > 4.00 and would be accepted by a firm in which .25 ≤ ρ ≤ 4.00. *Clearly there is something strange in the implication that a firm with* ρ *[discount rate, cost of capital] = .20 would not accept this project, but would accept the project if it could only increase its* ρ … *to over 25 %; moreover it would attach a greater and greater value (present value) to the project as it increased its cost of capital up to 100 %.* (Italics added)

Therefore, the three authors accept the *NPV* with a single discount rate only in certain cases, but they introduce several rates in the other cases: they then suggest a new technique to generalize the *NPV*, based on a recursive *fund method* that is applied on the series of balances of the project.

Other authors suggest using several discount rates to generalize discounting starting from a *flow method.* Solomon (1956) seems to be the first to apply this flow method to the 'pump project' case. He stresses that, if we apply the current method of the *IRR* and *NPV* in such a case, we will have odd results: 'The more the pump costs, the more 'profitable' the project becomes!' (1956, p. 128b). On the contrary:

The correct solution for the investment worth of the [pump project] is simple and straightforward. But it requires an explicit answer to a relevant question 'What is it worth to the investor to receive $10,000 one year earlier than he would have otherwise received it? (Solomon 1956, p. 129a)

He thus introduces a return x to which the investor replaces cash inflows from the project, i.e. he has recourse to the same 'replacement rate' as Duvillard (1787) did in his *Researches.*

If x is 23 per cent, for example, getting $10,000 a year earlier is worth $2,300. In other words, if he spent $1,600 on the larger pump now (at time t_0), he would end up at time t_2 having $2,300 more than he otherwise would have had. (Ibid., p. 129a).

This is the same logic that was applied by Duvillard. The 'pump project' allows the investor to gain $10000 at time t_1, but forces him to spend the same amount ($10000) at time t_2. Solomon (1956) then proposes calculating the rate at which the future value (at time t_2) of the start-up capital ($1600) is equal to the future value (at time t_2) of the series of cash inflows, the replacement rate for the latter being $x = 23$ percent.

This can be stated as an equivalent 'rate of return', which in this case would be about 20 per cent ($1,600 at 20 per cent per annum would amount to $2,304 at the end of two years). Using this approach, a unique and meaningful rate of return can always be found for any set of cash inflows and outflows (ibid., p. 129a).

This 'equivalent rate of profitability', which we called *MIRR*, was developed more fully by Baldwin (1959). This author refuses nevertheless to limit its application to such a case as the 'pump project'. On the contrary, he considers it as a comprehensive generalization, leading to a better comprehension of the principles that underlie discounting, to more effective planning and to higher profits.[66]

> It is to one critical assumption underlying the usual procedure [present value and *IRR*] that I take strong exception. The future receipts and payments are reduced to their present value by discounting them at the same rate as that which the proposed investment is estimated to provide.
>
> In other words, management assumes that, for the period between the base point and the time when the funds are spent or collected, the funds are, or could be, invested at the rate of return being calculated for the proposal.
>
> This is simply not true. Indeed, it is only by coincidence that the two would be at all alike. The funds would be at work during the interim period not at a rate similar to that of the proposed investment, but at the average rate at which general corporate funds are being invested – at the over-all value of money to the company ... It is at this rate that future cash flows must be discounted to reflect its present value in terms of the realities of the particular company's operations.[67] (Baldwin 1959, pp. 98b–99a)

In summary, some authors, such as Solomon (1956) or Teichroew et al. (1965a),[68] consider that the *MIRR* method applies only in the case where the *IRR* does not work well. Other authors, such as Baldwin (1959), Athansopoulos (1978) and also Lin (1976), nevertheless, consider it as a generalized criterion of choice, especially since it is unique and easy to calculate in all cases.

> The salient advantage of Effective Rate of Return [*ERR*] method [here, *MIRR*], compared to all others, is that it combines the recognized reliability of the net present value criteria with the ease of interpretation and understanding inherent in a rate of return (percentage) analysis ... .
>
> In view of this clear advantage for the *ERR* technique, serious consideration [to using this technique] as the sole criterion for investment profitability is merited. (Athansopoulos 1978, p. 132b)

From this perspective, the analysis carried out by Duvillard on the relation between the *MIRR* and time may acquire its own modernity. We have reviewed some of the classics of the last decades on the topic, without claiming comprehensive: the author who has dealt more thoroughly with this relationship is Baldwin (1959), but he does not refer to the existence of the maximum discovered by Duvillard. Bernhard (1979) mentions its existence, but only to criticize the use of such criteria as *MIRR*.

Appendix II Duvillard's *Recherches* (1787): the structure of the work

Duvillard (1787) organizes his essay in six parts:

1. Exposition of the subject (pp. 1–17)
2. Constant annuities (pp. 18–38)
3. Increasing or decreasing annuities (pp. 38–54)
4. Life annuities (pp. 54–83)
5. Means of making lenders gain the greatest advantages that they can from life annuities, without charging too much to the borrower (pp. 83–115)
6. Summary

We can distinguish two developments in the analysis provided by Duvillard (1787):

1. Theoretical analysis, i.e. the core of the work (parts 1, 2 and 3).
2. Its application to life annuities (parts 4 and 5).

According to the theoretical scope of our analysis, we have focused especially on the first development and examined Duvillard's economic views and analysis.

Notes

1. As Voltaire explains at the beginning of this novel, if we counted the income of the nation (in the eighteenth-century sense) and shared it among all the people, everyone would receive 40 Ecus. The Man of Forty Ecus, indeed, stands here for the common man.
2. Guy Thuillier (1997) has written a reference work on Duvillard, publishing a selection of texts that were for the most part not previously published. Giorgio Israël (1991, 1993) also carried out an in-depth study related to *Social Mathematics*. These two authors base their work on manuscripts of the Bibliothèque National Français (N.a.fr. 20576-20591) for which Thuillier (1997, pp. 495–508) gives the first inventory. Moreover, in the eighteenth century, Vasco and Condorcet became interested in the financial analysis developed by Duvillard. While, more recently, Baumol and Goldfeld (1968) and Crépel (1990) have addressed certain specific aspects of Duvillard's financial work, studies on the subject remain occasional.
3. See Thuillier (1997, pp. 391–448), which publishes the report of Dr Odier in the British Library and other significant materials.
4. See Dupâquier (1985, pp. 258–61). On the quarrel, see Desrosières (2000, pp. 48–54).
5. See Dupâquier (1985, pp. 245–6) and Israël (1991, pp. 29 and n. 113).
6. Second letter of M. Duvillard, Archives of the Academy of Sciences, Institute of France, Paris, meeting cover of 31 May 1813, quoted according to Israël (1991, p. 34 and 1993, p. 75), italics in the original text.
7. There are many studies on this subject in Thuillier (1997) and Crépel (1990). This question is also examined later in this chapter.
8. When the interest rate is equal to i, the present value of a sum S due at time t is equal, at time $t = 0$, to $S/(1+i)^t$.
9. On usury and the emerging spirit of capitalism, see, for example, the brief synthesis provided by Le Goff (1986).
10. On this tradition, see in general Poitras (2000).
11. However, we will leave aside his remarkable analysis of the mutual life insurance companies. Duvillard refers explicitly to the 'Equitable Society of London' (1787, p. 77, note), perhaps the first mutual life insurance company founded in 1762 on a scientific theory: Richard Price was a technical adviser to this company (Equitable Society) and contributed, through his calculations, to its almost fabulous success (Laboucheix, 1970; Poitras 2000). However, an Amicable Society had also been established in London since 1706 (Thiveaud 1996; Poitras 2000).
12. 'Le montant *m* de toutes ces annuités perçues, au moment où l'on cesse de les recevoir'.
13. Historians have insisted for two centuries on the role of this question in the political crisis which led to the French Revolution.
14. Knowing that the limit, when the number of terms n tends towards infinity, of the present value PV_r of an annuity with constant terms is a/r, this definition of r makes the initial capital c equal to the present value.
15. As noted by Vasco (1787). We could compare this to the modern view expressed by Schlacther (1989, p. 66).
16. 'Car il s'en faut bien qu'accumulant leurs rentes dans ce commerce à un intérêt si fort au-dessous de celui que l'Emprunteur supporte, ils puissent porter leurs profits aussi haut que les sacrifices de l'Emprunteur semblent le promettre.'
17. This original formula from the author (Duvillard 1787, p. 20) is obtained by replacing i by y in (1b).
18. We believe that his analysis rests first and foremost on the search for the real or effective rate of the transaction, an analysis close to the contemporary notion of the actuarial rate of borrowing, that is the rate which equalizes the present value of the cash flows corresponding to the respective engagements of the borrowers and lenders (Duvillard 1787, pp. 62, 70–72). Indeed, it should be noted that, from a technical point of view, the contemporary definitions of the actuarial rate and the internal rate of return (*IRR*) are equal; this influence of actuarial mathematics on contemporary financial analysis can be traced in particular to Walras (see subsection 3.2).
19. See Appendix I and Biondi (forthcoming).
20. See Duvillard (1787, p. 19, note 7), which refers to his graphs. Besides, the author gives other graphic interpretations for various calculations (ibid., pp. 3, 8, etc.).
21. Duvillard often reasons using joint graphs and explaining the relations between the variables by these curves. He does it, for example, in his presentation of the various manners of discounting (see subsection 3.1).
22. To see how Duvillard proceeds:

    With t being variable, what value should it take for y to be at a maximum? For this, will differentiate the equation and have ($L = ln$):

    $$aq^t dtLq - i(1+y)^t dtL(1+y) = ti(1+y)^{t-1} dy;$$

    putting $dy = 0$, we then have

    $$\frac{aq^t Lq}{i} = (1+y)^t L(1+y)$$

an equation which, divided by the equation given in (7) in the text, leaves

$$\frac{q^t Lq}{q^t - 1} = L(1+y) = \frac{1}{t} L\left(\frac{a}{i}(q^t - 1)\right)$$

or

$$q^{tq^t/(q^t-1)} = \frac{a(q^t - 1)}{i}$$

$$= (1+y)^t = Q^t.$$

(Duvillard, 1787, p. 22)

23. Here in the words of Duvillard ($L = ln$):

> In the given equation $a(q^t - 1)/i = (1 + y)^t = Q^t$ or $\sqrt[t]{a/i(q^t - 1)} = Q$, we will assume that we will solve for t, provided that the value from which y will result is positive; that is, we will assume $t > L(1 + i/a)Lq$. We will substitute the value of Q which will result from this assumption of t in the following equation $x = (L(aLq) - L(iLQ))/(LQ - Lq)$, for which all the logarithms can be taken from common tables, we make $t = x$ in the equation $\sqrt[t]{a/i(q^t - 1)} = Q'$; we will substitute the new value for Q' which will result in equation $x = (L(aLq) - L(iLQ'))/(LQ' - Lq)$ we will have a value already very approximate to the time for the maximum gain from interest; and we will also iteratively approach the actual solution every time that we repeat the operation. For example, either $a = 0.1 : i = 0.05 : \& \ t = 22$ from which $Q = 1.063199$; we will have … , $x = 37.2387$, $Q' = \sqrt[31]{a/i(q^{37} - 1)} = 1.0646737$; $x' = 31.906$; $Q'' = \sqrt[31]{a/i(q^{37} - 1)} = 1.0651546$; $x'' = 30.40076$, which is very near the time for the sought maximum. This method results from a remark that I make hereafter on another curve. (Duvillard, 1787, pp. 23–4)

24. Letter of Mr Duvillard, Archive of the Academy of Sciences, Institute of France, Paris, portfolio of the meeting of 31 May 1813, quoted according to Israël (1993, p. 74).
25. 'Il fait ainsi participer cette partie des Mathématiques mixtes aux progrès que les Géomètres modernes ont fait faire à l'Analyse'; see their report on Duvillard's work with respect to 'l'Etablissement d'une caisse national d'epargne' (session of the Academy of Sciences, the 11 vendémiaire year V (2.10.1796)). See also Thuiller (1997, pp. 188–234, p. 238 for the quote) and Israël (1993, pp. 61–6, in particular p. 63).
26. As usual in financial calculations of this kind, we proceed with simulations of the optimization. They show that this maximum has been accurately calculated by Duvillard.
27. That is, the number of years such that the net present value (*NPV*) is zero. Duvillard applies this calculation of the zero at the same time in the case of reinvestment with compound interest, with simple interest and with no interest.
28. In fact, Duvillard uses an interesting personal method on this subject, which we will not comment on here, because it has no remote relationship to our theme.
29. See Appendix I and Biondi (forthcoming).
30. This is the case of the famous 'bankruptcy of two thirds' (Thuillier 1997, p. 231), which occurred on 30 November 1797 (9 vendémiaire year VI). Two-thirds of the debt was then refunded in 'papers'.
31. Letter of Mr Duvillard, Archives of the Academy of Sciences, Institute of France, Paris, portfolio of the meeting of 10 May 1813, quoted according to Israël (1993, pp. 68–9). We can see several sentences in this text which resemble an autobiographical text of Duvillard published by Thuillier (1997, 'Souvenirs').
32. See Duvillard (1787, p. 117 and also p. 87). In other words, beyond the maximum, all occurs as if part of the money were sterilized. This idea is also taken up in the quotations below.
33. This is between paragraphs LXIII (p. 83) and LXXXXIX (p. 115).
34. This solution is adopted by Vasco (1787) in his report.
35. Ross M. Robertson (1949), pp. 524–7. Frisi's and Buquoy's use of the calculus is somewhat peripheral, and in an inspection of the latter one may well question whether his writing can reasonably be called as 'economics' (note from Baumol and Goldfeld).
36. Nevertheless, these two authors are the only ones who were interested specifically in the financial analysis developed by Duvillard. See also Crépel (1990).
37. They undoubtedly refer to the heroic assumption that no such things as multiple interest rates and diversified capital markets exist. In this case, we have one unique interest rate for investing and financing.
38. See Appendix I and Biondi (forthcoming).
39. For the definitions see for example (Schlacther 1989, p. 16). Poitras (2000) addresses discounting methods from a historical perspective in chapter V, 'Simple Interest and Compound Interest'. Some economists are more inter-

ested in simple or hyperbolic discounting from a theoretical perspective; see Laibson (1997, Loewenstein and Thaler 1989); for other references, see Biondi (2002).

40. See also Schlacther (1989). Further, note that compound discounting makes the greatest future value with the smallest discount rate.
41. In the contributions to the Kehi edition of the works of Voltaire, with the last volumes appearing in 1789, Condorcet does not seem convinced that the arrangements relative to the life annuities can be changed 'without injustice'; the life annuities loans have great disadvantages: 'we are always capable of changing, through regulated reimbursements, a perpetual annuity loan with a fixed term, and we can not, without injustice, change anything to the life annuities once established; … '. (Condorcet 1994, p. 663). We might infer that this undated fragment of Condorcet is posterior to Duvillard's work.
42. It has been named the 'Baldwin rate, effective rate of return' (Athansopoulos 1978) and finally the modified internal rate of return (Lin 1976); see Athansopoulos (1978). Cf. Biondi (forthcoming) for further analysis.
43. See also Alchian (1955), in particular on I. Fisher and J.M. Keynes. We should nevertheless note that the Keynesian concept of liquidity preference distinguishes the interest rate and inter-temporal preferences.
44. According to Gintschel (1999, p. 327), Fisher has the same perspective: 'Interestingly, Fisher (*Theory of Interest*, New York, 1930) fleshes out his theory by analyzing how the investment opportunity set can be derived from the underlying technology. Unlike most modern financial economists, Fisher interprets his investment opportunity set as more than a collection of cash-flow vectors. Rather, it is has a complete characterization of available technology.'
45. 'Dean's work triggered much academic activity on the discounted cash-flow technique. In 1956, a trade journal, *The Engineering Economist*, was founded to encourage the dissemination of ideas on newly developed capital budgeting techniques, and textbooks soon followed to establish the acceptance of discounted cash-flows among academic scholars and teachers' (Johnson and Kaplan 1987, p. 164); see also Miller (1998).
46. At that time, some empirical studies contested their concrete application. See Bierman-Smidt (1993, pp. 77–78 and Klammer 1972, p. 387).
47. Tirole (1999) refers to an 'optimal endogenous duration' applied to highway concession, calculated by a rule based on present values of future gross revenues. This retrospective renewal can also be supported if we consider two investments of different profitability, both used until their optimal duration. The optimal *DIRR* leads to choosing, as common sense would suggest, that investment which has the highest profitability *r*.
48. Flemming and Wright (1971) also refer to the statistical concept of the mean to frame *IRR*'s analysis. Cf. Biondi (2005) for further developments.
49. For simplicity, we do not generalize this formula to a series of rates instead of a single rate.
50. If the idea of funds' reinvestment is accepted, one knows that the internal rate is not directly comparable to the current interest rate; the usual comparison between the risk-free rate and the investment returns should be based on the simple discount rate, which we can derive as either the present or future value, or the related internal rate. Moreover, different *IRR*s calculated from the various reinvestment assumptions can constitute a ranking spectrum, while the usual techniques work on just one single value. Lastly, the case without reinvestment (where *i* is zero), excludes the time value of money from the analysis and could constitute a sort of borderline case, suitable for project assessment with a technological or strategic predominance (Baldwin 1959, p. 103a) rather than financial; in this case, the sums have the same value in every present or future instance. There is no established preference between present and future amounts (Biondi 2002 and 2005).
51. Cf. Biondi (2005) for further developments.
52. As with Duvillard, Price was critical of the opposition to life annuities; see Laboucheix (1970) and Poitras (2000).
53. See also Vasco (1787), who, within the general framework of a risky investment in capital, considers that any interest rate higher than the current level will be transformed into a present or future loss of capital.
54. It seems that there is an influence between the '*General Table*' of Condorcet and this '*Mémoire on the utility of a geometrician's place in government and a chair of applied mathematics to the social interest*' of Duvillard, see Israël (1993, pp. 48 and 58–9) and Thuillier (1997, pp. 144–5).
55. 'La théorie des grandeurs susceptibles d'accroissements proportionnels au temps, … renferme celle de l'intérêt de l'argent'.
56. See also Vasco (1787, pp. 715–16).
57. 'Subjective time-preference rate', according to an expression used by Hirshleifer (1958).
58. Nevertheless, if an agent can invest money, we can consider that he deprives himself of interest, which is the idea of opportunity cost.
59. Cf. Robertson (1949); Tubaro (2002).
60. 'Un ordre économique à établir dans les époques des payments'.
61. See also Thuillier (1997, p. 38).
62. See Theocharis (1983, p. 85).
63. On this topic, French reader can refer to Laboucheix (1970, pp. 32–6).
64. Cf. Biondi (2005) for further developments.

65. For generalization, Hirshleifer credits Solomon (1956). At this time, the controversy about the multiplicity of the internal rates of return led also to the theoretical development of the *truncation theorem*, based on the unrestrained possibility of truncating investment projects at any age different from their complete lifetime and at no extra costs (Arrow and Levhari 1969, Flemming and Wright 1971; Sen 1975, Eatwell 1975), a solution that factually is scarcely viable.
66. On the 'discounting approach', see also Price (1993).
67. We should note here that, even if a change in the level of *MIRR* modifies the internal profitability of the project, nevertheless this change does not modify the ranking between different alternatives.
68. See Athansopoulos (1978) for other references.

Bibliography

Historical references

Condorcet, Marquis de (1994), *Arithmétique politique. Textes rares ou inédits (1767–1789)* (*Political Arithmetic. Rare and Unpublished Texts (1767–1789)*), critical edition by Bernard Bru and Pierre Crépel, Paris: Institut National d'Études Démographiques. 1994.

Duvillard de Durand (Emmanuel-Étienne) (1787), *Recherches sur les rentes, les emprunts et les remboursemens* (*Research on Rents, Loans and Repayments*), Paris and Geneva.

Duvillard de Durand (Emmanuel-Étienne) (1806), *Analyse et tableaux de l'influence de la petite vérole à chaque âge et de celle qu'un préservatif tel que la vaccine peut avoir sur la population et la longévité* (*Analysis and Tables of the Influence of Smallpox at each Age and that which a Preventative such as a Vaccine can have on the Population and Its Longevity*), Paris: Imprimerie Impériale.

Price, Richard (1772), *Observations on Reversionary Payments* (3rd edn), Dublin: James Williams.

Vasco, Gian Battista (1787), 'Compte rendu des *Recherches sur les rentes, les emprunts et les remboursements*' ('Review of *Researches on Rents, Loans and Repayments*'), *Biblioteca Oltermontana*, XI (November 1787), pp. 115–16, in Vasco, G.B., *Opere*, I, Turin: Fondazione Einaudi, 1989, pp. 707–26.

Walras, Léon (1900), *Éléments d'économie politique pure* (*Elements of Pure Political Economy*), IV final edition, Lausanne.

Books and articles concerned with Duvillard's time

Bardet, Jean-Pierre (1977), 'Aux origines du Bureau de la Statistique: Duvillard de Durand (1755–1832)' ('On the origins of the Statistical Office: Duvillard de Durand (1755–1832)'), *Population et Société*, **4** (1980), pp. 154–64.

Baumol, J. William and Goldfeld, M. Stephen (eds) (1968), *Precursors in Mathematical Economics: An Anthology, ch. 10:* 'Duvillard de Durand, J.H.T.: *Recherches sur les rentes, les emprunts et remboursements*', Paris and Geneva, 1787, excerpts from pp. 1–22, London: London School of Economics.

Biondi, Yuri (2002), '*Les Recherches sur les rentes, les emprunts et les remboursemens* par M. Duvillard (Genève 1787) et le taux interne de rentabilité' ('The *Researches on Rent, Loans and Repayments* by M. Duvillard (Geneva 1787) and the internal rate of return'), CAMS no. 205, Série *Histoire du calcul des probabilitiés et de la statistique* no 47, Paris: EHESS, February.

Biondi, Yuri (2003), 'Les "Recherches sur les Rentes" de Duvillard (1987) et le Taux Interne de Rentabilité' ('The *Researches on Rents, Loans and Repayments* by Duvillard (1787) and the internal rate of return'), *Revue d'Histoire des Mathematiques*, **9**: 81–30.

Biondi, Yuri (forthcoming), 'The double emergence of modified internal rate of return: the neglected financial work of Duvillard (1755–1832) in a comparative perspective', *European Journal of Economic Thought*, **13** (3).

Crépel, Pierre (1990), 'Les calculs économiques et financiers de Condorcet pendant la Révolution' ('Condorcet's economic and financial calculus during the French Revolution'), *Économies et Sociétés*, série OEconomia, **13**, pp. 339–50.

Daston, Lorraine (1988), *Classical Probability in the Enlightenment*, New Jersey: Princeton University Press.

Desrosières, Alain (2000), *La politique des grands nombres, Histoire de la raison statistique,* Paris: La Découverte. English translation: *The Politics of Large Numbers. A History of Statistical Reasoning*, Cambridge, MA: Harvard University Press, 1998.

Dupâquier, Jacques et Michel (1985), *Histoire de la démographie. La statistique de la population des origines à 1914* (*History of Demography. Population Statistics to 1914*), Paris: Académique Perrin.

Hampsher-Monk, Ian (ed.) (2005), *The Impact of the French Revolution*, with an Introduction (pp. 1–24), a commented list of further readings (pp. 25–30) and a chapter on Richard Price (pp. 37–55), Cambridge: Cambridge University Press.

Israël, Giorgio (1991), 'El declive de la mathématique sociale y los inicios de la economia matematica en el contexto de los avatares del Institut de France' ('The fall of social mathematics and the rise of mathematical economics within and among the French Institut'), LLULL, *Revistad de la Sociedad española de historia de las ciencias y de las técnicas*, pp. 59–116.

Israël, Giorgio (1993), 'The two paths of the mathematization of the social and economic sciences', *Physics*, **30**, pp. 27–78.

Jonckheere, W.G. (1965), 'La table de mortalité de Duvillard' ('The mortality table of Duvillard'), *Population*, **20**, pp. 865–74.

Laboucheix, Henri (1970), *Richard Price, Théoricien de la Révolution américaine*, Paris: Didier. English translation: *Richard Price as Moral Philosopher and Political Theorist*, trans. S. and D.D. Raphael, Oxford: Oxford University Press (1982).

Le Goff, Jacques (1986), *La bourse et la vie, Économie et religion au Moyen Âge* (*Your Money or your Life: Economics and Religion in the Middle Ages*), Paris: Hachette.

Martin, Thierry (ed.) (2003), *Arithmétique politique dans la France du XVIIIe siècle* (*Political Arithmetic during the Eighteenth Century in France*), Paris: Institut National d'Études Démographiques.

Poitras, Geoffrey (2000), *The Early History of Financial Economics (1478–1776): From Commercial Arithmetic to Life Annuities and Joint Stocks*, Cheltenham, UK and Northampton, MA, USA: Edward Elgar.

Porter, M. Theodore (1995), *Trust in Numbers: The Pursuit of Objectivity in Science and Public Life*, Princeton: Princeton University Press.

Rashid, Salim (2002), 'Review of *The Early History of Financial Economics (1478–1776)*' (Poitras 2000), published by EH.NET, February, available at http://www.eh.net/Bookreview.

Robertson, M. Ross (1949), 'Mathematical Economics before Cournot', *Journal of Political Economy*, **LVII**, pp. 524–7.

Stelling-Michaud, S. et S. (1972), *Le livre du recteur de l'Académie de Genève (1559–1878)* (*The Dean's Book of the Geneva Academy (1559–1878)*), vol. III, Geneva: Droz.

Theocharis, D.R. (1983), *Early Developments in Mathematical Economics*, 2nd edn, London: Macmillan, pp. 84–5.

Thiveaud, Jean-Marie (1994), Condorcet, prévoyance, finance et probabilitiés entre raison et utopie' ('Condorcet: foresight, finance and probabilities among reason and utopia'), Monnaie et Finances chez Condorcet Conference, University of Lyon 2, Lyon, 17–18 June.

Thiveaud, Jean-Marie (1996), 'Le risque et son prix: genèse d'un concept et de son évaluation juridico-financière (XIVe–XVIIe siècles)', ('Risk and its price: the emergence of a concept and of its legal-financial valuation (14th–17th century)'), *Revue d'économie financière*, **37**, pp. 253–74.

Thuillier, Guy (1997), *Le premier actuaire de France: Duvillard (1755–1832)* (*The First French Actuary: Duvillard (1755–1832)*), Paris: Comité d'histoire de la Sécurité sociale.

Tubaro, Paola (2002), 'A case study in early mathematical economics: Pietro Verri and Paolo Frisi, 1772', *Journal of the History of Economic Thought*, **24** (2), June, p. 195–214.

Wise, Norton W. (ed.) (1995), *The Values of Precision*, Princeton: Princeton University Press.

Books and articles concerned with internal rate of return (IRR) and discounting

Alchian, A. Armen (1995), 'The rate of interest, Fisher's rate of return over costs and Keynes' internal rate or return', *American Economic Review*, **XLV** (December), pp. 938–42.

Arrow, J. Kenneth and Levhari, David (1969), 'Uniqueness of the internal rate of return with variable life of investment', *Economic Journal*, **LXXIX**, pp. 560–66.

Athansopoulos, P.J. (1978), 'A note on the modified internal rate of return and investment criterion', *The Engineering Economist*, **23**, pp. 131–3.

Baldwin, H. Robert (1959), 'How to assess investment proposals', *Harvard Business Review*, **37**, pp. 98–104.

Bernhard, R.H. (1979), 'Modified rates return for investment project evaluation. A comparison and critique', *The Engineering Economist*, **24**, pp. 161–7).

Bierman, Harold Jr and Smidt, Seymour (1993), *The Capital Budgeting Decision. Economic Analysis of Investment Projects*, 8th edn, New York: Macmillan.

Biondi, Yuri (2005), 'A generalisation of investment decision criteria to multiple discount rates of reference, and its application to project financing and public–private partnership', working paper of University of St Etienne.

Dean, Joel (1954), 'Measuring the productivity of capital', *Harvard Business Review*, **32** (1954), 120–30.

Eatwell, John (1975), 'A note on truncation theorem', *Kyklos*, **28**, pp. 870–75.

Fama, F. Eugene (1996), 'Discounting under uncertainty', *Journal of Business*, **69**, pp. 415–28.

Flemming, J.S. and Wright, J.F. (1971), 'Uniqueness of the internal rate of return: a generalisation', *Economic Journal*, **LXXXI**, pp. 256–63.

Gintschel, Andreas (1999), 'Beyond Fisher's NPV? Much ado about nothing!', in H.-E. Loef and H.G. Monissen (eds), *The Economics of Irving Fisher*, Cheltenham, UK and Northampton, MA, USA: Edward Elgar, pp. 326–34.

Hirshleifer, Jack (1958), 'On the theory of optimal investment decision', *Journal of Political Economy*, **LXVI**, pp. 329–52.

Hirshleifer, Jack (1987), 'Investment decision criteria', in *The New Palgrave. A Dictionary of Economics*, London: Macmillan, pp. 971–94.
Johnson, H. Thomas and Kaplan, S. Robert (1987), *Relevance Lost. The Rise and Fall of Management Accounting*, Boston, MA: Harvard Business School Press.
Jones, W. Thomas and Smith, J. David (1982), 'An historical perspective of net present value and equivalent annual cost', *Accounting Historians Journal*, **9**, pp. 103–10.
Klammer, Thomas (1972), 'Empirical evidence of the adoption of sophisticated capital budget techniques', *Journal of Business*, **45**, pp. 387–97.
Laibson, David (1997), 'Golden eggs and hyperbolic discounting', *Quarterly Journal of Economics*, **112**, pp. 443–77.
Lin, A.Y. Steven (1976), 'The modified internal rate of return and investment criterion', *The Engineering Economist*, **21**, pp. 237–47.
Loewenstein, George and Thaler, H. Richard (1989), 'Anomalies: intertemporal choice', *Journal of Economic Perspectives*, **3**, pp. 181–93.
Lorie, J. and L. Savage (1955), 'Three Problems in Capital Rationing', *Journal of Business*, **28**, pp. 229–39.
Miller, Peter (1998), 'The margins of accounting', *European Accounting Review*, **7**, pp. 605–21.
Negrete, L. Gabriel (1978), 'The modified internal rate of return and investment criterion: a reply', *The Engineering Economist*, **23**.
Parker, R.H. (1968), 'Discounted cash-flow in historical perspective', *Journal of Accounting Research*, pp. 58–71.
Price , Colin (1993), *Time, Discounting and Value*, Oxford and Cambridge: Blackwell.
Robinson, Romney (1956), 'The rate of interest, Fisher's rate of return over costs and Keynes' internal rate of return: comment', *American Economic Review*, **XLVI**, pp. 972–3.
Samuelson, A. Paul (1937), 'Some aspects of the pure theory of capital', *Quarterly Journal of Economics*, **LI**, pp. 469–96.
Schlacther, Didier (1989), *Calcul financier, Initiation pratique*, esp. ch. 7: 'Les choix d'investissement' (*Financial Calculus: Practical Introduction*, especially ch. 7: 'Investment choices'), Paris: Hachette, pp. 85–96.
Sen, Amartya (1975), 'Minimal conditions for monotonicity of capital value', *Journal of Economic Theory*, **11**, pp. 340–55.
Solomon, Ezra (1956), 'The arithmetic of capital-budgeting decisions', *Journal of Business*, **XXIX**, pp. 124–9.
Solomon, Ezra (1987), 'Capital budgeting', in *The New Palgrave. A Dictionary of Economics*, London: Macmillan, pp. 341–2.
Stigum, M. (1982), *Money Market Calculations*, New York: Dow Jones-Irwin.
Teichroew, Daniel, Robichek, A. Alexander and Montalbano, Michael (1965a), 'Mathematical analysis of rates of return under certainty', *Management Science*, **11**, pp. 395–403.
Teichroew, Daniel, Robichek, A. Alexander and Montalbano, Michael (1965b), 'An analysis of criteria for investment and financing decisions under certainty', *Management Science*, **12**, pp. 151–79.
Tirole, Jean (1999), 'Concessions, concurrence et incitations' ('Concessions, competition and incentives'), *Revue d'économie financière*, **51**, pp. 63–80.

PART III

THE NINETEENTH-CENTURY 'SCIENCE OF FINANCIAL INVESTMENTS'

7 Rational investors, informative prices: the emergence of the 'science of financial investments' and the random walk hypothesis*

Alex Preda

In the second half of the nineteenth century, popular investment literature flourished on both sides of the Atlantic. Consisting of advice manuals, stock exchange descriptions and financial periodicals, this literature presented itself as a 'science of financial investments' and as an indispensable means for successful transactions. At about the same time, core elements of the random walk hypothesis were first formulated in a book by Jules Regnault, called *Calcul des chances et philosophie de la Bourse* (*Chance Calculus and the Philosophy of the Stock Exchange*), published in 1863 in Paris (Jovanovic 2000, 2001; Jovanovic and Le Gall 2001). After Jules Regnault, authors like Henri Lefèvre developed graphic methods (Jovanovic 2002; Zylberberg 1990, p. 88) used later by Louis Bachelier in his *Theory of Speculation* ([1900] 1964).

Seen in this perspective, the 'prehistory of efficient capital markets' (Le Roy 1989, p. 1586) began in the 1860s. Some of its main contributors were stock market operators writing for investors. Jules Regnault and Henri Lefèvre saw themselves as financial speculators. Their publications explicitly addressed investors, and their aim was to provide practical advice. Henri Lefèvre invented several practical devices for horse-race gamblers and financial speculators. Jules Regnault stated explicitly in his *Chance Calculus* that his aim was to formulate 'rules of prudence for the speculator' (1863, p. 199). Writing with the aim of providing practical advice does not mean that the contributors were without an elite education.[1] Nevertheless, the drive behind their publications was a desire to educate investors, mixed with the belief that financial knowledge would attract popular investors into financial activities and thus attenuate class differences.

What then was the relationship between nineteenth-century vernacular finance, on the one hand, and the assumptions grounding the random walk hypothesis, on the other? How did vernacular finance contribute to the reconceptualization of investor behavior, of financial information, or of the relationship between investment and gambling? I explore here the ways in which this vernacular science promoted a set of assumptions which are central to a formalized theory of market efficiency. My standpoint is that of the sociologist of knowledge and science: I trace the ways in which practical problem-solving and cognitive shifts led to approaching financial investments in a systematic fashion. I will therefore follow the social practices which supported these cognitive developments. My purpose is neither to show that the one or the other author (fully) anticipated the random walk hypothesis, nor to contest the relevance of any author. Quite the contrary: I examine the cognitive and cultural background represented by popular efforts to transform financial investing into a science. The interest of such an enterprise is three: (1) from the perspective of the sociologist of science, it shows that vernacular knowledge generated notions and standpoints which were later brought together, focused and reconfigured by formal models of market efficiency; (2) from the perspective of the sociologist of economics, it shows that concrete, everyday problems related to financial securities influenced the shape of academic theories of financial markets; and (3) from the perspective of the sociology of financial markets, it shows how cognitive instruments and practices supported a set of key assumptions with respect to the hypothesis of market efficiency. These instruments and practices changed public perception of and the way in which financial markets worked.

I will structure my arguments in the following way: first, I provide an overview of the social processes which led to the emergence of a vernacular science of financial markets in the second half of the nineteenth century. I show how financial investments gained social legitimacy, how they were disentangled from gambling, and associated with a 'science of the market' grounded in systematic observation and inquiry. Next, I show how this popular science conceived investment behavior as foreseeable and analyzable in rational terms. This behavior was taken to be observable and repeatable, subject to systematic empirical inquiry, and not exclusively driven by irrational factors. More importantly, it was defined by rules for investment decisions; in their turn, rules were related to criteria of profit. Third, I examine how this vernacular science represented price information as the most important kind of financial information. I show that this was accompanied by substantial changes in the way price information was recorded and distributed. In the fourth section I examine explanatory models of prices changes. Finally, the conclusion spells out the overall relevance of the nineteenth-century popular 'science of financial investments' with respect to the later emergence of an academic financial theory.

1. The difficult relationship between vernacular and academic economics

Recently, historians of economic thought have begun examining the relationship between academic and vernacular economics. 'Vernacular economics' is understood to comprise heterogeneous sets of practices, know-how techniques and rationalization procedures with the help of which social actors make sense of their economic environment and of the economic consequences of their own actions. Rather than a body of homogeneous, abstract and formalized explanations of economic processes, vernacular economics mixes tacit, commonly shared assumptions and knowledge about economic processes with non-systematic rationalizations. It lacks the jurisdictional boundaries of academic economics and is not organized around professional bodies and institutions. Seen in this perspective, vernacular economics includes the mental computations used by buyers to make sense of supermarket prices and of affordability (Lave 1988), as well as the rationalization procedures through which popular investors justify their investment decisions (Lépinay and Rousseau 2000).

In a widely discussed paper, Arjo Klamer and Thomas Leonard (1993, pp. 5–7; see also Klamer 1999) argue that this relationship can be conceptualized as a translation, a pragmatic difference, or a consequentialist difference. The first implies that vernacular and academic economics are very much alike, only that the vernacular variety is less rigorous. In this perspective, vernacular economics is (logically and empirically) posterior to academic theory. The pragmatic difference implies that the two varieties serve different purposes: while vernacular economics is oriented toward solving everyday problems, the academic variety is more concerned with elaborating a unified conceptual framework. In this case, it is not clear whether they just coexist, or whether academic theories can emerge out of pragmatic concerns with everyday problems. Finally, the consequentialist difference implies that vernacular and academic economics are incommensurable: their aims and principles are radically different, and translations are only marginal. Following these arguments, Jack Amariglio and David Ruccio

(1999, p. 26) have recently argued that vernacular practices should be examined more closely, since they express the concrete interests of economic actors. However, Amariglio and Ruccio see vernacular economics as a quasi-closed system, which in no way influences academic theories. While transfers and translations from academic to vernacular economics are possible, the opposite lane remains forever closed. But if Regnault and Lefèvre were writing for a broader public (which they were), this lane seems to have been, at least in this case, open.

In the past decade, the sociology of science has examined the relationships between vernacular and academic theories in cases such as AIDS research (Epstein 1996), nuclear energy (Callon et al., 2001), or Down's syndrome (Rapp 1999), among others. The conclusion has been that, at least in the cases examined, this relationship is not a simple, linear one: vernacular varieties of science are irreducible to popularized academic theories. Rather, vernacular knowledge actively influences academic theories: among others, it provides them with rationalization devices, formulates competing explanatory models, and articulates interests which are later integrated in academic theories. In some cases, popular theories emerge in the early stages of academic ones (as was the case with AIDS research) and set the framework in which the broader public will interpret the results of scientific research.

In the case examined here, it seems that key assumptions were first articulated (even if disparately) by popular, practical concerns with financial investments. Examining these assumptions can lead to a better understanding of the cognitive, cultural and social processes that acted as a background for the scientific approach to financial market operations. Until now, these connections have not been thoroughly examined; we know fairly little about nineteenth-century popular ideas, representations and cognitive instruments related to financial markets. We also know little about the connections between these popular representations and academic theories of financial investments. Starting in the mid-nineteenth century, a wave of popular literature aimed at changing the attitudes of the public and at introducing new cognitive instruments for the evaluation of financial securities (Preda 2001). This raises the question whether these cultural and cognitive changes generated views which were later incorporated in more rigorous theories of financial securities.

2. The popular 'science of financial investments'

A popular science of financial investments flourished on both sides of the Atlantic from the mid-nineteenth century on; it was closely connected to the emergence of individual and institutional investors as an aggregate source of money to be reckoned with (Preda 2000, 2001). Starting in the 1840s, and (initially) related to the explosive growth in the number of railway companies, publications targeting the middle-class investor multiplied: manuals, journals, newsletters, how-to books were published by brokerage firms, newspapers, speculators, or railway engineers. For example, Pierre-Cyrille Hautcoeur (1997, p. 238) estimates that in 1881 there were 238 financial periodicals published in Paris alone. This literature parallels (and is closely related to) the first wave of financial globalization (O'Rourke and Williamson 1999, 2000, 2001; Officer 1996; Rousseau and Sylla 1999, 2001; Sylla 1999a, b) unfolding between 1850 and 1914, when financial markets became internationally integrated, with a continuous flux of capital and information between them. Attracting growing numbers of investors into market activities required not only that financial investments were economically rewarding, but also that they were socially legitimate and morally acceptable. The problem was that, since the eighteenth century, investments were associated with gambling (Fabian 1990) and therefore socially unpalatable.

The 'science of financial investments' was meant, among other things, to disentangle investment from gambling. It certainly helped that, at about the same time, gambling was dissociated from morals and transformed into a medical condition (Brenner and Brenner 1990, pp. 72–6). An effect of this double dissociation was that both gambling and investing became objects of scientific inquiry.

The modes of conceptualizing and representing financial investing changed. Self-styled 'scientific' manuals explicitly promoted an active attitude of observation, inquiry and intervention, as opposed to the passive contemplation of a theatrical spectator, an attitude so common in the eighteenth century (Agnew 1986; Preda 2000, 2001). Manuals and advice brochures disseminated cognitive instruments with the help of which readers could examine the markets and intervene in them. The most important instruments were financial charts, price tables and balance sheet analyses.

Manuals provided several rationales whereby financial investing was good for the individual, as well as for the nation. Investing was represented as the most important means of self-fulfillment, as enhancing individual and family happiness, strengthening the nation-state and, last but not least, as a means for achieving social harmony and justice. Already in the 1850s some publications wrote that criticisms of the stock exchange were meant 'to split the finance, the bourgeoisie and the working classes ... but this market is now democratized; while in the past it had looked like a monopoly profiting the financial aristocracy, it now embraces all the spheres of human activity and goes down to the people, this source of modern life, that transforms an investor's savings into a state bond or railway stock, certain that he will find not only an advantageous income, but to see his capital prosper' (*La Bourse* 1854, p. 3). Under the influence of Proudhon, this strain of thought was especially influential in France:

> The Stock Exchange imposes responsibilities on the bourgeoisie – responsibilities toward itself, toward the working classes and the poor, toward the state; the bourgeoisie has to sustain the equilibrium, prevent depreciation, initiate general measures for the welfare and the education of the masses. ... The bourgeoisie must contribute to paying the state's debt; the Stock Exchange is the parliament of the generous, intelligent, honest bourgeoisie. (Proudhon 1854, pp. 33–4)

Henri Lefèvre too saw financial markets as a tool for achieving a more just, egalitarian society. He firmly believed that financial investments were a means of empowering the middle classes, of attenuating class distinctions, of defusing social tensions, and of attaining social equality. In these respects, the stock exchange was the central organ of society (Lefèvre 1870, p. 245; see also Lefèvre 1874; Proudhon 1854, pp. 23–5).

A new analytical language emerged, different from that of pamphlets and comedies. It was riddled with metaphors borrowed from physics, engineering, medicine and meteorology, promoting the analogy between investing and the natural sciences. A language which stresses the similarities between financial and physical processes also suggests that both obey the same (or similar) laws, and can be studied by similar means. More precisely, it suggests that every investor can act as a scientific observer of the laws of financial markets. As Philip Mirowski (1989, 1994, 2002, pp. 7, 9) has shown, neoclassical economists set out to model economics after the causal, deterministic program of nineteenth-century mechanics. In turn, popular financial writers did what they could to promote this analogy. In a complementary way, the language of technology stock prospects from the late nineteenth century stressed economic competitivity as the main advantage of new technologies (Bazerman 1999, p. 156).

The drive toward making investment scientific had a direct impact on how activities like options trading were conceived. For the public of the eighteenth and early nineteenth centuries, speculation in options had raised many conceptual problems. The terms of trade could not be easily grasped; they were often associated with sorcery (especially in pamphlets and comedies), and were taken as thoroughly immoral. This was the more general background for the legal bans and regulatory restrictions enacted upon options trading throughout the early nineteenth century (e.g., Guillard 1875 for the French legislation). A science of financial investments did not have to bother much about explaining the moral character of options trading, or its relationship to gambling. Instead, it explained to the public the trading itself. Many manuals included chapters on problem-solving, so that investors could try their hand before engaging in trading proper. The transformation of investing into a scientific activity allowed two apparently opposite, yet simultaneous, movements: disentangling investment from gambling and transferring the methods of analysis from the latter to the former.

This self-styled 'science of financial markets' promoted the notion that financial investments are governed by principles that are not controlled by any single individual or group. Even if some persons may occasionally manipulate markets, these principles will ultimately prevail. Investors can learn the principles, provided they adopt the right attitude. This dovetailed with a rationalization which did not appeal primarily to ethics, but relied on the idea that financial markets require a systematic investigation and a scientific attitude on the part of the investors.

Therefore, legal changes in the regime of options trading – as they were enacted in France, for example – did not operate in a cognitive vacuum. These changes, which can be observed in France, England and the USA in the second half of the nineteenth century were – in all these countries – paralleled by a cognitive and cultural move toward transforming financial investing into a scientific activity. One of the most durable effects was on how investment behavior was understood.

3. The rational behavior of investors

In order to understand better the conceptual changes introduced by this vernacular science, we have to take into account that how-to brochures were not just a new literary form. They aimed to convince their readers that investments were not only lucrative, relatively sure, but also legitimate sources of income, given that a few rules were respected. These rules, incessantly repeated, concerned individual behavior, on which financial success was made dependent. Lack of emotions, capacity of self-control, continuous study of the markets, and monitoring of the joint-stock companies were made into fundamental conditions of successful investments.

This meant, in the first place, that the notion of market behavior was stripped of its emotional, unforeseeable side, of aspects like panic or hysteria: principles and cold blood, not passions, govern the stock exchange (De Mériclet 1854, p. 31). This did not mean that financial panics were no longer an object of reflection; quite the contrary. But panic behavior could now be examined and explained in thoroughly rational terms as lack of self-control. Errors were made by the investors who did not respect basic rules, did not properly evaluate information, or were letting themselves be manipulated by others. In other words, financial panics were tied to cognitive deficiencies on the part of investors who did not fit the model of permanent monitoring and dispassionate analysis of market events. Behavior was also stripped of its moral aspects, because nobody any longer asked whether it was moral to invest in financial securities or not.[2] While a moralizing discourse on financial investments continued to exist in the nineteenth century, it was by no means dominant; it was articulated mostly in novels and journalism, and was pitted against the 'scientific' character of investment manuals. Moreover, the morality (and necessity) of financial investments was amply legitimated with respect to the family, the state and the individual's happiness. Financial behavior was made dependent on knowledge and presented as thoroughly rational: it was a matter of studying, observing and analyzing. A successful investor has to rely on long studies and reasoning; one must always hear all the news (Crampon 1863, p. 48; *Notions générales* 1877, pp. 54–5).

While attention to information was one of the main components of rational behavior, another one, at least as important, was acting according to rules. As a consequence, investor manuals sought to devise clear rules of investing, of assessing risks, of picking up stocks, and of computing the value of financial securities. Two kinds of rules were devised: on the one hand, there were rules according to which investors should examine and assess the value of securities, or calculate interest rates.[3] A railway engineering manual, for example, stated that assessing the value of railway stocks has to go through a series of steps, such as examining gradients and curves, analyzing balance sheets, and computing profits per share (Lardner 1850, p. 310). The investor's aim should be the maximization of financial value, i.e., of the value of stocks and bonds in one's portfolio. This was no longer seen as a matter of sheer luck, but as dependent on the efforts of each individual. Publications stressed cognitive abilities as intrinsic to the rationality of financial behavior: analysis of balance sheets, reading of stock price diagrams, examination and evaluation of news.

At the same time, there were rules according to which investors should make decisions about buying and selling. For example, an English manual from 1870 advised its readers to build classes of financial securities and to select the cheapest stock in a class (*Beeton's Guide Book* 1870, pp. 6–7, 67). Problem-solving chapters – a must for every manual worth this name – showed the right decision for various trading situations, and how to act on the grounds of the information at hand. Here's such an example from a French manual published in 1877, a contemporary of Henri Lefèvre and Jules Regnault:

> Q: We sell 6,000 francs of French 3% bonds at 71.50 at 1 franc premium and we buy the same quantity at 71.90 at 50 centimes premium. Which limits do we impose by that to our gains? Which limits do we impose to our losses?
> A: We limit gains to 1,000 francs and losses to 800 francs. (*Notions générales* 1877, p. 62)

This and similar problems show that decisions are represented as thoroughly rational, and depending on rules for projecting profits and losses. Investor behavior was reduced to decisions according to certain, given situations; decisions were reduced to calculations. In order to decide, the investor needs to compute possible outcomes. Behavior was thus conceived as both embedded in calculations (of probable outcomes) and calculable – that is, foreseeable – since it took place according to standardized rules. While manuals did not solve once and for all the moral problems related to investing, they avoided them by transferring financial practices from the social to the scientific domain. Irrational mass psychology was superseded as an explanatory variable by the informed decisions of individuals. Since these decisions depended on information, and since information determined prices too, both could be represented and analyzed in a homogeneous, unitary framework.

As an overall consequence, this effort directly contributed to changing the premises on which financial behavior was conceived. It can thus be argued with good reason that this popular financial literature played an important role in making financial behavior apt for formal analysis.

The realization (and maximization) of financial value was made dependent on rational, cognitively founded individual behavior. With this, another fundamental premise for their formalization in a coherent theoretical framework was fulfilled.

4. Information, prices and rational behavior

Since investors had to rely on study and research, it followed that information was key with respect to market-related decisions. At the same time, some authors shifted to the notion that the price of financial securities should be treated as information – namely, as the most important kind of financial information. Systematic attempts to gather and process information on financial securities had been initiated before 1850. Already in 1844, the Court of Directors of the Bank of England had appointed 'John Beaton, of the 3 per cent Consols ... to make such confidential investigations and inquiries in the various Funds as may be required, and to attend the Courts of Law and Equity, in relation thereto,' a decision that may be regarded as the birth of the stock analyst. As one manual put it, the Stock Market is nothing more than the high organization of information:

> Taking the Stock Exchange as the pattern of high organization, it will be easy to point out the advantages and disadvantages which a market of this kind exhibits. It is too often forgotten that the eager speculation in securities makes it worthwhile for the keenest business men in the world to obtain good information on the value of what they traffic in; and as a bad thing falls, a good one rises in market value, a paying speculation is immediately advertised to those who will imitate it, a worthless concern is publicly expressed by a mere figure on a list. (*The rationale* 1876, pp. 25–6)

Investor manuals and brochures distinguished between several kinds of information: on the one hand, there was the information provided by newspapers and journals, gossip and rumors. On the other hand, there was the information an assiduous investor could gain from calculus, from examining the balance sheets and computing profits per share, or from examining the historical variations of securities' prices. With respect to the information disseminated by newspapers, one had to be careful, since a good portion of it was planted and not trustworthy; moreover, a successful operator always supplements public with private information (*Stock Speculation* 1875, pp. 4, 30). At the same time, calculating is key for successful investments; it is what makes investing a science. Accounts and balance sheets have to be examined in detail; the same goes for historical price variations. Therefore, investors' manuals published both, with the explicit aim of facilitating research and decisions (e.g., Train 1857, p. 213; Courtois 1862). Statistics of historical and seasonal price variations were relatively common in investor manuals after the late 1840s.

Since information was seen as key, and since manuals distinguished between narrative information and cognitive rules, they also tended to stress one more than the other. Some authors argued that newspaper and private information matters more; others emphasized the importance of rules and formulas for determining the value of financial securities. Accordingly, the first were viewed as 'speculators,' while the latter formed the camp of 'theorists' (e.g., Pinto 1877, p. 179). 'Speculators' considered that the value of a stock is determined by investors' expectations (Wayland 1837, p. 278). While they did not contest the role of (private) information, 'theorists' maintained that analytical models were required in order to understand the movements of securities and devised formal rules for determining the value of stocks.

The idea that the value of a stock is measured by the profit per share required formulae for evaluating income per share, as well as for extrapolating income – which served to estimate the future value of a railway company or any firm, for that matter (e.g., Blanchard 1861; Sourigues 1861, 1862; Lefèvre 1870, pp. 114ff., 122). *Beeton's Guide Book to the Stock Exchange* stated in 1870 that 'to calculate what a security at a certain price pays the investor, multiply the rate per cent paid by the security by 100, and divide by the price' (p. 90).

A standard technique for evaluating stocks was computing their relative value, which meant taking a (standard state) bond as a reference point and computing the variations in price differences (security to bond) over a chosen time interval. This method had been first introduced by Thomas Fortune's (1810) *An Epithome of the Stocks & Public Funds* at the beginning of the nineteenth century, replacing the old view according to which the value of a stock can best be estimated by comparing it with the value of land. Comparative tables of price variations were published (*Fenn's Compendium* 1854, pp. 52–3; Wright 1842, pp. 5–6), allowing readers to compare not only the variations in prices over a time interval, but also the variations in price differences, and to classify stocks according to these variations. An investors' guide from 1870 stated that this method has enriched all who have used it since 1800 (Medbery 1870, p. 209). Some publications went so far as to state that charts and tables of price variations were an indispensable instrument for any broker dealing in puts, calls and straddles:

> To guard against these disasters, the new system of operating in stock privileges (known as puts and calls) has been devised, by which any person may increase their chances of operating a thousand fold, with a very limited amount of capital. … It is as much the duty of a broker to pilot his customers safely through the sea of speculation, as it is his business to obtain such a customer. … Now for a broker to be able to judge with any degree of certainty the course that a stock is likely to take, he must have had actual experience in the market under many different conditions, and he must also base his opinion upon something more than the general indications at any moment, for appearances are often deceitful in a stock market. One of the oldest maxims of the street is, that 'where a stock has once sold, you may reasonably look for it to sell there again.' Therefore, it becomes almost a necessity that the broker or operator should consult a table of fluctuations of stocks before he can form an intelligent opinion of future prices. (*Secret of Success* 1875, p. 11)

Even more importantly, perhaps, prices and price variations began being acknowledged as intrinsic information, the most important an investor can get. The more detailed the price variations and the closer their recording was to the actual transactions, the more important was the information. Writers of popular manuals began to realize that real-time, minute price variations were important, and that investors should gather data on these. As I show below, Henri Lefèvre was very well aware of the importance of fresh prices. In order to better understand this shift of perception, one must keep in mind that the quotations published in financial newspapers and journals were not standardized until the late 1860s. Many authors of financial manuals complained about the difficulty of finding and accurately compiling securities' prices, advertising at the same time their own investigative and statistical skills (e.g., Martin 1886, p. iv). Price information depended on specific price-recording systems, which influenced the cognitive instruments available to investors.

5. Securities prices and price-recording technologies

Against this background, it is important to note that in the late 1860s and the early 1870s there was a sustained preoccupation with devising technical systems with the help of which price variations could be recorded minutely and accurately. Traditionally, prices were written down by brokers on paper slips, which were sent to brokerage houses by courier boys, rented by the hour from telegraph companies (Downey 2000, p. 130). Some of the effects of this system were that slips were lost, misdirected, misread or forged very frequently. Price compilation was difficult and inaccurate. More often than not, price compilers aggregated data. Price lists and diagrams showed prices by the day, week, month and year, but not by the minute or by the hour (Preda 2002).

Investors could not know if what they were reading in quotation lists were opening, closing, median prices, or something else. On the London Stock Exchange, only consols prices were published in standardized form at the beginning of the 1860s. In Paris, there was an official quotation in the French bonds, as well as an unofficial one, published by the curb brokers and called Cote Defossés. It gave the highest, lowest and closing quotations (Vidal 1910, pp. 37–8), as well as after-hours prices, but was not officially endorsed (Tetreau 1994, p. 77). Official stockbrokers, who were practically civil servants with a monopoly on trade, fought the curb brokers and continuously tried to undermine the credibility of their list (Hautcoeur 1997, p. 261). Parallel price data (official and unofficial), together with a lack of standardized price-recording procedure, contributed to informational uncertainties.

Uncertainty about prices and price variations was especially high in the unofficial French markets (the *coulisse*), with its multiple prices for a given security (Walker 2001, pp. 192–3). More often than not, traders negotiated directly with each other, without an auctioneer (p. 194). In New York and London the situation was similar. In the absence of technology that could record prices minutely and accurately, these latter were not standardized, and generated considerable uncertainties.

This began to change with the introduction of the ticker in 1867 and 1872 in New York City and London, respectively. It allowed (by comparison) a minute and accurate recording of price variations. The ticker was invented in New York City in 1867 by E.A. Callahan, an engineer associated with the American Telegraph Company, who in his youth had worked as a courier boy. The ticker's main innovation consisted in two type-wheels mounted on separate shafts, moving independently of each other. It could thus transmit names and quotations in real time; the names and prices were printed on the paper tape in two distinct lines. The first instrument was installed in the brokerage office of David Goesbeck in Manhattan in 1867; in 1872, it was adopted by the London Stock Exchange.

Among the social changes induced by the ticker was a decisive impetus given to chart analysis: it was now possible to produce charts of minute price variations, from which market movements could be deduced. Financial charts had previously been used as a source of financial information.[4] The ticker, however, revealed the full information potential of price variations. By 1900, the chart analyst had become a fixture of brokerage houses; the institutionalization of the profession was loudly requested by investor manuals. Detailed charts and analyses were regularly published by investors' magazines; they institutionalized a new technical language (like tops and bottoms, head and shoulders), together with the view that causal explanations of the market could be deduced from the sole variation of prices. Indexes like Dow Jones's and Standard & Poor's started at about the same time (Wyckoff 1972, pp. 31).

These changes left their imprint on how prices were perceived. Investor manuals began to assert that price variations were the most important kind of information. In this respect, there is a striking difference between Jules Regnault, who wrote in 1863, and Henri Lefèvre, who was writing in the 1870s. Regnault considered that the value of a security gravitates toward 'the absolute price' (1863, p. 51) and that this latter was approximated by the median price. By opposition, Lefèvre argued that statistically constructed prices are at best of historical interest. What counts are the quotations by the hour:

> The attentive reading and sustained observation of the documents containing the official quotations is of the highest importance for the investor as well as for the speculator and, for those who can read, the quotation is more instructive than all the journals' reports. Those who seriously want to benefit [from it] should record the median prices in a chart, on which the successive days are on the horizontal axis and the prices on the vertical axis. We obtain thus a market of movements, and operations which continue from month to month, and we gain extremely precious indications. The only thing that is missing is the quotation of options contracts as they happen. The opening and the closing [quotations] are important information, but the highest and the lowest have a real use only if we have the time at which they happened, otherwise they have only a statistical interest for obtaining the median price. (Lefèvre 1874, pp. 31–2)

Lefèvre's stance against statistically constructed prices may not be entirely alien to the aversion of a part of the French public toward statistics (Porter 1995, p. 83), an aversion shared by some French economists (Ménard 1980). While the explanation of prices as being influenced by political and economic events had a long tradition, going back to the eighteenth century, the explanation of price movements in their own terms was a relatively new development, made possible by advances in price-recording technology. These approaches differed in their premises: historical–political explanations stressed the role of political information; technical analysis renounced examining this kind of information altogether. It stressed the central role of price differences in understanding price movements; what counted were not absolute values, but differences between prices.

6. Price information and market explanations

While technical analysis was one way to promote the idea that price variations in themselves were the most important kind of information, there was a second way to promote the same message. Technical analysis was dependent on a specific technology (the ticker) and on a minute recording of prices. The alternative was to develop abstract models of price variations, ignoring the real ones.

Let us reexamine the picture: investors' manuals promoted a behavior anchored in observation, analysis and knowledge. They formulated decision rules, according to which investors should conduct themselves in the marketplace. Rational investor behavior was dependent on knowledge, and this meant in the first place knowledge of price variations. Behavior was made into a discrete variable and tied to price movements. This implied that knowledge, behavior and price movements could now be integrated and examined in a homogeneous framework. Hence, what counted was not so much an explanation of price movements based on causal external factors, but how behavior changed together with prices.

Jules Regnault, writing at the beginning of the 1860s, when price recording was not yet standardized, insisted on computing median prices as the absolute value toward which real prices tend. Under the influence of Quételet (Jovanovic and Le Gall 2001, pp. 333, 348), he insisted on the causal determination of prices. Regnault asserted that stock-price variations have causes which remain constant over time and can be examined in a rational fashion. He classified these causes as general or particular, constant or variable (pp. 17–18, 110) and proceeded to study them. Information determines the investors' expectations, and with that price variations. Since these expectations are individual, and since they determine price movements, it follows that these movements do not depend on each other; future movements cannot be inferred from past ones. But this does not mean that we cannot find a method for analyzing them: this method, dubbed by Regnault 'law of deviations' (*loi des écarts*), consisted in analyzing the relationship between time spans and price variations: the aim was to find a regular, probabilistic relationship between time and price differences.

Regnault considered that the causal influence of events diminishes with time; what happened a month ago has less influence on prices than what happened yesterday. This led him to argue that shorter time spans cause smaller differences in prices, while longer time spans cause bigger prices differences. His 'law of deviations' was that price differences are proportional to the square root of time (1863, p. 50); with its help, investors could compute how long they had to wait if they wanted to double or triple their profit.

While Quételet's influence is no doubt important, I argue here that it was not the only one. After all, the preoccupations with the causes of price movements were present almost everywhere on both sides of the Atlantic. My argument is that price-recording systems and technologies also played a role. In other words, we should take into account not only isolated conceptual analogies with the natural sciences, but how these analogies fitted together with the social perception of information and with the constraints introduced by communication technologies. Until the late 1860s, the accurate, real-time recording of securities prices was very difficult, if not impossible. Minute price variations could not be perceived as (reliable and valid) information. Compilers very often tied prices to political events; they simply introduced an additional column in their tables, showing what happened on the day when the price of the consols was at such-and-such a level. Under these circumstances, a deterministic view of price movements was not surprising.

After the introduction of the ticker, however, it became easier to analyze price movements without tying them to external events. Technical analysis, stressing pure price variations, became the vogue. At the same time, if (political and economic) events occurred less frequently than recorded price changes, they could not explain frequently changing prices. Differences between prices became important. It was relevant now to identify sets of patterns in price variations. The causal explanation of price movements was no longer the only alternative.

There is, however, an additional element: while the ticker triumphed in New York and London at the beginning of the 1870s, the Parisian marketplace continued to have multiple prices for the same security, as well as several quotation lists (Vidal 1910). At about the same time, we encounter authors who abandon the analogy between financial markets and mechanics – dominant since the eighteenth century – and argue that financial markets are to be conceived as a living organism and approached in a functionalist, not in a causal manner. I quote here again Henri Lefèvre:

> The Stock Exchange is a circulation organ, its function is to circulate, to appraise the quality of the materials submitted to its action. When you introduce poison, venom, in the veins of an animal, the heart makes it circulate through the entire organism. More or less grave disorders result, and the heart becomes a victim, but, again, its role is to produce movement and not to make chemical analyses. This is why most criticisms of the Bourse are off the mark, like the legal dispositions they pretended to impose upon [the Bourse]. It will go on like that as long as we continue to believe that society is a mechanism whose movements and wheels can be controlled at will, when in fact it is a natural *organism* whose spontaneous functioning must be studied with the aim of supporting its development. (Lefèvre 1874, p. 13)

While organic and anatomic metaphors were not a novelty in the banking language of the time (Alborn 1994), Lefèvre drew his consequences with respect to the explanation of prices. Accordingly, causal explanations of price movements, which rely on a mechanistic view of financial markets, are useless. What matters is to explain the functions fulfilled by markets in the society at large. A functionalist explanation, however, has to be supplemented by an adequate market model. Biological analogies and functionalist explanations did not exclude recourse to statistics; quite the contrary. As Claude Ménard (1980, pp. 533, 539) and Yves Breton (1992, p. 32) have shown, mainstream academic economists in France had a legal and literary education, being opposed to formal modeling and to statistics. It was the analogy with biology which justified the application of statistics to economic and financial phenomena.

My argument here is that in this situation, where causal explanations were no longer seen as adequate, and price-recording systems in France lagged behind those of other important marketplaces, observers and speculators alike were driven toward abstract market models as a means of reducing uncertainties about prices. This explains why, at a time of trans-Atlantic, almost frenzied preoccupation with analyzing financial markets, abstract models developed preponderantly in France.

We can observe this in the case of Henri Lefèvre, who wrote in the early 1870s. Lefèvre thoroughly rejected the deterministic approach. He considered that a causal explanation of price movements was totally superfluous. The (investing) public needed something completely different:

> The public does not need definitions and formulae, it needs images which are fixed in its mind (*esprit*), and with the help of which it can direct its actions. Images are the most powerful auxiliary of reason; thus, whatever properties of a geometric figure result from its definition and are implicitly contained within it, it would be almost impossible to extract them without the help of the eyes, that is, of images, in order to help the mind. ... Especially in the case of Stock Exchange operations, where the decisions must be prompt, it matters if one has in one's mind clear images instead of more or less confusing formulas, because the slightest hesitation or a false movement may cause considerable damages in some cases. (Lefèvre 1870, pp. 184–5)

But, at the same time, there is a second reason: a science of the stock exchange should not be concerned with explaining the causes of price movements, but with

> *differences*, one must look after the laws of *differences*, abstracting from the quotations in which they appear, which needlessly complicate the phenomenon, and abstracting from the concrete quantities with which one works, which confuse the reader. By eliminating from the problem any reference to quotations (*cours*) and quantities, in order to consider only the differences, we can easily determine their laws and make them visible to the eyes. ... We shall consider first and foremost the unity of value which is the object of the market. (Ibid., pp. 186–7).

An abstract, formal model of the market is required because real quotations obscure 'the unity of value.' Against the background of multiple, parallel quotation lists and in the absence of minute price charts, we can better understand this insistence on an abstract market model.

If only the laws of differences should be taken into account, then one can focus the analysis on the differences between the price of an option and that of the underlying security. Starting from these arguments, Henri Lefèvre proceeded to develop a graphical representation of decisions in the options trade, which was employed 30 years later by Bachelier in his doctoral thesis. When devising the payoff diagram and the *auto-compteur*,[5] Lefèvre's strategy was to visualize individual decisions in a space of coordinates. His space of decisions is defined by two axes: the horizontal axis of the market, with downward (*baisse*) and upward (*hausse*) situations as its extremities; and the vertical axis of the investment's outcome, having gains and losses as its upper and lower extremities, respectively. These axes define four angles: two of them are angles of gains (in a bear and a bull market, respectively); correspondingly, two are angles of losses. The diagonal lines intersecting these angles represent the various situations of the spot seller and buyer, respectively, in various market situations (Lefèvre 1870, p. 191).

Lefèvre then proceeded to show that options contracts can be visualized in this graphical space; he also described the outcome and the right decision for each type of contract traded in the French 3 percent bond. The payoff diagram, published first in his *Traité* in 1870, was repeated in 1874 in the *Principes de la science de la Bourse* – a booklet which was officially endorsed by the union of the stockbrokers of the Paris Bourse. Starting from this diagram, he devised the 'abacus of the speculator,' an instrument to be used by investors on the floor of the stock exchange. This was a wooden board, divided into squares, with the axes of loss and gains drawn on it; it had mobile letters (similar with those of the *auto-compteur*), with the help of which investors could visualize the course of various options with respect to the corresponding security. By repositioning the letters, an investor could see the outcomes of his decisions on each type of option contract. Lefèvre even devised a national plan of financial education based on his method, but the stockbrokers' union declined to invest any money in it. In 1873, the payoff diagram was taken over by Léon Pochet – an engineer from the École des Ponts et Chaussées – in an article published in the *Journal des Actuaires Français*, the stronghold of mathematical economy in France (Zylberberg 1990, pp. 92–3). Around 1900, this method was a fixture of investors' manuals, being known under the name of 'polégraphie'; it was advertised as the one with the help of which the laws of bull and bear markets could be discovered (Roussel 1904).

While Lefèvre's perspective was that of individual decisions, 30 years later Louis Bachelier used the payoff diagram (a) for examining the behavior of prices, not that of individuals, and (b) as a starting point for an algebraic, not a geometrical, model of price behavior. His dissertation (1964 [1900], p. 18) gives only one page to the actions of individual actors. Similar to Lefèvre, Bachelier considered a causal explanation of price levels only briefly (p. 17); he declared it impossible to achieve in mathematical terms and stated that the study of quotations would never be an exact science. Instead, one should focus on price changes.

Thus it can be argued that, by giving up looking for a causal explanation of price movements and by insisting on abstract models instead of real, all-too-confusing quotations, Lefèvre and other popular financial writers prepared the ground for their formal treatment.

7. Financial investing and formal market models

The question is now: to what extent did manuals develop abstract models? The answer to this question is twofold: on the one hand, some manuals applied algebra to the evaluation of financial securities. On the other hand, trading in futures and options was conceptualized in a way that made it apt for a formal, abstract treatment. I will begin here with this second aspect.

Against the more general background of rules and procedures concerning stock values, nineteenth-century manuals gave futures and options special attention. While options contracts were not enforced by law (for example, they were legalized in France only in 1885), and therefore not binding for any parties, options trade was a standard feature of manuals and how-to brochures. Manuals were confronted with the task of explaining trade operations, types of contracts, their consequences, and rules of behavior for each type of contract. Another, no less important, aspect was explaining the factors which determine the price of options. These were by no means simple questions: how can one formulate the rules for investing in these products, when so many said such rules did not exist? And how can one convey the complexities of financial products reputed to be the most refined ever to the average family father?

Manuals argued that futures and options fulfill clear economic functions, like raising short-time money or ensuring that the laws of supply and demand are working. I will quote here Pierre-Joseph Proudhon again, who in 1854 wrote in his *Manual* that forbidding futures markets was an economic folly:

> Let the press be gagged, a tariff be put on the library, let the post be spied on, the telegraph exploited by the state, but speculation, by the anarchy which constitutes its essence, escapes all state and police constitutions. To try putting a control on this last and infallible interpreter of opinions would mean governing in the darkness of Egypt, which, according to the rabbis, was so thick that even the candles and lanterns went out. How, for example, to forbid *futures markets*? In order to forbid futures markets, they should stop the oscillations of *demand* and *supply*, that is, guarantee to the trade the production, the quality, the placement, and the invariability of commodities' prices, and at the same time to eliminate all the aleatory conditions of the production, circulation, and consumption of goods, which is impossible and even contradictory. (p. 31)

Proudhon was no exception in this respect. Many authors argued that futures and options allow smaller investors to become active on the market and distribute the chances of gain more widely. A put or a call contract benefits both parties and nobody loses, since the money is attracted anyway from other sectors of the economy (Proudhon 1854, p. 31; Noel-Fearn 1866, p. 103; *Stock Speculation* 1875, pp. 22, 25; Playford 1855, p. 58). Some manuals declared futures and options to be so well known that it did not pay to discuss them again (*Stocks* 1848, p. 11). Glossaries of trading notions, together with problem-solving chapters, were a standard feature. Readers were required to compute the outcomes of trading puts and calls in a bull or a bear market (Rougemont 1857, pp. 11–12; Les écueils 1865, pp. 100–11). Most French manuals, however, followed the strategy of differentiating between speculating (*spéculer*) and gambling (*jouer*) (Proudhon 1854, p. 81; *La Bourse* 1866, pp. 31–5; Playford 1855, pp. 57–8). Jules Regnault (1863, p. 36), among others, operated with this distinction. While speculating involved the usual operations in stocks and bonds, gambling involved betting on price differences. Speculation was a legitimate activity for the middle-class investor and a basic feature of human creativity. But if gambling was nothing more than a second-order speculation (Crampon 1863, pp. 158–9), a speculation on the speculation in stocks, it would follow that it is useful and creative too – and hence acceptable for a family father. The consequence was that these transactions should be studied with the same scientific methods employed in studying gambling (Borel 1835, p. 9; *Les écueils* 1865, p. 12). Henri Lefèvre (1871, p. 7), as well as Léon Pochet (Zylberberg 1990, p. 94) considered that the stock exchange and the race-track are basically similar and should be studied with similar instruments (that is, Lefèvre's).

Probabilistic modeling of gambling and its outcomes already had a long tradition (Bernstein 1996; Todhunter 1965; Hacking 1990). Since financial gambling as such was not rejected wholesale, but only considered too risky for the middle-class investor, applying formal tools to it would reduce risks and increase its appeal to the investor. For the 'theorists,' devising investment rules with the help of such tools was an appealing idea. This rationalization dovetailed well with the project of abstract and formal market models, as pursued by Henri Lefèvre, among others.

A manual from 1854, for instance, although skeptical, clearly shows that probabilistic explanations of price variations were discussed at that time:

> I do not know about the power of probabilistic calculus applied to the operations of the Stock Exchange, but I know that Condorcet and the marquis of Laplace failed in all their calculations of the probability of moral events, judgments of a plurality of votes, and the results of parliamentary votes. A moral event depends on a thousand unknown causes which are not subject to any calculus. If we wanted to try our fortune by some calculus, the method of the viscount Saint-André would be better. The marquis of Laplace has made a science out of the probability calculus. This science can be applied to life insurance, to ship insurance, it has a basis in the mortality tables and the number of ships which founder every year, but it is impossible to find it in the lows and highs of bonds. What produces the movements of these bonds is as variable as the golden weathervane on the dome of the Stock Exchange. (De Mériclet 1854, pp. 88–9)

In their turn, 'speculative' authors contended that the causes of price variations were far too complex to be modeled probabilistically. In ranting against probabilistic calculus, they provided a clear view of how such methods were to be employed:

> I had a High Wrangler on my books (he is dead now), who thought that with his knowledge of mathematics he must succeed. He was not a gambler, but an experimental philosopher. What he told me was this, and I tell you, dear 'Outside Fools' – '*Multiply each gain or loss by the probability on which it depends, compare the total results of gains and losses, and then you will have the required average, or, as it is termed, the mathematical expectation.*' In fact, he started with a *petitio principii*. In other words, he assumed that he knew the probability on which the gain or loss depended, which was a totally unwarrantable assumption. In stock exchange speculation, and indeed, as I think, in all other things, it is impossible to gain such a complete knowledge of the '*sum of the conditions*' as to correctly predict the result of those conditions. The only people, my dear 'Outside Fools,' who have any approximate knowledge of this philosophical '*sum of the conditions*' are the powerful men who are behind the scenes, the directors, and wire-pullers, and financial magnates, who, possessing through their wealth enormous leverage on the markets, exercise it remorselessly; and I grant you this, that they, if anyone, have this knowledge. And yet it would not be theoretically correct to say that they had this knowledge, for a war might suddenly break out, they might die, a money panic might suddenly occur, or a division in their own camp to frustrate their plans. (Pinto 1877, pp. 376–7)

This is a biting critique of the attempt to develop a causal explanation of price movements based on probabilistic calculus and the evaluation of (insider) knowledge. It shows, however, that two lines of inquiry were entangled here: (1) the application of the probability calculus to market decisions and (2) the impossibility of causal explanations of price variations. 'Theorists' may have been derided for their belief that the complex and changing causes of financial volatility could be grasped in probabilistic terms, but they were clearly onto something (Eggleston 1875, p. 79; De Mériclet 1854, p. 87). The belief that probabilistic calculus was an adequate method for analyzing price variations was embedded in the popular science of the market. Irrespective of the concrete outcomes of these experiments and debates, they show the extent to which this vernacular science was preoccupied with finding strict rules for evaluating financial securities and for decision-making in the trade with financial products. Probabilistic calculus occupied a prominent place in these efforts, as did visual techniques like charts and tables showing variations in prices. Seen in this framework, the efforts of Henri Lefèvre (and Jules Regnault, respectively) appear as the ingenious continuation of already existing preoccupations.

At the same time, some authors began applying formal tools to the study of financial securities. In 1891, Adolphe Pierre Brasilier published the *Théorie mathématique des placements et des emprunts à long terme* (*The mathematical theory of long-term investing and credit*), a manual for commercial schools that dealt, among other things, with French corporate and city bonds. These were structured in such a way that periodically, a fixed number of bonds were drawn by lottery and reimbursed at a fixed price above the issue price. The drawing was repeated until the whole issue was reimbursed. The bonds not drawn continued to receive interest until the next drawing date. This system raised several practical problems for investors, not dissimilar with those of annuities: what were their chances of getting reimbursed quickly and what would be their real profit on the investment? Brasilier, who believed that 'all questions of long term investments are very often only algebraic questions' (Vol. 2, p. 1) set out to elaborate a formal model of the bonds' lifespan and of the real interest rate. These corporate bonds were to be treated as a lottery problem (Vol. 2, p. 183). As a concrete case, he analyzed the bonds of the city of Paris from 1855 to 1860 and computed the probability of having won on them.

Thus we encounter a manifold preoccupation with applying formal tools to financial investments: on the one hand, to the analysis of French bonds resembling lottery tickets; on the other, to the analysis (however misled) of the causes of price variations. These preoccupations weren't restricted to a small academic circle. Brasilier's manual was written for commercial schools; Regnault, Lefèvre and other authors explicitly addressed a broader investing public, familiarizing it with the idea that the probability calculus is applicable to the study of financial investments.

8. Conclusion

Let us reexamine the achievements of this vernacular science of financial investments. It promoted the notions that (1) financial behavior is grounded in knowledge and observation; (2) it is reducible to rules of decision-making; (3) information is the main factor determining price movements; (4) these are by themselves the most important information; (5) abstract market models are in certain circumstances quite useful and desirable; (6) formal tools can be applied to the analysis of financial securities.

The value of financial securities was thus liberated from any ethical considerations and particularities and made into something abstract and dependent on quantifiable relationships. In this respect, the popular science of the market (or at least a part of it) came to see financial securities as abstract and depending on quantifiable relationships. Second, there was the belief that the causes of price variations can be grasped in probabilistic terms and that strict rules of decision-making should be based on these terms. While the attempt to analyze these causes did not yield results, it was nevertheless the concrete form in which the probability theory made its way into the analysis of financial securities. Lefèvre's great innovation was in this respect that he shifted the focus from a probabilistic analysis of concrete causes to an abstract model of variations, or 'differences,' which could subsume particular cases. While some authors held a causal explanation of price variations, others shifted to functionalist explanations.

Of course, these arguments and cognitive practices did not converge into elaborate, rigorous models of price behavior. They were formulated as (more or less disparate) attempts to solve practical problems. But my main argument here is that the popular science of financial investments provided the cognitive and cultural background against which elaborate theories and models could appear. When contemplating the development of these notions, we can – from the standpoint of the sociologist of knowledge and science – argue the following:

1. The 'popular science of financial investments' made financial securities into a legitimate object of scientific analysis.

2. The boundaries between a vernacular and a high (or academic) science of financial markets have been more porous that one might think. Many underlying assumptions pertaining to the efficient market hypothesis are the offspring of a popular 'science of the market.' In this sense, it can be argued that vernacular financial theories acted as the necessary cultural and cognitive background for the formulation of a stochastic market model.

There is good reason to argue that Bachelier's ideas (as well as those of later theorists) have had an impact not only on academic theories of finance, but also on concrete investment activities: options pricing and portfolio management formulas are nowadays widely used by investment and hedge fund analysis and decision-makers. In this sense, they have considerably influenced popular (i.e., non-academic) beliefs about financial investments. Against this background, we should keep in mind that these ideas, after all, had their origins in popular preoccupations with investments.

Notes

* This is a revised version of an article published in HOPE 36/2, 2004: 351–86. Research for this chapter was supported by a Barra International Fellowship at the Library Company of Philadelphia and a Gilder Lehrman Fellowship at the New York Historical Society. I thank the anonymous reviewers for their valuable suggestions and criticisms. Yuval Millo and Franck Jovanovic have also provided very useful suggestions and information. A previous version of this chapter was presented in November 2000 at the workshop 'Financial Cultures' organized at the University of Bielefeld, Germany.

1. While Henri Lefèvre was a product of the French system of elite schools, it appears that Jules Regnault was an autodidact: he did not pass through an elite school and did not even have a high school degree (*baccalauréat*). I owe this information to Franck Jovanovic.
2. This is not to say that moral questions disappeared altogether; but, to a considerable extent, they were debated now in works of fiction, being thus relegated to the domain of disbelief. This, among other reasons, is why we witness such a preoccupation with the ethics of finance in Victorian fiction, for example Reed (1984) and Holway (1992).
3. Investor manuals showed in detail how to compute interest rates on state, city and corporate bonds, since their modalities of payment and maturities could differ considerably. French state bonds, for example, had annual payments; some city and corporate bonds worked like martingales, being redeemed according to a lottery principle. This required continuous recalculations of interest rates, and manuals had to explain the procedures for each type of bond.
4. Railway companies had used charts in their attempts to win the favor of the legislators and of the public. In the British Parliament, charts of railway tracks were often used when applying for operating licenses. Many brochures addressing potential investors made use of diagrams to convince them of the viability and efficiency of the projected lines. On the other hand, since the beginning of the nineteenth century, diagrams began to be used for visualizing the price of state bonds over longer periods of time, as well as for correlating price movements with political events, thus explaining the movements of financial markets. One of the first instruments of this sort was the collection of diagrams of bond prices published by James Vansommer, the secretary of the Committee of the London Stock Exchange in 1834, in which price variations were correlated with political events for a time span of 44 years. On yet another level, there was a geographical tradition (particularly strong in the UK), in which social and economic events were visually correlated with climatic ones (like variations in temperature). Thus British geographers were also producing charts superimposing temperature variations on wheat and bond prices. All in all, the idea of assessing stock value on the basis of a general model or principle opened up two interrelated possibilities: namely, (1) that of visual representation of financial securities, and (2) that of using visual representations as a homogeneous framework for heterogeneous entities.
5. The *auto-compteur* was a device for computing bets on horse-races. It consisted in a wooden board divided into 100 squares. Several wires were anchored at the squares 0, 55 and 100, and could be moved diagonally across the board, with the help of five wooden pieces mounted on rails on the four sides. The wooden pieces were lettered B, B′, C, A, A′. Each piece had a hook which held the wire. There were two wires permanently attached at 110. One of them went to A and from there to B′, so that moving B′ would also mean moving A. The other one went to A′, from there to C and from C to B, so that moving C would mean also moving A′ and B. Another line was permanently anchored at 0 and 55. This device enabled gamblers to compute the relative chances of race-horses.

References

Agnew, Jean-Christophe (1986) *Worlds Apart: The Market and the Theater in Anglo-American Thought, 1550–1750*, Cambridge: Cambridge University Press.
Alborn, Timothy L. (1994) 'Economic Man, Economic Machine: Images of Circulation in the Victorian Money Market', in Philip Mirowski (ed.), *Natural Images in Economic Thought. 'Markets Read in Tooth and Claw'*, Cambridge: Cambridge University Press, pp. 173–95.
Amariglio, Jack and David F. Ruccio (1999) 'The Transgressive Knowledge of 'Ersatz' Economics', in Robert F. Garnett Jr (ed.), *What Do Economists Know? The New Economics of Knowledge*, London: Routledge, pp. 19–36.
Bachelier, Louis (1900) 'Theory of Speculation' in Paul H. Cootner (ed.) (1964), *The Random Character of Stock Market Prices*, Cambridge, MA: The MIT Press, pp. 17–78.
Bazerman, Charles (1999) *The Languages of Edison's Light*, Cambridge, MA: The MIT Press.
Beeton's Guide Book to the Stock Exchange and Money Market. With hints to investors, and the chances of speculators, London 1870: Ward, Lock, and Tyler.
Bernstein, Peter L. (1996) *Against the Gods. The Remarkable Story of Risk*, New York: John Wiley & Sons.
Blanchard, Ch. (1861) *De la valeur des actions du chemin de fer du Dauphiné à l'époque de la fusion*, Paris: Castel.
Borel, L. (1835) *Traité de la Bourse et de la Spéculation*, Paris.
La Bourse, Paris, 1866: Michel Levy Frères.
La Bourse, Réponse à ses détracteurs, Lyon, 1854: Méra.
Brasilier, Adolphe Pierre (1891) *Théorie mathématique des placements et des emprunts à long terme*, Paris: Masson.
Brenner, Reuven and Gabrielle A. Brenner (1990) *Gambling and Speculation: A Theory, a History, and a Future of Some Human Decisions*, Cambridge: Cambridge University Press.
Breton, Yves (1992) 'L'économie politique et les mathématiques en France 1800–1940', *Histoire et mesure*, **7**(1–2), 25–52.
Callon, Michel, Pierre Lascoumes and Yannick Barthe (2001) *Agir dans un monde uncertain. Essai sur la démocratie technique*, Paris: Seuil.
Courtois, Alphonse (1862) *Tableau des cours des principales valeurs. Du 17 janvier 1797 (28 Nivose an V) à nos jours*, Paris: Garnier-frères.
Crampon, A. (1863) *La Bourse. Guide pratique à l'usage des gens du monde*, Paris: H. Durandin.
De Mériclet, A. G. (1854) *La Bourse de Paris. Moeurs, anecdotes, spéculations et conseils*, Paris: D. Giraud.
Downey, Greg (2000) 'Running Somewhere Between Men and Women. Gender in the Construction of the Telegraph Messenger Boy', *Knowledge and Society*, **12**, 129–52.
Eggleston, George Cary (1875) *How to make a living. Suggestions upon the Art of Making, Saving, and Using Money*, New York: G.P. Putnam's Sons.
Epstein, Steven (1996) *Impure Science. AIDS, Activism, and the Politics of Knowledge*, Berkeley, CA: University of California Press.
Fabian, Ann (1990) *Card Sharps, Dream Books, & Bucket Shops. Gambling in 19th-Century America*, Ithaca, NY: Cornell University Press.
Fenn's Compendium of English and Foreign Funds, London 1854: Effingham Wilson.
Fortune, Thomas (1810) *An Epithome of the Stocks & Public Funds*, London: T. Boosey.
Guillard, Edouard (1875) *Les opérations de Bourse. Histoire – Pratique – Législation – Jurisprudence – Reformes – Morale – Economie Politique*, Paris: Guillaumin & Cie.
Hacking, Ian (1990) *The Taming of Chance*. Cambridge: Cambridge University Press.
Hautcoeur, Pierre-Cyrille (1997) 'Le marché financier entre 1870 et 1900', in Yves Breton, Albert Broder and Michel Lutfalla (eds), *La Longue Stagnation en France*, Paris: Economica, pp. 235–65.
Holway, Tatiana (1992) 'The Game of Speculation: Economics and Representation', *Dickens Quarterly*, **9**(3), 103–14.
Jovanovic, Franck (2000) 'The Origin of Financial Theory. A reevaluation of the contribution of Louis Bachelier', *Revue d'économie politique*, **110**(3), 396–418.
——— (2001) 'Pourquoi l'hypothèse de marché aléatoire en théorie financière? Les raisons historiques d'un choix éthique', *Revue d'économie financière*, **61**, 203–11.
——— (2002) 'Instruments et théorie économique dans la construction de la "science de la Bourse" d'Henri Lefèvre', *Revue d'Histoire des Sciences Humaines*, **7**, 41–68.
Jovanovic, Franck and Philippe Le Gall (2001) 'Does God Practice a Random Walk? The 'financial physics' of a nineteenth-century forerunner, Jules Regnault', *European Journal of the History of Economic Thought*, **8**(3), 332–62.
Klamer, Arjo (1999) 'The Art of Economic Persuasion', manuscript.
Klamer, Arjo and Thomas Leonard (1993) 'Everyday versus Academic Rhetoric in Economics', paper given at the George Washington University.
Lardner, Dionysius (1850) *The Steam Engine Familiarly Explained and Illustrated*, 5th American edn, Philadelphia: A. Hart.

Lave, Jean (1988) *Cognition in Practice: Mind, Mathematics and Culture in Everyday Life*, Cambridge: Cambridge University Press.
Lefèvre, Henri (1870) *Traité des valeurs mobilières et des opérations de Bourse. Placement et speculation*, Paris: Lachaud.
——— (1871) *Le jeu sur les courses des chevaux*, Paris: Chez l'auteur.
——— (1874) *Principes de la science de la Bourse. Méthode approuvée par la chambre syndicale des agents de change de la Bourse*, Paris: Publications de l'Institut Polytechnique.
Lépinay, Vincent and Fabrice Rousseau (2000) 'Les **Trolls** sont-ils incompétents? Enquête sur le financiers amateurs', *Politix*, **13**(52), 73–97.
Le Roy, Stephen (1989) 'Efficient Capital Markets and Martingales', *Journal of Economic Literature*, **27**, 1583–621.
Les écueils de la Bourse, Paris 1865: Librairie du Petit Journal.
Martin, Joseph G. (1886) *Martin's Boston Stock Market. Eighty-eight years, from January, 1798, to January, 1886*, Boston: published by the author.
Medbery, James K. (1870) *Men and Mysteries of Wall Street*, Boston: Fields, Osgood, & Co.
Ménard, Claude (1980) 'Three Forms of Resistance to Statistics: Say, Cournot, Walras', *History of Political Economy*, **12**(4), 524–41.
Minutes of the Court of Directors, Bank of England, 10 October 1844. London: Archives of the Bank of England.
Mirowski, Philip (1989) *More Heat than Light: Economics as Social Physics, Physics as Nature's Economics*, Cambridge: Cambridge University Press.
——— (ed.) (1994) *Natural Images in Economic Thought. 'Markets Read in Tooth and Claw'*, Cambridge: Cambridge University Press.
——— (2002) *Machine Dreams. Economics Becomes a Cyborg Science*, Cambridge: Cambridge University Press.
Noel-Fearn, Henry (1866) *The Money Market: What it is, what it does, and how it is managed*, London: Frederick Warne & Co.
Notions générales de Bourse, de Banque & de Change, Paris, 1877: Le Moniteur des Fonds Publics.
Officer, Lawrence (1996) *Between the Dollar–Sterling Gold Points: Exchange Rates, Parity and Market Behavior*, Cambridge: Cambridge University Press.
O'Rourke, Kevin and Jeffrey Williamson (1999) *Globalization and History. The Evolution of a Nineteenth-Century Atlantic Economy*, Cambridge, MA: The MIT Press.
——— (2000) *When Did Globalization Begin?*, Cambridge, MA: NBER Working Paper No. 7632.
——— (2001) *Globalization and Inequality*, Cambridge, MA: NBER Working Paper No. 2685.
Pinto, Erasmus (1877) *Ye Outside Fools! Glimpses into the London Stock Exchange*, New York: Lovell, Adam, Wesson & Company.
Playford, Francis (1855) *Practical Hints For Investing Money: With An Explanation Of The Mode Of Transacting Business on the Stock Exchange*, London: Smith, Elder &Co.
Porter, Theodore M. (1995) *Trust in Numbers. The Pursuit of Objectivity in Science and Public Life*, Princeton, NJ: Princeton University Press.
Preda, Alex (2000) 'Financial Knowledge and the "Science of the Market" in England and France in the 19th Century', in Herbert Kalthoff, Richard Rottenburg and Hans-Jürgen Wagener (eds), *Facts and Figures. Economic Representations and Practices*, Marburg: Metropolis, pp. 205–28.
——— (2001) 'The Rise of the Popular Investor: Financial Knowledge and Investing in England and France, 1840–1880', *The Sociological Quarterly*, **42**(2), 205–32.
——— (2002) 'On Ticks and Tapes: Financial Knowledge, Communicative Practices, and Information Technologies in 19th Century Financial Markets', paper presented at the Columbia University Workshop on Social Studies of Finance.
Proudhon, Pierre-Joseph (1854) *Manuel du spéculateur à la Bourse*, Paris: Garnier-frères.
Rapp, Rayna (1999) *Testing Women, Testing the Fetus. The Social Impact of Amniocentesis in America*, New York: Routledge.
The rationale of market fluctuations, London, 1876: Effingham Wilson.
Reed, John (1984) 'A Friend to Mammon. Speculation in Victorian Literature', *Victorian Studies*, **27**(2), 179–202.
Regnault, Jules (1863) *Calcul des chances et philosophie de la Bourse*, Paris: Mallet-Bachelier.
Rougemont, Henri (1857) *Guide-Manuel du placement et de la spéculation à la Bourse*, Paris: Passard.
Rousseau, Peter and Richard Sylla (2001) *Financial Systems, Economic Growth, and Globalization*, Cambridge MA: NBER working paper No. 8323.
——— (1999) *Emerging Financial Markets and Early US Growth*, Cambridge, MA: NBER Working Paper No. 7448.
Roussel, Etienne (1904) *Manuel du spéculateur et du capitaliste*, Paris: Guillemin.
Secret of Success in Wall Street, New York, 1875.
Sourigues, M. (1861) *De la valeur des actions de la Cie du Chemin de Fer de Lyon à Genève*, Paris: Castel.
——— (1862) *De la valeur des actions du Credit Foncier de France*, Paris: Castel.

Stock Speculation. A Daily Market Report, New York, 1875: L.W. Hamilton & Co.
Stocks and Stock-Jobbing in Wall-Street, with Sketches of the Brokers, and Fancy Stocks, New York, 1848: New York Publishing Company.
Sylla, Richard (1999a) 'Emerging Markets in History: The United States, Japan, and Argentina', in R. Sato (ed.), *Global Competition and Integration*, Boston, MA: Kluwer, pp. 427–46.
——— (1999b) *The State, the Financial System and Economic Modernization*, Cambridge: Cambridge University Press.
Tetreau, François (1994) *Le Développement et les Usages de la Coulisse aux XIXe et XXe Siècles*, Ph.D. diss., University of Paris II.
Train, George Francis (1857) *Young America in Wall Street*, New York: Derby and Jackson.
Todhunter, I. (1865) *A History of the Mathematical Theory of Probability from the Time of Pascal to that of Laplace*, New York (1965): Chelsea Publishing Co.
Vidal, E. (1910) *The History and Methods of the Paris Bourse*, Washington: Government Printing Office.
Walker, Donald (2001) 'A Factual Account of the Functioning of the 19th Century Paris Bourse', *European Journal for the History of Economic Thought*, **8**(2), 186–207.
Wayland, Francis (1837) *Elements of Political Economy*, New York: Leavitt, Lord & Co.
Wright, G.S. (1842) *A Letter to British Capitalists, upon the present and prospective advantages of investing capital in railway stock*, London: James Baker.
Wyckoff, Peter (1972) *Wall Street and the Stock Markets. A Chronology (1644–1971)*, Philadelphia: Chilton.
Zylberberg, André (1990) *L'économie mathématique en France 1870–1914*, Paris: Economica.

8 Economic instruments and theory in the construction of Henri Lefèvre's 'science of the stock market'

Franck Jovanovic

> It is in speculative trade that political economy will discover the theory of the circulation of wealth, which is one of the principal objects of its investigations.
>
> (Henri Lefèvre 1879a, 19)

The history of financial theory remains a rarely studied, and ultimately little-known, area. The first theoretical financial model is generally considered to have been formulated in Louis Bachelier's[1] doctoral thesis of 1900. But if we accept this genesis too readily, we risk overlooking a number of other attempts to construct a financial theory, especially in nineteenth-century France. These attempts – which played their part in the development of Bachelier's model – were particularly fruitful, and provided financial theory with some of its main instruments of analysis: in 1863 Jules Regnault[2] was the first to put forward the idea of using a random walk model to represent stock price fluctuations; in 1870, the French actuary Henri Lefèvre constructed the first graphical representations – now in common use – for analysing the outcome of complex combinations of stock market operations, most notably combined options.[3]

Henri Lefèvre was born in Châteaudun in 1827 and died in or around 1885.[4] He took a degree in natural sciences in 1848, but from the 1850s onwards steered his career towards economics, working his way into the selective circle of economic journalists. His interest in the 'dismal science' initially led him to work as economic correspondent for a number of different newspapers, eventually becoming chief editor of a Spanish-language economic journal, *El Eco Hispano-Américo*. After 1865, he turned to activities more directly related to finance, offering financial packages in the name of a company called the Comptoir Central de Souscription (Lefèvre 1865).[5] At various times he held positions as a banker, as the private secretary of Baron de Rothschild,[6] and also worked for the Union, one of the largest insurance firms in Paris. In 1869, he founded the Agence centrale de l'union financière with a group of partners, managing and acting as chief editor of its press organ, the *Journal des Placements Financiers*.[7] He also took an interest in accounting. In 1882 he published a brochure of which Mr Harang, president of the education section of the Seine Accountancy Committee, writing in the 1 August 1882 issue of the *Revue de la Comptabilité*, proclaimed that 'the teaching of accounting will soon be divided into two schools: one consisting of the partisans of practical education and the other, the partisans of theoretical education. *Without any doubt, the theoretical school will have been founded by Mr H. Lefèvre*' (italics added). This initial brochure was supplemented by a later work published in 1885. He also examined the 'theory of currency and exchange' in an article published in 1879 in the *Journal des actuaires français*. He probed the subject at greater depth in his treatise of 1881, *La Change et la Banque*, in which he sets out an original set of technical rules of exchange. This work, presented to the Académie des Sciences Morales et Politiques by Léon Say as 'containing, with regard to exchange operations, a discovery to some extent comparable with Monge's discovery of descriptive geometry' (1885a), was awarded a gold medal by the Société d'Encouragement pour l'Industrie Nationale. Finally, it is interesting to note that Lefèvre made several attempts to alert public opinion to the need for specialist financial and commercial education in France, along the lines of the German business schools. At the Institut Polytechnique – not to be confused with the École Polytechnique – he created a course in 'higher financial education' and published a number of pedagogical works, such as his *Principes de la science du commerce* of 1874 or his two works of 1885. One characteristic already stands out clearly: there is strong practical streak in Lefèvre's work, which also runs through his contributions to financial theory.

The historical background to Lefèvre's financial analysis is marked by the development of the Parisian stock market. During the nineteenth century, France's financial markets began to assert their economic status. Their activities spread out beyond financing the public debt and into the sphere of private sector finance, a new dimension which led to the development of the Paris Bourse[8] in the second half of the century: in 1800, there were three listed stocks; by 1850, there were 197; this rose to 689 by 1876, and more than 1000 in 1900.[9] This 'prodigious growth in securities in the portfolios of French capitalists ... mainly between 1850 and 1870' (Neymarck 1888, 8) indubitably left its mark on French society. In the 1860s and 1870s, a specialist press flourished: as Pierre-Cyrille Hautcœur (1994, 238) reminds us, Paris had 16 stock market journals in 1857 and 228 in 1881, not counting the financial sections of the 94 general newspapers. Neymarck (1903, 17) observes that, contrary to the prevailing view of the time, 'the vast majority of stock market investors are small shareholders, and the great majority is made up of those who have but one share and those who have between two and ten shares'.[10] The National Assembly and Senate were regularly called upon to legislate on legal and moral issues related to financial markets.[11] From the 1850s, French economists tried to raise public awareness of the economic role played by the financial markets, especially in the industrial development of the private sector.[12]

Paradoxically, however, the theoretical content of their economic analyses was relatively weak: more often than not its focus was limited to the history of the financial markets, or of the assets traded therein. With their literary bias, the 'traditional' economists remained highly descriptive, and had difficulty accounting for the workings of the stock market or apprehending its general mechanisms.[13] Consequently, they contributed very few original elements, whether practical or theoretical.[14] Shaken by the crisis in the field of political economy,[15] some economists tried to broaden its scope to encompass new problems and areas, including financial theory.

Decrying the lack of theoretical studies, a number of practitioners and more pragmatically minded economists tried to apply the new instruments at their disposal – graphical methods, statistics, probabilities, etc. – to the analysis of financial markets. Thus it was that, in 1863, the first theories and first financial models came to be constructed. These theoretical reflections on the stock market and finance – which ultimately led to the first Congrès international des values mobilières of 1900, among other things – developed independently from the traditional economists, for the reasons set out above. The work of the French actuaries, most notably Lefèvre, is worthy of particular attention here.[16] Lefèvre himself paints a sorry picture of the state of financial theory prior to his *Traité ... des valeurs mobilières et des opérations de bourse* (*Treatise on Securities and Stock Market Operations*) of 1870:

> Works about the stock market and banking that promise more than they provide, and do nothing to help the reader understand the inner workings of the operations they purport to explain ... . There is Courtois' *Treatise on Stock Market Operations*, which teaches no-one how to operate; Proudhon's

> *Speculator's Manual in the Stock Exchange*, which teaches no one how to speculate, and a plethora of minor works which serve as advertisements for the proponents of spurious financial schemes. (1885a, III)

From this starting point, Lefèvre set out on an ambitious quest to build a 'science of the stock market' that would determine the laws governing stock market activity. The new discipline was to focus on the circulation of goods. His analysis had a profound impact on other thinkers of the day: Léon Walras (1880a, 1880b) adopted his organic representation of society and his recommendations on access to the financial markets;[17] his work also inspired a number of eminent late-nineteenth-century economists and statisticians with an interest in financial theory, such as Paul Leroy-Beaulieu, Arthur Raffalovich[18] and Alfred Neymarck; finally, his graphical representations were widely circulated – by 1874, they were already known and much appreciated in stockbroking circles[19] – and re-used in theoretical works by other actuaries, notably Léon Pochet (1873),[20] as well as economists and mathematicians, including Louis Bachelier.

Such was the historical context that led Lefèvre to venture one of the first attempts at creating a new field of economic economics: financial theory. It was, of course, a very different concept to the one we know today. Analysis of Lefèvre's works should, however, shed some light on the way in which financial economics has come to be constructed, and the role played by technical instruments in its evolution. The aim of this chapter is to show that – by contrast with their current, highly restrictive, application – Lefèvre's graphs were originally part of a theoretical reflection on the stock market's economic role and the modalities of its contribution to economic development. Specifically, we look at how Lefèvre placed stock markets at the heart of economic theory by focusing on the circulation of goods and by developing theoretical instruments that would enable them to circulate with optimal efficiency.

This chapter is in two sections. The first discusses Lefèvre's thinking – highly original for its day – on how economic theory interfaces with financial theory. It emerges that his analysis of the economic organization of the circulation of goods and of exchange mechanisms is akin to the construction of a theoretical norm – i.e. an incipient ideal – designed to provide guidance for economic policy and for structural reforms of the financial markets. Lefèvre's goal was to determine which technical instruments and which economic policies could be employed to smooth the way towards this ideal situation. This is the object of the second section, which presents Lefèvre's practical recommendations for attaining greater economic efficiency by optimizing the stock markets as far as possible. This concern would notably lead him to formulate the graphical method that we know today, designed to facilitate stock market transactions.

1. The elaboration of a theoretical norm

Unlike almost every other nineteenth-century author who wrote on the subject, Lefèvre's aim was not to describe the stock market as it existed, but to conduct a general theoretical inquiry into the economic organization of society. He specifically analysed an ideal form of social and economic organization in which the stock market played a central role, sitting at the heart of economic activity and indirectly directing it. The integration of stock markets into economic theory – and the resulting outline of financial economics – can be seen as a product of Lefèvre's ideal representation of the economic organization of society. By projecting the form of organization to which society is heading, his approach amounts to the construction of a theoretical norm. This approach is presented in two stages, looking first at the origin of the norm, then at its nature.

1.1 The origin of the norm

Lefèvre's representation of the economic organization of society is a synthesis of elements drawn from two models of knowledge: on the one hand, that of Auguste Comte ; on the other, that of animal physiology. From the first, he takes the historical determinism inherent in the progress of civilization, according to Comte's law of the three stages: every society tends towards the stage of greatest perfection, i.e. positivism. The second, by analogy with the human organism, provides a representation of how such a perfect society should be organized. The synthesis of these two elements enables him to prefigure the ideal economic organization for society, from which perspective he analyses the economic transformations which were then taking place – in particular the emergence of stock markets.

In the field of research that he opened up in the 1820s, Auguste Comte focused on the evolution of civilizations and of the sciences. He was especially interested in the social organization that would be dictated by 'scientific policy', given the stage of civilization that had been reached. To understand this stage of development, one must first determine the process by which societies evolve, which can be discovered, according to Comte, by observing the past and analysing the data thus collected. From this one can determine the evolutionary direction of any civilization, and foresee its future development. Thus, 'scientific policy' seeks first to determine the system that history tends, of its own devices, to generate, and subsequently to optimize that system.

On the basis of his own historical observations, Comte considered that all civilizations passed through three stages of development: the theological stage, the metaphysical stage and the positive stage. This succession of stages always leads in the direction of the third and final stage of social development, that of the greatest perfection, culminating in the triumph of science and industry. The sole and constant goal of social activity becomes production; inevitably, in such a society, the economy has pride of place.

The historical determinism of Comte's model encouraged Lefèvre to construe the evolution of the economic organization of society as a historical process tending towards the state of greatest perfection:

> [Human societies] are, in a real sense, living organisms. Their degree of perfection varies, depending on whether they have developed slowly or quickly, and one finds, in different places and at different times, societies at different levels of organization … . Society initially organizes itself into slaves who feed it, warriors who defend it, and priests who govern it. But this is not the moment to recount the history of the various stages of humanity, of which the laws have been mapped out by our illustrious master, Auguste Comte. (1870a, 242)

Lefèvre saw, in the rise of the nineteenth-century stock market, a sign of society's economic progress. At that time, moreover, the large centralized stock exchanges, such as the Paris Bourse and the London Stock Exchange, were starting to list physical goods such as corn and sugar.[21] For Lefèvre, the stock market was not limited to capital transactions alone: it was that great organized marketplace in which raw materials, as well as capital, could be exchanged (1879a, 15).[22] Goods were no longer destined for local markets alone, as was the case, according to Lefèvre, in less developed societies; they could circulate freely over a wide network to meet the needs of any individual. Society was therefore moving towards the creation of a vast economic marketplace in which every agent, thanks to the great stock exchanges, had direct access to the whole range of goods produced. This vast marketplace could only operate perfectly – indeed, could only exist – in the final stage of development of human society. Lefèvre's assimilation of human societies to living organisms, explicit in the quotation above, reveals another characteristic of his 'perfect society', and here we touch on the second model of knowledge from which he drew inspiration, that of animal physiology.

While Comte's historical determinism offered an explanation for social evolution, it provided no clear picture of how society was organized at the final stage. The physiological model of knowledge, however, gave Lefèvre a template for the final-stage society, by positing that human societies had living characteristics. After all, as society was evolving towards the stage of greatest perfection and could be assimilated to a living organism, the organization of final-stage society would ultimately be identical to that of the most perfect of living organisms. To find out what that was, one need look no further than the science which studies the organic functions of living creatures, i.e. physiology. And physiology told Lefèvre that the most perfect living organism was … man. The organization of the most perfect society should, therefore, be analogous to the organization of the human body: in other words, it should be characterized by a perfect fit between the organization and functions of society and those of the human form:

> We must obstinately proclaim, as a truth which can no longer be disputed, that societies are living organisms in constant development, successively perfecting their various functions, and their organs – which are the agents of those functions – in reaction to their ever more complete knowledge of Man himself. (1870a, 242)

The analogy between economic systems and the human body was not a new one: it crops up in many economists, even in the twentieth century, such as Théret (1995) or Ménard (1978, 111 ff.). In order to assert its scientific status, economics has frequently borrowed models or instruments from disciplines already recognized as scientific, such as biology or mechanics. Indeed, as Ménard (1981, 138) reminds us, one of the first mathematical economists, Canard (1801), represented the social body with the image of a living organism in which 'traders occupy "the centre of circulation", of which the two ventricles are the store and the cash-register and where work and its products represent the arterial system, while the movement of money is analogous to the venous system' (Ménard 1981, 138). Canguilhem (1968, 73) also makes the point that the nineteenth century was a heyday for determinist theories about biological phenomena.

The belief that society is evolving towards a final stage, characterized by an increasingly developed and highly perfected social organization, inevitably leads to a modification in the nature of that final stage. In Lefèvre's analysis, the nature and role of the final stage are made clear by the synthesis of the two models of knowledge. It is no longer just the culmination of a process of development; it becomes an ideal: 'Clearly, we are still a long way from a perfect conformity of this type; it is, in my view, an ideal' (1870a, 243). This touches directly on the nature of this final stage: by definition, an ideal can never be attained; it is something towards which one strives. In this particular case, moreover, society has an inherent tendency, because of the way it develops, to move towards a form of organization analogous to that of a living organism. The course of its evolution cannot be diverted; on the contrary, our constantly enriched knowledge about the organism guides political action by showing us 'that which must be'. The role of the final stage is clear: it is an ideal to which society inherently aspires. In the political sphere, it fulfils the role of a theoretical norm.

By identifying a deterministic process of historical evolution and defining the ideal towards which we are moving, Lefèvre constructed a theoretical norm that enabled him to represent society as it should be. But his synthesis also allowed him to go further. Since society is 'in constant development', it evolves towards the final stage by perfecting its various functions and organs. Consequently, the study of the human body should offer us a preview of the way in which this ideal society will be organized, allowing us to identify the functions of the various social and economic agents: it enables us to examine in detail the nature of the norm.

1.2 The nature of the norm

Having discovered the ideal organization of society, Lefèvre sought to determine, in the economic sphere, the role of each element involved in the circulation of goods in the final stage of social evolution. One of the characteristics of any living organism, necessary for its general viability, is the separation of functions: each organ has a specific role. With Comte's law of the three stages, one can foresee that the evolution of economic organization will lead to local stock exchanges being integrated into a single stock exchange, in which all commodities are traded; but the physiological model of knowledge allows one to go further still, identifying point by point the analogies (or identities, to use Cohen's (1993) term) between the economy and the human body. Thus,

> In superior creatures and societies, these scattered centres all disappear, giving way to a single organ, namely the heart – or the stock exchange – and the social circulatory system tends increasingly, albeit empirically, to model itself on that of the individual. The individual is the standard which the collective organism seeks ever more closely to approach. (Lefèvre 1873, 213)

This involves proceeding by analogy to identify, empirically, the factors that must be modified in order to attain the ideal model.

The human analogy offered Lefèvre an opportunity for a further insight into the final stage of social development: he used it to sketch the outlines of the ideal economic organization. Just as living creatures are organized around their vital organ, the heart, so economic organization centres on the stock market, that 'organ of circulation' whose 'function is to circulate' the goods produced (Lefèvre 1874a, 12) – in other words, it is only through the stock market that commodities come to be exchanged. The stock exchange becomes the only point of encounter between supply and demand. More exactly, the stock market centralizes the commodities produced by the various industries dotted around the country and redistributes them according to intermediate and end consumer needs (Lefèvre 1873, 213). It would be wrong to conclude, however, that the stock market operates autonomously, independently from the rest of society. It is open to two influences: on one side, government; on the other, speculation. The first element, government, can regulate – or at least orient – stock market activity up to a certain point. But this dependency operates indirectly: 'the stock market is absolutely free in society, and governments cannot act directly on its fluctuations' (ibid., 214). For this reason, Lefèvre identifies the government with the brain: it is the cerebral organ 'which thinks and calculates, but which also hesitates, tires and falls asleep' (1873, 215). The government's scope for action is constrained by the economic context and economic activity. The second element, by contrast – speculation – is the real driving force behind the economy; it keeps the stock market moving, even if only slowly at times, and exercises 'deliberate direct action': 'Speculation is the – as yet incompletely formed – organic nervous system of society: it presides over the circulation, and thus over nutrition, and it gives the stock market, i.e. the heart of society, its constant impetus' (ibid.). Lefèvre uses the analogy with the human body to isolate two of the key elements that drive the circulation of goods: stock markets[23] and speculation. These two elements help him to resolve a fundamental economic problem raised by the circulation of goods: time.

The issue of temporality in the circulation of goods is not limited to the financial sphere; it is very much a real-world question. There is a time gap, in the 'real' sphere, between the moment when a good is produced and the moment when it is effectively sold. A comparable gap exists in the financial sphere between the moment when the capital is advanced to produce a commodity, and the moment when the consumer buys it. This double gap entails two types of risk. In the real sphere, there is a risk that consumer tastes will change between the two instants in time, burdening the producer with unwanted stock. In the financial sphere, the risk is that commodity prices will vary, forcing the producer to sell at a loss.[24] So, although the production quantities and costs of commodities are known elements, the same is not true for their consumption, i.e. the quantities bought and the selling prices. But given that society's system of organization – modelled on that of the human body – is ideal, these risks can be avoided by simply identifying the factors that promote good blood flow, and developing their counterparts in the economic sphere. Lefèvre therefore sought, through the analogy with the human body, to determine how the stock market and its constituent elements could ward off these two dangers.

The first temporal problem concerns the real sphere. Lefèvre starts out from the observation that it takes a certain amount of time to produce a commodity. Between the moment when an enterprise buys in raw materials and the moment when the output is produced, there is inevitably a lapse of time. Likewise, goods cannot suddenly be produced as and when the demand for them arises. More specifically, it takes less time to produce goods than it does to distribute and consume them. By raising the question of temporality, Lefèvre automatically brings in the issue of the circulation of goods between the different economic moments, and the problem of unforeseen events and changes in consumer behaviour or taste during the intervening period.

This built-in uncertainty of economic activity carries over onto the stock markets where the goods are – or, in their finished state, will be – exchanged. This was an important element for Lefèvre, one that had often, he felt, been under-estimated or ignored by economic theory:

> For the last hundred years, economists have been striving to found a science encompassing the production, distribution and consumption of wealth; but have they thought to examine the remarkable mechanism of the uncertain market, designed precisely to correspond to the uncertain conditions to which human existence, both individually and collectively, is constantly subjected? (1879a, 16)

What mechanism, therefore, will cover producers against the risk of variation in consumer tastes? In other words, what mechanism will keep the whole economy in supply despite changes in consumer behaviour?

The aim of Lefèvre's approach was to identify, by analogy with human physiology, the 'social organs' that fulfil the same role as those which, in the human body, enable the blood to supply any organ with what it requires, no matter what changes occur. In other words, one must identify the factors that will give society advanced warning of its supply needs, allowing it to modify supply flows at any moment without adversely affecting the producers. For Lefèvre, this is precisely the role that the stock market should play:

> Neither the public, nor the traders, nor even the economists are yet fully cognizant of the need for these large markets by means of which, ultimately, the existence of a whole society is ensured several months in advance. How many of them, at the present time, truly understand the process by which the entire floating volume of a commodity or stock can remain in suspension on the market, ready to meet all probable and even possible needs, and in a state of unstable equilibrium that only some great political catastrophe could disrupt? (1879a, 16)

Specifically, it is the futures markets that are able to redirect production in response to unforeseen variations in demand. These markets make it possible to terminate a contract at any moment if the economic conditions so require. In this case, speculation will perform the task of redirecting the goods towards other needs: 'It is the forward markets – the options markets, in a word – which force capital to preserve the current surplus of production over consumption, or to deliver it in accordance with the needs of that consumption' (Lefèvre 1873, 362). Stock markets keep goods permanently available. Speculation enables the economy to respond to unforeseen variations in tastes and requirements.

By resolving the problem of the time gap between production and consumption, the stock exchange should enable markets to attain equilibrium in time as well as in space. And while the stock exchange is the forum where supply and demand rub shoulders, it is the speculator who really makes them connect. 'The law of supply and demand truly comes into play between the speculators, and not at all between the real buyers and sellers, who represent the consumers and producers' (Lefèvre 1874a, 49). Stock markets therefore unburden the producers of the risk of not selling their output. The problem of selling off the goods produced is then borne by the entire collectivity (as represented by the stock markets) which takes care of finding the necessary outlets. Moreover – as a result of arbitrage operations – improvements in means of communication and in market organization have, Lefèvre explains, levelled prices on different markets by smoothing out the price differentials found on alternative markets at any given moment. This uniqueness of pricing from one stock exchange to another has led speculation to focus instead on price differentials between points in time, which may be nearer or further apart. Thus, by operating on futures markets, speculation establishes equilibrium in the temporal dimension.

However, the stock markets still need to address a second temporal problem, specific to the financial sphere. There is a time gap between the moment when capital is advanced and the moment when payment is received. This time gap exposes the producer to the risk of prices changing and may, at the end of the day, result in negative earnings. Once again by analogy with the human body, Lefèvre tries to identify a system in the economic sphere that will prevent the repercussions of retail price variations at the level of the consumer reflecting back on the producer; in other words, a system of insurance against the risk of variation in retail prices. And indeed, a defining role of any futures market is to ensure that a given quantity of a commodity will be delivered at a given date and at a price agreed in advance. For Lefèvre, this insurance function of the stock market[25] is analogous with the cardiovascular valve in the human organism, which prevents blood from flowing backwards. Options markets thus avoid the problem of price variations being passed back from one player to another. The potential this offers for insuring against price variation has benefits for the consumer, as well as the producer:

> The baker cannot escape the conditions of existence to which the whole of industry is subject, and above all the requirement that he should have the necessary capital or credit to ensure his supplies well in advance, rather than going to market in the morning to buy the few sacks of flour he needs for that evening's batch, thereby enduring and making the public – so easily panicked in such matters – endure all the fluctuations that grand speculation is wont to impose upon it.
>
> We need a certain number of bakers, but not too many. Those who know their trade, who have a degree of business acumen …, will drive out some of their competitors by learning to buy their supplies on the options markets … and by selling … their bread more cheaply than those who have to buy their supplies for spot cash. (Lefèvre 1873, 357–8)

Ultimately, the consumer gains as much as the producer from being insured against price variation. Options trading thus protects the interests of the various players – producers, consumers, retailers – and prevents society's supplies from being threatened by an excessive drop in prices. The ability to insure against uncertainty acts as a stimulus to economic activity by enabling the players to cover themselves against the various risks. This system offers security for producers and consumers alike, an especially important consideration when it comes to supplying large conurbations, and thus in the overall organization of the economy.[26] This second function of speculation ultimately helps to smooth out prices and avoid instability in the price of finished goods due to unforeseen fluctuations in the price of raw materials.

The focus on the economic roles played by speculation underlines the closeness of the interaction between financial theory and economic theory. Both functions illustrate how speculation acts as an engine, indispensable to the smooth running of the economy and to its equilibrium. This leads Lefèvre (1873, 219) to account for financial or commercial disasters as the direct result of ignorance or non-compliance with the fundamental laws governing the circulation of goods. One can see how important it was for him to be able to identify the processes that lead to the ideal state of society. The norm thus derived must enable real problems to be assessed, by comparing the ideal with the reality, and political action must steer reality closer towards the norm. In this respect, society is 'a natural *organism* whose spontaneous workings we must first study in order subsequently to improve its development' (Lefèvre 1874a, 13). We must therefore turn our attention to the means for improving the organization and efficiency of the stock markets which will in turn accelerate society's convergence towards the ideal.

2. Practical recommendations for improving the circulation of goods

As we have just seen, the stock market acquires a central economic position because all goods must come to it to be exchanged. Given the central function of the stock exchange and of speculation in the economy, Lefèvre poses the question of how the stock market can be made as efficient as possible. The previously defined norm enables us to measure reality against the norm and thus to recommend ways of narrowing the gap that separates us from the 'final stage'. Although this process is already under way with a momentum of its own, it can be speeded up. In other words, Lefèvre seeks to identify the political actions that might hasten the advent of stock markets operating at optimal efficiency. The methods he envisages are of two types; we will look at each in turn. First, he applies the principle of organ specialization to the organization of stock markets, separating out the various agents involved in the circulation of goods in a way that isolates the role played by each one. He goes on to suggest rationalizing access to markets and to financial operations in line with each player's need, with the aim of avoiding such abuses as stockjobbing. Second, he outlines a method of analysis, specific to his field of research, designed to improve the way the various agents intervene on the markets. The method is a graphical one, and it enables the stock exchange to exercise its function (the circulation of goods) more effectively, and thus move closer towards the ideal situation analysed in the first section.

2.1 Rationalizing access to financial markets

One of the characteristics of the ideal social organization, as described above, is the division of functions. Each part of the human body fulfils a precise function for which it is uniquely adapted. The division of labour is, consequently, a sign of social progress: 'it is as necessary in society as it is in industry; the confusion of the different functions is encountered only in the savage condition, and among inferior creatures' (Lefèvre 1874a, 55, note 2). Lefèvre therefore set out to determine how the division of labour operated in the financial markets. To this end, he drew on observations of the most efficient and highly developed enterprises of his time – the major trading companies – to deduce the division of functions that best served the circulation of goods in the ideal society to which we are all heading.

The circulation of goods via the big trading companies of the late nineteenth century depended on the actions of three key agents: the wholesaler, the broker and the retailer. Each agent constituted an intermediate step between producer and consumer, one that was necessary for the smooth circulation of goods:

> As we know, the division of labour in business calls for three sorts of agent: one, the wholesaler, deals with the product; another, the retailer, deals with the consumer; and then there is the intermediary between these two, the broker, a retail-wholesaler or commission merchant, who has nothing directly to do either with the public, nor even with the product. (1874a, 114)

This division of functions governs the relationships between the different players. At either end of the equation we have the wholesaler and the retailer. The first stores the finished goods while the second sells them as products to the consumer. Liaison between the two agents, who are not in direct contact, is made possible by 'an intermediary, who has no store, nor outlet, nor commodity, who has no need to handle a bail of cotton or a sack of flour or coffee ... , but who runs between the wholesaler and the retailer: the broker [*courtier*] or runner [*couratier*], as he used to be called, is the man who runs and who sets the price [*qui court et qui fait le cours*]' (Lefèvre 1873, 216). Each agent is therefore characterized by a precise function which should logically correspond to a particular type of stock market operation.

This view of how financial markets are organized offers an interesting window on Lefèvre's thinking about social organization. But it also opens up a quite different set of questions: who are the agents whose role it is to participate in the various markets? This was one of the burning issues of the day: which operations could be considered permissible, and which illicit (Jovanovic 2001)? Lefèvre's answer is to shift the debate away from the nature of the operation (e.g. selling short or selling long) to its end: any operation that does not serve the circulation of goods must be prohibited. In this system, each agent has a precise function and practises a particular type of stock market operation, which leads him to operate only within certain markets. Accordingly, any operation not justified by the agent's economic function is illicit.[27] The consumer, for instance, who buys the good from the retailer, wants to consume it immediately and pays for it on the spot. He is not subjected to temporal constraints – even if he doesn't consume the item immediately, he has no stock management to worry about: the thing is his to use when he pleases. Consequently, since he pays for commodities on the spot, he has access only to the spot market. Futures markets should be closed to him: he does not require access to the futures markets to perform his operations. However, when the retailer takes the customer's money, it is not in fact a spot transaction but part of a forward transaction. The retailer, after all, had the goods well before the consumer approached him. He is therefore bound by a temporal constraint that leads him to purchase forward, buying goods from the broker that he then sells on to the consumer for cash. He must therefore have access to both spot and futures markets. As for the broker, he needs to hedge against unforeseen changes in consumption. It is thanks to him that the market readjusts to variations in demand. He needs to be able to exercise great flexibility of supply in order to insure against such uncertainties.

To this end, he must have access to the options markets to establish his contract with the wholesaler:

> The holder of large quantities of commodities or stocks puts some of them into circulation, where they float between probable consumption and possible consumption, and are sold to a buyer for more than they would have made by firm sale, by means of a written or verbal contract under which the vendor promises to take them back at a certain date if the buyer considers it in his interest not to demand delivery. (Lefèvre 1873, 218)

It only remains for the wholesaler to source the goods from the producer, who sells them firm, whether forward or spot.[28] From the basis of this division of functions in the circulation of goods, Lefèvre argues for restricted access to the different stock markets – spot and futures – in accordance with each player's social role. This form of access to the financial markets can thus be considered rationally grounded.[29]

The purpose of this rationalization is to ensure the efficient circulation of goods. As each agent operates in accordance with requirements specific to his own particular profession or line of business, he cannot operate on a market for personal reasons outside his professional capacity, for example, in order to gamble. Failure to comply with the rules of stock market access would transform speculation into mere gambling, a socially unproductive activity that can only be condemned:[30]

> [Respect for the natural hierarchy of the different social functions] is the only viewpoint which one should need to adopt in order to resolve the question of stock market gambling, a subject which has aroused such controversy, and on which there have been so many empty pronouncements, all without arriving at any criterion of judgment. Gambling, whatever form it may take, is not a social act, as it produces nothing of utility; society has no need to acknowledge its existence … . Between the retailer and the non-trading individual, who is a pure consumer, there can only be cash purchase and sale operations … . However, speculative or trading agreements between two non-trading individuals, or between one non-trading individual and a retailer, a wholesaler or a broker, should be considered a form of gambling, since one of the parties, if not both, is unqualified for such a trade … . Between different orders of trader, by contrast, it is not gambling, but legitimate speculation, since certain formalities have been completed in order for the effects of their mutual relations to be recognized. (Lefèvre 1874a, 116–17)[31]

Unlike gambling, which does not respect the natural order, legitimate speculation increases the welfare of the collectivity. On the basis of this analysis, Lefèvre feels able to judge the realities and economic policies of his day. He exposes what he sees as absurdities in market organization which, by violating this specialization, diminish the collective welfare.[32] Having established the case for rationalized (i.e. restricted) access to the stock markets, Lefèvre puts forward another method for optimizing the circulation of goods by improving the effectiveness of stock market operatives.

2.2 An original graphic method

The rationalization of access to the different stock markets is connected to the efficiency of trading. Financial markets need to organize themselves with a limited number of players and a growing number of commodities presented for exchange on the market. The growing number of commodities will be accompanied by an increase in the complexity of stock market operations, as the market must maintain a continuous temporal equilibrium. And if the circulation of goods is to be made efficient, everything must be done to allow players to act promptly.

Lefèvre therefore needed to find a way to facilitate stock market operations, i.e. by increasing the rapidity with which they could be performed by traders.

One of the goals of any market player is to have instant visibility of the outcome of any set of stock market operations, however complex, and for any listed stock. If the price subsequently varies, each player can react immediately on the basis of his position; and the faster a player can establish the accounting situation of his operations, the sooner he can intervene on the market – in other words, the more efficient he will be. The ability to establish one's accounting situation at any moment thus becomes a factor of economic efficiency, and a criterion that can easily be acted upon:

> When several operations have been performed by a wholesaler or by a speculator, it is important that one should know the resulting situation at any moment. To this end, one must learn directly to conjugate any number of markets, be they firm or options markets, by means of simple rules that anyone can apply. (Lefèvre 1873, 363)

As Lefèvre points out, there should be no need to be a specialist, since stock market operations are accessible to certain agents whose main line of business is not speculation. The earlier example of the baker who makes use of the stock market to avoid passing on price fluctuations to his customers is a case in point. One must therefore find an easily used instrument capable of analysing potential combinations of operations in terms of a player's trading outcome for any listed stock.

This quest takes us back to the models of knowledge from which Lefèvre drew his inspiration. As we saw in the first section, he draws partly on Comte's model. For Comte, the most advanced scientific disciplines – the positive sciences – eschew theoretical abstraction and advocate empirical observation. Positivism allows no other scientific method than induction, rejecting the use of abstract mathematics in favour of the concrete mathematics that structures the visible world, as used in mechanics and geometry (Callens 1997, 270–72). Thus, for Lefèvre:

> Although arbitrage trading represents a very interesting application of common algebra, speculative trading must borrow from analytical geometry to find a way of explaining its combinations; it is impossible to gain a clear picture of the subject by using arithmetic, algebra or ordinary language. (Lefèvre 1879a, 19)

Lefèvre's aim is to develop a geometry-based analytical tool to study combinations of operations and compare their outcomes. Arithmetical calculations have the advantage of being accurate, but they tend to be long and intricate, and thus impractical for many people. Geometry, by contrast, offers a simple, graphic mode of representation that anyone can understand. For example, the gain y from a security transaction can be expressed by the equation:[33]

$$y = n(l - a) - f,$$

where n is the number of shares, l the settlement price, a the purchase price and f the brokerage fees. By assuming a single share and leaving aside the question of brokerage fees – as we will continue to do from here on – we get:

$$y = l - a.$$

The profit from such an operation, as expressed by the gain function, can easily be depicted on a graph by plotting settlement prices on the x axis and outcomes on the y axis. The above equation yields a line (AA in Figure 8.1) in Lefèvre's example.

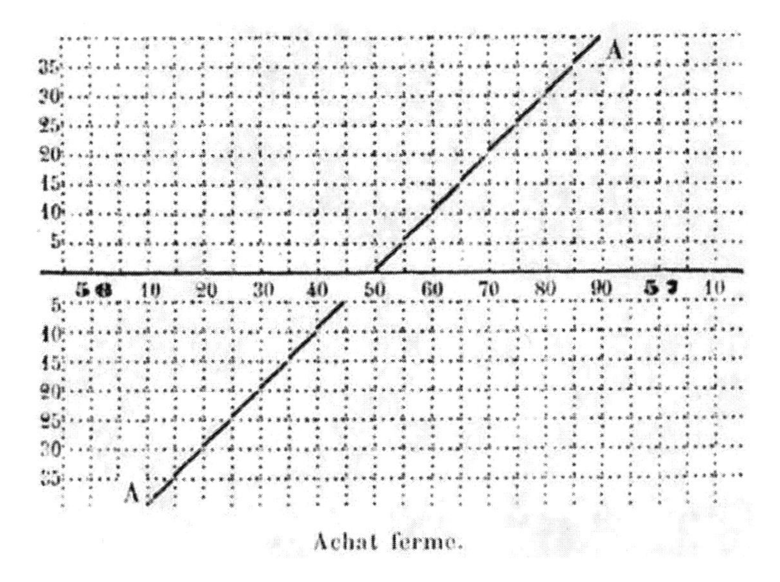

Figure 8.1 Firm purchase (Lefèvre 1873, 224)

The profit or loss arising from the firm purchase of a stock – or a commodity – for 56.50 francs can simply be read off the graph. If, for example, at the end of the period, i.e. when the operation is performed, the price of the stock (x axis) is Fr 56.80, 30 centimes above the price fixed by the firm contract, the profit (y axis) is 30 centimes. Likewise, the gain y of an option transaction will depend on whether the option is taken up. In the simplest case, the profit will be expressed by:

$$y = l - a.$$

The loss, however, will be equal to the amount of the option premium, p. In all, three cases need to be considered: if $l > a - p$, the option is exercised; if $l < a - p$, the option is surrendered; finally, if $l = a - p$, it makes no difference whether it is exercised or not. Lefèvre offers a graph (Figure 8.2) for the gain function of a call option with a 25c premium – an option to buy with a premium value (or option price) of 25 centimes – where the exercise price of the underlying asset is Fr 56.45.

The x axis represents the price of the stock, the y axis the outcome of the operation. According to this graph, if, on expiration, the underlying asset is priced at Fr 57.00, a profit of 30 centimes can be made;[34] if the price on expiration is Fr 56.20, then there will be a loss of 25 centimes.

These two illustrations are rather rudimentary. Their interest lies in the many permutations that can be generated by combining them, and in the ability to derive the total gain function

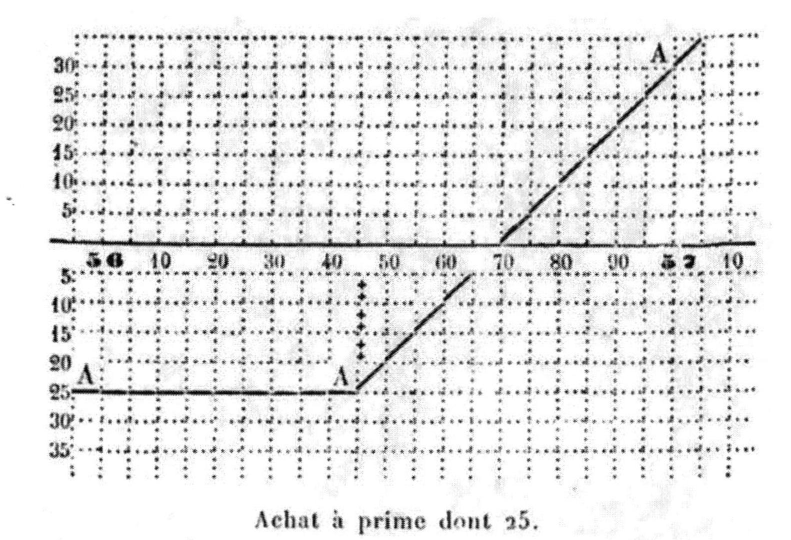

Figure 8.2 *Call option with a 25c premium (Lefèvre 1873, 228)*

using this system, dispensing with complex calculations. Lefèvre envisaged two types of application.

First, it could be used for complex hedging operations. For example, in Figure 8.3, by combining the sale of one option (curve VV) with the purchase of another (curve AA), Lefèvre suggests a hedge against strong volatility in prices (curve RR).

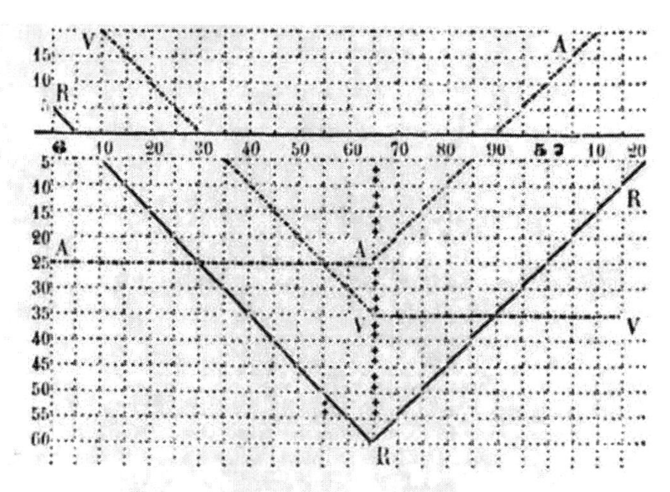

Figure 8.3 *Direct call with converse put, or purchase of two options with a premium of 25c for Fr 56.90 versus firm sale at Fr 56.55 (Lefèvre 1873, 242)*

In this instance, the option holder covers himself against the underlying asset being priced at less than Fr 56.05 or more than Fr 57.25 on expiration, in other words, against excessive volatility in the price of the underlying asset: his maximum loss is limited to the premiums paid on the two options, i.e. 60 centimes.

Second, on any given settlement date, a player will often have a number of stocks where he is sometimes in a position to sell and sometimes in a position to buy. The basic graphs described above can be combined to represent the player's final situation and thus assess the gain function of such operations, however complex they may be.[35] In this case, Lefèvre's graphic method fulfils its role perfectly, since 'however expert the calculations of those with long experience in this kind of operation, they cannot, through ordinary means, attain the accuracy and speed of execution' (Lefèvre 1873, 245) obtained by this method. In Figure 8.4, for example, Lefèvre derives the final situation for a series of operations on French 5 per cent bonds.[36]

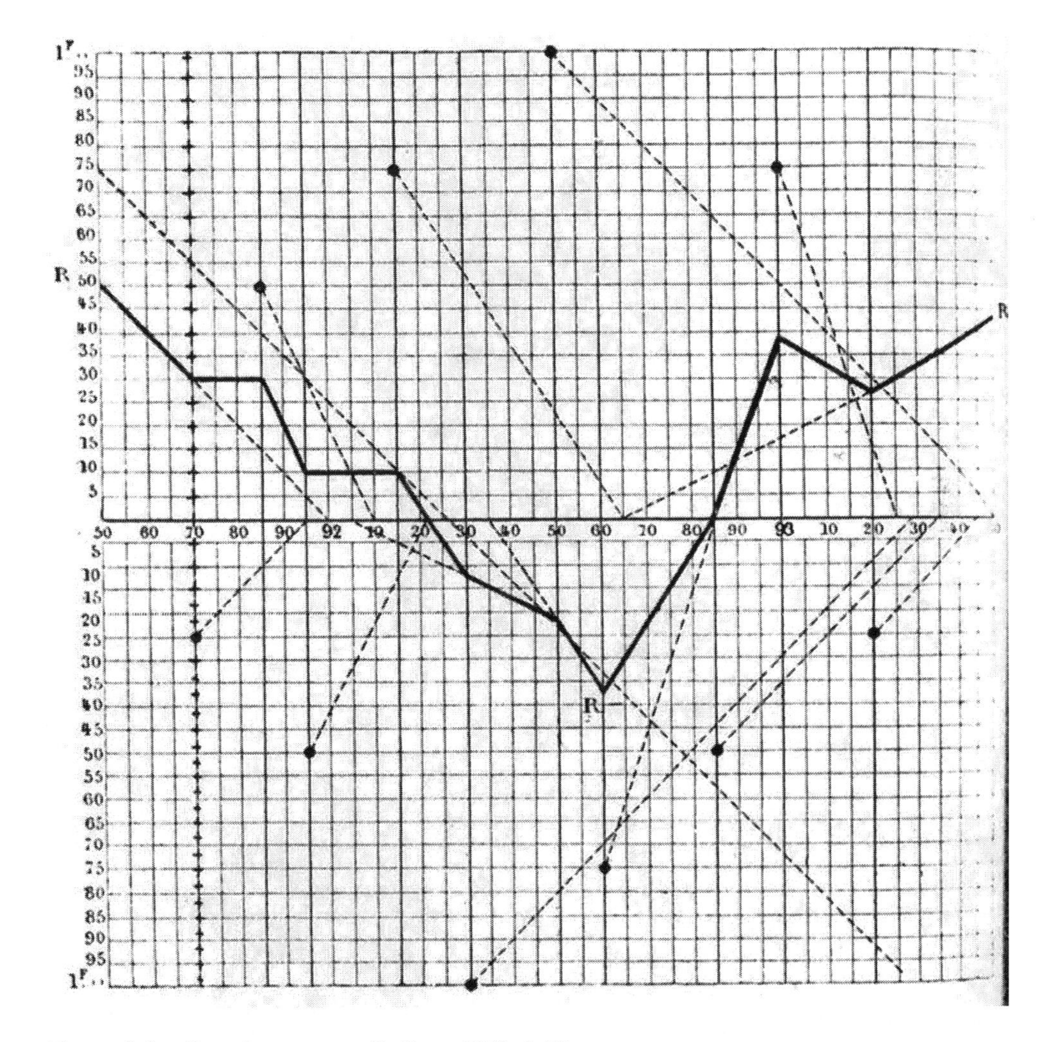

Figure 8.4 Complex strategy (Lefèvre 1873, 248)

The profit or loss at any given price point of the asset can be read directly off the graph, and the position adjusted if necessary. Thus, for any price between Fr 92.20 and Fr 92.85, the overall outcome from this set of operations is negative. What Lefèvre is finally suggesting, in an original way, is that a player's final situation should be evaluated relative to the total gain function, which can be represented in graphic form.

To enable every player easily to express any combination of stock market operations, Lefèvre goes back to the principle of the nomogram[37] and proposes nothing less than a 'typological alphabet of the stock market'[38] designed to represent the gain function for any combination of stock market operations, thereby providing a powerful instrument of analysis:

> Thanks to [the speculator's nomogram] ... it is simplicity itself for anyone to perform stock market operations, no matter how complex, to take perfectly precise account of each operation, and to reflect quickly and accurately on the figures thus derived, something that no one has previously been able to do. (Lefèvre 1870b, 1870c, 3)

This instrument has a dual advantage. For one thing, the benefit of such an 'alphabet' resides in the ease with which – by virtue of its simple construction – it can be distributed, particularly in the newspaper medium. Lefèvre circulated his graphs widely, through his teaching, in the press and even on posters.[39] But they also enabled any player to work out his position at any moment, without the need for painstaking calculations. With this simple accounting control tool, everyone was equipped to operate efficiently:

> I have attempted to shed light on the workings of the Stock Exchange [*Treatise on Securities and Stock Market Operations*, 1871] and for this purpose have created an auditing instrument [the speculator's nomogram] with which everyone can be aware of what he is doing and thus avoid the traps which are set for him. (Lefèvre 1871, 7)

The advantage of the graphical instrument is that it relieves players of the need to perform tricky accounting calculations. Its ease of use considerably reduces response times to market fluctuations and speeds up the flow of transactions, thus improving the circulation of goods and, beyond that, the functioning of the economy as a whole. Lefèvre's graphs therefore fulfil a necessary social function by regulating and stimulating economic activity in a way that takes us closer to his 'norm' – the ideal standard described at the outset.

3. Conclusion

Lefèvre's work, drawing on two models of knowledge – animal physiology and Comte's historical model – can be read as an interesting attempt to apply economic theory to the financial markets of the late nineteenth century. By retaining only his graphical instruments, however, history casts a broader light on the direction taken by financial theory throughout its development. Lefèvre's graphs were adopted by theoreticians in two different ways. One group – whose standpoint is exemplified by Alexandre Masseboeuf (1923) – held onto their primary vocation as a pedagogical tool, offering an easily used mechanism for the uninitiated. The graphs obviate the need for complex and abstract formalization. For the other, they served as a starting point for a line of abstract reasoning that incorporated mathematical developments in order to formalize financial theory. The graphical tool was no longer an end in itself, but a support for mathematical analysis. For Bachelier (1900) and Alfred Barriol (1908), for example, graph-based approximations were no longer sufficient: they set out to formalize these graphic representations in order to calculate an exact value. In his thesis, Bachelier made use of this graphical reasoning to determine mathematically the price of an option, but the graphs were isolated out from Lefèvre's wider work.

These authors used the same method as Lefèvre, but in a very different perspective. Bachelier and Barriol completely lost sight of the norm, keeping only the graphical tool, which thus breaks free from the philosophy and the particular model of society which brought it into being. These diverging paths signal an evolution in the methods used in financial economics. But beyond the methodological considerations, this 'emancipation' of the graphical tool reflects above all a radical shift in the nature of the theoreticians' goals, and even in the way that financial economics is conceived. With Lefèvre, we have a reflection on the utilization and social utility of stock markets. They must promote society's economic development and avoid non-professional exploitation. In becoming independent, his graphical method also became considerably poorer: an economic tool primarily for practitioners, with all ideas of wider social evolution abandoned and forgotten. It became no more than a technical expedient, with a new – and limited – purpose: playing the stock market.

Notes

1. The French mathematician Louis Bachelier (1870–1946) defended his doctoral thesis 'Théorie de la speculation' on 29 March 1900. He taught mathematics in Paris, Dijon, Rennes and Besançon – most of the elements of his biography are presented in Courtault et al. (2000) and in Mandelbrot (1995). His thesis, and his article of 1901, 'Théorie mathématique du jeu', are pioneering works in mathematical finance, and in the theory of random processes in continuous time. Long overlooked, as they were so far ahead of their time, they influenced both random process theory (especially the work of Itô) and probability theory (notably Kolmogorov's breakthroughs). His thesis was rediscovered by economists in the 1950s and 1960s and for a long time was mistakenly hailed as the first work of modern financial economics. On the mathematical repercussions of Bachelier's work, see Taqqu (2001); on his economic work, see Jovanovic and Le Gall (2002); on his contribution to financial economics, see Jovanovic (2000).
2. Little is currently known about this author. He was born in Bethencourt in 1833 and worked as a stockbroker at the Paris Bourse. His model provided a starting point for Bachelier's study (1900), enabling the latter to discover Brownian motion before Einstein. On this model, see Jovanovic and Le Gall (2001); on the link between Regnault and Bachelier, see Jovanovic (2000).
3. An option contract confers the right, but not the obligation, to sell or buy a financial or tangible asset for a predetermined price – the 'exercise price' or 'strike price' – at a set date, the 'expiration date'. In Paris, in Lefèvre's day, this type of financial asset was known as a '*prime*' and only European-style options were exchanged – for which the right could only be exercised just before the actual expiration date.

   One of the advantages of options is precisely that they can be combined ad infinitum to obtain any particular end result as a function of stock price movements. For example, one can, if so desired, determine a strategy that yields a profit if prices fluctuate beyond a certain interval, and a loss if they remain within that interval – a so-called 'straddle'. The outcomes of such strategies can be plotted on graphs, presented in greater detail in the final section.
4. Certain biographical elements are taken from Taqqu (2001, 14, note 14).
5. This was in all probability a small company set up by Lefèvre to manage stock investments for people who could not come to Paris in person or who had no direct access to the Bourse. Such firms were common at the time.
6. This particular position, which he casually mentions on the cover of most of his publications, may have had more to do with name recognition (and its effect on sales) than with any real employment.
7. At the time, financial journals offered to manage their readers' financial investments. This type of service, of obvious interest to those in the provinces who could not visit Paris regularly, gave rise to numerous financial scandals. Note surprisingly, some journals would sing the praises of certain especially effective investments with the sole aim of fleecing their readers. Likewise, small investment banks – like the one for which Lefèvre worked – were legion.
8. This evolution in the Parisian financial landscape was accompanied by a change in the attitude of the public – and of successive governments – towards the stock market (Reznikow 1990). A similar development marked the history of the British and American stock markets (Banner 1998); in France it was notable for the birth of financial economics (Jovanovic 2001).
9. These data, for stocks listed on the official market, are taken from Courtois (1877) and from the records of the

Congrès International des Valeurs Mobilières of 1900. Neymarck (1888, 8) tells us that in March 1888, '767 different stocks were traded at the Paris Bourse; 208 were traded on the spot and futures markets; 559 were traded on the spot market alone', to which must be added some 200 stocks traded on the free market. The nominal year-end stock market capitalization – in millions of current francs – was 9407 in 1851, 23 247 in 1861, 84 012 in 1880 and 130 304 in 1902 (Moreau-Nérêt in Hautcœur 1997, 245). However, these statistics are merely indicative of the development of the Paris stock market; since the sources are neither homogeneous nor easily verified, the data differ from one study to another.

10. For the six major railway companies, the average number of shares per French shareholder varied, depending on the company, from 22 to 47.24 in 1860, falling to the lower range of 10 to 13.6 by 1900. For bonds, the average was 42.10 in 1860, falling to within the range 24.69–32.00 by1900. Sixty-seven per cent of nominative bonds belonged to holders who had no more than 24 bonds.
11. For an overview of these issues, see Boboeuf (1864) and Jovanovic (2001).
12. The liberal economists' mouthpiece, the *Journal des Economistes*, regularly published articles about financial markets and the Société d'Economie Politique organized debates on the subject. The specialists on financial questions were Alphonse Courtois and his son Alphonse. The liberal economists were not the only ones, however, to stress the economic role of the stock market. In 1857, for example, Proudhon published his *Speculator's Manual*, in which he emphasized this function of the financial markets.
13. The field of political economy in nineteenth-century France was marked by a series of methodological disputes, notably regarding, on the one hand, the relationship between economics and mathematics, and, on the other, the relationship between economics and statistics (Ménard 1987; Breton 1991). Courtois was opposed to the use of probability in economics: 'with all due respect for the genius of those who created this science and for the higher intelligence of those – distinguished in so many ways – who have followed them down this path, I cannot but protest against stretching the laws of mathematics and nature in this way' (1879, 14–15).
14. For example, a large part of Proudhon's *Speculator's Manual* is taken up with descriptions of the status of stocks traded on the Paris market.
15. This troubled period was marked by a flurry of methodological debates, and the development of economic sociology, which 'criticized certain limitations of political economy in order to enrich economic theory by incorporating previously neglected or poorly studied phenomena' (Gislain and Steiner 1995, 14, our transl.).
16. In 1872, Hyppolyte Charlon founded the Cercle des Actuaires Français. The circle's periodical, the *Journal des Actuaires Français*, regularly published economics articles, especially with a mathematical bent. For example, Septime Avigdor (1874) proposed – almost simultaneously with, and independently from, Walras – that one should 'seek out the harmony that must surely exist, and consequently the relations that must come into play, between the prices of different objects of consumption' (1874, 300) using a model of general equilibrium very similar to Walras's own. The contributions of the French actuaries, highly innovative in terms of theory, are a perfect illustration of how economic and financial theory in France developed outside the traditional schools. We should also remember that Hermann Laurent, vice-president of the Institut des Actuaires Français (set up in 1890 as the successor to the Cercle), was strongly committed to introducing mathematical economics, especially the works of Walras, into France. For more details on the economic works of the French actuaries and their role in propagating mathematical economics in France, see Zylberberg (1988, 1990), Le Gall (1997) or Breton (1998).
17. See also Rebeyrol's analysis (1999, 194–5) of certain roles played by financial markets in Walras, who also cites Lefèvre in his 'bibliography of works on the application of mathematics to political economy' and recommends them to readers seeking a deeper understanding of stock market mechanisms (Walras 1880a, 370).
18. This Russian economist – an official correspondent of the Institut, and one of the greatest economists of the end of the nineteenth century (Gislain and Steiner 1995, 14) – takes up some of Lefèvre's ideas in his writings.
19. Lefèvre published a letter dated 27 February 1874, sent to him by the Paris stock exchange committee: 'Sir, The Committee has listened with interest to the report given by one of its Members, charged with studying your method for stock market operations. The Committee has decided that as your tables may be useful to the Company of Stockbrokers, a subscription should be placed for 60 copies, which I trust you will kindly have delivered to our treasury …' (Lefèvre 1874a, opening citation). In 1874, he also published a poster (100 × 60 cm) presenting his graphs and his theory of stock market operations. The poster was available from the Correspondence Bureau of the Paris Bourse.
20. This publication, which failed to acknowledge the works of Lefèvre, stirred up a controversy in this review (see Zylberberg 1988).
21. At the time, prices for raw materials were listed and some of them were already traded on a regular basis at stock exchanges, in both spot and futures markets. The Chicago Board of Trade, the great raw materials exchange founded in 1848, allowed American cereals producers to defer delivery of the harvest relative to the date on which the price was determined. In 1874, this market was extended by the new Chicago Mercantile Exchange.
22. In the nineteenth century, the term '*Bourse*' referred primarily to a forum of exchange, which was accordingly not limited to financial markets alone. For example, in the France of the 1840s, the idea emerged of organizing *Bourses de travail* or labour exchanges. Subsequently, a number of local initiatives were set up in France, and

the first long-term labour exchange was established in Paris in 1881. The concept was later expressed in theoretical form by Gustave de Molinari (1893). On the social aspect of labour exchanges in France, see Soriot (1999).

23. For Lefèvre, as mentioned earlier, the stock market must be understood as a forum for the exchange of commodities as well as financial assets.
24. The time at which Lefèvre was writing was marked by an ongoing debate about the risks generated by industrialization and assembly-line production, and particularly about how best to manage the risks incurred by industrialization. This debate eventually led, among other things, to the development of the welfare state in European countries; an acknowledgement is due here to the conference held in Paris on 12 January 2000 by the Association pour la Défense de l'Histoire Economique on the theme 'The Welfare State, from Construction to Crisis'.
25. In his analysis, Lefèvre (1873, 220) makes a clear distinction between commercial or financial insurance, on the one hand, and life or fire insurance on the other. By dissociating the different types of insurance, Lefèvre was generalizing out from the type of insurance that actuaries normally dealt with. His only point of interest in the matter lay in the uncertainty phenomena surrounding economic and financial risk. He left to his actuarial colleagues – Lefèvre joined the Cercle des Actuaires Français in 1873 and remained a member up until his death in 1890 – the task of analysing other types of risk and insurance.
26. This function of speculation was clearly set out later by Leroy-Beaulieu: 'speculation is a regulating force ..., it is the marvellous worker-bee that regulates markets, apportions supply to demand and demand to supply and which, through its various oscillations, restores equilibrium everywhere ... . The question has often been asked as to how, without government intervention, without directives from administrative departments, countries with populations of 40 or 50 million, towns of 2, 3 or 4 million souls, can be regularly supplied every morning with all their needs, and without any shortages. The credit for this feat is due to speculation, and price variations are its means of action. Abolish rises and falls in price, attempt to establish constant prices, contrary to the nature of things, and our markets will no longer be supplied' (Leroy-Beaulieu in Raffalovich 1893, foreword).
27. Walras (1880a, 1880b) later echoed this proposal for restricted access to the financial markets.
28. Lefèvre toyed with the idea of a fourth intermediary, the *agent de change* (stockbroker), acting as an intermediary between merchant brokers and thus barred from operating on his own account. The need for such a role, in Lefèvre's eyes, explained 'the natural origin of the sworn broker who, at the Stock Exchange, is the *agent de change*, at a higher level of the business and financial hierarchy' (1874a, 114). Consequently, he must be 'as far removed as possible from the public, with whom he should have no direct contact' (ibid.).
29. This idea pops up again in Walras (Rebeyrol 1999, 195).
30. There was much debate at the time about the utility of stock markets, and especially about whether useful speculation could be distinguished from gambling. For an overview, see Jovanovic and Le Gall (2001).
31. Walras in turn picked up on Lefèvre's argument when setting out his own vision of how stock markets should be organised: 'my proposal, in line with the opinion of Mr Lefèvre, differs from current practice in law and jurisprudence ... . I would like ... all stock market operations between merchants to be legal, and all forward transactions, for future settlement, to be illegal between non-merchants or between merchants and non-merchants. Thus, the market for capital would be reserved for professional speculators' (1880a, 393).
32. For example, Lefèvre notes that the division of labour specific to stock markets is not always observed. This lack of observance leads to dysfunctions in social organization: 'the broker, who should act only as an intermediary between merchants, is in direct contact with the public: he 'does retail' as well as 'wholesale and retail-wholesale' ... . This is absurd; it makes it impossible for the retailer to exercise his own trade. ... The general consumer has no business dealing directly with the Stock Exchange, which is the great market for all stock, or with the brokers who are – or at least should be – intermediaries between merchants, and whose interest logically lies in respecting the natural hierarchy of the different social functions, the absence of which leads only to disorder and fraud' (Lefèvre 1874a, 115–16).
33. These equations are used here only to illustrate Lefèvre's thinking and approach. He does not of course present them himself, since he rejects abstract mathematics. A number of theoreticians who later made use of Lefèvre's graphs, notably mathematicians such as Barriol (1908), formulated these equations explicitly.
34. To assess this profit, one simply assumes that the holder takes up the option, i.e. buys a share of the underlying asset for Fr 56.45 and sells it immediately at the market price of Fr 57. His net profit, after deducting the cost of the option premium (Fr 0.25 francs), is therefore 57 – 56.45 – 0.25 = 0.30 francs.
35. On the complexity of possible graphic representations, see Lefèvre (1873, 377 or 382).
36. Fr 91.95 call option with a premium of 25c; Fr 92.20 call, premium 25c; Fr 92.85 call, premium 25c; Fr 93.30 call, premium 100c; Fr 93.35 call, premium 50c; Fr 93.45 call, premium 25c; Fr 92.10 put option with a premium of 25c; firm sale at Fr 92.25; Fr 92.65 put, premium 50c; Fr 93.25 put, premium 25c; Fr 93.50 put, premium 100c.
37. Nomograms date back to the Cartesian coordinate system. They began to be commonly used from 1843 onwards by French engineers who saw the graphic method not only as a pragmatic mode of expression but also as an instrument of research in its own right (Marey 1885, introduction). Nomogram usage subsequently became

widespread and led the French mathematician Maurice d'Ocagne to advocate a whole new field of science called 'nomography' (Ocagne 1908). Nomograms have several applications in finance, notably for calculating the value of securities.

38. This alphabet is based on four fundamental characters: a mute character, a character representing a profit or loss on the purchase, another representing a profit or loss on the sale, and finally one representing stagnation of profit and loss (Lefèvre 1870a, 3).
39. They were taken up by French stockbrokers from 1874 onwards (Lefèvre 1874a, opening citation).

References

Avigdor, Septime (1874), 'Question d'économie sociale' ('A question of social economics'). *Journal des Actuaires Français*, **3**, 300–306.

Bachelier, Louis (1900), 'Théorie de la spéculation' ('Theory of speculation'). Reproduced in *Annales de l'Ecole Normale Supérieure, 3ème série* 17 January: 21–86. Reprint, 1995, Paris: J. Gabay.

——— (1901), 'Théorie mathématique du jeu' ('Mathematical theory of games'). *Annales de l'Ecole Normale Supérieure, 3ème série* 18 January: 77–119. Reprint, 1995, Paris: J. Gabay.

Banner, Stuart (1998), *Anglo-American Securities Regulation: Cultural and Political Roots, 1690–1860*. Cambridge and New York: Cambridge University Press.

Barriol, Alfred (1908), *Théorie et pratique des opérations financières* (*Theory and Practice of Financial Operations*). Paris: Doin.

Boboeuf, Pierre-Alexis-Francis (1864), *Marchés à terme. Pétition adressée au Sénat par M. Boboeuf pour rendre obligatoires les marchés à terme* (*Future Markets. Petition Addressed to the Senate by M. Boboeuf to Make Futures Markets Obligatory*). Paris: C. de Mourgues frères.

Breton, Yves (1991), 'Les économistes français et les questions de méthode' ('French economists and questions of method'). In *L'Economie politique en France au XIXe siècle*, edited by Yves Breton and Michel Lutfalla. Paris: Economica.

——— (1998), 'Hermann Laurent (1841–1908): In search of a new political economy'. In *European Economists of the Early 20th Century*, vol. 1, edited by Warren J. Samuels. Cheltenham, UK and Northampton, MA, USA: Edward Elgar.

Callens, Stéphane (1997), *Les maîtres de l'erreur* (*Masters of Error*). Paris: PUF.

Canard, Nicolas-François (1801), *Principes d'économie politique* (*Principles of Political Economy*). Paris: Boisson.

Canguilhem, Georges (1968), *Etudes d'histoire et de philosophie des sciences* (*Studies in the History and Philosophy of Science*). Paris: J. Vrin.

Cohen, I. Bernard (1993), 'Analogy, homology and metaphor in the interactions between the natural sciences and the social sciences, especially economics'. In *Non-Natural Social Science: Reflecting on the Enterprise of 'More Heat than Light'*, edited by Neil De Marchi, Durham, NC: Duke University Press.

Courtault, Jean-Michel, Youri Kabanov, et al. (2000), 'Louis Bachelier on the century of Théorie de la spéculation'. *Mathematical Finance*, **10** (3): 341–53.

Courtois, Alphonse (Jr) (1877), *Tableaux des cours des principales valeurs négociées et cotées aux bourses des effets publics de Paris, Lyon et Marseille du 17 janvier 1797 à nos jours* (*Tables for the Prices of the Main Securities Traded and Quoted on the Stock Markets of Paris, Lyon and Marseille between 17th January 1797 and our Time*) Paris: Garnier frères.

——— (1879), *Défense de l'agiotage* (*Defence of Gambling*). Paris: A. Hennuyer (second printing).

Gislain, Jean-Jacques and Philippe Steiner (1995), *La sociologie économique 1890–1920* (*Economic Sociology 1890–1920*). Paris: PUF.

Hautcœur, Pierre-Cyrille (1994), *Le marché boursier et le financement des entreprises françaises (1890–1939)* ('The stock echange and financing of French companies (1890–1939)'). Ph.D. thesis, University of Paris 1.

——— (1997), 'Le marché financier de 1870 à 1900' ('The stock exchange between 1870 and 1900'). In *La Longue Stagnation en France. L'Autre Grande Dépression (1873–1897)*, edited by Yves Breton, Albert Broder and Michel Lutfalla, Paris: Economica.

Jovanovic, Franck (2000), 'L'origine de la théorie financière: une réévaluation de l'apport de Louis Bachelier' ('The origin of financial economics: a reappraisal of Louis Bachelier's contribution'). *Revue d'Economie Politique*, **110** (3): 395–418.

——— (2001), 'Pourquoi l'hypothèse de marche aléatoire en théorie financière? Les raisons historiques d'un choix éthique' ('Why the random walk hypothesis in financial theory? The historical reasons for an ethical choice'). *Revue d'Economie Financière*, **61**: 203–11.

Jovanovic, Franck and Philippe Le Gall (2001), 'Does God practice a random walk? The "financial physics" of a 19th century forerunner, Jules Regnault'. *European Journal for the History of Economic Thought*, **8** (3): 323–62.

——— (2002), 'Genèse et nature de la Théorie de la spéculation: les contributions de Louis Bachelier et de Jules Regnault à la théorie financière et à l'économétrie' ('Birth and nature of the theory of speculation: Louis Bachelier's and Jules Regnault's contributions to financial economics and econometrics'). In *Louis Bachelier, aux origines de la finance mathématique*, edited by Jean-Michel Courtault and Youri Kabanov, pp. 165–202. Besançon: Presses Universitaires Franc-Comtoises.

Le Gall, Philippe (1997), 'Une autre science économique durant la longue stagnation: la pensée économique des actuaires français' ('Another economics during the long stagnation: the economic thought of the French actuaries'). In *La longue stagnation en France. L'autre grande dépression (1873–1897)*, edited by Yves Breton, Albert Broder and Michel Lutfalla. Paris: Economica.

Lefèvre, Henri (1865), *L'art de bien placer son argent et de le faire fructifier* (*The Art of Making Good Investments and Making One's Money Work*). Paris: author.

——— (1870a), *Traité théorique et pratique des valeurs mobilières et des opérations de Bourse* (*Treatise of Financial Securities and Stock Exchange Operation*). Paris: Lachaud.

——— (1870b), 'Spéculation' ('Speculation'). *Journal des placements financiers*, **22** (2), June: 1–4.

——— (1870c), 'Spéculation' ('Speculation'). *Journal des placements financiers*, **23** (8) June: 1–3.

——— (1871), *Le jeu sur les courses de chevaux* (*Betting on Horse Races*). Paris: Kugelmann.

——— (1873), 'Physiologie et mécanique sociales' ('Social physiology and mechanics'). *Journal des Actuaires Français*, **2**: 211–50 and 351–88.

——— (1874a), *Principes de la Science de la Bourse* (*Principles of the Science of the Stock Exchange*). Paris: Publication de l'Institut Polytechnique.

——— (1874b), *Théorie générale des opérations de bourse* (*General Theory of Stock Exchange Operations*). Large-format poster.

——— (1874c), *Principes de la science du commerce, méthode et programme d'enseignement* (*Principles of Trading Science, Method and Teaching Programme*). Paris: Delagrave.

——— (1879a), *Quelques mots sur l'enseignement commercial en France* (*A Few Words on Teaching Trading in France*). Paris: Martinet.

——— (1879b), 'Théorie des monnaies et des changes' ('The theory of money and exchange'). *Journal des actuaires français*, **8**.

——— (1881), *Le Change et la Banque* (*Exchange and Banking*). Paris: Ch. Delagrave.

——— (1882), *La Comptabilité. 1er fascicule: Théorie générale et enseignement de la comptabilité* (*Accounting. First Part: General Theory and Teaching*). Paris: author.

——— (1885a), *La Comptabilité. Théorie, pratique et enseignement* (*Accounting. Theory, Practice and Teaching*). Paris: Librairie Illustrée.

——— (1885b), *Le Commerce, théorie, pratique et enseignement, suivi du Dictionnaire du commerçant* (*Business, Theory, Practice and Teaching*). Paris: Librairie illustrée.

Mandelbrot, Benoit (1995), *Objets fractals* (*Fractal Objects*). Paris: Champs Flammarion.

Marey, Etienne-Jules (1885), *La méthode graphique dans les sciences expérimentales et principalement en physiologie et en médecine* (*The Graphical Method in Experimental Sciences, and Particularly in Physiology and Medicine*) (2nd printing). Paris: Masson.

Masseboeuf, Alexandre (1923), *Des marchés à primes dans les bourses de valeurs (Paris – Londres – Berlin)* (*Option Markets (Paris – London – Berlin)*). Paris: Garnier frères.

Ménard, Claude (1978), *La Formation d'une rationalité économique, A. A. Cournot* (*The Fomation of an Economic Reationality, A.A. Cournot*). Paris: Flammarion.

——— (1981), 'La machine et le coeur. Essai sur les analogies dans le raisonnement économique' ('The machine and the heart'). In *Analogie et connaissance*, edited by André Lichnerowicz, François Perroux and Gilbert Gadoffre. Paris: Éditions Maloine.

——— (1987), 'Why was there no probabilistic revolution in economic thought?' In *The Probabilistic Revolution, vol. 2, Ideas in the Sciences*, edited by Lorenz Krüger, Gerd Gigerenzer and Mary S. Morgan, Cambridge, MA: MIT Press.

Molinari, Gustave de (1893), *Les bourses du travail* (*The Work Exchanges*). Paris: Guillaumin et Cie.

Neymarck, Alfred (1888), 'Les valeurs mobilières en France' ('Securities in France'). *Journal de la Société de Statistique de Paris*. 10 June.

——— (1903), 'Une Statistique nouvelle sur le morcellement des valeurs mobilières (chemins de fer, rentes, Banque de France, Crédit foncier, etc.)' ('A new statistic for the division of securities'). *Société de statistique de Paris (séance du 18 février)*. Paris: Guillaumin.

Ocagne, Maurice d' (1908), *Calcul graphique et nomographie* (*Graphical Calculus and Nomography*). Paris: Doin.

Pochet, Léon (1873), 'La géométrie des jeux de Bourse' ('Geometry of stock exchange gambling'). *Journal des Actuaires Français* **2**: 153–65.

Proudhon, Pierre Joseph (1857), *Manuel du spéculateur à la Bourse* (*The Manual of Stock Market Speculation*). Paris: Garnier frère.

Raffalovich, Arthur (1893), *Le marché financier en 1892* (*The Stock Market in 1892*). Paris: Libraire Guillaumin et Cie.

Rebeyrol, Antoine (1999), *La pensée économique de Walras* (*Walras's Economic Thought*). Paris: Dunod.

Reznikow, Stéphane (1990), 'Les envolées de la Bourse de Paris au XIXème siècle' ('The Paris stock exchange rises during the 19th century'). *Histoire économique et financière de la France, Etudes et recherches*, **2**: 223–44.

Soriot, Annie (1999), *Le travail et la question sociale: histoire de la construction d'une synthèse entre le socialisme et l'économie politique au XIXème siècle* (*Work and the Social Question: A History of the Construction of a Synthesis between Socialism and Political Economy during the 19th Century*). Ph.D. Thesis, Université de Paris 1.

Taqqu, Murad S. (2001), 'Bachelier and his times: A conversation with Bernard Bru'. *Finance and Stochastics* 5 (1): 3–32.

Théret, Bruno (1995), 'Du statut des métaphores médicales en économie politique: essai d'approche archéologique' ('The status of medical metaphors in political economy: an archaeological approach'). *Cahiers Charles Gide*, **1**: 293–341.

Walras, Léon (1880a), 'La Bourse, la spéculation et l'agiotage' ('Stock exchange, speculation and gambling'). *Bibliothèque universelle et Revue suisse*, **85** (March): 452–76. Reprinted 1992 by Economica, Paris, vol. X.

——— (1880b), 'La Bourse, la spéculation et l'agiotage' ('Stock exchange, speculation and gambling'). *Bibliothèque universelle et Revue suisse*, **85** (April): 466–94. Reprinted 1992 by Economica, Paris, vol. X.

Whelan, S.F., D.C. Bowie, et al. (2002), 'A primer in financial economics'. *British Actuarial Journal*, **8** (1): 27–74.

Zylberberg, André (1988), 'L'économie mathématique chez les actuaires français au temps de Walras (1870–1914)' ('The mathematical economics of the French actuaries at Walras's time (1870–1914)'. *Economie et Sociétés, Oeconomia*, **9** (March): 35–63.

——— (1990), *L'économie mathématique en France 1870–1914* (*The Mathematical Economics in France 1870–1914*). Paris: Economica.

9 A nineteenth-century random walk: Jules Regnault and the origins of scientific financial economics

Franck Jovanovic

L'homme s'agite, Dieu le mène (Man fidgets, God guides him).

(Jules Regnault 1863, 52)

Until the 1990s, the canonical history of modern financial economics provided what was known about the construction of this discipline.[1] As with any canonical history, it was a means to structure and to legitimize a scientific discipline. However, it did not provide a full understanding of its construction, in particular its origin. This chapter presents a seminal early study in financial economics – a work that the canonical history of modern financial economics does not mention: Jules Regnault's book, the *Calcul des chances et philosophie de la bourse*. This book laid the basis of modern stochastic models of price behavior. It lays bare the origins of one of the most important models used in financial economics, the random walk model, and consequently the modern approach to capital markets. It deserves close attention and contains many original ideas: for instance, Jovanovic (2000) shows that the majority of Bachelier's reasoning came directly from Regnault – most importantly the random walk hypothesis.

This chapter analyses Regnault's work in its own context: it suggests that this author was a highly typical figure of the mid-nineteenth century. His approach to financial markets was deeply rooted in the new interest in financial markets that occurred in France during the period: at a time when speculation was morally denounced, Regnault followed Quételet's program of social physics, designed to form the foundation for an exact science of human societies, and approached 'scientifically' the issue of speculation. His work tried to show that short-term speculation – based on the search for immediate gains – leads to ruin but that, by contrast, another kind of speculation, based on the long term, was socially useful. Interestingly, this piece of work relies on a typically nineteenth-century philosophical and methodological framework: it belongs to the deterministic paradigm, based on the belief that exact laws rule the phenomena and can be unveiled by mean values – Regnault was more interested in mean values than in variations for their own sake, seen as kinds of vices. As other economists and social scientists of that time, he also perceived analogies with the natural sciences and imported some methods, concepts and laws from these disciplines. Nevertheless, his approach to economics was also certainly pioneering: as early as 1863, his work took the shape of theoretical and mathematical models – that were exposed and discussed in literary terms[2] – and, at a time when the application of statistics to economics was controversial in France, some of these models were combined with statistical procedures. In other words, a historical analysis of Regnault in his own context leads us to think that this author sheds new light on the origins and early uses of economic models, of econometrics, and of course of financial economics.

This chapter is organized as follows. Section 1 explains Regnault's aim and framework. It examines how his work is embedded in the context of its time and how this author looked for tools, methods and hypotheses considered as scientific at his time to analyze stock markets. Section 2 examines his first model, which aims at analyzing short-term speculation. It first took the shape of a random walk, model but the introduction of brokerage fees enabled him to show that short-term speculation leads to bankruptcy. Section 3 presents Regnault's model of long-term speculation, which aims at evaluating the mean value of the French 3 percent bond.[3] Finally, the Appendix presents a biography of Jules Regnault.

1. Regnault's framework

In this section, we suggest that Regnault's work cannot be separated from the context of his time. First, the *Calcul des chances et philosophie de la bourse* was mainly stimulated by the development of financial markets and by debates on speculation in France that followed this development. This book demonstrates 'scientifically' the usefulness and the morality of one kind of speculation. Second, it must be regarded as an extension of the research program of Condorcet, Laplace and Quételet to a new field: the determination of 'scientific laws' that rule financial markets. Regnault's framework is inherited from Quételet and Laplace and is highly representative of the scientific and deterministic views of the mid-nineteenth century; this section also explains why reductionism led Regnault to consider that similar laws governed natural phenomena and human phenomena.

1.1 The historical context of French financial markets

The democratization of financial markets as a preamble to the emergence of theoretical works in finance For a full understanding of the origin of the *Calcul des chances et philosophie de la bourse*, the development of financial markets during the nineteenth century, which occurred in all developed countries, must be recalled (Preda 2001). However, we will focus here on the Paris Stock Exchange, where Regnault, as well as his brother, was a broker. The Paris Stock Exchange was created during the eighteenth century, but it became an important financial marketplace and an important economic actor only during the nineteenth century. If we compare its situation at the beginning and at the end of the nineteenth century, we find a considerable contrast. From a market devoted solely to the financing of the public debt, it became an important actor in the financing of the private sector. This change occurred between the end of the 1850s and the end of the 1860s, precisely when Regnault published his book.

During the first part of the nineteenth century, the general public was largely ignorant of the financing function of stock markets. These markets were only known by the links they had with the State, which made it responsible for its financial disappointments. Thus, stock price changes were associated with political events and not with the economic results and profits of companies.[4] Because the Stock Exchange concerned very few private agents – the most influential part of them was a minority called *Haute Banque*[5] – the general public remained largely unaware of its functioning, especially its economic function. General public knowledge was mainly shaped by a financial literature that caricatured traders and scoffed at the image of these 'big businessmen' inherited from Law's system bankruptcy. This system was initially supported by the French government – in the hope it could lead to a reduction of its debt. However, it rapidly initiated a speculative phenomenon that ended in a financial crash. Because of this crash, the legislation immediately and severely denounced the presumed culprit: gambling (*agiotage*).[6] This literature had developed since the beginning of the nineteenth century and reached its peak in the 1850s.[7] However, the Second Empire led to some changes.

During the Second Empire (1852–70), the importance of the Paris Stock Exchange as well as its part in the economy had been increasing. It is well known that many new inventions and innovations appeared in developed countries at the end of the eighteenth century and at the beginning of the nineteenth. Moreover, French economic growth was very strong during the period 1840–60 (Asselain 1985, 103–10). In France, the 1840s and 1850s saw a marked creation of companies, reaching its apogee between 1855 and 1859 (Caron 1995, 80). Although most of these new companies were limited partnership companies, more and more limited companies were created and were quoted on the Paris Stock Exchange. This progressive development of private securities rested on new financial institutions. The great credit establishments (Crédit Lyonnais, Société Générale, etc.) were created during the 1850s and1860s, and many banks during the 1880s. Two reasons explain the important part that these financial institutions played in the development of the Paris Stock Exchange. First, their activities led these financial institutions to find equity capital for themselves. They gave savers the possibility of buying their securities. Thus they became the first stock issuers and they supplanted railways companies, which were the first companies to use the financial market.[8] Second, they gave other activity sectors the possibility of having access to financial markets, because they could diffuse securities among their numerous customers. The Paris Stock Exchange took advantage of the introduction of these news companies to develop.[9] From then on, it financed the public sector as well as private sector, not only catching the savings of the main banks specialized in state debt. Because of this development, French financial markets had a strong bull period during the first years of the Second Empire. Then, from 1857 to 1874, in the economic slowdown that followed, the Paris Stock Exchange had a crisis period with high volatility in stock prices. This rise and crisis accentuated debates and reforms, in particular during the 1860s.

These financial and economic developments led the general public to change its mind about the Stock Exchange as a scary place. By the end of the 1870s, lampoons and moralizing plays on the Stock Exchange disappeared.[10] The general public no longer considered financial markets from the political viewpoint. It tried to understand their functioning and their economic status. These changes in general public opinion were supported by an increase of specialized publications, which developed financial and economic analysis.[11] These manuals and newspapers aimed at familiarizing the general public with financial techniques and participated in the emergence of the knowledge of financial market functioning. They also gave a new vision of financial markets: 'Investor manuals and journals disseminated a view on financial investing as promoting social harmony and as being patriotic[;] financial investing meant striving to attain happiness and to improve one's social position' (Preda 2001, 219).[12] 'With these arguments disseminated … via newspapers, brochures, and manuals, financial investing appeared as a legitimate, desirable activity' (ibid.).[13] Manuals and financial newspapers created 'a knowledge framework mutually recognized and accepted over such a geographic area' (ibid., 209). Moreover, since March 1854, the State used the financial markets directly, not through the Haute Banque. The result was that the number of persons of independent means, who came from all social classes,[14] strongly increased.

This democratization of financial markets and of finance was progressive. However, the main changes appeared at the end of the 1850s, with a peak at the beginning of the 1860s. Two parallel movements allowed this: the first dealt with debates on the adaptation of financial markets law to the new economic deal; the second with the creation of a financial science.

Legal debates to legitimize financial markets This new economic context made the law obsolete. Until the 1850s, the legal system which ruled financial markets and financial operations had been built to defend the State and its financial interests. It was largely elaborated to prevent the private sector from accessing financial markets. Because it was not possible to cater to these new financial needs with the old legal system, many debates occurred in which economists exerted a strong influence on jurisprudence.[15] These debates were often presented in front of the courts[16] or the Senate,[17] and they strongly contributed to modifying the public conception of financial markets.

It is easy to understand this conflict by analyzing the laws that had governed futures markets. These markets were legally recognized in France on 28 March 1885, although French jurisprudence implicitly recognized futures operations on 19 January 1860.[18] However, from the beginning of the eighteenth century to the second half of the nineteenth, there was a conflict in France, as in other European countries and in the USA, between the economic need for futures markets and moral issues. This conflict can be illustrated by the fact that during the nineteenth century, the gap constantly increased between restrictive legislation – decided by the French government – and jurisprudence, which took into account the growing financial needs of the time. The repressive legislation was motivated by reasons of both a moral and a political nature: on one hand, the government denounced enrichment based on a kind of gambling; on the other hand, condemnation of such practices aimed at a purification of the futures markets that were a means of financing the French public debt. At that time, these markets were mainly composed of public bonds, and any lack of public confidence had to be avoided.

It soon appeared that this repressive legislation was inadequate, in the sense that several kinds of speculation were condemned although they were economically useful and even necessary.[19] The courts scrupulously respected the law until financial scandals occurred. Then they were led to search for criteria that were necessary to characterize various kinds of operations on the stock markets and thus to identify those that should be condemned. They suggested several criteria to make a distinction between licit and illicit operations[20] – i.e. between speculation and gambling.

A new environment favorable to financial science As explained above, the new interest in financial markets and operations led to the development of specialized publications. These publications 'made financial markets into an object of inquiry and a field of activity: investing required a science' (Preda 2001, 228). It could be called, according to Preda (2004, 10), 'a popular science of financial investments'. This expression characterizes a new sociological context, in particular the emergence of financial journals, newspapers and books that shared common knowledge and language, but it does not mean that a new science existed. The authors of these publications did not share a scientific aim and did not adopt a method that could be considered as scientific at that time or even now. They aimed to describe stock market functioning, financial operations and financial securities, but did not look to establish laws or regularities that rule stock markets. As Bru explains, 'there is a gigantic body of literature on the Exchange [in the nineteenth century]. But these are not interesting books ("How to Make a Fortune", etc.)' (Taqqu 2001, 14). However, these publications strongly contributed to laying the foundations of this new context that could support attempts to construct a science of financial economics, although these attempts came neither from these authors nor from French economists.

Among these new financial publications, very few came from French economists, and very few of them dealt with financial markets. There was one notable exception: Alphonse Courtois 'fils'.[21] From a theoretical viewpoint, he was a liberal economist and a member of the French classical tradition – his ideas were close to those of Say. He claimed the usefulness of the stock market as a whole. From a methodological point of view, his approach was purely literary and descriptive and was characterized by a rejection of mathematics and probability. It seems that he was not preoccupied with the construction of a science of financial markets.

At the same time, a few authors, such as Henri Lefèvre[22] and Regnault, claimed the need for 'something new': the construction of a 'scientific' approach to the stock market.

> The existing books on Stock markets and banks are of no help towards the understanding of the very mechanism of their operations, although such was their aim … . The *Traité des Opérations de Bourse*, by Courtois, is of no help … no precise idea that could help towards teaching or a scientific approach can be found here. (Lefèvre 1885, III)

Indeed, financial manuals published during the same period did not have requirements of demonstration, of empirical validation, and of insertion in scientific debates. For these reasons, Regnault's and Lefèvre's books are different from other financial publications of the mid-1860s. On theoretical grounds, both authors stressed the need for an understanding of the very nature of the way the stock market was functioning: their aim was not to present a collection of examples, but to identify laws that ruled this market. On methodological grounds, they rejected the literary style and approached the problem 'scientifically': Lefèvre followed a graphical path while Regnault followed a statistical and probabilistic path.

The aim of Regnault was the identification of 'new laws of the variations of the stock market' (Regnault 1863, 7). It has to be noted that he saw his investigations as undoubtedly scientific – his agenda was the construction of a 'Science of the stock market' (ibid., 47). The book is closely linked to the nineteenth-century debates that came with the democratization of financial markets: the goal was to 'demonstrate the dangers of gambling [*jeu*] and to discover the aim that Speculation [*Spéculation*] should propose' (ibid., 1). But the approach was a pioneering one: it was not based on moral presuppositions *per se* but on a rational demonstration of the consequences of immoral behavior of individuals – driven by their sole 'personal interest' (ibid.) – on society as a whole as well as on individuals, proving that such behavior led to their inexorable ruin. He indeed believed that unlike morals as such, a 'scientific proof' was definitively convincing:

> Morals, in their various forms, were not lacking, at this point, to attack the abuses of speculation, and to try to correct them; but morals, in order to persuade, have to convince … ; truths that are convincing have to be obvious, irrefutable. (Ibid., 1–2)

His aim was thus, from a scientific perspective, to separate two kinds of speculation: short-term speculation (gambling) and long-term speculation (speculation).[23] As explained above, these two kinds of speculation were highly debated at that time. His choice was Adolphe Quételet's scientific program.

1.2 Regnault's methodological framework and worldview

On God's clockworks Regnault embedded his program into the main scientific program of his time for social sciences, that of Adolphe Quételet. Quételet's influence on Jules Regnault's thought is undeniable:[24] the two main authors he quoted are Quételet and Laplace.[25] Regnault was educated in Belgium during the 1840s and the 1850s when Quételet's influence was especially strong (see Appendix). The *Calcul des chances et philosophie de la bourse* contains almost all the principles and the methods that Quételet set out in his *Lettres ... sur la théorie des probabilités*. We know that Quételet was the first to concretize the Condorcet and Laplace program, which aimed at applying the theory of probability to the social universe. With his book, Jules Regnault followed exactly this program. He defended the use of mathematics and statistics to study human and social facts. From Quételet, he took the tools, the hypothesis, the method, the worldview as well as the way to demonstrate the results[26] – for example, the limited presentation of mathematical calculations as Quételet suggested in his *Lettres ... sur la théorie des probabilités*.[27] One can also note the closeness of the moral positions of these two authors, for instance the importance of labour value or individual prudence. Thus, the *Calcul des chances et philosophie de la bourse* must be regarded as an extension of the research program of Condorcet, Laplace and Quételet to a new field: the determination of 'scientific laws' that rule financial markets.

Following Laplace and Quételet, Regnault believed that the terms 'scientific' and 'deterministic' were synonymous and inseparable. His fundamental postulate was that chance does not exist: 'nothing in nature is arranged arbitrarily' (1863, 2). Nature was characterized by 'general and unchanging [*immuables*] laws' (ibid., 7), society was 'a huge machine in which all the springs are connected' (ibid., 202): both were precision clocks that are regular, orderly and highly predictable.

Four features of this deterministic framework deserve attention.[28] First, these deterministic views are, of course, associated with the issue of causality. Regnault constantly argued that 'nothing happens without having been prepared by a previous cause' (ibid., 2) and that 'anytime, anywhere, the same causes reproduce the same effects' (ibid., 135). The *Calcul des chances et philosophie de la bourse* was then based on a fundamental distinction between two kinds of causes: 'accidental' causes and 'constant' causes – a distinction inherited from Laplace and which is also present in Quételet's work (Porter 1986, 108). The former were produced 'without any apparent law and fortuitously' (Regnault 1863, 11) and were the concern of the short term. As far as the stock market is concerned, such causes were new and exogenous information. By contrast, the 'constant causes' were acting 'continuously and regularly, always in the same direction and with always a constant intensity' (ibid.). They were associated with long-term trends and linked to exact laws, although masked by the existence of accidental causes at work.

Second, the deterministic laws were only accessible to us in a state of perfect knowledge: it would then be possible to discover what the future had in store for us. However, individuals have bounded knowledge and have to content themselves with an approximate knowledge of these laws. This imperfection of knowledge has two consequences. On the one hand, individuals can only try to control the future through the elaboration of probabilities that are, of course, of a subjective nature:

> There is no chance, but there is our ignorance that serves instead of it. (Ibid., 2)
> All our calculus cannot have another basis than personal observation. (Ibid., 18)

On the other hand, he emphasized that the underlying uncertainty favored errors and deviations: 'Ignorance, that ... maintains our illusions and our errors, it is the first cause for all our excesses [*débordements*], all our passions, all our misfortunes (ibid., 2).

Third, science was seen as a means to approach a harmonious state of perfect knowledge – the aim of science was the constant reduction of 'the limits of doubt' (ibid.), through the discovery of the mechanisms that rule the universe. In that perspective, his goal and his methodological framework – his greater interest in mean values than in variations – were well matched. On one hand, deviations from the mean were associated with accidental causes and considered to be errors and moral vices; error was thus banished from the universe. On the other hand, the mean value represented a harmonious equilibrium in the social world, the ideal in morals:[29] it was the sign for an order that he supposed to prevail beneath the whirl of observed phenomena. The mean was seen as the manifestation of the deterministic laws that rule natural and human affairs, and statistics was seen as a means to approximate determinism. Once these exact laws were discovered by scientists, the individuals could reach 'a stable and quiet state' (ibid., 163). Deviations should thus be reduced through the progress of civilization or of advancement in scientific knowledge; men could then behave in conformity with God's will.

Fourth, and finally, Regnault saw the underlying order and structure of the universe – from the formation of prices on the stock market to the trajectory of planets (ibid., 98) – as created by God. He constantly referred to the existence of 'superior and providential' laws (ibid., 185) that each individual should respect. Indeed, man was or should be subordinated to God's laws:

> What a subject for amazement and admiration is offered by the views of Providence, what reflections are suggested to us by the marvelous order that characterizes the least details of the most hidden events! What! The variations of the Stock market are ruled [*soumises*] by immutable mathematical laws! Events that are generated by the caprice of men, the most unpredictable shocks of the political movement, the most cleverly studied financial combinations, the result of a multitude of events that are not related, all these effects are tied up in an admirable set [*ensemble*], and *chance* is now a meaningless word! And now, you, the princes of the Earth, have to learn and to be humble, you who in your pride, are dreaming of holding in your hands the People's destiny; you, the kings of finance, who have at your disposal the wealth and the credit of nations, you are nothing else than frail and docile instruments in the hands of *the One who masters* [*embrasse*] *the whole causes and the whole effects in a same order*, and who, according to the expression of the Bible, has measured, calculated, evaluated and distributed everything according to a perfect order.
>
> Man is stirring, God rules them. (Ibid., 51–2)

His identification of a divine law ruling financial affairs should pave the way for the speculator's happiness and for the stability of society – 'the discovery of the future ... leads to wisdom' (ibid., 140).

A unified conception of the world: analogies and transfers at work Another feature of Regnault's deterministic framework is to be found in the idea of reductionism: the various bodies that constitute the universe were seen as ruled by the same kinds of laws. A unified conception of nature means here that some laws were constantly at work, through time and through space, and at very different levels, and that various sciences and disciplines have principles, methods and also laws in common. It is well known that several social scientists of the nineteenth century and of the turn of the century developed similar ideas, and were consequently led to approach economics with the light of the natural sciences.[30] Regnault is a perfect illustration of this reductionism: he indeed claimed that 'the moral world is not ruled by other laws than the physical world' (1863, 5).

Consequently, he looked for financial translations of existing natural laws and identified some analogies with the natural sciences. The analogies perceived by Regnault are close to what Israel labels the 'mechanical analogies', which took place in a unified conception of the world: 'Science has to construct a unitary and objective picture of the universe. ... The various parts of science, as well as the theories which apply to various kinds of phenomena, have to be connected and to be consistent' (Israel 1996, 19). The laws identified by natural scientists would thus have counterparts in the social world and could be transferred into that field. This feature is exemplified by the testing procedure he used. As Jovanovic (2000, 2002b) argued, this procedure was original, in the sense that it included two steps. First, an 'economic test' was based on a comparison of theoretical laws with observed data – this test is sometimes close to an econometric one. Second, a 'non-economic test' was based on a comparison of the theoretical laws with existing natural laws; this was a means for Regnault to ensure that his own work in the social field was connected to the fundamental mechanisms of nature.[31]

2. The model of short-term speculation

The aim of the first model – which he labeled the model of gambling ('*le Jeu*') or the model of short-term ('*courte période*') speculation – is to demonstrate that gambling inexorably leads to ruin. First, Regnault built a symmetrical random walk model, and then he deduced from empirical data a 'law of deviations' that he tested. Second, he introduced brokerage fees in the model and posited the ruin of gamblers – i.e. short-term speculators.

2.1 The random walk model

On random walk: Regnault ahead Regnault's first aim was to construct a model that explains stock price variations in the short term. In that perspective, he analyzed the stock market in the light of 'a game of heads or tails' (Regnault 1863, 34). This choice deserves two comments. First, he analyzes the variations of the prices in a probabilistic perspective. The main interesting feature of the model is precisely a modeling of price behavior that is similar to the binomial probabilistic model of a game of heads or tails: 'On the stock market, the whole mechanism of gambling comes down to two opposite possibilities [*chances*]: the rise and the fall. Each one can always occur with an *equal* facility' (ibid.).

Second, this choice was also motivated by moral considerations linked with the debates mentioned earlier. Regnault aimed here at constructing a model of moral short-term speculation, which can show that speculation is moral because each agent has perfectly equal chances to make profits: 'at any moment, no advantage exists for one possibility over the other and, because of our ignorance about the future effect, it is absolutely indifferent to bet for or against, to take position in one way rather than another, to buy rather than to sell' (ibid.). In such a case, the expected profit is zero for each operation[32] and consequently he aimed to show that the stock market should not to be condemned *per se*. In a very pioneering way, price behavior took the shape of a random walk model – although he never used the term.[33]

This was undoubtedly an important step in the construction of financial economics as well as in its theoretical basis.[34] Bachelier was to follow this path in his 1900 dissertation[35] – in which he first offered a formalization of Brownian motion and thus initiated the mathematical theory of stochastic processes in continuous time. The random walk model was also used in the construction and the test of the informational efficiency theory, which was built during the 1960s and the 1970s (Jovanovic 2004b). Given this relation between the theory of efficient markets and the random walk model, it is not surprising to discover in Regnault's book the main lines of the contemporary theory of informational efficiency of financial markets although he did not create it: information is seen as a cause that generates the short-term variations of stock prices.

The movement of prices with new information An important issue at work in this book is indeed that of information. The short-term speculator is only interested in immediate profits – more precisely, profits that are made during a period which is shorter than the settlement period.[36] He thus tries to make a gain from any variation of prices – i.e. from accidental causes. Regnault's originality lies in this association of these causes with the new information that arrives on the market. In addition, he claimed that at every moment of time, the price contains all the information:

> When the gambler [*joueur*] buys or sells, expecting a rise or a fall of prices [*cours*], he thinks that prices are below or above the true *value* [*valeur*]: because of this determination, it is necessary for him to perceive in the current situation a cause of rise or fall which is not yet taken into account. In vain, he could pretend that it is only in future and distant consequences he sees these reasons for rise or fall; we know that these consequences, if they exist, are contained in the current price; however, if we think about what the word *value* [*valeur*] means, we will see that the value is and can only be determined by the *price* [*cours*] itself. (Regnault 1863, 29–30)

Moreover, Regnault clarifies that price variations result from the arrival of new information on the market. From these ideas, Regnault identified two assumptions relative to the distribution and the independence of the variations that he translated into the language of probability.

Indeed, he explained that 'on the stock market, all possible events can only determine two opposite effects, the *rise* and the *fall*' (ibid., 15). From his conviction that the price contains all the information and that its variations result from new information, he deduced that the probability for the price to rise is equal to the probability for the price to fall, i.e. ½. If such was not the case, agents could arbitrage – a word explicitly used by Regnault (ibid., 40) – and choose systematically the strategy that has the greatest probability:

> In all the games of chance that contain two opposite chances, relative equality precisely results from the possibility of the player choosing one chance or the other as he wants: these two conditions cannot be separated, because if one of the two possibilities generated a greater advantage than the other one, it would be constantly chosen. (Ibid., 41)

Regnault also claimed that, as in a game of heads or tails, the movements of stock prices are independent: neither the variations nor previous prices are useful to predict future variations:

> When I toss up, it is certain that each toss is completely independent from the previous ones … . In a similar way, the speculator on the Stock market always attempts to conjecture what has to happen from what has already happened, in such a way that after three or four days of fall, he will be led to believe in rise for the next day, or, other times he will see a motive for the continuation of the movement, although a complete independence is after all existing between these various effects. (Ibid., 38)

Otherwise stated, the only thing that agents know for certain is the fact that, at every moment of time, the price can increase or decrease with the same probability of 1/2 thanks to new information, independently of the previous prices. In addition to the arrival of new information, Regnault identifies another feature of price fluctuation, which comes from the subjective nature of probability.

The movement of prices without new information Regnault shows that the subjective nature of probability affects the evaluation of securities and therefore their price. However, these evaluations also lead prices to fluctuate according to a random walk. To demonstrate this, Regnault analyses prices movements when there is no new information.

Indeed, and despite the fact that public information is known by every agent, the evaluation of the consequences of any accidental cause on the price remains particular to every agent: 'There are perhaps not two speculators among one thousand that have the same opinion on all the set of the causes and of their effects' (ibid., 20). Thus each agent attributes his own probability that the price will increase or decrease. Of course, this variety of opinions makes exchanges possible – if everybody ... evaluates similarly the same causes, no possible counterpart would exist ... and consequently, no variation should exist' (ibid., 22). However, Regnault suggests that a law rules the evaluations made by individuals. He justifies this idea by an example, that of the evaluation of the height of a building by a group of individuals. When such a group tries to evaluate this height, most of these individuals make an error on the true value. However, according to Regnault, these evaluations are ruled by a law like the Gaussian one, considered as the law of chance.[37] He then applies this example to the stock market, and deduces from it two groups of agents that are equally distributed around the mean value: the *bulls* (*haussiers*) and the *bears* (*baissiers*), to use our modern vocabulary. This evaluation distribution explains short-term movements of prices without new information: the price has the same probability of being quoted under the value as over, because the probability, 1/2, that an operation is realized by a speculator who undervalues the security is the same as the probability that a transaction is realized by a speculator who overvalues it. Thus the price will fluctuate around the value of the security, which is for Regnault the long-term value. Moreover, its variations are independent, because evaluations are independent.

Finally, according to Regnault's hypothesis about price variation with or without new information, in the short term, stock market prices can be considered as a symmetrical random walk model around the mean value. If we give a mathematical interpretation to this model, securities prices should fluctuate according to $P_{t+1} = \overline{P} + \varepsilon_{t+1}$, where $\varepsilon = \{\varepsilon_t, t \in N\}$ is white noise and $\overline{P}$ the mean value of the bond.[38] Thus the expected profit between periods is zero, $E(P_{t+1} - P_t) = 0$.

The law of deviations His model established, Regnault tests the hypothesis that short-term price fluctuations conform to a random walk model. We know that, if stock prices follow a random walk, because of the independence of this process, the deviation of the prices increases with the square root of time, $\sigma(n\tau) = n^{1/2}\sigma(\tau)$, where n is a multiple of the reference scale.[39] It is precisely what Regnault finds for the 3 percent French bond, which was the main State bond and also the main security traded on the Paris Stock Exchange. According to his own words, Regnault tests the following problem. If a security is bought at time t with the plan to sell it in n periods, what will be the price deviation in $t + 1, t + 2, \ldots, t + n$ (with $n \leq 30$ days, because of the liquidation)? By investigating the way the prices vary through time, Regnault discovered a relation between the mean deviation of prices and time.[40]

Regnault explains that when an agent is involved in a new operation, he is in a relatively uncertain situation: an agent can choose a certain deviation – i.e. the profit he wishes or the loss that he is ready to bear – but the time of the operation remains uncertain or, by contrast, he can choose a determined period but an undetermined deviation (ibid., 48). In the latter case, a mean deviation for a given period can be calculated, and Regnault looked for a relation between time and that deviation. He remarked that the mean deviations for a given period of time were approximately equal and that the shorter the period of time considered, the smaller the deviations.

Moreover, if the period of time is only half as much, the deviation is divided by a number below 2. This observation led him to claim:

> A mathematical law thus exists and rules the variations as well as the mean deviation of the prices on the Stock market, and this law, which apparently has never been suspected until now, we will formulate for the first time as: THE DEVIATION OF THE PRICES IS IN DIRECT PROPORTION TO THE SQUARE ROOT OF TIME [*L'ÉCART DES COURS EST EN RAISON DIRECTE DE LA RACINE CARRÉE DES TEMPS*]. (Ibid., 50)

Otherwise stated, it is not possible for an agent to anticipate in an exact way the future price of a security, but he can anticipate its mean deviation over a given period of time.

Regnault then carefully tried to examine the robustness of this law using two kinds of testing procedures: a non-economic one, based on a parallel with existing scientific laws, and an economic one, close to an econometric one. The first section of this chapter showed that, according to him, the various parts of the world were ruled by similar and universal laws. He thus suspected that the law of deviations was not only at work in the field of finance but was also at work in other sciences:

> The security [*La valeur*], in its variations, is constantly in search of its true price [*véritable prix*], or an absolute price, that we can represent as the *center* of a circle, the *radius* of which will represent the deviation that can equally appear in the one or the other direction and on each point of the surface, in a period of time consequently equal to this surface, and all the points of its *circumference* will represent the limits of deviation. In all its variations, the security [*valeur*] is only moving away or getting closer to the center, and from the basic notions of geometry, we know that the radius or the deviations are proportional to the square root of areas or of times. (Ibid., 51)

In addition to this geometrical analogy, we know that Quételet had established this law in his works on social physics (Quételet 1848, 43 and 48). Then, Regnault empirically tested the law, using monthly data relative to the 1825–62 period. He determined the mean deviation for various periods (a month, a quarter, a year): for instance, he found that the monthly mean deviation was 2.73 and that the yearly mean deviation was 9.50. He tried to ensure that these deviations obeyed the theoretical law: he thus verified that 9.50 (the observed mean deviation) was close to $2.73\sqrt{12} = 9.45$ (the theoretical mean deviation). His conclusion was very enthusiastic: 'is there a more striking example of matching theory and experience!' (ibid., 175).

According to these tests, stock price variations seem to fluctuate randomly. However, it is important to emphasize that Regnault derived the law of the square root of time from his empirical observation: he did not demonstrate it.[41] In fact, Regnault's hypothesis does not permit of deriving this law. Indeed, in his random walk model with reversion to the mean, $P_{t+1} = \overline{P} + \varepsilon_{t+1}$, stock price variations are not independent because of reversion to the mean. If these variations have been modeled by a random walk without bias, as a Bernoulli process, $P_{t+1} = P_t + \varepsilon_{t+1}$, then the law of the square root of time could be deduced from the model. In other words, two models coexist in Regnault's analysis.[42] Nevertheless, this author is the first to model stock price variation by a random walk model and to establish that stock price deviations are proportional to the square root of time.

This first model was for him a means to show that stock markets are moral, in the sense that they are based on equal chances for all participants (the price can increase or decrease with the same probability of 1/2). However, in his first model, Regnault introduces brokerage fees that enabled him to demonstrate the inexorable ruin of short-term speculation, a speculation that disturbs the economy and that is not moral (see Jovanovic 2001, 2002b).

2.2 *The introduction of brokerage fees*

The nature of the costs Given this law of price variations, Regnault became interested in the costs that affect the gambler or the speculator when he trades: the risk of dealing with an informed trader, the risk that the order will not be executed, and the risk that agents manipulate prices or information. However, these were considered as negligible – they can be avoided or reduced, or are kinds of exceptions. For instance, the risk that an agent deals with an informed trader can be reduced by an appropriate choice of bonds – those whose market is large: 'Other things equal, the unfavorable possibilities [*chances*] are largely reduced on a large market, where the business is very important, and they proportionally increase on a small and especially an easily influenced market' (Regnault 1863, 43–4). Similarly, the manipulation of information was seen as marginal (ibid., 97–8), and the risk that the order will not be executed (ibid., 43–4) can be reduced by a change in the limits of the order price.

By contrast, a fourth element plays a key role in Regnault's model: the brokerage fees that concern every operation and that modify the equal probability of winning and losing a certain amount of money. Indeed, without any brokerage fee, the probabilities for the price to increase or to decrease on the average of an amount of x francs, during a period of time t, are equal (1/2). By contrast, when a brokerage fee c exists, the probability for the price to increase on an average of $x - c$ or to decrease on an average of $x + c$ is 1/2: the mean deviation is thus changed, and the expectation to win becomes negative ($-c$). In order to get back the same mean deviation x, it is necessary to have a probability of winning that becomes inferior to the probability of losing. Consequently, 'The equal chances to win or to lose different amounts of money [leave room for] unequal chances to lose or to win an identical amount of money' (ibid., 212). But in such a case, the probability of losing a given amount becomes greater than the probability of winning that amount and the expected profits become negative. Regnault thus had in his hands the elements that can pave the way for a 'law of ruin'.

A law for the ruin of the short-term speculator Each time an agent transacts, he has to pay a brokerage fee. In such a case, his mean loss is equal to the amount of brokerage fees multiplied by the number of operations – the frequency of operations being considered as constant. Regnault then put forward three results. First, '*the chances of loss are increasing with the power given by the amount of wealth* [*les chances de perte s'élèvent à la puissance donnée par le rapport direct des fortunes*]' (ibid., 91) – i.e. it is better to have initially a small amount of money. Second, '*the chances of loss are increasing with the power of the inverse ratio of amounts* [*les chances de perte s'élèvent à la puissance donnée par le rapport inverse des quotités*]' (ibid.) – i.e. it is better to have a predilection for important operations. These two elements are not specific to the financial market: they are relevant to every kind of random game. Third, he identified a specific element that exerts an influence on the chances of losing on the stock market: time. Indeed, 'THE CHANCES OF LOSS ARE INCREASING WITH THE POWER OF THE INVERSE RATIO OF TIME [*LES CHANCES DE PERTE S'ÉLÈVENT À LA PUISSANCE DONNÉE PAR LE RAPPORT INVERSE DES TEMPS*]' (ibid.).

Regnault can then demonstrate that short-term speculation inexorably leads to ruin. In the long term, the sum of accidental causes can compensate themselves; the short-term speculator, who constantly wants to benefit from the variations that result from these accidental causes, has to transact rapidly and frequently. However, rapid trades generate only small profits – according to the law of deviations – and frequent trades lead him to lose his capital – because of brokerage fees. Consequently, this kind of speculation – based on the search for immediate profits – inexorably fails: the profits cannot compensate for the brokerage fees.

Regnault thus 'scientifically' demonstrated that the ruin of the short-term speculator could not be avoided and that short-term speculation was a deviation – in the sense of a vice:

> *The frequency of operations is an abuse*; and since the unique motivation of each exchange is and has to be *usefulness* [*utilité*], each time this usefulness disappears, there is an error or a bad use; from this, we can thus clearly separate gambling [*agiotage*] from speculation [*spéculation*] (Ibid., 105)

He thus demonstrated the dangers of gambling on the stock market, and from his law he believed that he could predict the exact moment when an agent would be ruined:

> It is even possible to predict the moment when the short-term speculator [*joueur*] will be ruined … . The brokerage fees [*droits de courtage*] generally represent ⅛% or 1/800 for the game business and for the serious business … . As a result, if the amount of money that he can lose represents for instance a twentieth of the capital that enables him to transact each time, the brokerage fees represents for him twenty times more, that is 2.5%. As a consequence, since the gain and the loss equilibrate [*se balançant*], no more that forty operations will lead to the loss of his capital. (Ibid., 95)[43]

Given this law of ruin, another kind of behavior had thus to be considered: long-term speculation.

3. The model of long-term speculation: a non-random walk down econometrics street

The aim of this third section is to analyze Regnault's second model, that of 'true speculation' ('*la spéculation*' or '*la véritable spéculation*') or of 'capital', which is presented in the second part of the *Calcul des chances et philosophie de la bourse*. It mainly aims at showing that, in the long term, deterministic laws rule the stock market. We shall first examine how long-term speculation was defined, how it was seen as being socially useful, and explain its relations with constant causes. Then, it will be possible to shed some light on Regnault's methodological choices: he thought that accidental causes compensate in the long term and consequently that the underlying order that rules society could be discovered. In Quételet's style, his approach was closely associated with the determination of mean values and this was an opportunity to claim the usefulness of a statistical approach to the social world. Finally, we shall present the model, constructed in four stages: it aimed at identifying a new kind of 'attraction' and undoubtedly deserves its place in the history of econometrics.

3.1 Some speculation about long-term causal laws

The construction of this second model originates in the belief that true deterministic laws were permanently at work, although masked by the accidental causes previously studied in section 2 of this chapter. As seen in section 1, these laws were associated with constant causes at work. One can straight away note that two kinds of constant causes were identified: 'general' ('*générales*') versus 'special' ('*spéciales*') constant causes. The first related to events that concern all general conditions (for instance the whole security market):

> They encompass all of a political, commercial and financial situation, they lead to a rise or a decline of the general interest rate, or exert an indirect influence on prices [*prix*] via imposition taxes … or only a financial measure whose main effect is an acceleration or a reduction in the circulation of securities [*valeurs*]. (Ibid., 111)

By contrast, the 'special' constant causes related to a particular security (ibid.).

Regnault first looked for a special constant cause that contributes to the formation of 'the true price of the bond [*valeur*]' (ibid.) and that could form the skeleton of a theoretical and simple model. This identification resulted from the main feature of a bond – the payment of interest, defined as 'the representation of the risk capital incurs' (ibid., 124). He thus believed that 'the *interest* rate is the most important element in the composition of a security' (ibid., 120). This focus on interest deserves two comments. First, risk was here considered as a source of instability and Regnault thus claimed his predilection for bonds offering low interest: agents have 'to avoid carefully the too important risks that can compromise [their] capital' (ibid., 123), since 'numerous dubious enterprises offer unjustified dividends … as a misleading lure' (ibid., 124). Second, a similar idea can also be found in his distaste for variable interest securities: this variability was seen as generating uncertainty about future dividends and was consequently offering a basis for gambling (ibid., 122–3). These two comments help to explain Regnault's study of a particular security, the French 3 percent bond: the identification of the constant cause was certainly eased by the constant nature of the interest; moreover, we guess that this choice gave him the opportunity to claim the morality of such a bond.

The knowledge of such a constant cause was indeed delineating the outlines of a moral behavior that leads to social usefulness. At that stage, Regnault clearly opposed short-term gambling to long-term speculation. The former was largely independent of interest and capital, and consequently resulted in a 'ghost market' which is insignificant as a game practiced in 'a gambling-den' can be (ibid., 108). By contrast, long-term speculation was undoubtedly a fruitful path: it was generating trust.[44] Moreover, this path was a moral one, in the sense that it was associated with labor from two points of view. First, an agent has to spend a considerable amount of time and labor to choose appropriate securities, i.e. to identify those that have serious economic counterparts. Second, these counterparts were precisely seen as sets of labor: profits result from 'an accumulation of Labor, of Savings and of Production' (ibid., 103). Securities are here seen as portions of capital, which have to be cultivated as sets of labor forces. In that sense, it seems to us that he remained close to the Classical paradigm and had a certain taste for the labor theory of value: he indeed believed that '*labor* is the real and closest measure' of price (ibid., 111) and this was closely linked to what Regnault considered as the *raison d'être* of men: labor.

'True speculation' was thus defined as 'an accumulation of labor' (ibid., 6). Whereas short-term gambling was based on the search for immediate profits and had no economic counterpart, long-term speculation was associated with the development of capital and labor, and was seen as leading to moral behavior: 'the only possible wealth is the one which is the product of labor; any other one is purely chimerical' (ibid., 137). In that sense, it should be clear that Regnault approached the stock market with a harsh condemnation of the search for immediate individual interest in mind: collective interest should prevail. But how was it possible for Regnault to demonstrate these views? We now present his methodological choices.

3.2 A hymn to a statistical approach in economics

A case of attraction for social statistics The second part of Regnault's book can be described as a hymn to a statistical approach in the economic and social worlds. At a time when the application of statistical and probabilistic procedures in economics was controversial in France (Ménard 1987), Regnault posited a way in which the knowledge of society benefited from the statistical approach initiated by Quételet. He extensively discussed its applications to numerous issues and focused on the resulting possibility of forecasting. More precisely, statistics was for him a way to discover and to approximate deterministic laws:[45]

> Statistics ... succeeded in subjecting its laws, not only to material things, whose functioning [*marche*] belonged to a certain extent to the domain of mechanics, but most importantly, it has also included within a rigorous system the *moral* facts, even those which are apparently less likely to belong to a stable or normal state. Births, marriages, diseases, suicides, crimes, etc. can change from year to year under the influence of accidental causes, but in a rather long period, they will follow each other in a very regular way .... More surprisingly, our mistakes, our distractions, our biases, and even our caprices are ruled by the law of probabilities. What is more indiscernible, uncontrollable, than human thinking? Yet, the phenomena that produce it ... appear even more regular than the physical phenomena when men are free, that is when they are not disturbed by private causes of personal interest. (Ibid., 156–7)

Like Quételet, Regnault had in mind a statistical approach that was closely associated with the calculus of mean values, seen as signs of stability and order – every kind of variation from an average was considered as an error or a vice.

Observation and time-series: Regnault's methodology The basis of Regnault's model is thus to be found in his claim that the key to knowledge was observation:

> Knowledge, or rather the intuition of future facts, is a precious faculty that allows men, who own it to the supreme degree, to be considered supernatural beings and that was pretentiously called *divination*, when its true name is *experience*, this faculty is nothing than the fruit of a careful study of past facts: this is one of the truths that can never be repeated too frequently. The future inexorably follows from the past, as the effect invariably derives from the cause. (1863, 140)

Consequently, the discovery of the laws that rule the stock market led him to a statistical analysis of previous observed prices.

Basically, Regnault thought that all data resulted from two components, and this idea was based on an analogy with the decomposition of movement in physics:

> When we study the natural laws of motion, in mechanics, physics, astronomy, etc., we soon see that motion is subject to laws that are always made of two simple, separate, and crucial movements. [For instance], the Earth, in its path through space, is ruled by *two* well separated movements: the first on itself, in one day; the other around the Sun, in one year. In order to represent the movement made up of these various bodies, it is necessary to study separately, to *decompose* the two simple movements that constitute it (Ibid., 142–3)

He thus showed that the data included a short-term or accidental component and a long-term or constant component. The short-term components were seen as the product of causes that 'inexorably cancel each other' (ibid., 146). By contrast, the long-term components are 'admirably regular' (ibid., 144), and 'the demonstration of this fact is given by the use of averages' (ibid., 150). In accordance with his deterministic views, he thus believed that some averaging procedures, associated with the law of large numbers, should be useful in revealing long-term tendencies. Although he did not construct a formal decomposition of time-series such as those devised during the early twentieth century,[46] Regnault deserves a place in the history of time-series analysis: he explicitly had in mind a decomposition of time-series that would be at the forefront during the first years of the twentieth century, when early econometricians faced the problem.

With the help of these statistical procedures, Regnault zealously dealt with the discovery of deterministic laws in the field of stock market prices. His analysis was based on monthly data, relative to the highest and the lowest prices of the French 3 percent bond, and ranging from May 1825 to October 1862.[47] The model of speculation was constructed in four steps.

3.3 The model of speculation: on constant discoveries

The first step: mean values and seasonal variations The first step began with a statistical analysis of the data and was based on the determination of several mean values. For each month, during the 1825–62 period, he determined the mean value for the lowest prices and the highest prices, from which he deduced for the whole period the monthly mean values and then the general mean value (72.48F).

Then Regnault discovered, in a quite pioneering way, the existence of seasonal effects.[48] He found that the lowest monthly averages occurred in June and December and that the highest monthly mean values occurred in May and November. He associated this evidence with a feature of the French 3 percent bond: coupon payments (*détachement du coupon*), i.e. the money that the holder of the bond gets twice a year.[49] He thus defined a theoretical hypothesis – the price constantly increases between the coupon payments: 'Within the interval defined by the payment of two coupons, we should expect a regular increase of the prices, that would define a perfectly straight line (see the figure), because of the influence of the interest' (ibid., 153). He then statistically examined the robustness of this hypothesis. Of course, he had no formal testing procedures available; however, he proceeded just like turn-of-the-century pioneers of econo-

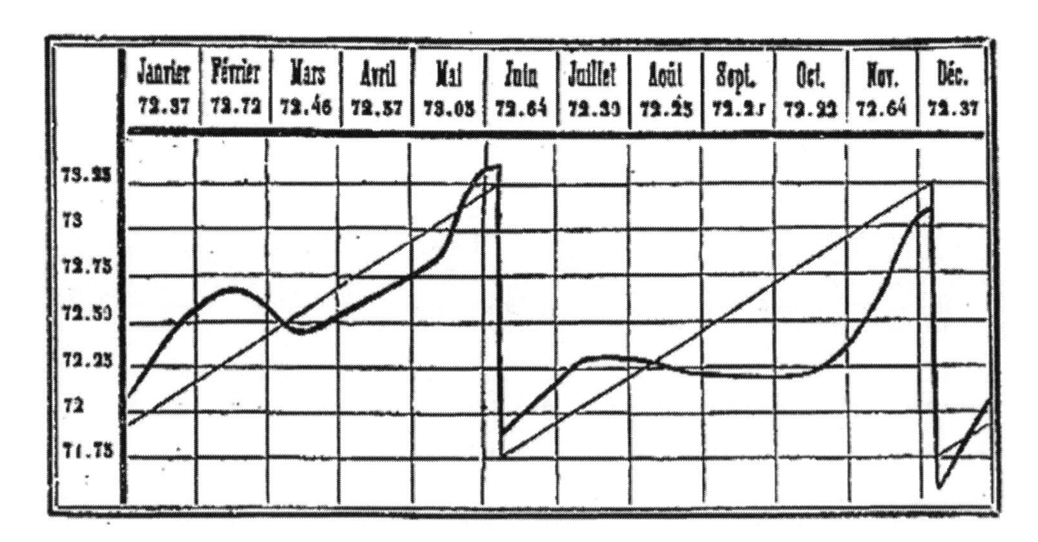

Note: Observed mean values: thick line; theoretical averages: thin line.

Figure 9.1 The evolution of monthly mean values of the price of the French 3 percent bond (Regnault 1863, 153)

metrics did,[50] and used a graphical approach. The observed and theoretical monthly averages are plotted on Figure 9.1. He found that the two curves were matched and concluded that:

> Among the most capricious variations, the price of the Rente is thus ultimately and solely influenced by the *constant* causes; the main one, the amount of *interest* [*le montant de l'intérêt*], is clearly identified ... this cause, so weak, apparently will inexorably triumph over the other causes .... (Ibid., 154).

However, he noted that the deviations of observed data from the theoretical curve could also be generated by other constant causes of a seasonal nature – such as the summer holidays.

This first step needs two comments. First, it seems perfectly clear that this kind of comparison between theoretical data and observed data is an anticipation of early econometric work. Such a graphical analysis was an important characteristic of the French econometric tradition that arose from the 1880s – with the work of Emile Cheysson – to the 1910s – with the pioneering work of Lucien March and Marcel Lenoir.[51] Second, Regnault got confirmation that the interest rate was a dominating cause at work.

The second step: from the mean value to the median value The second step can be characterized as the search for the best approximation of the mean value of the price of the French bond. Regnault believed that the previous value (72.48F) was a rather good approximation but, interestingly, he was led to consider other kinds of 'mean values'.

His starting point is here to be found in a criticism of his data: he saw them as 'crude', and consequently saw the 72.48F mean value as perfectible:

> It seems that we can get the true mean value of the price only from a careful record, for each day of the year, of the *mean prices* [*cours moyens*], determined from the highest and the lowest daily prices at the end of each day. Such a record, that would include more than 11000 numbers, would give a price around 73F, even closer than the previous ones, but this is still not the true price of the Rente. (Ibid., 159)

He thus decided to approach the issue in a 'roundabout manner' (ibid., 160), on the basis of monthly data. This procedure, based on the probable error, was explained as follows:

> Once we have obtained any mean value, the exactitude of which is in proportion to the number of observations that contributed to form it, it is always possible to calculate the error or the probable difference between this result and the true result we are looking for, on the basis on the very number of observations that were used. (Ibid.)

Considering an equal weight[52] for the 900 data he used, he thus computed a probable error:

$$\xi_p = \frac{1}{\sqrt{900}} \times 0.67 = 0.0223.$$

The absolute value of the probable error could then be calculated on the basis of the observed deviation, 54.15:[53]

$$E_p = \frac{1}{\sqrt{900}} \times 0.67 \times 54.15 = 1.20.$$

Regnault then investigated how these probable errors were distributed around the mean value and an analysis of the observed deviations led him to think that no symmetry was prevailing:

> The fluctuations in the prices of public bonds give variable quantities that, in their extraordinary deviations, show a marked tendency to fall *below* the mean value [and] far more often than they exceed it. From this, we can consider that the increasing state, more than the decreasing state, is the normal one; what the decrease gains in *vivacity*, it should necessarily lose in *duration*, and this condition is essential for restoring the balance [*rétablir l'équilibre*] and the absolute equality of these two kinds of states. In other words, the causes that generate the decreasing are less numerous than the causes that generate the increasing, but what they lose in *number*, they regain it in *force*. (Ibid., 161)

From this observation, he concluded that the observed price was more frequently superior than inferior to the mean price. He then embarked on a quantification of the 'intensity of the deviations' (ibid., 162) and found that one quarter of them occurred below the mean value. Consequently, 'one has to add approximately ¾ of the probable difference 1.20 to the price of 72.48 to get the probable price of the Rente, as close as possible, given the number of data we used' (ibid., 164). The 'probable price' was thus $P_p = 72.48 + \frac{3}{4}1.20 = 73.40$, and he concluded that 'the variations of the *Rente* are stirring around this price' (ibid., 166).

This price, that would 'separate the number of operations in two equal parts' (ibid., 164), was in fact, in Cournot's language (Porter 1986, 144), the median value. It should be remarked that it illustrates Regnault's predilection for the mean value: in our case, the mean value and the median value are not equal, but he believed that in the ideal case, both would be equal.

The third step: the structural changes The third step can be seen as a historical analysis of the deviations from this 'probable price', and he discovered that other constant causes, of a 'general' nature, were at work: they were related to historical circumstances and led him to suggest the evidence of homogeneous periods as well as structural changes.

Once more, the analysis was based on a visual approach. Considering the monthly data for the 1825–63 period, he represented the frequency of the various prices of the *Rente* (Figure 9.2). Regnault brought to the fore the existence of four maximum frequencies (46F, 57F, 70F and 80F) – that he labeled 'the attraction centers' ('*centres d'attraction*') (ibid., 168) – and a particular dispersion of the observed prices around these centers: their frequency 'decreases, symmetrically on the two sides' (ibid., 166).[54] Within the global population, he thus discovered the existence of four normally distributed sub-populations that he carefully analyzed.

The first one (46F) was generated by the year 1848, characterized by political disorders. The second one (57F) mainly occurred in 1830–31 and from 1849 to 1851, and was seen as the consequence of political revolutions. Consequently, these two sub-periods were 'abnormal' moments of French history and interpreted as 'deviations' (ibid., 169). The third 'attraction center', 70F, occurred during the successive waves of the development of industry and trade in France (in the 1830s and the 1850s). It was thus considered as a 'normal' but transitory and 'unstable state' (ibid., 170). Finally, the fourth one (80F) occurred during the years 1833–47 and 1852–53 – the most prosperous years of the nineteenth century. This price was thus seen as a 'normal' one.[55] This historical analysis was thus an opportunity for Regnault to complete his results: he concluded that the 'value of the French *Rente* lies between 70 and 80F' (ibid., 172). It was then possible to know if 'we should buy or sell, in a given context' (ibid., 144).

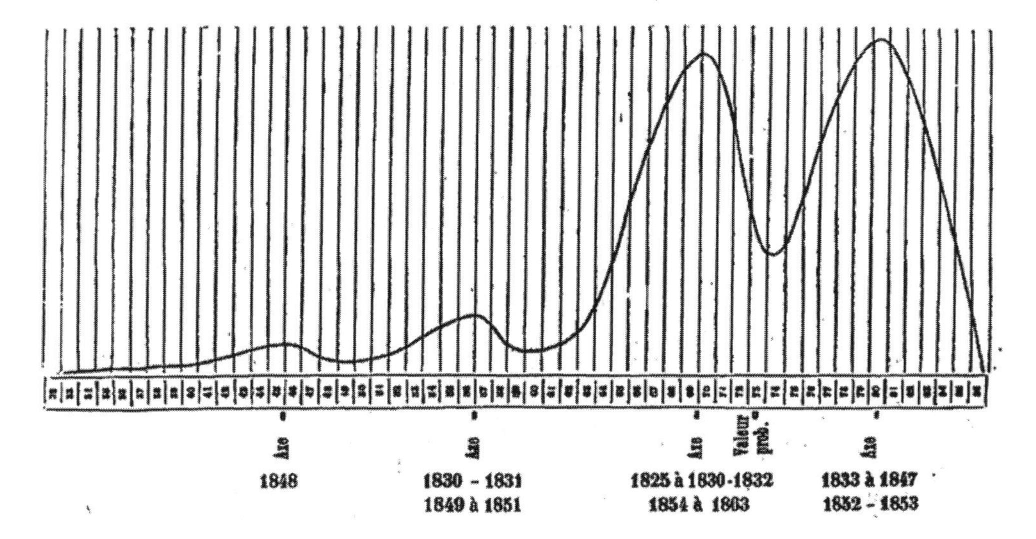

Figure 9.2 The evolution of monthly mean values of the price of the French 3 percent bond (Regnault 1863, 167)

The final step: The law of attraction The final step was that of the deduction of a deterministic law that rules long-term speculation: a kind of attraction mechanism that constantly moves the price toward the mean.

In the first part of his book, Regnault presented a law of deviations, according to which 'The deviation of the prices increases with the square root of time' and is also independent of the price itself. This law could not, of course, contribute to explaining a possible relation between the observed price and the mean price. However, on the basis of the preceding steps, he put forward the existence of a second law that stipulates a relation between these deviations and the mean price. The normal distributions around the 'attraction centers' led him to think that a kind of 'force' was acting. This second law at work states that: '*The value, in all its deviations, is permanently attracted to its mean price, in direct proportion with the square of its distance* [*La valeur, dans tous ses écarts, est sans cesse attirée vers son prix moyen, en raison directe du carré de son éloignement*]' (ibid., 187). However, it should be remarked that the demonstration of this second law was based on a unique example, that of 1848:

> Why, when the price of the Rente fell to 32.50F in 1848, did it increase so rapidly and with vigor, although it stayed quoted during several years at the extreme prices of 85 and 86? Because the distance to the mean value was three times more important in the first case, the Rente ... had a force *nine* times more important to rise than to fall. (Ibid., 188)

Apart from this example, Regnault himself dealt cautiously with this law, and confessed that he ignored 'the measurement of this force, and the moment when it has to be at work' (ibid.). However, he had good reason to suppose the existence of this law: the 'law of attraction' was indeed seen as a 'universal law' (ibid., 168) and, in accordance with his unified conception of the world, he believed that it was also at work in financial affairs. This is also an illustration of the fact that 'at the apogee of classical mechanics ... , there existed no scientific project or political utopia which did not seek a secret principle of attraction' (Ménard 1989, 90).

This 'law of attraction' was undoubtedly the law Regnault was looking for. It crystallized the various constant causes at work and, consequently, aimed to prove that short-term speculation was a mere illusion: in spite of its apparent randomness, the price of the French 3 percent bond was dependent on a deterministic law. The short-term speculator was thus considered as 'blind' (Regnault 1863, 198), whereas the 'true speculator' behaves 'with the interests in mind; he focuses less on the current circumstances, than on a more or less distant future' (ibid.). The end of the story was thus a moral one: the short-term speculator was favoring – and took advantage of – the existing (moral) deviations of society, but 'extreme things are always fatal, to peoples and to individuals' (ibid., 210). The deterministic laws Regnault put forward had thus to induce a (moral) change in the behavior of the economic agents: they have to learn the crucial importance of time – 'it is necessary to WAIT' (ibid., 198), since 'Time always takes care to bring back the price to its true value and to correct the deviations of speculation' (ibid., 205). The knowledge of these laws could then lead to a kind of convergence towards a state of certainty. Like several nineteenth-century scientists, Regnault was praising an end of history to the skies.

3. Concluding comments: a scientific discovery without scientific field

The *Calcul des chances et philosophie de la bourse* is a seminal work in financial economics. More precisely, before the twentieth century, there is no equivalent of Jules Regnault's quantitative and theoretical approach to stock price variations in other countries.[56] The book was published in a specific period characterized by a democratization of financial markets and by the development of vernacular financial literature. However, it differs from other manuals published at the same time, which aimed at educating investors. In fact, other books gave, in the better cases, a description of financial markets, and generally they only gave 'recipes' for how to become rich. Contrary to these publications, a scientific spirit marks Regnault's book. Two elements of his work must be recalled here. First, Regnault inserted his book into the scientific debates and into the scientific conventions of his time. Second, it is concerned with empirical validation, which constitutes one of the two criteria identified by Bourdieu (2001) to characterize a scientific work. Once his model was established, Regnault tested it. The constant focus on the test of the relations, the way these relations were also deduced from observation, the statistical procedures he used – the whole can undoubtedly be considered as the sign of an econometric approach at work. In that perspective, Regnault's book is an illustration of the fact that econometrics rose quite early in France, in separate places and in various fields of economics, as suggested by recent work on the history of econometrics in France (Le Gall forthcoming). Financial manuals published during the same period did not have requirements of demonstration, of empirical validation, and of insertion in scientific debates. For these reasons, Regnault's book differs from other financial publications of the mid-1860s, as Bru explains: 'there is a gigantic body of literature on the Exchange [in the nineteenth century]. But these are not interesting books ('How to Make a Fortune', etc.). There's Regnault's book which is unique, and which we know about' (Taqqu 2001, 14).

Although Regnault inserted his book into scientific debates, we should note that he was not part of an academic community. In fact, the nineteenth-century French academic community was prepared to receive neither Jules's attempts nor those of the French actuary Henri Lefèvre, who published his works between 1870 and 1885.[57] At this time, in France, there was no such community for a financial science. Indeed, it is well known that France was late to institutionalize economics in comparison with other developed countries. In France, economics was only institutionalized in 1877 (Le Van-Lemesle 1991, 2004). Before that date, the system of education was informal: 'in France, an informal system of economics diffusion had been slowly built during the nineteenth-century, at liberal practitioners' instigation, elaborated and created by them' (Le Van-Lemesle 2004, 9).[58] Thus, until the 1870s there were French economists but no academic economics.[59] Economists were practitioners, autodidacts self-educated by books, private conferences, *sociétés savantes* – like the *Société d'économie politique* – and a few courses (ibid., 163–4). Among French liberal economists, who constituted the most structured group of French economists, few were concerned with economic science: the majority of them considered that economic science was achieved by Jean-Baptiste Say.[60] Thus they did not try to develop new theory or new subjects. Consequently, it is not possible to find academic adherence to financial science. Moreover, we note that French economists,[61] who had 'temporal power' (journals, etc.),[62] do not quote Regnault's book. Three reasons can explain this. First, financial markets were of interest to only few French economists. Until the end of the nineteenth century, the two principal authors who analyzed these markets, Alphonse Courtois and his son, Alphonse Courtois, remained descriptive. They gave no explanation for price fluctuations and they elaborated neither natural laws nor mechanisms from models or theoretical analyses.[63] Second, at this time in France, economics was marked by controversies on methods to be used. More precisely, most French economists were against the use of mathematics and probability in economic science.[64] Thus it is natural that the first theoretical works in financial economics developed outside the group of French economists.[65]

The *Calcul des chances et philosophie de la bourse* is thus undoubtedly the first scientific work in financial economics, although it was developed outside an academic community. Indeed, the academic community of modern financial economics only a rose during the 1960s. One of its major preoccupations was the creation of a canonical history, which glorified its past (Jovanovic 2004b). However, that is another story.

Appendix: a biography of Jules Regnault

This appendix presents, first, a biography of Jules Regnault, and then discussed the influence and the diffusion of the *Calcul des chances et philosophie de la bourse*.

1. Jules Regnault's biography

Jules Augustin Frédéric Regnault was born on 1 February 1834 in Béthencourt, département du Nord, France. His father, Augustin Frédéric Regnault, was a customs officer. His paternal grandfather, Jean Baptiste François Regnault, was a bailiff, and his maternal grandfather, Louis Haye, a manufacturer and a property owner. During the first years of his life, Jules Regnault lived in the département du Nord where his father worked. His family moved often but always stayed near Cambrai. When his father died on 16 January 1846, in Paris,[66] Jules was 12 years old. His family moved to Brussels, where two of his uncles, both professors, lived.[67] Odilon, Jules's brother, became a writer[68] and a student in advanced mathematics at the Université Libre de Bruxelles.[69] Although he was registered for several years, Odilon did not graduate from this university. However, we do not know about Jules's education,[70] but the move to Brussels suggests that he was educated in this city. Two points are apparent. First, Jules was not the only member of his family to be interested in mathematics. In addition to his brother, one of his cousins, Albert Picard, was a teacher of mathematics at the high school in Tours. Second, at this time, Jules's family was not rich. His father left no fortune.[71] Thus Odilon was exempt from serving in the military service and from paying his university registration. When Jules Regnault arrived in Brussels, he probably benefited from the law of 1 June

1850, which created the foundations of high school public education. However, the modest financial resources of his family do not favour the view that he was an undergraduate, or that he was a graduate.

Whatever Jules Regnault's educational level, one point that contributes to understanding the origins of his work can be made: at this time in Belgium, education was completely reorganized, in particular under Adolphe Quételet's (1796–1874)[72] influence. After his doctorate from Ghent University in 1819, Quételet obtained the chair of elementary mathematics and afterwards the chair of advanced mathematics at the Athenaeum of Brussels. His first mathematical work led him to be elected to the *Académie Royale de Belgique*, which he later managed. From 1824, he lectured in several scientific fields at the military college and the museum. He also participated in the creation of the first public office of statistics, several scientific journals and the Brussels observatory. He also published several handbooks in which he explained the principles of his 'social physics' and his method for applying the theory of probability to the social and moral sciences. Quételet had a great influence and audience in the country. His positions led him to reform both natural education and research. One must remember that, before the 1820s, this country was an intellectual desert; Quételet gave a new impetus to its intellectual life. His publications and courses exerted a decisive influence on the new generation of Belgian students as well as the new Belgian researchers. This setting had a significant influence on Jules Regnault, because it is most probably during his education in Belgium that he elaborated the main principles of his financial theory.

Quételet's influence on Jules Regnault's thought is undeniable. From Quételet, he took the tools, the hypothesis, the method, the worldview, as well as the way to publish the results. As we explained, the *Calcul des chances et philosophie de la bourse* must be regarded as an extension of the research program of Condorcet, Laplace and Quételet to a new field: the determination of 'scientific laws' that rule financial markets.

At some point, Jules Regnault and his brother left Brussels for Paris.[73] Jules was 28 years old when his name appeared in the electoral lists of the ninth district of Paris, in 1862. Thus, even if we do not exactly know when he moved to Paris, because several electoral lists have been lost, he probably arrived at the beginning of the 1860s. Between 1862 and 1866, it seems that he shared an apartment with his brother, Odilon, at 13 rue Neuve-des-Martyrs (which is nowadays rue Manuel; the house numbers have also changed).[74] From 1862 until his death in 1894, Jules lived in Paris. He lived only in the ninth and tenth districts, and always near the Paris Stock Exchange. This closeness is not a coincidence: Jules and his brother were brokers (*employés d'un agent de change*) in the Paris Stock Exchange. Through his job, Jules was obviously interested in the debates and reforms concerning the Paris Stock Exchange and financial operations which occurred during the 1860s.

In all probability, when Jules and Odilon arrived in Paris, their financial resources were low because they lived in one (or two) garret room(s), for which no tax had to be paid.[75] From 1866 onwards, their resources were more plentiful. They could rent two separate apartments on rue de Belzunce: Jules moved to number 20 and Odilon to number 12. Odilon married Eliza Damoye (1830–76) on 9 April 1870[76] and died about one year later, on 10 September 1871. Because he had no children, his heirs were his wife, his mother, his sister and his brother. The declared amount of the inheritance was very low (442.64 francs, that is, around 1500 euros 2004[77]) and it was mainly constituted of bonds.[78] Eliza died a little over four years later, on 18 June 1876. In her testament, Jules was her only heir. The declared amount of this inheritance was also very low (624 francs, that is around 2400 euros 2004).[79]

Jules lived at 20 rue de Belzunce until 1875, then he moved to 17 rue de Montyon, where he stayed until 1880.[80] In 1881, he stopped being a broker and became a rentier. He moved into a new apartment, 13 rue de Maubeuge (tenth district), in which he lived for five years and then, in 1886, he moved to 83 rue de Maubeuge. He lived there until 1894, when he moved to 25 rue de Rocroy, where he lived with his mother and his sister, both widows.[81] These 13 years correspond to a very easy financial period for him. His apartments were large and had servants' quarters. In fact, Jules had several servants: a maid, a carriage-man and a gardener. From 1887 until his death, he rented a stable and a garage for his three carriages and three horses, at 140 boulevard Magenta. At that address there was also a room for his carriage-man. Although Jules always rented his Parisian apartments, he bought a large plot in Saint-Gratien (near Paris) for 45 000 francs (171 500 euros 2004) in 1887. He expanded this in 1887, by buying the plot next to it for 6100 francs (23 250 euros 2004). Then, in 1888 and 1893, Jules bought two plots in Enghien-les-Bains (near Paris) for a total of 47 928 francs (182 500 euros 2004). He built two houses on them as his summer houses. Finally, in 1894, Jules bought a burial plot in perpetuity (*concession perpétuelle*) in the Père Lachaise cemetery. During this period, he also lent significant amounts to several persons for more than 65 000 francs total (that is around 248 000 euros 2004).

Jules died on 9 December 1894. His body was buried in his vault in the Père Lachaise cemetery.[82] When he died, his fortune was estimated at 1 026 510.03 francs (more than 3.8 million euros 2004). Jules never married; consequently, he had no direct heir. He left a testament with a Parisian lawyer. His testament gives a good idea of his financial means and his lifestyle.[83]

2. *On the influence of the* Calcul des chances et philosophie de la bourse

We have seen that Jules Regnault and his brother were brokers, i.e. they worked for an *agent de change*. At this time, the Paris Stock Exchange had only 60 such *agents*. It was not easy to become an *agent de change* because such posts were very expensive, and generally the *agents* had their own successors. The *agents de change* were public officers who had the monopoly of transactions on the stock exchange. They employed many people.[84] Because Jules was a broker, we can assume that other brokers and financial analysts of the second half of the nineteenth century read his book or knew of his ideas. It was probably in this way that Jules Regnault's ideas influenced Louis Bachelier. As Bachelier explains (1912, 293), before 1900 and probably since 1895 (Courtault et al. 2002, 22), he was interested in finance. As I explained in Jovanovic (2000), Bachelier used Regnault's hypotheses and presented them in the same order, although he referred to no financial work. This influence also appears with several identical mistakes that exist in the Regnault and Bachelier books. The influence of Regnault's book in the community of brokers probably continued after 1900, because Maurice Gherardt used the work in his book, *Le gain mathématique à la bourse*, published in 1910. This speculator was interested in the statistics and calculus of probabilities and their applications to games of chance. He extended Regnault's calculus and associated it with Bachelier's thesis.

We also know that French actuaries used the *Calcul des chances et philosophie de la bourse*. Emile Dormoy referred to it in his 1872 and 1873 articles. It should be remembered that, in France during the second half of the nineteenth century, actuaries and French economist-engineers were the main supporters of the use of mathematics in the social sciences, in particular in economics. They played an important role in the creation and diffusion of mathematical and statistical methods in economics. It is well known that Léon Walras found some supporters in the French actuary community. Moreover, Henri Lefèvre, who also tried to create a stock exchange science, was a French actuary too (see Chapter 8 in this volume).

Finally, Jules's book had an international diffusion, although it is not easy to evaluate its effective impact. This international diffusion reminds us that Louis Bachelier's works, which, until the 1960s, were rather familiar in France, were well known in the USA, the United Kingdom and Russia (Jovanovic 2004a). In the case of Regnault, however, his book does not seem to be quoted outside France.

To give an idea of the influence of Regnault influence, we list below, classified chronologically, the libraries which have a copy of the *Calcul des chances et philosophie de la bourse* and the authors who mention it.

Libraries which have a copy of the Calcul des chances et philosophie de la bourse

The Bibliothèque Nationale de France, received in 1863.
The British Library, received in the second part of March 1864.
The Library of Congress (USA), received in 1884 (classified as a financial/gambling book).
The Library of the University of Toronto, received in 1892 (classified as a probability book).
The Library of the Katholieke Universiteit Leuven.

Books which refer to the Calcul des chances

Laurent, Hermann[85] (1873). *Traité du Calcul des Probabilités*. Paris: Gauthier-Villars.
Laurent, Hermann (1893). *Théorie des jeux de hasard*. Paris: Gauthier-Villars.
Piéron, Henri et Nicolas Vaschide[86] (1903). Les Applications du Calcul des Probabilités. In *L'Enseignement Mathématique*, 5ème année (1–2): 1–44.
Barriol, Alfred[87] (1908). *Théorie et pratique des opérations financières*. Paris: Octave Doin.
Keynes, John M.[88] (1921). *A Treatise on Probability*. London: Macmillan.

Articles and books which use the Calcul des chances

Dormoy, Emile[89] (1872, 1873). Théorie mathématique des jeux de hasard. *Journal des Actuaires Français*, tome 1: 120–46 and 232–57; tome 2: 38–57.
Gherardt, Maurice (1910). *Le gain mathématique à la Bourse*. Paris: Charles Amat.
Massebeuf, Alexandre[90] (1923). *Des marchés à primes dans les bourses de valeurs (Paris–Londres–Berlin)*. Paris: Garnier frères.
Laferrière, Julien[91] (1951). *La loi juridique et la loi scientifique de la Bourse*. Unpublished. Paris: Cujas Library (call number: MS 196).

Notice that there is a mistake in the *Grand dictionnaire universel du XIXe siècle* published by Pierre Larousse.[92] In the Jules Regnault bibliographical note, he wrote 'Regnault (Jules), French scholar, died in 1866'. This note attributes several books to Jules. However, with the exception of the *Calcul des chances et philosophie de la bourse*, all the other books were written by Jean-Joseph Regnault (1797–1863),[93] who signed some of his books 'J. Regnault'. This signature may explain the mistake. However, these two authors have no family relationship. The *Catalogue général de la librairie française*,[94] published in 1871, made the same mistake.

Resources used

Archives Crédit Lyonnais.
Archives départementales des Ardennes: Certificates issued by the Registry Office.

Archives départementales de l'Aube: Certificates issued by the Registry Office.
Archives départementales de la Marne: Certificates issued by the Registry Office.
Archives départementales du Nord: Certificates issued by the Registry Office, military registration tables, bursaries and scholarship, Business school student lists.
Archives départementales de l'Oise: Certificates issued by the Registry Office.
Archives départementales du Val d'Oise: Certificates issued by the Registry Office, Land register (*Cadastre*), donations and bequests, *minutes notariales* (Notarial Inventory records).
Archives économiques et financières du Ministère des finances et de l'industrie.
Archives Nationales: *minutes notariales* (Notarial Inventory records).
Archives de la mairie d'Enghien-les-Bains: Regnault's bequest.
Archives de la ville de Bruxelles: Certificates issued by the Registry Office, Land register (*Cadastre*).
Archives de la ville de Paris: Certificates issued by the Registry Office, electoral lists, Land register (*Cadastre*), direct taxes and 'patentes', estate, military registration tables.
Archives of the Université catholique de Louvain: student graduation lists.
Archives of the Université Libre de Bruxelles: student graduation lists.
Archives of the University of Ghent: student lists.
Centre des archives contemporaines: *minutes notariales* (Notarial Inventory records).
Cimetière du père Lachaise: perpetual grant of grave file.

Notes

1. This canonical history, which is widely known, is analyzed in Jovanovic (2004b).
2. The mid-nineteenth century was indeed characterized in France by some resistance to the use of mathematics in economics (Ménard 1978), and this might explain Regnault's predilection for a literary exposition. However, while presenting his results, he explicitly referred to 'mathematical laws' (see for instance 1863, 50), and mathematical formulae explicitly appear in the book when he turned to the empirical testing of the theoretical laws he put forward.
3. The French 3 percent (or the '*Rente*') was then the most important bond related to the French public debt. The coupon payment – that is, the payment of interest – occurred twice a year (in June and December). Three points can be noted here. First, approximately 450 securities were quoted on the Paris Stock Exchange and among them approximately 160 (French and foreign) bonds. Second, most existing forward (or futures) contracts or option contracts dealt with these securities. Third, Bachelier's dissertation (1900) was also devoted to the analysis of the bond.
4. See Reznikow (1990, 225).
5. The *Haute Banque* was constituted by new banking houses – Rothschild, Eichthal, Fould, etc. – which were created during the 1810s and 1820s. These banking houses were the only ones that had enough money to finance the public debt. That is why their activities were closely linked to the State.
6. The definition of '*agiotage*' changed repeatedly during the eighteenth and nineteenth centuries (Courtois 1879). At the time of Regnault (1863, 102), the word – which he used – was related to short operations, made 'without any resource, credit or capital, or a low amount of capital'. It should be noted that the French government was here paradoxically condemning a practice that it largely contributed to spread. See for instance Roussel (1859, 179–80) on the way the French government encouraged speculation (*l'agiotage*) to obtain some funds, then created some *chambres de justice* (courts of justice) in order to intimidate the speculators (*agioteurs*) when it no longer needed them.
7. See Reznikow (1990, 230) and Dupont-Ferrier (1926, 212–18).
8. The first private companies that used heavily financial markets were the railway companies. From the 1820s, they issued a large number of bonds that broke the quasi-monopoly of public bonds. Through a 1839 law the French State guaranteed a minimum interest on the bonds of railways companies, thus making them very popular (Adam 1972, 83). This kind of guarantee contributed to developing the 'railwaymania' (Studeny 1995, 228) in the 1840s. See also Preda (2001).
9. The number of securities strongly increased after the mid-nineteenth century: three securities were quoted in 1800, 197 in 1850, 689 in 1876 and more than 1000 in 1900. These data correspond to securities quoted on the official market of the Paris Stock Exchange (*le Parquet*). They do not take into account securities quoted on the non-official market (*la Coulisse*). They come from Courtois (1877) and the annals of the Congrès international

des valeurs mobilières in 1900. Moreover, Hautcœur (1997, 245) shows that stock market capitalization also strongly increased.

10. See Reznikow (1990, 235) and Dupont-Ferrier (1926, 212–18).
11. See Hautcœur (1994, 238).
12. During the nineteenth century in France, the question of social harmony was emphasized in the views of the liberal economists who tried to heighten the general public awareness of financial markets. Their aim was 'to work for the transformation of the French economy in order to enable it … to realize the social peace in France through the development' (Le Van-Lemesle 1991, 356). They defended the following argument: 'progress in production always remains the source of universal happiness and of social peace' (ibid., 361).
13. We observe the same movement of democratization on all European stock markets. See Michie (1999) and Preda (2001).
14. See Neymarck (1903).
15. The *Journal des Economistes* – the most influential economic journal of the time – recurrently published debates among the members of the *Société d'Economie Politique* (see for instance the number 47 of the *Journal des Economistes* published in 1857).
16. For example, the proceedings of the *coulissiers* in 1860.
17. For instance, the petitions presented by Corbin on 3 February 1863, which asked for the abolition of short operations, by Boboeuf in March 1864 which asked for the legalization of all futures operations, or by Véry and Lavallée presented on 8 May 1864.
18. On that issue and on the juridical debates during the nineteenth century, see Tetreau (1994).
19. The main bankers, financiers and merchants (*négociants*) of Paris signed numerous petitions to the Senate. Their number increased in the 1860s.
20. See Frèrejouan du Saint (1893) and Boboeuf (1864) on this issue.
21. Alphonse Courtois – the father of the former Alphonse Courtois – published in 1852 in the *Journal des Economistes* a study that aimed to defend speculation by arguments based on its economic need. Note that the 1850s were characterized by a rapid development of the stock market, illustrated by the number of quoted enterprises and the amount of capitalization. The ratio capitalization/GNP was 1.9 in 1820, 6.7 in 1850 and 17.5 in 1855 (Arbulu 1998).
22. On Lefèvre, see Chapter 8 in this volume.
23. However, he recognized that the separation between short-term and long-term speculation was merely a theoretical one, just like the one between right and wrong (1863, 103–4).
24. This link was first analyzed in Jovanovic (2001, 2002b).
25. Regnault makes few references and they are always very targeted. He only quotes two economists, who are liberal, Say and Courtois, a speculation manual – by Calemard de la Fayette's, to which he is opposed, and secondarily philosophers – Pascal and Locke. His more numerous references, which are also the most precise and the most important for his demonstrations, concern mathematicians or scholars interested in probability. He refers to 'the solution of the 5th Huyghens' problem'; he quotes Bernoulli for his work on the law of large numbers; and he quotes also Hume, Laplace, Quételet and Cabanis for their involvement in and their works on the link between ignorance and probabilities as well as on the application of the probabilities to the social world.
26. For instance: the predilection for mean values; the search for deterministic and long-term laws; the interpretation of variation as error, vice or imperfection; human progress as narrowing changes, etc. On Quételet, see Hankins (1908) and Porter (1986).
27. Note also that, in this book, Quételet suggested the extension of his analysis to prices. He offered several analyses of grain prices (1846, 183).
28. See Hacking (1990) on nineteenth-century determinism.
29. According to Armatte, the contemporary meaning of the mean value ('*la moyenne*') appeared in the French language at the very beginning of the seventeenth century and came from the Latin words '*mediocris*' and '*mediocitas*'. Neither word was used in a pejorative sense but meant an intermediate place between two extremes. 'Thomas Aquinas is the theologian of this mediocrity that becomes the place of all the virtues. Then the just middle became the model of religious and non-religious morals' (1995, chap. 5, 24), in the sense that it became a model of justice and rational decision.
30. See for instance Cohen (1994), Israel (1996), Le Gall (1999, 2002) and Schabas (1990).
31. Le Gall (forthcoming) participantes in this kind of test in 'natural econometrics', which arose in France during the nineteenth century.
32. Such moral issues stimulated the emergence of probability theory. See Coumet (1970) and Hacking (1975).
33. The word *random* appeared in a statistical sense in 1898 (Frankfurter et al. 1999, 166–7), while the expression *random walk* was used for the first time by Karl Pearson (see Pearson 1905a, 1905b, Rayleigh 1905).
34. For a long time, financial 'theory' only related to the finances of the government, actuarial practice and legal problems linked to financial operations.
35. See Jovanovic (2000) on the relation between Regnault and Bachelier.
36. In the opposite case, the speculator has to pay an amount of money (the '*report*').

37. Regnault explains that 'the values given by each individual will not be randomly ruled, or without any order; they will be distributed [*se grouperont*] according to *a certain law*, and *in the most symmetrical way around* [*des deux côtés*] *the mean value*; if we divide in equal parts the distance from this value to the extreme values, the numerical value of each group would constantly and progressively decrease with the distance from the mean value' (1863, 25, our italics). At that time, this example was a classical one (see Feldman et al. 1991), and Porter (1986, 107) shows how it was also used by Quételet. Note that the term 'normal law' was only introduced by Karl Pearson in 1893 (Klein 1997). Although this law was never explicitly put forward by Regnault, his diagrams as well as numerous parts of his book led us to think that his analysis was based on the Gaussian law (see for instance 1863, 167), which was a means to bring deviations within the domain of order.
38. This model is similar to the Ornstein–Uhlenbeck process in continuous time of which the dynamic is $dP_t = a(\bar{P} - P_t)d_t + dW_t$, where $dP_t = \bar{P}$ is the mean, W_t a Brownian and a a constant. With $a = 1$, we obtain $dP_t = (\bar{P} - P_t)d_t + dW_t$. Translated into discrete time, we have $P_{t+1} - P_t = \bar{P} - P_t + \varepsilon_{t+1}$, with $\varepsilon_{t+1} = W_{t+1} - W_t$. Then we obtain a random walk model with mean reversion $P_{t+1} = \bar{P} + \varepsilon_{t+1}$.
39. For instance, if $t = 1$ day and we have $n = 5$, it leads to change the scale from a daily resolution to a weekly one, because 1 week = 5 working days.
40. The mean deviation was the mean value of the extreme prices during a certain period. He also calculated a probable deviation (i.e. the median deviation). The difference between these two deviations reveals the instability of the market. If the prices were affected by no large variation, there would be no difference between the mean and the probable deviations. He saw this difference as a measure of the 'morality' of the market: a mean deviation superior to a probable deviation indicates that the short-term speculation dominates and the market can then be considered as volatile. In Regnault's own words: 'We can note … the remarkable ratio that links the probable deviation to the mean deviation, approximately 2/3, a ratio that we frequently find, for instance the one which links the probable life to the mean life. Moreover, this ratio is not constant, it is used for giving a measure of the regularity of the movement of prices [*cours*], and depending on whether this movement is following less violent shocks … , the probable deviation gets closer to the mean deviation; they could even be identical if the movement of prices [*cours*] were perfectly regular and continuous. And just as the tendency for the probable life to get closer to the mean life is a sign [*indice*] of the progress of the well-being [*bien-être*] and of the civilization in a nation, the ratio of deviations for prices, which tends to get closer to unity … , is an exact measure of the morality of speculation … ' (Regnault 1863, 53). See also the conclusion of Regnault's book.
41. Bachelier (1900) is the first who did this demonstration.
42. We have exactly the same problem in Bachelier's thesis: the economic hypothesis led to a model different from the mathematical model developed by Bachelier (Jovanovic 2003).
43. See also Regnault (1863, 77–95).
44. 'What makes the prices on the stock market significant is the fact that, at a given time, at a given price [*cours*], there will be a buyer who can demand to obtain a security in exchange for his capital, there will be a seller who will demand the payment of capital in exchange for his security … . The rise will then not be a simple phenomenon, fruitless and without any result, because its direct effect is the appreciation [*une plus-value*] of the other existing securities … whereas the decline will result in their depreciation. It is true that the rise has contributed neither to the creation of any security, nor to add a centime to social assets. Its result is the creation of a *moral* value [*valeur morale*] that we label trust or *creditworthy* [*crédit*] and that can perfectly be measured [*susceptible d'une appréciation chiffrée*] just like concrete and material wealth would be' (Regnault 1863, 109).
45. This relation between statistics and determinism is analyzed in Hacking (1990) and Porter (1986).
46. We have for instance in mind the methods devised by Lucien March (1905), which were based on the estimation of a trending factor (a moving average); the deviations from the observed data were seen as oscillatory short-term components, see Jovanovic and Le Gall (2001), Klein (1997) and Le Gall (forthcoming).
47. The data are presented in Regnault (1863, 148–9).
48. In a paper read to the British Association for the Advancement of Science in 1862, Stanley Jevons took a similar approach to seasonal fluctuations. This paper is reproduced and analyzed in Hendry and Morgan (1995). Note moreover that seasonal effects were also put forward by Quételet.
49. More precisely, he remarked that the maximum price of the French bond precedes the days of its coupon payment (6 June and 6 December), whereas its minimum price happens on the following day.
50. See Morgan (1997).
51. See Ekelund and Hébert (1999) and Zylberberg (1990) on Cheysson's econometric work on demand. See Jovanovic and Le Gall (2001) on March's views on statistics and econometrics. See Le Gall (forthcoming) on Lenoir's econometric work on demand and supply.
52. This choice was based on the conviction that the data were the product of a homogeneous trend.
53. The figure 54.15 is the difference between the highest monthly mean value (86.65F in July 1840) and the lowest one (32.50F in April 1848).
54. This was, once more, a confirmation that the world was normally ruled: this result 'is in accordance with the universal laws that rule the world' (Regnault 1863, 168).
55. Regnault claimed that a well-organized society would only admit one 'center of gravity'. One can also note that

he had an ideal society in mind, and history was for him that of a possible convergence toward it, *à la* Cournot.

56. Girlich (2002) notes three others works that were published before 1900: Castelli (1877), Edgeworth (1888), Macleod (1855, 1866). However, there are major differences between these and Regnault's book. The works of Edgeworth and of Mcleod deal with bank and not with financial markets – at this time banking was a subject already theoretical studied. Castelli's book is about finance but, in contrast with Regnault's book, it remains descriptive and takes no theoretical steps.
57. On Lefèvre's work, see Chapter 8 in this volume.
58. Economics education was promoted by liberal economists and was mainly based on Jean-Baptiste Say's theoretical works.
59. There were some courses but these were very isolated and not definitive. For instance, the first course in economics was given at the Ecole normale in 1795, but it only lasted for four months (Le Van-Lemesle 2004, 47–54).
60. See Breton and Lutfalla (1991).
61. On the French economists during the nineteenth century, see Breton and Lutfalla (1991).
62. According to Bourdieu, it is necessary to distinguish 'two kinds of scientific capital: an authoritative capital specifically scientific and the capital of power within the scientific world, which can be accumulated by ways that are not purely scientific ... and which is the bureaucratic principle of temporal power within the scientific field' (Bourdieu 2001, 113). 'These temporal powers are principally national *i.e.* linked to the national institutions, in particular those that govern the reproduction of the scientific corpus – as academicians, comities, commissions, etc. – whereas the scientific capital is rather international' (Bourdieu 2001, 113–14).
63. However, we can note that the *Journal des Economistes* regularly published articles that dealt with financial markets. Moreover, the *Société d'économie politique* organized several meetings on this subject.
64. See Breton (1991) and Ménard (1987). Note that Courtois was opposed to the use of probabilities in economics (Courtois 1879, 14–15).
65. In addition to Regnault's book, we can mention the work of the French actuary Henri Lefèvre, who, in 1870, for the first time suggested representing the result of a complex combination of financial operations – in particular of options – by graphs, which are still commonly used nowadays. See Chapter 8 in this volume.
66. The death certificate of Regnault's father can be found at the Archives de la ville de Paris (call number: 5mi 1/1338).
67. This information comes from the Archives of Brussels: marriage certificate of Jean Baptiste Haye and Marie Louise Goffin in Brussels on 7 March 1846 (certificate no. 239), and that of Lucien Regnault and Thérèse Keyser in Brussels on 1 June 1837 (certificate no. 438).
68. This information comes from the Archives départementales du Nord (*registre du conseil de révision de recrutement* of Valenciennes for the year 1847, call number: 1R534).
69. He was registered for the university year 1846–47, and he cancelled his registration during the university year 1850–51. This information comes from the Archives of this University.
70. He did not graduate at any of the four Belgian universities that existed in the middle of the nineteenth century: Brussels, Ghent, Liège and Leuven. However, it must be noted that the registration lists of the Université Catholique de Louvain were destroyed in 1914 by a fire. Thus, it is possible that Jules studied in this university without graduating.
71. The bequest of Frédéric Augustin Regnault is recorded at the Archives de la ville de Paris (call number: DQ8/2093).
72. On Quételet, see Hankins (1908).
73. Their mother and sister remained in Brussels, probably until 1870 for the former and until 1876 for the latter.
74. This information comes from electoral lists (call numbers: D1M2/77, 85, 92, 100 and 111) and Paris's land register (*cadastre*) (call numbers: D1P4/792 and D1P4/770). These documents can be consulted at the Archives de la ville de Paris.
75. At this time, direct taxes were calculated on the basis of the windows and the size of the lodging.
76. Eliza came from a poor family: her father was a laborer, her mother a seamstress (see their marriage certificate, at Grandvilliers, on 22 November 1815; this certificate is in the Archives départementales de l'Oise, call number: 5 MI 614). In all probability, it was at that time that Jules's mother moved from Brussels to Paris. His sister, Delphine, stayed in Brussels where she married Albert Lescuyer, a journalist, on 8 October 1872. Albert Lescuyer came from the Parisian upper class (see the inventory of his father's wealth after death on 20 March 1879, which is in the Archives de la ville de Paris, call number: DQ7/12397).
77. For information, around 1890, the *franc-or* at that time was worth about 4 euros 2004, and the daily wage of a skilled worker was between 8 and 10 euros 2004.
78. On the French tax system during the nineteenth century, see Bouvier and Wolff (1973).
79. The property inventory after death is in the Archives de la ville de Paris (call number: DQ7/12629). Eliza's testament can be consulted in the Archives nationales françaises, but it gives no further information.
80. This information comes from Paris's land register (*Cadastre*). It can be consulted at the Archives de la ville de Paris (call numbers: D1P4/769 and D1P4/106).

81. This information comes from Paris's land register (*Cadastre*). It can be consulted at the Archives de la ville de Paris (call numbers: D1P4/671, D1P4/709, D1P4/710 and D1P4/969). Note that this apartment should be his sister's because, when she and her husband lived in Brussels, their personal address was precisely 25 rue de Rocroy – see their marriage certificate in the Brussels archives (year 1872, register no. 1544).
82. His burial vault is number 2 in div. 25, i.1/26 (on the left side of Molière's and de La Fontaine's graves). The perpetual grant of grave number is 10 PA of 1894. His mother and his sister are also buried in it.
83. The Centre des archives contemporaines holds Jules's testament and the inventory of his wealth after death (call numbers: 19860 351 art. 156 and 19860 351 art. 157). There is a copy of it in the donations file in the Archives départementales de l'Oise.
84. A non-official market also existed, the Coulisse, that dealt with financial securities. Recall that the Coulisse arose because the small number of *agents de change* could not cope with the development of the Parisian market.
85. This French actuary mentioned at the end of his treatise the major books on the calculus of probability, including Jules's book. However, he did not read all the books mentioned in this bibliography.
86. They were two French psychologists very interested in experimental psychology, of which they were the founders. They were also interested in the application of rigorous measurement techniques, in particular psychophysics, to social science topics from the viewpoint of mental activity.
87. This author was the first professor of finance at the Institut de Statistique of the University of Paris. His book was used by generations of students of finance and insurance.
88. His bibliography would contain 'a much longer list of what has been written about probability than can be found elsewhere'. It was based on two books: Todhunter's *History of the Mathematical Theory of Probability* and Hermann Laurent's *Calcul des probabilités*. According to Keynes, 'the bibliographical catalogue at the conclusion of Laurent's *Calcul* (published in 1873) is the longest list published hitherto of general works on probability' (p. 472). Thus, Keynes probably never read Jules's book.
89. Emile Dormoy was a French actuary.
90. His book is a Ph.D. thesis in law and economics. Note that, at this time, in France, departments of economics and law were not separate.
91. From 1929 to 1951, Julien Laferrière was professor at the Sorbonne. This manuscript is most probably his course notes. It is presented in Jovanovic (2002a).
92. The publication of Pierre Larousse's *Grand Dictionnaire universel du XIXème siècle* took 13 years, from 1863 to 1876.
93. There are two obituaries of Jean-Joseph Regnault, published in 1863: the first in the *Annales des Chemins vicinaux*, première partie, tome XIX, pp. 169 and 170; the second in the *Annales des conducteurs des ponts et chaussées*, première partie, tome VII, pp. 205 and 206.
94. This is a bibliography of French books published between 1840 and 1925. This book can be consulted from the Gallica database on the Bibliothèque Nationale de France website.

References

Adam, Jean-Paul (1972), *Instauration de la politique des chemins de fer en France* (*The Creation of the Politics of Railways in France*). Paris: Presses Universitaires de France.

Arbulu, Pedro (1998), 'La Bourse de Paris au XIXe Siècle: l'exemple d'un marché émergent devenu efficient' ('The Paris stock exchange during the 19th century: an example of an emergent market that became efficient'). *Revue d'Economie Financière*, **49**: 213–49.

Armatte, Michel (1995), *Histoire du modèle linéaire. Formes et usages en Statistique et en Econométrie jusqu'en 1945* (*The History of the Linear Model. Forms and Uses in Statistics and Econometrics until 1945*). Ph.D., Paris: EHESS.

Asselain, Jean-Claude (1985), *Histoire économique: de la révolution industrielle à la première guerre mondiale* (*Economic History: From the Industrial Revolution to the First World War*). Paris: Presses de la fondation nationale des sciences politiques & Dalloz.

Bachelier, Louis (1900), 'Théorie de la spéculation' ('Theory of speculation'). Reproduced in *Annales de l'Ecole Normale Supérieure, 3ème série*. **17**, January: 21–86. Reprint, 1995, Paris: J. Gabay.

——— (1912), *Calcul des probabilités* (*Probability Calculus*). Paris: Gauthier-Villars.

Boboeuf, Pierre-Alexis-Francis (1864), *Marchés à terme. Pétition adressée au Sénat par M. Boboeuf pour rendre obligatoires les marchés à terme* (*Futures Markets. Petition Addressed to the Senate by M. Boboeuf to Make Futures Markets Obligatory*). Paris: C. de Mourgues frères.

Bourdieu, Pierre (2001), *Science de la science et réflexivité: cours du Collège de France, 2000–2001*. Paris: Raisons d'agir.

Bouvier, Jean and Wolff Jacques (eds) (1973), *Deux siècles de fiscalité française, XIXe–XXe siècles: histoire, économie, politique* (*Two Centuries of the French Fiscal System, 19th–20th Centuries*). Paris: Mouton.

Breton, Yves (1991), 'Les économistes français et les questions de méthode'. In *L'Economie politique en France au XIXe siècle*, edited by Yves Breton and Michel Lutfalla. Paris: Economica.

Breton, Yves and Michel Lutfalla (1991), *L'Economie politique en France au XIXe siècle*. Paris: Economica.
Caron, François (1995), *Histoire économique de la France XIX–XXème siècles* (*Economic History of France, 19th–20th Centuries*). Paris: A. Colin (2nd edn).
Castelli, Charles (1877), *The Theory of 'Options' in Stocks and Shares* (pp. 77). London: F.C. Mathieson.
Cohen, I. Bernard (1994), *The Natural Sciences and the Social Sciences: Some Critical and Historical Perspectives*. Dordrecht and London: Kluwer Academic.
Coumet, Ernest (1970), 'La Théorie du Hasard est-elle née par Hasard?' ('Was the theory of chance born by chance?') *Annales ESC*, **25** (3): 574–98.
Courtault, Jean-Michel, Youri Kabanov et al. (2002), 'Louis Bachelier on the centenary of Théorie de la spéculation'. In *Louis Bachelier: aux origines de la finance mathématique*, edited by Jean-Michel Courtault and Youri Kabanov (pp. 5–86). Besançon: Presses Universitaires Franc-Comtoises.
Courtois, Alphonse (Jr) (1852), 'Étude sur l'agiotage' ('A study on agiotage'). *Journal des économistes*, **7**, **8**, **9** and **10**.
——— (1877), *Tableaux des cours des principales valeurs négociées et cotées aux bourses des effets publics de Paris, Lyon et Marseille du 17 janvier 1797 à nos jours* (*Tables of the Prices of the Main Securities Traded and Quoted on the Stock Markets of Paris, Lyon and Marseille, between 17th January 1797 and our Time*). Paris: Garnier frères.
——— (1879), *Défense de l'agiotage* (Defense of Gambling). Paris: A. Hennuyer.
Dormoy, Emile (1872), 'Théorie mathématique des jeux de hasard' ('Mathematical theory of games of chance'). *Journal des Actuaires Français*, **1**: 120–46 and 232–57.
——— (1873), 'Théorie mathématique des jeux de hasard' ('Mathematical theory of games of chance'). *Journal des Actuaires Français*, **2**: 38–57.
Dupont-Ferrier, Pierre (1926), *Le Marché financier de Paris sous le second Empire* (*The Paris Stock Exchange during the Second Empire*). Paris: Presses universitaires de France & libr. Félix Alcan.
Edgeworth, Francis Ysidro (1888), 'The Mathematical Theory of Banking'. *Journal of the Royal Statistical Society of London*, **51**: 113–27.
Ekelund, Robert B. and Robert F. Hébert (1999), *Secret Origins of Modern Microeconomics: Dupuit and the Engineers*. Chicago: University of Chicago Press.
Feldman, Jacqueline, Gérard Lagneau et al. (1991), *Moyenne, milieu, centre. Histoires et usages* (*Mean, Median, Center. History and Uses*). Paris: Editions EHESS.
Frankfurter, Georges M. and Elton G. McGoun (1999), 'Ideology and the theory of financial economics'. *Journal of Economic Behavior & Organization*, **39**: 159–77.
Frèrejouan du Saint, Georges-Marie-René (1893), *Jeu et pari, au point de vue civil, pénal et réglementaire, loteries et valeurs à lots, jeux de bourse, marchés à terme* (*Gambling and Betting*). Paris: L. Larose.
Girlich, Hans-Joachim (2002), *Bachelier's Predecessors*. Mathematisches Institut Preprint.
Hacking, Ian (1975), *The Emergence of Probability: A Philosophical Study of Early Ideas about Probability, Induction and Statistical Inference*. London and New York: Cambridge University Press.
——— (1990), *The Taming of Chance*. Cambridge, UK and New York: Cambridge University Press.
Hankins, Frank Hamilton (1908), *Adolphe Quetelet as Statistician*. Ph.D. thesis, Columbia University, New York.
Hautcœur, Pierre-Cyrille (1994), *Le marché boursier et le financement des entreprises françaises (1890–1939)* (*The Stock Exchange and Financing of French Companies (1890–1939)*). Ph.D. thesis, University of Paris 1.
——— (1997), 'Le marché financier de 1870 à 1900' ('The Stock Exchange between 1870 and 1900'). In *La Longue Stagnation en France. L'Autre Grande Dépression (1873–1897)*, edited by Yves Breton, Albert Broder and Michel Lutfalla. Paris: Economica.
Hendry, David F. and Mary S. Morgan (eds) (1995), *The Foundations of Econometric Analysis*. Cambridge, UK and New York: Cambridge University Press.
Israel, Giorgio (1996), *La mathématisation du réel. Essai sur la modélisation mathématique* (*The Mathematization of Reality: An Essay on Mathematical Modeling*). Paris: Le Seuil.
Jovanovic, Franck (2000), 'L'origine de la théorie financière: une réévaluation de l'apport de Louis Bachelier' ('The origin of financial theory: a reappraisal of Louis Bachelier's contribution'). *Revue d'Economie Politique*, **110** (3): 395–418.
——— (2001), 'Pourquoi l'hypothèse de marche aléatoire en théorie financière? Les raisons historiques d'un choix éthique' ('Why the random walk hypothesis in financial theory? The historical reasons of an ethical choice'). *Revue d'Economie Financière*, **61**: 203–11.
——— (2002a), 'La Loi Juridique et la Loi Scientifique de la Bourse par Julien Laferrière' ('Juridical law and scientific law of the stock exchange by Julien Laferrière'). *Revue d'Histoire des Sciences Humaines*, **7**: 181–91.
——— (2002b), *Le modèle de marche aléatoire dans la théorie financière quantitative: fondements historiques, théoriques et épistémologiques* (*The Random Walk Model in quantitative Financial Theory: Historical, Theoretical and Epistemological Foundations*). Ph.D. thesis, University of Paris 1, Panthéon-Sorbonne: Paris.
——— (2003), *Le modèle de marche aléatoire dans l'économie financière de 1863 à 1976*. Working paper, University of Orléans.

——— (2004a), *The Construction of Financial Economics: A Sociological and Historical Analysis*. Working paper, Glendon College, University of Toronto.

——— (2004b), 'The construction of the canonical history of financial economics'. Presented at History of Economics Society Conference, Toronto.

Jovanovic, Franck and Philippe Le Gall (2001), 'March to numbers: the statistical style of Lucien March'. In *History of Political Economy, annual supplement: The Age of Economic Measurement*, edited by Judy Klein and Mary S. Morgan, pp. 86–100.

Klein, Judy L. (1997), *Statistical Visions in Time: A History of Time Series Analysis, 1662–1938*. Cambridge, UK and New York: Cambridge University Press.

Larousse, Pierre (1866–1876), *Grand dictionnaire universel du XIXe siècle (The Large Universal Dictionary of the 19th Century)*. Paris: Larousse.

Le Gall, Philippe (1999), 'A world ruled by Venus. On Henry L. Moore's transfer of periodogram analysis from physics to economics'. *History of Political Economy*, **31** (4): 723–52.

——— (2002), 'Les Représentations du Monde et les Pensées Analogiques des Econometres. Un Siècle de Modélisation en Perspective' ('Econometric representations of the world and thinking with analogies'). *Revue d'Histoire des Sciences Humaines*, **6**: 39–64.

——— (Forthcoming), *From Nature to Models: An Archaeology of Econometrics in France, 1830–1930*. London: Routledge.

Le Van-Lemesle, Lucette (1991), 'L'institutionnalisation de l'économie politique en France' ('Institutionalization of French political economy'). In *L'Economie Politique en France au XIXe Siècle*, edited by Yves Breton and Michel Lutfalla, pp. 335–88. Paris: Economica.

——— (2004), *Le Juste ou le Riche. L'enseignement de l'économie politique: 1815–1950 (The Just or the Rich. The Teaching of Political Economy: 1815–1950)*. Paris: Comité pour l'histoire économique et financière de la France.

Lefèvre, Henri (1885), *La Comptabilité. Théorie, pratique et enseignement (Accounting. Theory, Practice and Teaching)*. Paris: Librairie Illustrée.

Lorenz, Otton (1871), *Catalogue général de la librairie française (tome quatrième) (The General Catalog of the French Bookshop (Volume 4))*. Paris: Lorenz éditeur.

Macleod, Henry Dunning (1855), *The Theory and Practice of Banking; With the Elementary Principles of Currency; Prices; Credit; and Exchanges*. London: Longman, Brown, Green, and Longmans.

——— (1866), *The Theory and Practice of Banking*. London: Longmans, Green, Reader, & Dyer.

March, Lucien (1905), *Les Représentations Graphiques et la Statistique Comparative (Graphical Representations and Comparative Statistics)*. Nancy: Berger-Levrault.

Ménard, Claude (1978), *La Formation d'une rationalité économique, A.A. Cournot (The Formation of Economic Rationality, A.A. Cournot)* Paris: Flammarion.

——— (1987), 'Why was there no probabilistic revolution in economic thought?' In *The Probabilistic Revolution, vol. 2, Ideas in the Sciences*, edited by Lorenz Krüger, Gerd Gigerenzer and Mary S. Morgan, Cambridge, MA: MIT Press.

——— (1989), 'The machine and the heart'. *Social Concept*, 4: 81–95.

Michie, R.C. (1999), *The London Stock Exchange: A History*. New York: Oxford University Press.

Morgan, Mary S. (1997), 'Searching for causal relations in economic statistics: reflections from history'. In *Causality in Crisis? Statistical Method and the Search for Causal Knowledge in the Social Sciences*, edited by V.R. McKim and S.P. Turner, South Bend, IN: University of Notre Dame Press.

Neymarck, Alfred (1903), 'Une Statistique nouvelle sur le morcellement des valeurs mobilières (chemins de fer, rentes, Banque de France, Crédit foncier, etc.)' ('A new statistic for the division of securities'). *Société de statistique de Paris (séance du 18 février)*. Paris: Guillaumin.

Pearson, Karl (1905a), 'The problem of the random walk'. *Nature*, **72** (1865): 294.

——— (1905b), 'The problem of the random walk (answer)'. *Nature*, 72 (1867): 342.

Porter, Theodore M. (1986), *The Rise of Statistical Thinking, 1820–1900*. Princeton, NJ: Princeton University Press.

Preda, Alex (2001), 'The rise of the popular investor: financial knowledge and investing in England and France,1840–1880'. *Sociological Quarterly*, **42** (2): 205–32.

——— (2004), 'Informative prices, rational investors: the emergence of the random walk hypothesis and the 19th century "science of financial investments"'. *History of Political Economy*, **36** (2): 351–86.

Quételet, Adolphe (1848), *Du système social et des lois qui le régissent (The Social System and the Laws that Govern It)*. Paris: Guillaumin et Cie.

Quételet, Adolphe (1846), *Lettres à S.A.R. le duc régnant de Saxe-Coburg et Gotha, sur la théorie des probabilités, appliquée aux sciences morales et politiques (Letters Addressed to H.R.H. the Grand Duke of Saxe Coburg and Gotha, on the Theory of Probabilities: As Applied to the Moral and Political Sciences)*. Brussels: M. Hayez.

Rayleigh (1905), 'The problem of the random walk (answer)'. *Nature*, **72** (1866): 318.

Regnault, Jules (1863), *Calcul des chances et philosophie de la bourse (Chance Calculus and the Philosophy of the Stock Exchange)*. Paris: Mallet-Bachelier and Castel.

Reznikow, Stéphane (1990), 'Les envolées de la Bourse de Paris au XIXème siècle' ('The rise of the Paris stock exchange during the 19th century'). *Histoire économique et financière de la France, Etudes et recherches*, **2**: 223–44.

Roussel, Pierre-Antoine-Eugène (1859), *Des Agents de Change et des Jeux de Bourse* (*Stock Brokers and Gambling*). Imp. du Moquet.

Schabas, Margaret (1990), *A World Ruled by Number: William Stanley Jevons and the Rise of Mathematical Economics*. Princeton, NJ: Princeton University Press.

Studeny, Christophe (1995), *L'invention de la vitesse: France, XVIIIe–XXe siècle* (*The Invention of Velocity: France, 18th–20th Centuries*). Paris: Gallimard.

Taqqu, Murad S. (2001), 'Bachelier and his times: a conversation with Bernard Bru'. *Finance and Stochastics*, **5** (1): 3–32.

Tetreau, François (1994), *Le Développement et les Usages de la Coulisse aux XIXe et XXe Siècles* (*Development and Uses of the Coulisse during the 19th and the 20th Centuries*). Ph.D. dissertation, Université Paris II: Paris.

Zylberberg, André (1990), *L'économie mathématique en France 1870–1914* (Mathematical Economics in France 1870–1914). Paris: Economica.

PART IV

EARLY TWENTIETH-CENTURY CONTRIBUTIONS

10 Louis Bachelier

Robert W. Dimand and Hichem Ben-El-Mechaiekh

Introduction

After half a century's neglect, Louis Bachelier's 1900 dissertation achieved remarkable recognition. Benoit Mandelbrot (1989) proclaims that the field of finance 'has its Gregor Mendel in Louis Bachelier' (see further the chapter on Bachelier in Mandelbrot and Hudson 2004), and Nobel laureate Robert C. Merton (1990, xiv) affirms that 'the lineage from Bachelier to modern continuous-time finance is direct and indisputable.' Beyond its pioneering treatment of option pricing, efficient financial markets and rational expectations, Bachelier's dissertation provided a mathematical formalization of the stochastic process later identified with the Brownian motion of molecules, an achievement celebrated by Jeremy Bernstein (2005) in the *American Journal of Physics* on the occasion of the centenary of Albert Einstein's independent formalization of Brownian motion in 1905, five years after Bachelier (Einstein 1956).

Bachelier (1900) remained little known and not readily accessible until A. James Boness's translation appeared in Cootner (1964) and until William Feller (1966 [1971], 181) introduced the term Wiener–Bachelier process as a synonym for Brownian motion, with a similar acknowledgement appearing on the opening page of Itô and McKean (1965). Osborne (1960) reported that he was able to find Bachelier (1900) only in the Rare Book Room of the Library of Congress. Feller (1966 [1971]), who did not cite Bachelier (1900), apparently had to rely on Lévy (1948), although Feller (1950 [1957], 354) had cited Bachelier (1912) to argue that Bachelier's heuristic work 'had inspired A. Kolmogorov to develop the formal foundations of Markov processes.' The *International Encyclopedia of Statistics* has only a single mention of Bachelier, in a list of names of contributors to the probability theory of motion (Kruskal and Tanur 1978, 1099).

Many scholars and scientists, when ignored by their contemporaries and frustrated in their academic careers, have taken comfort in the belief that posterity would recognize the importance of their path-breaking innovations. Louis Bachelier was exceptional in that the verdict of posterity fully justified this faith. Even though research by Franck Jovanovic and Philippe Le Gall has shown that Bachelier was not completely lacking in predecessors and followers (Jovanovic 2000, 2002a; Jovanovic and Le Gall 2001; Jovanovic and Le Gall in Courtault and Kabanov 2002), Bachelier is viewed as the Newton of the Bourse while Jules Regnault (1863) is its Kepler (according to Bernard Bru in Taqqu 2001 and in Courtault and Kabanov 2002, 98).

Because Bachelier (1900) was his first statement of his theory of speculation and the only one as yet published in English translation, it has overshadowed his repeated restatements and refinements of his approach, so that Bernstein (2005, 395) notes only that after 1900, 'Bachelier continued to publish occasionally, including a long paper in 1901, a treatise on the mathematical laws of chance underlying gambling' (contrast the bibliography of six books and 15 articles by Bachelier given by Courtault et al. 2000, 347–8). On the contrary, Bachelier continued to try to find an audience for his theory of speculation. Bachelier (1912), the substantial first volume of a never-completed scholarly treatise, included three chapters (Chapters XII–XIV, pages 277–322) applying his analysis of stochastic processes to financial speculation, chapters that were overlooked in an uncomprehending review by John Maynard Keynes (1912), one of the great lost opportunities for intellectual interchange. Bachelier (1914, 176–213), aimed at a more popular audience, also devoted a chapter to financial speculation. When Bachelier restated his life's work in a series of three short books from 1937 to 1939, he devoted a 49–page monograph (Bachelier 1938) to a more mathematically elegant treatment of his theory of speculation, in keeping with the increasingly sophisticated presentation of probability theory associated with the axiomatization of probability by Kolmogorov (1933). Bachelier's 1912 presentation of his theory of speculation was more rigorous than that of 1900, his 1914 version was less technical and more accessible, and that of 1938 more concise, mathematically elegant and readable, but the central message remained the same.

The theory of speculation

Louis Jean-Baptiste Alphonse Bachelier was born in Le Havre on 11 March 1870 to a wine merchant (who was also Venezuelan vice-consul in Le Havre) and a banker's daughter. The death of both his parents in 1889 left him head of the family wine business, which was renamed Bachelier fils, but, after compulsory military service, Bachelier was able to go to Paris in 1892 to study mathematics at the Sorbonne, attending the lectures of the three future examiners of his doctoral dissertation: Paul Appell, Joseph Boussinesq, and the outstanding figure among French mathematicians of the time, Henri Poincaré (whose 1893–94 lectures were published as Poincaré [1896] 1912). Bachelier graduated from the Sorbonne with a bachelor's degree in sciences in 1895 and a certificate in mathematical physics in 1897, but at least two of his classmates received higher marks in mathematics in 1895. Then, on 29 March 1900, 'the birthdate of mathematical finance' (Courtault et al. 2000, 341), Bachelier successfully defended his thesis on the theory of speculation for the degree of Docteur ès Sciences Mathématiques (along with a secondary thesis on fluid mechanics).

Bachelier's thesis is now recognized as

> the origin of mathematical finance and of several important branches of stochastic calculus such as the theory of Brownian motion, Markov processes, diffusion processes, and even weak convergence in functional spaces. Of course, the reasoning was not rigorous but it was, on the intuitive level, basically correct. (Courtault et al. 2000, 344)

Bachelier (1900) published his results five years before Karl Pearson's and Lord Rayleigh's exchange on random walks in *Nature*, five years before Einstein's paper on Brownian motion (the continuous-time analogue to a discrete-time random walk), and six years before A.A. Markov began to study Markov chains. Bachelier's contribution was overlooked by physicists studying the motion of molecules, who did not think to look for guidance to a study of the movement of asset prices, and tended to be overlooked even in later histories of Brownian motion (compare Maiocchi 1990 and Dimand 1993). However, the dust jacket of Peter Bernstein (1992), which credits Bachelier with having 'anticipated Einstein's work on relativity,' confuses Einstein's first paper on relativity, published in 1905, with his article on Brownian motion the same year. Bachelier (1912, 277; 1938, Preface, v) insisted to the contrary that his theory of speculation was not merely an application of the calculus of probabilities, but the necessary point of departure for the theory of continuous probability, providing simple and extremely clear new conceptions of stochastic processes because the analysis of financial speculation posed problems that required continuous solutions.

Bachelier (1900) analyzed the pricing of call options on French government bonds, exercisable only on their expiration date (see Sullivan and Weithers 1991 on Bachelier's place in the history of option pricing theory leading up to the Black–Scholes formula of 1973). His derivation of the diffusion of probability consisted of working out the mathematical implications of two statements, which Bachelier (1900, 26, 28, 42) italicized for emphasis: '*At a given instant, the market believes in neither a rise nor a fall of true prices* ... Clearly the price considered most likely by the market is the current true price: if the market judged otherwise, it would quote not this price, but another price higher or lower' and '*The mathematical expectation of the speculator is zero.* ... The mathematical expectation of the buyer of an option is zero.' Notice that these are not mathematical concepts, but economic concepts with mathematical implications. If unexploited profit opportunities existed (speculations with a positive expectation), speculators would take advantage of these opportunities until their speculation had caused the prices to change so that no further profitable speculation was possible. If participants in the market expected the price of an option to be at a certain level in the future, the price must be at that level now, or else speculators could make a profit (have a positive mathematical expectation) by taking advantage of the spread between current and future prices. Buyers may expect a price increase, sellers may expect a price decrease, but neither group has better information than the other, and the market as a whole expects an unchanged price. The implication, brought out by Bachelier (1900, 1912, 1914, 1938), is at the heart of the efficient markets hypothesis: the current price is the best predictor of future prices and incorporates all available relevant information. At any moment, prices are equally likely to rise or fall, and the best prediction is that they will not change. Past prices cannot be used profitably to predict the future course of prices, since all the information they can convey is already incorporated in current prices. These implications of the efficient markets hypothesis contradict the ingrained beliefs of financial market participants, whose intuition is that profitable predictions are possible and that valuable information can be extracted from the study of past prices. Since the market is right to believe that prices are equally likely to rise or fall, Bachelier's italicized statements about financial markets also imply the rational expectations hypothesis: market participants make no systematic mistakes in forming their expectations, which are correct except for unpredictable random errors with a mean of zero. This was not only six decades before John Muth's statement of rational expectations, but three decades before Jan Tinbergen (1932) used the concept and the German equivalent of its later name (Keuzenkamp 1991). There is, on average, no profit to be made by trying to outguess the expectations held by the market as a whole. Turning to empirical verification, Bachelier concluded that 'The observed and calculated figures agree on the whole, but they show certain discrepancies.'

Given this view of price formation in financial markets, Bachelier turned to the question of the probability of the price rising (or falling) by a given amount in a specified time. Option prices follow a random walk, with only a random, unpredictable change from one period to the next, equally likely to be an increase or decrease. The limit of such a random walk, as the length of the time period shrinks to zero, is the continuous process of diffusion of probability now identified with Brownian motion (originally a term for the motion of molecules). Drawing a parallel between financial markets and physical phenomena, Bachelier (1900, 1912, 1914, 1938) analyzed the radiation of probability, showing that the probability function P for price changes obeys the diffusion equation for heat. As Cootner (1964, 3) notes, in Bachelier (1900):

> we find the Chapman–Kolmogorov–Smoluchowski equation for continuous stochastic processes, the derivation of the Einstein–Wiener Brownian motion process and the recognition that this process is a solution of the partial differential equation for heat diffusion. ... In addition, Bachelier solves the first passage problem for the Wiener process, the probability law for diffusion in the presence of an absorbing barrier and other problems of interest, all of these solutions occurring many years before they were solved independently by the men who laid the basis for the modern theory of stochastic processes.

However, Bachelier did have a predecessor, Jules Regnault (1863), rediscovered by Franck Jovanovic (2000) and Jovanovic and Philippe Le Gall (2001). Regnault, aged 30 at the time of his only known publication, was influenced by Quetelet's 'social physics.' In contrast to Bachelier's mathematical development of the implications of his economic principles, Regnault expounded his theory in literary terms (even though describing them as the consequences of 'mathematical laws'), using mathematical formulae only in the empirical verification of his results. Nonetheless, Regnault (1863), like Bachelier (1900), was concerned with what the course of bond prices must be if there are to be no unexploited profit opportunities for speculators, and even found that 'The deviation of the prices increases with the square root of time,' a result also obtained by Bachelier. Bachelier's failure to cite other writers makes it difficult to be certain that he knew Regnault's book, which Jovanovic and Le Gall think is likely. The development of the mathematical implications of efficient financial markets is due to Bachelier, but the underlying economic ideas about the informational efficiency of financial markets were shared with Regnault, who held that 'On the stock market, the whole mechanism of the game comes down to two opposite possibilities: increasing and decreasing. Each one can always appear with *equal* facility ... at any moment, no advantage is existing for one possibility or the other' (Regnault 1863, 34, as translated by Jovanovic and Le Gall 2001, 340). Further, in confronting their theories with observations, both Regnault and Bachelier were pioneers of financial econometrics (see Jovanovic and Le Gall in Courtault and Kabanov 2002).

Bachelier made a number of minor mathematical slips, comparable to those found and corrected by Irving Fisher in his notes to his brother-in-law's 1898 translation of Cournot (1838). A more serious problem with the economic interpretation of Bachelier's theory is that his assumption that price changes are normally distributed (follow the Gaussian law) implies that option prices can become negative, even though the owner of an option is not obliged to exercise it. Later writers such as Osborne (1959) and Samuelson (1965a, 1965b) avoided this problem by assuming that the logarithm of the price relative (the ratio of future price to current price), rather than the price relative itself, is normally distributed.

Beyond theory, Bachelier's thesis also contained an extensive and careful empirical verification of his results for the market for options on French government bonds. Bachelier's detailed calculations, both in his thesis and in later works, were remarkable for an era before computers. Jeremy Bernstein (2005) checked some of the numbers from a table of the Gaussian error function in Bachelier (1901), and found that they agreed to the fourth decimal place with results obtained using a modern computer program.

Bachelier (1912) was reviewed, along with Poincaré's lectures on probability ([1896] 1912), another French book on probability, and a German translation of Markov (Markoff 1912), by John Maynard Keynes (1912), and consequently was also mentioned in Keynes's *Treatise on Probability* (1921). What better audience could there have been for a path-breaking analysis of financial markets based on probability theory? Yet Keynes was inclined to doubt the value and in some cases the validity of Bachelier's results, held that 'they can be capable of few applications,' and failed even to notice that the book included three chapters on financial speculation: 'This is a book on which those who are interested in the calculus of probabilities for its own sake ought to form their own opinion, and which statisticians, who are chiefly interested in the practical application of the calculus, can safely neglect.' Keynes (1921), originally written before the First World War as a fellowship dissertation submitted to King's College, Cambridge, only recapitulated Keynes's earlier negative review of Bachelier. The barrier to communication between Bachelier and Keynes was Keynes's emphasis on probability as the degree of belief in the likelihood of a discrete event, in contrast to which Bachelier 'regards the total gain or loss of the gamesters at each point in the game as a continuous variable, which changes by infinitesimal increments, and he is thus enabled to make free use of the methods of the differential calculus' (Keynes 1912, 571). Keynes's lack of sympathy is shown by his remark about Markoff (1912) that 'It is, in the first place, a great pleasure to read a treatise which is not influenced by the exhausted French tradition of mathematical probability, and is yet able to emulate the purity and elegance of French mathematical style' (Keynes 1912, 572). Keynes (1921) also included Regnault (1863) in his bibliography of works on probability. However, Keynes stated at the start of the bibliography that for the sake of completeness he included works that he had not seen, and the partial nature of the Regnault citation (omitting his first name) suggests that Regnault's book was one of those not directly known to Keynes. Another lost opportunity was in 1911 when Poincaré and Einstein both attended the Solvay Congress, at which Brownian motion was among the topics discussed. 'Poincaré did not use the occasion to mention Bachelier's work … Einstein was rather disappointed with Poincaré's views on the quantum theory and did not spend much time talking to him' (J. Bernstein 2005, 398).

Pursuing an academic career

Poincaré began his report on Bachelier's thesis by remarking that 'The subject chosen by M. Bachelier is somewhat removed from those which are normally dealt with by our applicants', much as Lévy, even after his reconciliation with Bachelier, recorded in his notebook that Bachelier's thesis had 'Too much on finance' ('trop question de Bourse'; Courtault et al. 2000, 348, 346). The leading mathematicians did not consider stock market speculation quite suitable as a subject for mathematical research, while financial operators lacked the mathematical background to read Bachelier. Such reservations about its subject matter may have been responsible for the dissertation's grade of *honorable*, rather than the *très honorable* usually needed to launch a successful academic career. Nonetheless, Poincaré's report was generally favorable, and he was helpful to Bachelier, whose thesis and subsequent books were published by Gauthier-Villars, a leading scholarly publisher which published Poincaré's works. Poincaré communicated one of Bachelier's papers to the Academy of Sciences for publication in its proceedings in 1910, as did Appell in 1913, after Poincaré's death. Bachelier (1938, Preface) stresses that Poincaré had Bachelier's work published and was responsible for Bachelier being able to present his work at the Faculty of Sciences of Paris for a number of years.

After a delay, during which Bachelier perhaps returned to running the family wine firm or worked on the Bourse, Bachelier started an academic career. From 1909 to 1914, Bachelier gave annually a 20-lecture course on 'Probability Calculus with Applications to Financial Operations and Analogies with Certain Questions from Physics' at the Faculty of Sciences at the University of Paris, although only from 1913 did the university provide a regular salary and assign Bachelier additional teaching in general mathematics. Such unsalaried lecturing was then common at the start of an academic career, and Paris was where all French academics hoped to teach. In 1914 the Council of the University unanimously authorized the Dean of Faculty of Sciences to try to find funding to make Bachelier's position permanent. His teaching at the university followed some published attention to his work.

Another 'free lecturer' at the Faculty of Sciences with a doctorate in mathematics who published through Gauthier-Villars, Vicomte de Montessus de Ballore (1908, 94–107) expounded, with full acknowledgement, an abridged version of Bachelier's theory of speculation in a volume of elementary lectures on the calculus of probabilities and its application to subjects from insurance to ballistics. De Montessus gave the name 'Bachelier's theorem' to the proposition that the speculator's mathematical expectation of profit is zero. Alfred Barriol ([1908] 1931, 374–84), a graduate of the Ecole Polytechnique, member of the Institute of French Actuaries, and first professor of finance at the Institute of Statistics of the University of Paris, made use of Bachelier's equations and Henri Lefèvre's diagrams in his only book, a work on the theory and practice of financial operations that went into four editions as part of a 'Library of Applied Mathematics' (see Jovanovic 2002a on Lefèvre). Unlike de Montessus, Barriol did not cite Bachelier (or Lefèvre) in his textbook (even though he cited Regnault), but this appears not to have been unusual at the time, especially in textbooks, and Bachelier himself did not mention Regnault or other probability theorists. Maurice Gherardt (1910), a speculator on the Bourse, cited both Regnault (1863) and Bachelier (1900), but presented statistical results to support his claim that it was possible to devise a mathematical formula for winning on the Bourse, contrary to Regnault and Bachelier (Jovanovic and Le Gall in Courtault and Kabanov 2002, 168). Keynes (1912, 571) protested against Bachelier (1912) 'giving no reference to other writers, even when he is borrowing from them. Save that on one occasion he calls Bernoulli's theorem after Bernoulli, there is, I think, no single reference throughout the book to any other author.'

Other scholars also helped Bachelier's career before 1914. As a member of the Council of the Faculty of Sciences, the eminent mathematician and probability theorist Emile Borel (best known to mathematicians for Borel spaces and contributions to measure theory and to economists as a pioneer of strategic games) supported Bachelier's successful applications for grants of 2500 francs in 1910–11 and 2400 francs in each of the next two academic years (Courtault and Kabanov 2002, 32), and it was on a motion by Borel that the Assembly of the Faculty of Sciences agreed to Bachelier offering a course (ibid., 31), but Borel does not appear to have taken an interest in the content of Bachelier's work. Borel was in fact a year younger than Bachelier, but had received his doctorate in 1894 at the age of 23, was appointed to the Sorbonne the following year, and was Appell's son-in-law (Bru in Taqqu 2001). Bachelier (1914), a work of popularization that sold seven thousand copies, was published as a volume in a 'Library of Scientific Philosophy' edited by the sociologist Gustave Le Bon, best remembered for his book on crowds. By 1914 Bachelier held a junior but desirable academic position, and members of the French scholarly community were summarizing and citing his work, supporting his grant applications, publishing his books and articles, and communicating his papers to the Academy of Sciences.

The First World War interrupted Bachelier's career. He was a soldier from September 1914 to the last day of 1918. When he returned, he no longer had a position at the Faculty of Sciences in Paris even though in 1914 the Council of the University had supported a move to make his position permanent (Courtault et al. 2000, 345), and his mentor Poincaré had died in 1912. De Montessus, who had taken up Bachelier's theory of speculation, changed fields, and after the First World War wrote books published by France's National Meteorological Office. Barriol, who had made (unacknowledged) use of Bachelier's equations in his textbook on financial operations, published new editions of his textbook but no new books after the First World War. From 1919 to 1922, Bachelier taught as an assistant professor at Besançon, as a temporary replacement while Professor Claude-Emile Traynard was on leave. Bachelier married in 1920, but was soon widowed. After Traynard's return from leave, Bachelier taught in Dijon from 1922 to 1925, again as an assistant professor replacing a full professor on leave, and then was an associate professor (*professeur sans chaire*) in Rennes from 1925 to 1927, when, at the age of 57, he finally received the professorship of differential and integral calculus in Besançon in succession to Traynard. Bachelier did not publish during his ten years as professor, during which time he suffered from ill health. In a letter to the rector of the university in 1928 requesting a leave of absence (in Courtault and Kabanov 2002), Bachelier stated that he had only just been able to get up after 71 days confined to bed by gout.

In 1926, a year before succeeding Traynard, Bachelier was rejected in favor of another candidate to succeed René Baire, the professor for whom Bachelier had substituted at Dijon. Bachelier was rejected on the basis of a letter from Paul Lévy of the Ecole Polytechnique confirming an error that a Dijon professor of mechanics had found in a 1913 paper by Bachelier, an apparent error reflecting only Bachelier's overly terse explanation of his notation. Bachelier was, in Lévy's phrase, blackballed. He no longer had a powerful mentor such as Poincaré to defend him. Bachelier replied with just but unavailing indignation (in Courtault and Kabanov 2002, 63–5, excerpts translated in Courtault et al. 2000, 365–6). Bachelier was particularly galled that Lévy, who had not read any of Bachelier's other works, sharply criticized Bachelier because the first equation of Bachelier's 1913 paper was nothing other than the equation of Brownian motion. Unaware that Bachelier himself had introduced that result in 1900, Lévy implied that in 1913 Bachelier had taken undeserved credit for a well-known finding of others.

As Lévy recounted much later in a letter to Benoit Mandelbrot on 25 January 1964 (in Courtault and Kabanov 2002, 66), he subsequently found a reference to 'der Bacheliers Fall' (the Bachelier case) in Kolmogorov's important article on diffusion processes (Kolmogorov 1931). Curious, he turned to Bachelier's writings, and discovered not only that the failure to define a symbol in Bachelier (1913) did not keep Bachelier from going on to derive correct results, but that, before Einstein or Norbert Wiener, Bachelier (1900) had discovered several important properties of what became known as the Wiener or Wiener–Lévy function, notably the heat equation for the diffusion of probability. Lévy wrote to Bachelier regretting that the impression made by an apparent error at the start of Bachelier's 1913 paper had kept him from reading further in works so full of interesting ideas, and received in reply a letter testifying to Bachelier's continued enthusiasm for research. Lévy (1948) drew attention to Bachelier's contribution.

Bernard Bru (interviewed in Taqqu 2001) tells a story that differs from Lévy's recollections of 1964. According to Bru, the reconciliation with Bachelier followed from Lévy's reading, not of Kolmogorov (1931), but of Bachelier (1941), while Lévy was in Lyon, to which the Ecole Polytechnique was evacuated during the war and occupation. Lévy's interest in Brownian motion was stimulated when the Polish mathematician Marcinkiewicz was in Paris in 1938 (cf. Marcinkiewicz 1939). Upon reading Bachelier (1941), and then turning to Bachelier's earlier writings and to Kolmogorov (1931), Lévy discovered that results reported in Lévy (1939, 1940), and results published by Einstein in 1905, Smoluchowski in 1906, and Chapman in 1928, had been previously published in overlooked works by Bachelier. Bru's account of the circumstances and timing of Lévy's discovery of Bachelier's contributions is supported by Bru's quotation of a letter from Lévy to Maurice Fréchet in September 1943, asking for verification that a result published by Bachelier in 1906 was in fact equivalent to Chapman's equation. Given the contrast between the post-1914 careers of Bachelier (temporary leave-replacement positions in the provinces) and Lévy (international recognition and a chair at the Ecole Polytechnique in Paris), it is poignant that their reconciliation occurred at a time when Lévy, as a Jew, was barred from publishing by the racial laws of the Vichy regime and then, after the German occupation of the Vichy zone, hid under an assumed name in Grenoble and Macon.[1]

Bachelier retired as a professor in 1937, and in retirement published three short monographs, from 36 to 69 pages each, restating and refining his approach to the calculus of probabilities (Bachelier 1937, 1938, 1939). His final article, in the proceedings of the Academy of Sciences in 1941, concerned the distribution of functionals of Brownian motion: 'Remarkably, the importance of these results in mathematical finance – for instance, the pricing of barrier options – was revealed only relatively recently' in 1996 (Courtault et al. 2000, 345). Bachelier died at the age of 76 on 28 April 1946, in Saint-Servan-sur-Mer and was buried in Sanvic, near Le Havre.

Influence – and lack thereof

Bachelier (1900) influenced a set of university lectures on applications of probability theory, a successful textbook on financial operations, and a speculator's attempt to devise a formula for beating the market, all in Paris (de Montessus 1908, Barriol 1908, and Gherardt 1910, respectively), and by 1914 he was on the verge of a permanent appointment at the University of Paris. The First World War brought this period of Bachelier's career to a close, and, without his mentor Poincaré to support him, he had great difficulty in achieving even a minor academic career in the provinces. Jovanovic and Le Gall (in Courtault and Kabanov 2002, 168) find a couple of later citations of Bachelier (1912), one of which, by Maurice Boll in 1936, attributed to Bachelier (1912) 'la théorie des jeux équitables et de la speculation,' and Julien Lafferière discussed Bachelier, Regnault, de Montessus and Barriol in a course on 'La loi juridique et la loi scientifique de la Bourse' at the Sorbonne's Faculty of Law from 1943 to 1951 (Jovanovic 2002b). Alexandre Massebeuf (1923), in a thesis on options markets supervised by Albert Aftalion, cited Regnault, Gherardt and Lefèvre, but not Bachelier (Jovanovic and Le Gall in Courtault and Kabanov 2002, 168). But Bachelier failed to capture the attention of Borel or, before 1941, of Lévy, the dominant figures in French mathematics and probability theory after the death of Poincaré. Keynes (1912) was so repelled by the very idea of continuous probabilities that he failed to notice Bachelier's chapters on financial speculation. After Barriol and Gherardt, those interested in financial markets were disinclined to tackle books and articles on stochastic processes. The comments of Poincaré in his report on Bachelier's dissertation and much later of Lévy show that the mathematicians were unsympathetic to the prominence of financial markets in Bachelier's work (just as, half a century after Bachelier's thesis, Milton Friedman was reluctant to accept Harry Markowitz's Nobel Prize-winning dissertation on portfolio selection because it could not be neatly classified as economics, mathematics, or business administration; see P. Bernstein 1992, 60). It did not occur to the physicists and mathematicians to look for guidance to a work on financial speculation, and so Einstein, Smoluchowski, Markov, Chapman, Wiener and Lévy laboriously reinvented Bachelier's results for Brownian motion, Wiener processes and Markov chains. The British economists William Stanley Jevons and Francis Ysidro Edgeworth each published scientific papers on the motion of particles, but it did not occur to either of them to relate these studies to their economic research. When Alfred Cowles presented his empirical studies on the inability of stock market forecasters to forecast stock prices in the early volumes of *Econometrica* and Cowles Commission conferences in the 1930s, and, contemporaneously, Holbrook Working published on the absence of serial correlation in price series, they were unaware of Bachelier or that their work on efficient markets had any parallel in Bachelier's writings in the 1930s and at the turn of the century, until works of Cowles, Working and Bachelier were reprinted together in Cootner (1964).

One may be tempted to conclude that Bachelier (1900) had no influence because at the time there was no scientific community to receive a work in mathematical finance. But such a conclusion is too simple. Bachelier influenced Kolmogorov (1931) on diffusion processes, and one of the two channels of rediscovery of Bachelier runs from Kolmogorov (1931) through Lévy (1948) to William Feller. To influence Kolmogorov in the 1930s was to be part of the development of probability theory at that time. Furthermore, the lack of a scientific community to receive Bachelier's work is contingent on the outbreak of the First World War. Had this war not started when it did, Bachelier would have had a permanent position at the University of Paris, where not only was he able to lecture on his own research, but de Montessus and Barriol were also lecturing on his theory of speculation and covering it in their textbooks. Would Borel have continued to ignore the work of a permanent colleague of his at the Sorbonne? Barriol belonged to a tradition of French actuaries, such as Hippolyte Charlon (1878), Henri Lefèvre, Emile Dormoy and Léon Pochet (1873), interested in mathematical analysis of the workings of financial markets (Zylberberg 1990). There was another potential audience, which Bachelier's writings seem not to have reached but might have if he had become a tenured academic in Paris, continuing to publish in prestigious journals and through a noted publisher: the mathematical economists who followed the general equilibrium analysis developed by Léon Walras and Vilfredo Pareto at the University of Lausanne. While the Lausanne School was very much a minority stream in French academic economics at the time, Zylberberg (1990) reports three books on general equilibrium theory published in French in Paris in 1914 alone, by French, Italian and Polish authors. One older contemporary of Bachelier, Hermann Laurent, bridged the two scientific communities of probability theorists and the Lausanne School, writing books on both Walrasian general equilibrium analysis and the calculus of probability (see Breton 1998) but not combining the two subjects in a single book, just as Cournot had written on mathematical economics and on probability in separate books, and as Edgeworth kept his writings on mathematical economics apart from those on probability and statistics (apart from index numbers).

According to Paul Samuelson's recollections, as recounted to Peter Bernstein, the Bayesian statistician Leonard Jimmie Savage of the University of Chicago chanced upon Bachelier's short 1914 volume of popularization 'some time around 1954, while rummaging through through a university library': 'Fascinated, [Savage] sent postcards to his economist friends, asking "Ever heard of this guy?"' (Bernstein 1992, 23). Three early papers by Emile Borel on minimax solutions to two-person, zero-sum games, originally published from 1921 to 1927, were published in *Econometrica* in 1953, translated into English by Leonard J. Savage with introduction and concluding comment by Maurice Fréchet, the recipient of Lévy's 1943 letter inquiring about Bachelier. Savage's discovery of Bachelier (1914) was thus not quite the isolated fluke Bernstein suggests. Savage was then browsing in the writings of early twentieth-century French probability theorists, and was receptive to the discovery of lost treasures comparable to Borel's contribution to game theory. When Samuelson received Savage's postcard asking about Bachelier, he found that the MIT Library did not have a copy of Bachelier (1914) – but it did have Bachelier (1900). Bernstein (1992, 23) quotes Samuelson's remark, 'Bachelier seems to have had something of a one-track mind. But what a track!' (a comment recalling Cezanne's appreciation of Monet as only an eye, but what an eye!). One of Samuelson's doctoral students, Richard Kruizenga, was just finishing three years of work on a dissertation on option pricing when 'Jimmie Savage stumbled across Bachelier's work, brought it to Samuelson's attention, and torpedoed poor Kruizenga's claim to originality' (Bernstein 1992, 115–16).

Knowledge of Bachelier (1900) radiated from Samuelson through MIT, and especially its Sloan School of Management. Another graduate student, A. James Boness, who was also writing on the valuation of stock options (Boness 1964), translated Bachelier's dissertation into English, and it was published in a volume on *The Random Character of Stock Market Prices* (Cootner 1964), edited by Samuelson's MIT colleague Paul Cootner and published by the MIT Press. Samuelson's papers on the rational pricing of warrants and on proving that properly anticipated prices fluctuate randomly (Samuelson 1965a, 1965b), following on the unpublished manuscript on Brownian motion in financial prices that he wrote in 1955 upon discovering Bachelier, appeared in the Sloan School's *Industrial Management Review* and in Cootner (1964). Henry P. McKean, Jr (1965) contributed an appendix to Samuelson (1965a) relating Samuelson's model of warrant pricing to the heat equation, and Bachelier was acknowledged on the first page of the influential book on diffusion processes by Itô and McKean (1965). Robert C. Merton (1990), a Samuelson doctoral student who won the Nobel Prize for his work on continuous-time finance and the intertemporal capital asset pricing model, stressed the links of his research to Bachelier (1900). However, the application of Brownian motion to percentage changes in stock prices by the astrophysicist M.F.M. Osborne (1959) at the Naval Research Laboratory was independent, as he only learned of Bachelier from post-publication comments (see Osborne 1960).

Conclusion

Louis Bachelier's path-breaking work on stochastic processes was based on his theory of speculation in informationally efficient financial markets. He shared his view of how financial markets work and forays into empirical verification of economic theory with a neglected earlier writer, Jules Regnault (1863), whose work may or may not have been known to Bachelier, but it was Bachelier who used the theory of speculation to work out a mathematical theory of stochastic processes, anticipating Einstein, Smoluchowski, Markov and Chapman on Brownian motion, diffusion of probability and Markov chains, and influencing Kolmogorov (1931) on diffusion processes. Bachelier's career looks like the stereotype of the lonely, misunderstood innovator, but until 1914 he was on the way to a solid academic career at the Sorbonne (although not matching the stellar path of Borel) and his work was read, appreciated and taught by Paris-based authors (de Montessus, Barriol, Gherardt). He survived the war, but his career in Paris did not. As he moved from one leave-replacement position to another in the provinces, finally securing a chair in the Franche-Comté (where illness and teaching interrupted his publications), Bachelier's work was ignored, except by Kolmogorov: mathematical physicists did not read books on financial markets, participants in financial markets did not read mathematical tracts on stochastic processes, and Keynes (1912) was so averse to the concept of continuous probability that he missed the point when reviewing Bachelier (1912). The exception is important, however: to have influenced Kolmogorov in the 1930s is no small matter. At the end of Bachelier's life, Paul Lévy, a great scholar then banned from publishing and hiding from Nazi and Vichy persecution under a false name, belatedly recognized Bachelier's brilliance and priority, and reconciled with him, apologizing for blackballing Bachelier's application for the chair at Dijon.

The rediscovery of Bachelier (1900) by Savage, Samuelson, Cootner and Boness was closely associated with the rise of the efficient markets hypothesis that asset price fluctuations are unpredictable and that it is impossible to systematically beat the market because asset prices efficiently incorporate available information (Cootner 1964), but the independence of Osborne's 1959 study of Brownian motion of percentage changes of stock prices suggests the possibility that these ideas might have developed at that time with or without the rediscovery of Bachelier (1900). Because Bachelier's 1900 dissertation has been translated into English, subsequent literature in mathematical finance has accorded much less notice to Bacheliers restatement and refinement of his theory of speculation in 1912, 1914 and 1938, as he continued to seek an audience for his theory into the 1930s, when Cowles and Working were, without awareness of Bachelier, pursuing an empirical route to the efficient markets hypothesis. Research, notably by Franck Jovanovic, has illuminated Bachelier's French context from Regnault in 1863 to Barriol's fourth edition in 1931. Bachelier's lifetime body of work, initiated by but not limited to his dissertation, establishes his place in the history of Brownian motion and diffusion process, of the efficient markets hypothesis and rational expectations, of mathematical finance and financial econometrics. Many unappreciated innovators have believed that posterity would recognize the brilliance and importance of their work. Bachelier was one who was right about the verdict of posterity.

Note

1. However, the opening footnote of Lévy (1940) is inconsistent with Lévy recognizing Bachelier's achievement upon reading Kolmogorov (1931) soon after its original publication (as implied in Lévy's 1964 letter to Mandelbrot) and also inconsistent with Bachelier (1941) being the occasion of their reconciliation (as surmised by Bru from Lévy's 1943 letter to Fréchet). While Lévy (1939) made no mention of Bachelier, the first footnote of Lévy (1940, p. 487) cited Bachelier (1912) and then stated: 'A cette date, Bachelier apparaît comme un précurseur. Si la manière dont sont introduits les problèmes où le temps joue le rôle d'une variable continue laisse à desirer, il n'en reste pas moins que c'est dans cet ouvrage que l'on trouve pour la première fois l'idée que la loi de Gauss s'introduit nécessairement comme conséquence de la continuité d'un processus additif, et la relation entre ce processus et l'équation de la chaleur. Il faut aussi signaler plusiers formules relatives à l'écart maximum, et peut-être la formule (que j'ai cherchée en vain dans un grand nombre d'ouvrages antérieurs) qui, dans le cas des lois absolument continues, définit la loi dont dépend la somme de deux variables aléatoires indépendentes.' Lévy's 1940 article, handsomely recognizing Bachelier's priority while still expressing reservations about the details of Bachelier's execution of his ambitious project, was received by the editors on 17 October 1939.

References

Bachelier, Louis (1900), *Théorie de la Spéculation*, Paris: Gauthier-Villars, and in *Annales de l'École Normale Supérieure*, 3rd series, **17**, 21–86, trans. A. James Boness in Paul Cootner (ed.), *The Random Character of Stock Market Prices*, Cambridge, MA: MIT Press, 1964.

Bachelier. Louis (1901), 'Théorie mathématique de jeu', *Annales de l'École Normale Supérieure*, 3rd series, **18**, 77–119. Reprinted (with Bachelier 1900) Paris: Editions Jacques Gabay, 1995.

Bachelier, Louis (1912), *Calcul des Probabilités*, vol. I, Paris: Gauthier-Villars. Reprinted Paris: Editions Jacques Gabay, 1992.

Bachelier, Louis (1913), 'Les probabilités cinématiques et dynamiques', *Annales Scientifiques de l'École Normale Supérieure*, 3rd series, **30**, 77–119.

Bachelier, Louis (1914), *Le Jeu, la Chance, et le Hasard*, Paris: Flammarion. Reprinted Paris: Editions Jacques Gabay, 1993.

Bachelier, Louis (1937), *Les lois des grands nombres du Calcul du Probabilités*, Paris: Gauthier-Villars.

Bachelier, Louis (1938), *La Spéculation et le Calcul des Probabilités*, Paris: Gauthier-Villars, trans. H. Ben-El-Mechaiekh (unpublished, 2005).

Bachelier, Louis (1939), *Les nouvelles methodes du Calcul des Probabilités*, Paris: Gauthier-Villars.
Bachelier, Louis (1941), 'Probabilités des oscillations maxima', *Comptes Rendus de l'Académie des Sciences*, **212**, 836–8 (erratum **213**, 220).
Barriol, Alfred ([1908] 1931), *Théorie et pratique des operations financières*, 4th edn, Paris: Octave Doin.
Bernstein, Jeremy (2005), 'Bachelier', *American Journal of Physics*, **73** (5), 395–8.
Bernstein, Peter L. (1992), *Capital Ideas: The Improbable Origins of Modern Wall Street*, New York: Free Press.
Boness, A. James (1964), 'Elements of a Theory of Stock Option Value', *Journal of Political Economy*, **72**, 163–75.
Breton, Yves (1998), 'Hermann Laurent (1841–1908): In Search of a New Political Economy', in Warren J. Samuels (ed.), *European Economists of the Early 20th Century*, Vol. I, Cheltenham, UK and Northampton, MA, USA: Edward Elgar Publishing.
Charlon, Hippolyte (1878), *Théorie Mathématique des Opérations Financières*, Paris: Gauthier-Villars.
Cootner, Paul, ed. (1964), *The Random Character of Stock Market Prices*, Cambridge, MA: MIT Press.
Cournot, Antoine-Augustin (1838) *Recherches sur les Principes Mathématiques de la Théorie des Richesses*, Paris: Hachette; trans. Nathaniel T. Bacon with introduction and notes by Irving Fisher, New York: Macmillan, 1898.
Courtault, Jean-Michel, Yuri Kabanov, Bernard Bru, Pierre Crépel, Isabelle Lebon and Arnaud Le Marchand (2000), 'Louis Bachelier, On the Centenary of *Théorie de la Spéculation*', *Mathematical Finance*, **10** (3), 341–53. Reprinted with an additional documentary appendix in Courtault and Kabanov (2002).
Courtault, Jean-Michel and Youri Kabanov (eds) (2002), *Louis Bachelier, aux origins de la finance mathématique*, Besançon: Presses Universitaires Franc-Comtoises.
Dimand, Robert W. (1993), 'The Case of Brownian Motion: a Note on Bachelier's Contribution', *British Journal for the History of Science*, **26**, 233–4.
Einstein, Albert (1956), *Investigations on the Theory of the Brownian Movement*, ed. R. Fürth, trans. A.D. Cowper New York: Dover Publications.
Feller, William (1950 [1957]), *An Introduction to Probability Theory and Its Applications*, Vol. I, 2nd edn, New York: John Wiley & Sons.
Feller, William (1966 [1971]), *An Introduction to Probability Theory and Its Applications*, Vol. II, 2nd edn, New York: John Wiley & Sons.
Gherardt, Maurice (1910), *Le Gain Mathématique à la Bourse*, Paris: Charles Amat.
Itô, Kiyoshi, and Henry P. McKean, Jr (1965), *Diffusion Processes and their Sample Paths*, New York: Academic Press.
Jovanovic, Franck (2000), 'L'origine de la théorie financière: une réévaluation de l'apport de Louis Bachelier', *Revue d'Économie Politique*, **110** (3), 395–418.
Jovanovic, Franck (2002a), 'Instruments et théorie économiques dans la construction de la "science de la Bourse" d'Henri Lefèvre', *Revue d'Histoire des Sciences Humaines*, **7**, 41–68.
Jovanovic, Franck (2002b), 'Document: *La Loi Juridique et la Loi Scientifique de la Bourse* par Julien Lafferière', *Revue d'Histoire des Sciences Humaines*, **7**, 181–91.
Jovanovic, Franck, and Philippe Le Gall (2001), 'Does God Practice a Random Walk? The "Financial Physics" of a Nineteenth-Century Forerunner, Jules Regnault', *European Journal of the History of Economic Thought*, **8** (3), 332–62.
Keuzenkamp, H.A. (1991), 'A Precursor to Muth: Tinbergen's 1932 Model of Rational Expectations', *Economic Journal*, **101**, 1245–53.
Keynes, John Maynard (1912), Review of Bachelier (1912) and books on probability by Henri Poincaré, E. Carvallo and A.A. Markoff, *Journal of the Royal Statistical Society*, as reprinted in D.E. Moggridge (ed.), *Collected Writings of John Maynard Keynes*, XI, London: Macmillan, and New York: Cambridge University Press for the Royal Economic Society (1983), pp. 567–72.
Keynes, John Maynard (1921), *A Treatise on Probability*, London: Macmillan.
Kolmogorov, Andrei N. (1931), 'Über die analitischen Methoden in der Wahrscheinlichkeitsrechtnung', *Mathematischen Annalen*, **104** (3), 413–58.
Kolmogorov, Andrei N. (1933), *Grundbegriffe der Wahrscheinlichkeitsrechnung*, Berlin: Springer, trans. N. Morrison as *Foundations of the Theory of Probability*, New York: Chelsea Publishing, 1956.
Kruskal, William H. and Judith M. Tanur (eds) (1978), *International Encyclopedia of Statistics*, New York: Free Press.
Lévy, Paul (1939), 'Sur certains processus stochastiques homogènes', *Compositio Mathematica*, **7**, 283–339.
Lévy, Paul (1940), 'Le mouvement brownien plan', *American Journal of Mathematics*, **62**, 487–550.
Lévy, Paul (1948), *Processus Stochastiques et Mouvement Brownien*, Paris: Gauthier-Villars (2nd edn 1965). Reprinted Paris: Editions Jacques Gabay, 1992.
Maiocchi, Roberto (1990), 'The Case of Brownian Motion', *British Journal for the History of Science*, **23**, 257–83.
Mandelbrot, Benoit B. (1989), 'Louis Bachelier', in John Eatwell, Murray Milgate and Peter Newman (eds), *The New Palgrave Finance*, New York: Stockton Press, pp. 86–8.
Mandelbrot, Benoit B. and Richard Hudson (2004), *The (Mis)behavior of Markets*, New York: Basic Books.
Marcinkiewicz, J. (1939), 'Sur une propriété du mouvement brownien', *Acta Litterarium Scientarium*, 77–87.

Markoff, A.A. (1912), *Wahrscheinlichkeitsrechnung*, trans. from 2nd Russian edn by H. Liebermann, Leipzig: Teubner.

Massebeuf, Alexandre (1923), *Des Marchés à Primes dans les Bourses de Valeurs (Paris–Londres–Berlin)*, Paris: Garnier-frères.

McKean, Henry P., Jr (1965), 'Appendix: A Free Boundary Problem for the Heat Equation Arising from a Problem in Mathematical Economics', *Industrial Management Review*, **6**, 32–9 (also in Cootner 1964).

Merton, Robert C. (1990), *Continuous-Time Finance*, Malden, MA and Oxford: Blackwell.

Montessus de Ballore, Robert, Vicomte de (1908), *Leçons élémentaires sur le calcul des probabilités*, Paris: Gauthiers-Villars.

Osborne, M.F.M. (1959), 'Brownian Motion in the Stock Market', *Operations Research*, **7**, 145–73, reprinted in Cootner (1964), pp. 100–128.

Osborne, M.F.M. (1960), 'Reply to Comments on Brownian Motion in the Stock Market', *Operations Research*, **8**, 806–10.

Pochet, Léon (1873), 'La Géométrie des Jeux de Bourse', *Journal des Actuaries Français*, **2**, 153–65.

Poincaré, Henri ([1896] 1912), *Calcul des Probabilités*, 2nd edn, Paris: Gauthier-Villars.

Regnault, Jules (1863), *Calcul des chances et philosophie de la bourse*, Paris: Mallet Bachelier & Castel (Bibliothèque Nationale, Paris, Inventaire V.51.066).

Samuelson, Paul A. (1965a), 'Rational Theory of Warrant Pricing', *Industrial Management Review*, **6**, 13–31 (also in Cootner 1964).

Samuelson, Paul A. (1965b), 'Proof that Properly Anticipated Prices Fluctuate Randomly', *Industrial Management Review*, **6**, 41–69.

Sullivan, Edward J. and Timothy M. Wethers (1991), 'Louis Bachelier: The Father of Modern Option Pricing Theory', *Journal of Economic Education*, **22** (2), 165–71.

Taqqu, Murad S. (2001), 'Bachelier and His Times: A Conversation with Bernard Bru', *Finance and Stochastics*, **1** (5), 3–32.

Tinbergen, Jan (1932), 'Ein Problem der Dynamik', *Zeitschrift für Nationalökonmie*, **3**, 169–84.

Zylberberg, André (1990), *L'Economie Mathématique en France, 1870–1914*, Paris: Economica.

11 Vincenz Bronzin's option pricing theory: contents, contribution and background

Heinz Zimmermann and Wolfgang Hafner

1. Introduction

The doctoral thesis of Louis Bachelier (1900) is widely considered as the seminal work in option pricing theory. However, only a few years later, in 1908, Vincenz Bronzin, who was a professor of arithmetic at the Accademia di Commercio e Nautica in Trieste, published a booklet entitled Theorie der *Prämiengeschäfte* (*Theory of Premium Contracts*), written in German and some 80 pages long. While the small booklet got some attention in the academic literature when it was published, it seems later to have been almost forgotten,[1] and more recent academic mentions are virtually nonexistent.[2]

While Bronzin's approach is more pragmatic than Bachelier's, every element of modern option pricing can be found: risk-neutral pricing, no-arbitrage and perfect-hedging pricing conditions, the put–call parity, and the impact of different distributional assumptions on option values. In particular, he shows how the normal law of error – which is the normal density function – can be used to price options, and how it is related to a binomial stock price distribution. His equation (43) is closer to the Black–Scholes formula than anything published before Black, Scholes and Merton. Moreover, he develops a simplified procedure to find analytical solutions for option prices by exploiting a key relationship between their derivatives (with respect to their exercise prices) and the underlying pricing density. Besides pricing simple calls and puts, he develops formulae for chooser options and, more important, repeat options.

Our 'discovery' also raises questions over and above the technical ones: why did the results of Bachelier, Bronzin, and possibly others yet to be rediscovered, not get broader acceptance? Why did their research not find immediate successors, academics who made it a subject of ongoing scientific research? Finding answers to these questions could help us better understand the cultural background of financial economics, and would probably add an interesting chapter to the sociology of science.

A general difficulty in the attempt to write about Bronzin's book is that the text is written in German, and many of his finance-related expressions (which may or may not reflect the commonly used terms at the time) cannot be translated easily. We therefore use the most appropriate English terms, and add the original German wording in parentheses where it seems to be useful. Moreover, we have adapted Bronzin's mathematical notation with only minor changes. In discussing or extending certain results (particularly in section 5, subsection 5.6), we have tried to make a clear distinction between Bronzin's results and our own.

The structure of the chapter is as follows. Section 2 describes the basic terminology as well as the range of derivative contracts analysed in Bronzin's book. Section 3 deals with his thoughts on hedging, replication and arbitrage – although he does not formally use these terms. Section 4 outlines the major elements of his valuation approach: the probabilistic foundations, zero-profit conditions and a characterization of the (risk-neutral) pricing density. Section 5 gives an overview of the major section of the book, namely the derivation of option prices under alternative specifications of the probability (or pricing) density function. This section also shows the close relationship between one of these specifications, the error function, and the Black–Scholes/Merton model. Section 6 tries to make an overall assessment of the scientific contribution of Bronzin's book in the light of the history of option pricing. Finally, in section 7, we give a brief description of the scientific and socio-cultural background of Bronzin's work and professional activities, which also includes reflections on the state of probabilistic thinking in physics and actuarial science as the key analytical prerequisites of modern option pricing.

It should be mentioned that this chapter is only a partial appreciation of Bronzin's work on option pricing. We try to highlight the most important elements of his analysis. A more complete characterization is provided by Zimmermann and Hafner (2004). Also, the content of section 7 is somewhat preliminary – and reflects ongoing research which is far from complete. Nevertheless, we think that it is important to highlight the cultural, social and scientific role of the kaiserlich und königlich (k.u.k)-Academy (Imperial and Royal Academy) in Trieste within the Hungarian–Austrian empire, where V. Bronzin started his career at a young age and was affiliated until he died in 1970, aged 98.

2. Basic structure and terminology

2.1 *Structure of the book*

Bronzin's book contains two major parts. The first is descriptive and contains a characterization and classification of basic derivative contracts, their profit and loss diagrams, and basic hedging conditions and (arbitrage) relationships. The second, more interesting part, is on option pricing and starts with a general valuation framework, which is then applied to a variety of distributions for the price of the underlying security in order to get closed-form solutions for calls and puts. Among these distributions is the 'error function', which is closely related to the normal distribution. It is interesting to note that the separation of topics between 'distribution-free' and 'distribution-related' results is in perfect line with the modern classification of option pricing topics, following Merton (1973).

In the second part, Bronzin's methodological set-up is completely different from Bachelier's, at least in terms of the underlying stochastic framework. He develops no stochastic process for the underlying asset price and uses no stochastic calculus, but directly makes different assumptions on the share price distribution at maturity and derives a rich set of closed-form solutions for the value of options. This simplified procedure is justified in so far as his work is entirely focused on European-style contracts (not to be exercised before maturity), so intertemporal issues (e.g. optimal early exercise) are not of premier importance.

2.2 *Contracts and basic terminology*

Bronzin's analysis covers forward contracts as well as options, but his main focus is on the latter. The term 'option' is not used. Instead, his analysis is on 'premium contracts' (*Prämiengeschäfte*), which is an old type of option contract used in many European countries up to the 1970s, before warrants and traded options became popular.[3] The buyer of a premium contract has the right to step down from a forward contract at maturity – not before, so the contract is always European-style. The four resulting positions are clearly characterized, analytically as well as in terms of payoff diagrams (pp. 2–7). The buyer of a premium contract acquires either the right to buy (*Wahlkauf*) or to sell (*Wahlverkauf*) the underlying security at maturity, while the seller of the contract has the obligation to sell (*Zwangsverkauf*) or buy (*Zwangskauf*) it. Forward contracts are called 'fixed contracts' (*Festgeschäfte*) in Bronzin's terminology (pp. 1–2).

Within the category of option contracts, Bronzin distinguishes between 'normal' and 'skewed' (*schiefe*) contracts. A normal option contract exhibits an exercise price equal to the forward price, the latter being denoted by B throughout the book. For obvious reasons, we will refer to this case as 'at-the-money' (ATM) contracts. Skewed call and put contracts exhibit exercise prices which deviate by a magnitude M from the forward price. We will denote exercise prices by K in this chapter, which implies that $K \equiv B + M$.

In addition to these standard (or simple) options, Bronzin analyses two special contracts: chooser options (called *Stella-Geschäfte*), where the buyer has the right to determine whether he wants to buy or sell the underlying security at maturity;[4] and a special kind of 'repeat option' (called *Noch*[5]*-Geschäft*), which adds a (multiple) option component to a forward transaction. The latter contract will be analysed briefly in section 6.[6]

Throughout the book, Bronzin does not refer to a specific underlying security in his analysis,[7] nor to other institutional characteristics of the contracts he analyses. The underlying security is often just called 'object' (*Wertobjekt*), and its price is referred to as 'market' price.

3. Valuation fundamentals: hedging, replication and arbitrage

Two key concepts, 'coverage' (*Deckung*) and equivalence (*Äquivalenz*), play an important role in the first part of Bronzin's book (see sections 4 and 5 in chapter 1, and section 3 in chapter 2). Although the author's focus is not always clear, this part of the text is nevertheless interesting because, in the light of modern[8] option pricing theory, it is an early notion of perfect hedging and replication of option positions, and the conditions for their general feasibility. Unfortunately, at this stage of analysis, the author does not introduce the concept of arbitrage (or what he later calls 'fair pricing'), but discusses the pricing implications as 'full hedging conditions'.

Bronzin defines a 'covered' position as a combination of transactions (options and forward contracts) which is immune against profits and losses. Two systems of positions are called 'equivalent' if one can be derived (*abgeleitet*) from the other, or, stated differently, if they provide exactly the same profit and loss for all possible states of the market. From a linguistic point of view, it is interesting to note that Bronzin explicitly uses the word 'derived' in this context.

Bronzin also stresses the relationship between the two concepts: we can always get two systems of equivalent transactions if we take a subset of contracts within a complex of covered transactions and reverse their signs. This basic insight is then followed by a lengthy characterization of conditions under which combined call and put option positions can be fully 'covered' (hedged) – by large systems of equations, which are not easily accessible.

In this context, the put–call parity is derived:

(i) For symmetric, i.e. ATM call and put positions (chapter 1, section 4): The number[9] of long and short options must be equal, and the (net or residual[10]) number of long call (put) options must be matched by the same number of forward sales (buys). Moreover, the call and put prices must be equal.

This is a slightly complicated way to state that a long position of calls (puts) plus a short position of puts (calls) produces a synthetic long (short) forward contract. The more interesting part in the statement is the equivalence of option prices:

$$C[K = B] = P[K = B] \tag{1}$$

(K denotes the exercise price) which is a special case of the well-known put–call parity.

(ii) For skewed positions, i.e. calls and puts with arbitrary but equal exercise price (chapter 2, section 1): The same conditions as before must hold, but the equality of call and put prices is replaced by the 'remarkable' (*bemerkenswerte*) condition:

$$P[K = B + M] = C[K = B + M] + M \tag{2}$$

which is the put–call parity, because measures the 'moneyness' of the options. For $M > 0$, the put option is in-the-money, and the equation shows that the put price exceeds the call price by exactly the amount of the 'moneyness', M. The reverse is true if $M < 0$.

It is important to note that Bronzin derives this parity relationship as a necessary condition for the feasibility of a perfect hedge. It is apparently obvious to him that a position which is fully hedged against all states of the market cannot exhibit a positive price – but there is no explicit statement of this kind.

Relating his equation to the standard formulation of the put–call parity, it is easy to recognize that the moneyness of the (put) option, M, must be specified in terms of current dollars as

$$M = Ke^{-r(T-t)} - S_t \tag{3}$$

to get the traditional parity relationship (r is the continuously compounded risk-free rate, $T - t$ time to maturity, and S_t the current stock price).

Unfortunately, the notion of arbitrage does not show up explicitly in Bronzin's text[11] – but he is close to it. In part I, the put–call parity is derived as part of the perfect hedging condition for joint put–call positions, without assuming a specific probability distribution for the future market price. It is a distribution-free result. However, no explicit mention is made of arbitrage in the modern sense of the word.[12]

In part II (chapter 1, p. 44 for symmetric contracts, p. 47 for asymmetric contracts) the put–call parity is again derived, but this time from an explicit *pricing* relationship. Based on a particular price distribution, Bronzin postulates a general valuation principle according to which no profit or loss should be expected for either of the two parties (the buyer or the seller) involved in the transaction when the contract is negotiated. This is a 'fair pricing' or 'zero expected profit' condition, but not an arbitrage condition because it refers to expectations, and no (risk-free) profits as required by arbitrage. However, Bronzin recognizes that this derivation has a different qualitative nature than in the previous part: the parity relationship now no longer has the character of an artificial condition but emerges from the 'incontestable' principle of reciprocity in business transactions. Of course, his remark that the parity only gets its 'full justification and importance' at this stage of analysis is not correct, because the derivation in a distribution-free setting is more general. But Bronzin apparently recognizes that deriving the parity by using some kind of 'equilibrium' relation adds a new dimension to the pricing of options – although this is not necessary for the put–call parity itself, but for the other pricing relationships he is about to derive.

4. The probabilistic setting and general valuation framework

Bronzin recognizes that his analysis in part I of his booklet leaves open the fundamental question about the appropriate (*rechtmässig*) size of the option premiums. He also recognizes that further assumptions and tools[13] are necessary to achieve this goal: probabilistic assumptions about the market,[14] and a rule to translate expected profits and losses from the contracts to current values.

4.1 The probability density

The market model which Bronzin has in mind can be characterized as a driftless random walk. In this respect, the approach is virtually identical to Bachelier (1900).

- *Random walk.* When discussing the possible specification of the probability density function of the underlying market price (p. 56), he finds himself in substantial difficulties: he argues that he does not know any general criteria to characterize the random (regellos) market movements for the various underlying securities analytically. Instead, he proposes to estimate possible distributionsstatistically (see section 5).
- *Spot and forward price.* The starting point of Bronzin's probabilistic market model is the forward price B. He assumes that this price is 'naturally' close or even identical to the current spot price. Since there is no mention of interest rates, the time value of money, or discounting anywhere in the book, this also implies that he assumes an efficient market.
- *Price expectation.* He repeatedly argues that the forward price is the most likely among all possible future market prices (pp. 56, 74, 80), i.e. the forward price is an unbiased predictor of the future spot price. Otherwise, he argues, one could not imagine sales and purchases (i.e. opposite transactions) with equal chances if strong reasons existed leading people ultimately to predict either a rising or falling market price with higher probability. Thus the forward price is regarded as the most advantageous price for both parties in a forward transaction.[15] A slightly different reasoning is used when discussing the payoff diagram of a forward contract, where he states that the forward price B must be such that the two 'triangle parts' to the left and the right of B, i.e. to the profit and loss of the contract, must be 'equivalent' because otherwise, selling or buying on spot should be more profitable. This does not necessarily imply an unbiased forward price, although there is little doubt that he wants to claim this.

While the issue of price expectations seems to be important for Bronzin, it is not relevant for the development of his model. The important point is that the mean of the price distribution is based on observable market price (spot or forward price), not price expectation or other preference-based measures.[16]

However, whether the forward price matches the expected future price or not is irrelevant for Bronzin's subsequent analysis. It would be relevant if statements about risk premiums or risk preferences were made, which is not the intention of the author. Instead, his focus is on consistent (or in his wording, 'fair') pricing relationships between spot, forward and option contracts – which qualifies his probability density as a risk-neutral density.

4.2 Fair pricing: zero expected excess returns

As noted before, Bronzin understands the forward price as the cutting edge for modelling the ups and downs of the underlying market price. He consequently characterizes the random behaviour of the market price by its deviation from the forward price

$$\tilde{x} \equiv \tilde{S}_T - B, \tag{4}$$

where $\tilde{S}_T$ is the stock price at maturity (which is, however, never focused on throughout the text). He also applies this characterization to his definition of expected profits and losses:

- *The 'expected value' of a contract is zero.* Bronzin (pp. 41–2) states the important valuation principle that at contract settlement, no profit or loss should be expected[17] for either of the two parties (the buyer or the seller) involved in the transaction. For this purpose, the conditions of each transaction must be determined so that the sum of expected profits of both parties (taking losses as negative profits) is zero. Bronzin calls this the 'fair pricing' condition (*Bedingung der Rechtmässigkeit*).

Note that profits and losses are defined with respect to the forward price – very different from Bachelier's martingale assumption, which is defined relative to the current stock price. Hence Bronzin considers a pricing rule as 'fair' if expected profits and losses of a contract are derived from a 'pricing' density of the underlying security which is centred at the forward price.

Based on these assumptions, Bronzin derives the general pricing relationship for call options

$$P_1 = \int_M^{\infty} (\tilde{x} - M) f(x) dx$$

where $f(x)$ is the probability density, or in modern usage, the state price or risk neutral pricing density. Recall that there is no riskless discounting in Bronzin's models. It may appear speculative to interpret $f(x)$ as a pricing density; however, it is shown in the next section that Bronzin establishes a direct analytical relationship between option prices and $f(x)$ which supports this interpretation.

4.3 Substituting probabilities by prices

The most amazing part of Bronzin's booklet is in section 8 of the first chapter in part II, where he relates the probability function $f(x)$ to option prices. This was explicitly done in an unpublished paper by Black (1974),[18] and a few years later by Breeden and Litzenberger (1978). By referring to the rules of differentiation with respect to boundaries of integrals, and expressions within the integral (generally known as Leibnitz rules), he derives the 'remarkable' expression

$$\frac{\partial P_1}{\partial M} = -\int_M^{\omega} f(x) dx = -F(M) \quad \text{(equation 16, p. 50)} \tag{5}$$

Remember that $F(M)$ is the probability that the stock price exceeds the exercise price at maturity, i.e. that the options gets exercised. Equation (5) thus postulates that the negative of the exercise probability is equal to the first derivative of the option price with respect to the exercise price (respectively, M). Remarkably, he notes that by this expression it is much easier to solve for P_1 than in the standard valuation approach: Based on (5), the option price can be computed by the indefinite integral

$$P_1 = -\int F(M)dM + c \quad \text{(equation 19, p. 51)} \tag{6}$$

where c is a constant which is not difficult to compute (it will be zero or negligible in most cases). Equation (6) is a powerful result: option prices can be computed by integrating $F(M)$ over M. Depending on the functional form of $f(x)$, this could drastically simplify getting option values. Thus, knowing (or determining) the function $F(x = M)$ showing the exercise probabilities as a function of M is the key element in determining option values in this approach. From there, it is straightforward to show that the second derivative

$$\frac{\partial^2 P_1}{\partial M^2} = f(M) \quad \text{(equation 17, p. 51)} \tag{7}$$

directly gives the value of the (probability density) function at $x = M$.[19] As Breeden and Litzenberger (1978) have shown, this derivative multiplied by the increment dM can be interpreted as the implicit state price[20] in the limit of a continuous state space. Bronzin also shows that equation (7) can be applied without adjustments to put options.

It is apparent from Bronzin's equations (16), (17) and (19) that he was aware that information on the unknown function $f(x)$ is impounded in observed (or theoretical) option prices, and just needs to be extracted. It establishes $f(x)$ as a *pricing* function (or density), or, to put it more directly: it demonstrates the key relationships between security prices and probability densities.

The analytical implications of equations (5) and (6) are of key interest to Bronzin, and we therefore provide a brief illustration using the 'triangle distribution' which he uses later in his analysis. $f(x)$ is specified as a linear function $f(x) = a + bx$, defined over the interval $[0; +\omega]$; and respectively $f_1(x) = a + b|x|$ if x is in the negative range $[-\omega; 0]$. For $f(\omega) = f_1(\omega) = 0$ to hold, the parameters must be specified as, $a = (1/\omega)$, $b = -(1/\omega^2)$ which implies $f(x) = (\omega - x)/\omega^2$.

The standard pricing approach requires the solution of the integral

$$P_1 = \int_M^\omega (x - M)F(x)dx = \int_M^\omega (x - M)\frac{\omega - x}{\omega^2}dx$$

which is a quite complicated task (see p. 66). In contrast, the procedure suggested by Bronzin is much simpler:

- Compute $F(M)$, i.e. the probability that $\tilde{x}$ exceeds $x = M$. This given by

$$\frac{(\omega - M)^2}{2\omega^2}$$

- Solve

$$\frac{\partial P_1}{\partial M} = -F(M) = -\frac{(\omega - M)^2}{2\omega^2}$$

for P_1, which is given by the integral

$$P_1 = -\int F(M)dM + c = -\int \frac{(\omega - M)^2}{2\omega^2} dM + c$$

The solution is

$$P_1 = \frac{(\omega - M)^3}{6\omega^2}$$

Note that the constant is zero because $P_1(M = \omega) = 0$ (see p. 62).

4.4 Summing up

The major task in pricing options and other derivatives is to find an appropriate pricing function $f(x)$ which translates future random payoffs into current prices. In Bronzin's own perspective, $f(x)$ is a standard probability density function. However, the mean of his density is not an ordinary, unspecified or subjective expected value, but a market price which can be observed – namely the forward price of the security. His pricing density can thus be regarded as a risk-neutral pricing function – which does not necessarily provide the 'correct' statistical probabilities, but prices options in a consistent way with the underlying, respectively the forward, contract. Based on his equations (16), (17) and (19), Bronzin suggests three ways to specify the pricing function $f(x)$:

- Estimate volatilities and probabilities, and fit $F(x)$ by least squares (the derivative $f(x)$ can then be derived).
- Try alternative functional specifications (see Section 5).
  Compute the second derivative $(\partial^2 P)/(\partial M^2) = f(M)$ for alternative $M = x$ from existing market prices, as shown in equation (7).

5. Option pricing with specific functional or distributional assumptions

5.1 General remarks

The specification of the pricing density $f(x)$ and the derivation of closed-form solutions for option prices is the objective of the second chapter in part II. Bronzin discusses six different functional specifications of $f(x)$ and the implied shape of the density for a given range of x. From a probabilistic point of view, this part of the book seems to be slightly outdated, because the first four 'distributions' lack any obvious stochastic foundation. The function $f(x)$ seems to be specified rather ad hoc, just to produce simple probability shapes for the price deviations from the forward price: a rectangular distribution, a triangular distribution, a parabolic distribution and an exponential distribution.

This impression particularly emerges if Bachelier's thesis is taken as a benchmark, where major attention is given to the modelling of the probability law governing the dynamics of the underlying asset value. This was an extraordinary achievement on its own. In order to be fair about Bronzin's approach, one should be aware of the state of probability theory at the beginning of the last century. As Bernard Bru mentioned in his interview with Murad Taqqu (see Taqqu 2001, p. 5), 'probability did not start to gain recognition in France until the 1930's. This was also the case in Germany'.

However, the fifth and sixth specification of $f(x)$ are the (normal) law of error (*Fehlergesetz*) and the Bernoulli theorem, or in modern terminology, the normal and binomial distributions. This enables a direct comparison with the Bachelier and the Black–Scholes and Merton models.

For the subsequent discussion it is useful to recall that x denotes the market price of the underlying asset at maturity *minus the forward price*. Bronzin now makes the simplifying assumption that functions $f(x)$ and $f_1(x)$ are symmetric around B, i.e. that $f(x) = f_1(x)$ (p. 55). This assumption makes the expected market price equal to the forward price. At the same time, he is entirely aware that a symmetric probability density is not consistent with the limited liability nature of the underlying 'objects': while price increases are potentially unbounded, prices cannot fall below zero. However, he plays down this argument by saying that these (extreme) cases are fairly unlikely, and price variations can be regarded as more or less uniform (*regelmässige*) and generally not substantial (*nicht erhebliche*) oscillations around. Based on this reasoning, he seems very confident about the results derived from this assumption.

Table 11.1 Option prices under alternative distributional assumptions

	Density function	Standard deviation	Bronzin's call option price
Uniform distribution	$f(x)=\frac{1}{2\omega}, x\in[-\omega;+\omega]$		$P_1=\frac{(\omega-M)^2}{4\omega}$
Triangular distribution	$f(x)=\frac{\omega-x}{\omega^2}, x\in[-\omega;+\omega]$		$P_1=\frac{(\omega-M)^3}{6\omega^2}$
Parabolic distribution	$f(x)=\frac{3(\omega-x)^2}{2\omega^3}, x\in[-\omega;+\omega]$		$P_1=\frac{(8\omega-M)^4}{8\omega^3}$
Exponential distribution	$f(x)=ke^{-2kx}$	$\sigma_{\exp}(x)=\frac{1}{2k}$	$P_1=\frac{e^{-2kM}}{4k}$
Error distribution	$f(x)=\frac{h}{\sqrt{\pi}}e^{-h^2x^2}$	$\sigma_{err}(x)=\frac{1}{h\sqrt{2}}$	$P_1=\frac{e^{-2M^2h^2}}{2h\sqrt{\pi}}-M\psi(hM)$
Bernoulli (binomial) distribution	$\frac{1}{\sqrt{2\pi}}\int_0^{z^*} e^{-1/2z^2}dz+\frac{e^{-z^2}}{\sqrt{2\pi}\sqrt{Bq}}$ $z^*=\frac{x^*}{\sqrt{Bq}}, \tilde{z}=\frac{\tilde{x}}{\sqrt{Bq}}$	$\sigma_{bin}(x)=\sqrt{qB}$	

Source: Bronzin (1908).

5.2 Option prices under specific distributional assumptions

Table 11.1 displays the densities derived from the various (six) functional specifications of the terminal price, as well as the implied call option prices (P_1). In what follows, we only add a few comments for each specification – except for the error (i.e. normal) distribution, which constitutes a direct link to the Black–Scholes formula. More details can be found in Zimmermann and Hafner (2004).

Uniform and triangular function distributions Assuming the same boundaries ω for the uniform and triangular distribution,[21] it is interesting to notice that the ATM option prices decrease from one-quarter of ω (uniform distribution) to one-sixth (triangular). This nicely shows the impact of the shifting part of the probability mass (i.e. one-eighth on each side of the distribution) from the 'tails' to the centre of the distribution, or the reverse. To put it differently, the 'riskier' uniform density implies an ATM option price which is $\omega/4 \div \omega/6 = 1.5$ times, or respectively 50 per cent, higher than the price implied by the triangular distribution – although only 25 per cent of the probability mass is shifted from the tails to the centre.

Parabolic distribution Bronzin suggests using this distribution for modelling extreme values with small probabilities by setting ω sufficiently large (p. 67). Nevertheless, we now assume that ω is the same as in the previous two sections in order to facilitate comparisons. Since extreme values have again become less likely compared to the triangular distribution, it is not surprising that the value of ATM options is again lower, i.e. it decreases from one-sixth of ω to one-eighth. The other results are similar and need no further comment.

Exponential function The range of x values is unbounded, and rare events with small probabilities can be handled much more easily by this functional specification. The parameter k determines the variability of x – a bigger k reduces the variability. As shown in the next section, the standard deviation (volatility) of the distribution is given by $\sigma = 1/2k$. Then the price of ATM option is *half* the volatility! Again, the general option prices separate the impact of the volatility and moneyness in an extremely satisfying way. The ATM option price under our calibration for k is

$$P\left(k = \frac{3}{2\omega}\right) = \frac{1}{4k} = \frac{1}{4 \times \frac{3}{2\omega}} = \frac{1}{\frac{6}{n}} = \frac{\omega}{6}$$

which exceeds the respective option price from the parabolic distribution by

$$\frac{\omega/6}{\omega/8} - 1 = \frac{1}{3},$$

i.e. one-third.

The normal law of error (normal distribution) The most exciting specification of $f(x)$ is the law of error (*Fehlergesetz*) defined by

$$f(x) = \frac{h}{\sqrt{\pi}} e^{-h^2x^2}. \tag{8}$$

[22]

Unlike the previous specifications of $f(x)$, this is now a direct specification of the probability density. Reasoning that market variations above and below the forward price B can be regarded as deviations from the markets' most favorable outcome, Bronzin suggests using the law of error as a very reliable law to represent error probabilities. Of course, the density corresponds to a normal distribution with zero mean and a standard deviation of $\sigma_{err} = 1/(h\sqrt{2})$. Or alternatively, setting $h = 1/(\sigma\sqrt{2})$ gives us the normal $N\{0, \sigma^2\}$.[23]

In order to compare the ATM option price with the previous section, it is necessary to have equal variances.

$$\sigma_{err}(x) = \frac{1}{h\sqrt{2}} \tag{9}$$

which shows the standard deviation of the error distribution implied by a specific choice of parameter h. Since h is inversely related to the standard deviation of the distribution, it measures the precision of the observations, and is called *precision modulus*; see Johnson et al. (1994), p. 81.

The relationship between the volatility of the exponential and the error distribution is then given by the equality $2k = h\sqrt{2}$ or

$$h = k\sqrt{2}. \tag{10}$$

The implied ATM option price is therefore

$$P_{err}\left(h = k\sqrt{2}\right) = \frac{1}{2k\sqrt{2}\sqrt{\pi}} = \frac{1}{k\sqrt{8\pi}} = \frac{1}{5.013 \times k} \tag{11}$$

which is only about 80 per cent of the exponential ATM option price $P_{\exp} = 1/4k$. This is not surprising: compared to the exponential distribution, the error (or normal) distribution has more weight around the mean and less around the tails – given the same standard deviation.

The binomial distribution ('Bernoulli theorem') While sections 2 through 6 in the second chapter of part II in Bronzin's book are direct specifications of the pricing density $f(x)$, the approach taken in his final section 7 is slightly different. It can be understood as a mere specification of the (inverse) volatility factor h in the error function. The starting point of his analysis is almost identical to the binomial model of Cox et al. (1979). Assume that s (consecutive) price movements[24] are governed by 'two opposite events' (e.g. market ups and downs) with probability p and q, which can be thought of as Bernoulli trials. The expected value of the distribution is sp (or alternatively, sq). Of course, the events can be scaled arbitrarily by choosing the parameter s appropriately. Therefore, one of the expected values (of which one is arbitrary) can be set equal to the forward price, e.g. $B = sp$. The price distribution can then be understood as being generated by cumulative deviations of market events from their most likely outcome, the forward price. The standard deviation of this distribution is $\sqrt{spq} = \sqrt{Bq}$.

Extensions and generalizations by Gustav Flusser (1911) We found[25] only one explicit reference to Bronzin's work, which is an article by Gustav Flusser[26] published in the Annual (*Jahresbericht*) of the Trade Academy in Prague. Although the article is highly mathematical, the author merely extends and generalizes the second part of Bronzin's option pricing formulae for alternative distributions for the underlying price:

- polynomial funtions of *n*th degree
- rational algebraic functions
- irrational functions
- goniometric (periodic) functions
- logarithmic functions
- exponential functions.

However, the author does not add original contributions to Bronzin's work, in the sense of general pricing principles or extensions thereof, so there is no need to discuss the paper further here.

5.3 A comparison with the Black–Scholes model

Obviously, the specification of the pricing function in the previous section is particularly interesting, because it promises a direct link to the celebrated Black–Scholes model.[27] As seen before, setting $h = 1/\sigma\sqrt{2}$ in the error function generates the normal distribution. The problem is, however, that the Black–Scholes model assumes a normal distribution for the *log* prices, while Bronzin makes this assumption for the price *level* itself. In terms of the underlying stochastic processes, Bronzin's distribution can be regarded as the result of an arithmetic Wiener process, while the Black–Scholes model relies on a geometric Wiener process.

Since there is an immediate link between the two processes, why not interpret Bronzin's price levels as log prices? This is, however, not adequate in the option pricing framework because the value of options is a function of the payoff emerging from the (positive) difference between settlement *price* and exercise *price* of the option, not their logarithms. In this respect, the approach of Bronzin is the same as that of Bachelier.

We show how to rewrite Bronzin's general valuation equation for calls (11) on p. 44 to get the Black–Scholes formula. For this purpose, we replace

$$\tilde{x} - M = [\tilde{S}_T - B] - [K - B] = \tilde{S}_T - K, \tag{12}$$

and assume that $\tilde{S}_T$ is lognormally distributed, which we write in terms of the standard normal $\tilde{z}$ as

$$\tilde{S}_T = S_t e^{\mu(T-t)+\sigma\tilde{z}\sqrt{T-t}}, \text{ with } \mu = \frac{E\left[\ln\left(\frac{S_T}{S_t}\right)\right]}{T-t}, \sigma^2 = \frac{Var\left[\ln\left(\frac{S_T}{S_t}\right)\right]}{T-t}. \tag{13a}$$

Adapting the risk-neutral valuation approach of Cox and Ross (1976), the drift of the log stock price changes can be replaced by $\mu = r - 1/2\sigma^2$. In order to facilitate the comparison with Bronzin, we subsequently assume an interest rate of zero and one time unit to maturity, $T - t$

= 1 (e.g. one year if volatility is measured in annual terms). The forward price is then equal to the current stock price, implying

$$\tilde{S}_T = Be^{-\frac{1}{2}\sigma^2+\sigma\tilde{z}}. \tag{13b}$$

The Black–Scholes valuation equation can then be written as

$$P_1 = \int_{-z_2}^{\infty}\Bigg(\underbrace{Be^{-\frac{1}{2}\sigma^2+\sigma\tilde{z}}}_{S_T} - K\Bigg)N'(z)dz, \tag{14}$$

where the remaining task is to adjust the lower integration boundary, here denoted by $-z_2$ in anticipation of the Black–Scholes model. For this task, we just have to transform the probability range of the normal $\tilde{x}$, $pr(\tilde{x} > M)$, to a new range $pr(\tilde{S}_T > K)$ expressed relative to the standard normal density $N'(z)$. Note that $pr(\tilde{S}_T > K)$ is equal to $pr(\ln S_T > \ln K)$, and that $\ln(S_T)$ is normally distributed with mean $\ln S_0 - 1/2\sigma^2 = B - 1/2\sigma^2$ and standard deviation σ. Thus we can standardize both sides of the inequality $pr(\ln S_T > \ln K)$ to get

$$pr\left(\underbrace{\frac{\ln\tilde{S}_T - \left[\ln B - \frac{1}{2}\sigma^2\right]}{\sigma}}_{\tilde{z}} - K > \frac{\ln K - \left[\ln B - \frac{1}{2}\sigma^2\right]}{\sigma}\right)$$

where $\tilde{z}$ is the standard normal. The expression on the right-hand side can be written as

$$\frac{\ln K - \left[\ln B - \frac{1}{2}\sigma^2\right]}{\sigma} = \frac{\ln B - \ln K - \frac{1}{2}\sigma^2}{\sigma} = -\frac{\ln\frac{B}{K} - \frac{1}{2}\sigma^2}{\sigma} \equiv -z_2 \tag{15}$$

which is exactly the Black–Scholes boundary typically expressed as

$$pr(\tilde{z} > -z_2) = pr(\tilde{z} < z_2) \equiv N(z_2).$$

Summing up, we have shown that the Bronzin equation (11) can be easily transformed to the Black–Scholes model if the stock price $B + \tilde{x} = \tilde{S}_T$ is specified as a lognormal instead of a normal variable and the integration boundary is adjusted correspondingly.[28] Thus, the pricing relationship looking most similar to the Bronzin equation is

$$P_1 = \int_K^{\infty}\left(\tilde{S}_T - K\right)L'(S_T)dS_T = \int_{-z_2}^{\infty}\left(Be^{\frac{1}{2}\sigma^2+\sigma\tilde{z}} - K\right)N'(z)dz, \quad z_2 = \frac{\ln\frac{B}{K} - \frac{1}{2}\sigma^2}{\sigma}$$

The explicit solution using the standard Black–Scholes procedure in transforming the integral[29] is

$$P_1 = BN\left\{z_2 + \sigma\sqrt{T-t}\right\} - KN\{z_2\}$$

or re-adapting time and interest,

$$P_1 = Be^{-r(T-t)}N\left\{z_2 + \sigma\sqrt{T-t}\right\} - Ke^{-r(T-t)}N\{z_2\}$$

where $Be^{-r(T-t)} = S_t$ can also be written as the current stock price. This derivation shows that Bronzin's valution equation (11) is fully consistent with the Black–Scholes, and, respectively, the Black (1976) forward price based valuation models. It is also a risk-neutral valuation approach – he makes no assumptions on preferences or expected values – simply because the option price relies on the forward price and zero (random) deviations from there.

6. Option pricing in historical perspective

Judgements about scientific originality are always difficult with a delay of a century, in a field which has progressed so rapidly as option pricing, and where statistical and stochastic methods are used which were hardly developed at this time. It is even questionable whether scientific originality is a fair criterion to apply – because nothing is known about its purpose or target audience. Given that he published it as a 'professor', and given that he had published a textbook on actuarial theory for beginners two years before (Bronzin 1906), it may well be that he regarded his option theory as a textbook, or a mixture of textbook and scientific monograph. Finally, Bronzin definitely did not overstate his own contribution – he even understates it by regularly talking about his 'booklet' (Werkchen) when referring to it. Why he was talking about his textbook as a 'booklet' is an open question: was it because it was not good for his reputation as an academic to write about financial mathematics – or worse, on a topic typically associated with speculation? Was it because the subject was too far away from his profession as a professor of arithmetic? We do not know. Further research needs to be done.

Originality in the field of option pricing is difficult to assess. Who deserves proper credit for the Black–Scholes model? The early Samuelson (1965) paper contains the essential equation.[30] Even more puzzling is a footnote in the Black–Scholes paper (p. 461) where the authors acknowledge a comment by Robert Merton suggesting that if the option hedge is maintained continuously over time, the return on the hedged position becomes certain. But it is the notion of the riskless hedge which makes the essential difference between Black–Scholes and the earlier Samuelson and Merton–Samuelson models![31, 32] Surprisingly enough, Merton was kind enough to delay publication of his (accepted) 1973 paper until Black–Scholes got theirs accepted.[33]

An open question is to what other publications Bronzin is referring: he surely knew the most important publications in German about probability and options. Options (*Prämiengeschäfte*) were well-known instruments at this time in the stock exchanges in the German-speaking part of Europe. There were many different forms. And, at least about the legal aspect of options, different books containing financial transactions had been published.[34] But the mathematical background of options didn't seem to be an issue. Another question is, whether Bronzin knew about Bachelier's work. Honni soit qui mal y pense ... – but extensive quoting was not the game at the time anyway. Bachelier did not quote any of the earlier (but admittedly, non-mathematical) books on option valuation either. For example, Regnault's book (1863) was widely used and contains the notion of random walk, the Gaussian distribution, the role of volatility in pricing options, including the square-root formula.[35] According to Whelan (2002), who refers to a paper by Émile Dormoy published in 1873, French actuaries had a reasonable idea of pricing options well before Bachelier's thesis, although a clear mathematical framework was missing. Einstein in his Brownian motion paper (1905) did not quote Bachelier's thesis, but it is a generally accepted view that he did not know it. Distribution of knowledge seems to have been pretty slow at this time, particularly between different fields of research, and across different languages. And again, extensive references were simply not common in natural sciences (e.g. Einstein's paper contains only one reference to another author).

If Einstein did not know Bachelier's thesis, it is even less likely that Bronzin knew it; based on what we know from his other work (Bronzin 1906), his general mathematical interests were also quite different from those of Bachelier. But after all, we do not know what Bronzin knew about others' work on option pricing, nor is the question very relevant, because there are enough innovative elements in his treatise. It is also surprising that (almost) no references are found to his work, particularly in the German literature. Although it is generally claimed that Bachelier's thesis was lost until the Savage–Samuelson rediscovery, it was at least quoted since 1908 in several editions of a French actuarial textbook by Alfred Barriol (at least until 1925).

Bronzin's book had a similar recognition. As stated earlier, it was mentioned in Leitner's book about banking in Germany, published in four editions. And with Bronzin's more pragmatic pricing approach, it is difficult to understand why the seeds for another, more scientific, understanding of option pricing did not develop, or the formulae did not get immediate practical attention. Bronzin was not a doctoral candidate, as was Bachelier, but (apparently) a distinguished professor; moreover, the flourishing insurance industry in Trieste should have had an active commercial interest in his research. While Poincaré's reservation about Bachelier's thesis is, at least, limited to his 'queer' subject[36] and can, somehow, be understood from a purely academic point of view, it is more difficult to understand why a reviewer of Bronzin's book, in 1910, commented that 'it can hardly be assumed that the results will attain a particularly practical value'. However, it justifies Hans Bühlmann's and Shane Whelan's[37] claim that the contribution of actuaries to financial economics is generally underestimated (see Whelan 2002 for detailed references).

7. Beyond finance: the probabilistic and historical background of Bronzin's work

Applying probabilistic models to financial problems was common in actuarial science, particularly life insurance, at the end of the nineteenth century, but not in areas related to speculation, financial markets, or derivative contracts. In this respect, the work of Bronzin as well as of Bachelier marked a substantial breakthrough.

It is not easy to identify the intellectual foundations of Bachelier's and Bronzin's works. It might be found in the 'probabilistic' revolution[38] which took place in physics, and to some extent in economics, in the second part of the nineteenth century. In this context, it may be regarded as another amazing parallel between of the lives and achievements of Bachelier and Bronzin that they were both students in an environment of theoreticians in search of new analytical tools for gaining a deeper and new understanding of the intrinsic structure of the world: entropy and probability. As noted earlier, Bachelier submitted his thesis to Henri Poincaré, and Bronzin took courses and seminars with Ludwig Boltzmann at the Technical University of Vienna.[39] Both, Poincaré and Boltzmann, building on the foundations laid by Maxwell, laid the mathematical foundations of modern physics – although their approaches were different.[40] Is there a relationship between the work of Bachelier and Bronzin?

7.1 Probabilistic modelling in physics and finance

Maxwell's achievement was a statistical formulation of the kinetic theory of gas in the 1860s. According to kinetic theory, heat is due to the random movement of atoms and molecules, so it looks much like kinetic energy. In contrast to other forms of energy, however, these movements cannot be observed or predicted, while other energies result from orderly movements of particles. Maxwell argued that, although random in nature, the velocity of molecules can be described by mathematical functions – derived from the laws of probability.

It is the same reasoning which is found in the introductory sections of Bachelier's and Bronzin's writings: they both argue that although speculative markets (prices) behave in a completely random and unpredictable way, this does not prevent, but rather motivates, the use of mathematical – probabilistic – tools. This marked a fundamental change in the perception of risk in the context of financial securities.

Back to Poincaré and Boltzmann – things become slightly more complicated. Their approach to model the unpredictability, irreversibility, or chaotic behaviour of dynamical systems was quite different and created much controvery. It was not clear how to reconcile probabilistic and statistical laws with the mechanical laws of Newtonian physics.

Boltzmann addressed the problem by proving the irreversibility of macroscopic systems through kinetic gas theory – which is, after all, a purely mechanic, deterministic point of view: while any *single* molecule obeys the classical rules of reversible mechanics, for a large *collection* of particles, he claimed that the *laws of statistics* imply irreversibility and force the second Law of Thermodynamics to hold. From any arbitrary initial distribution of molecular velocities, molecular collisions always bring the gas to an equilibrium distribution (as characterized by Maxwell). In a series of famous papers included as chapters 2 and 3 in Boltzmann (2000) he showed that, for non-equilibrium states, the entropy is proportional to the logarithm of the probability of the specific state. The system is stable, or in thermal equilibrium, if entropy reaches its maximum – and hence the associated probability. So maximum entropy (disorder) is the most likely – and hence equilibrium – state in a thermodynamic system. In short, Boltzmann recognized 'how intimately the second Law is connected to the theory of probability and that the impossibility of an uncompensated decrease of entropy seems to be reduced to an improbability'.[41]

This theorem is widely regarded as the foundation of statistical mechanics, by describing a thermodynamic system using the statistical behaviour of its constituents: it relates a *microscopic property* of the system (the number or probabilities of states) to one of its *thermodynamic properties* (the entropy).[42] However, he was heavily criticized, because, after all, it was a purely *mechanical* proof of the second Law of Thermodynamics: he used 'laws of probability' to bridge the conflict between *macroscopic* (thermodynamic) irreversibility and *microscopic* (mechanical) *reversibility* of molecular motions.

It is therefore not surprising that Boltzmann's probabilistic interpretation of entropy was not accepted by all researchers at that time without reservation, and created much quarrel, controversy and polemic. While Boltzmann (and Clausius) insisted on a strictly mechanical interpretation of the second Law, Maxwell still claimed the statistical character of the Law. A major objection came in 1896 from one of Planck's assistants in Berlin (E. Zermelo) which is particularly interesting in our context – it is the place where Poincaré enters the scene. Zermelo referred to a mathematical theorem published by Poincaré in 1893 which implies that any spatially bounded, mechanical system ultimately returns to a state sufficiently close to its initial state after a sufficiently long time interval. This was inconsistent with Boltzmann's theorem (and a kinetic theory of gas in general). If the validity of mechanical laws is assumed for thermodynamic processes on a microscopic level, entropy cannot increase monotonically, and irreversible processes are impossible: hence, the world is not a mechanical system!

It is amazing to see how notable scientists refused to 'swap the solid ground of the laws of thermodynamics – the product of a century of careful experimental verification – for the ephemeral world of statistics and chance' (Haw 2005, p. 19). Boltzman himself considered kinetic theory as a purely mechanical analogy; after all, nobody had ever physically observed the particles that kinetic theory was all about.

This was actually done by Albert Einstein's investigation of Brownian motion, i.e. the old observation from Robert Brown in the early nineteenth century that small particles in a liquid were in constant motion, carrying out a chaotic 'dance' – not being caused by any external influence. Was this a violation of the second Law on the level of single particles? Einstein was able to prove that liquids are really made of atoms, and experiments moreover demonstrated that the movement of Brownian particles was perfectly in line with Boltzmann's kinetic gas theory! Thus Einstein successfully integrated the thermodynamics of liquids with Boltzmann's interpretation of the second Law with statistical mechanics – Boltzmann's vision at the end of his 1877 paper proved to be right: he claimed that it is very likely that his theory is not limited to gases, but represents a natural law applicable to, for example, liquids as well, although the mathematical difficulties of this generalization appeared 'extraordinary' to him.

Einstein formulated a theory of Brownian motion in terms of a differential equation – the celebrated diffusion equation (Einstein 1905). But again – while Einstein could easily live with statistical concepts in the context of atoms, he was never in favour of a statistical or probabilistic interpretation of quantum mechanics ('God does not play dice'...). Today, much of the controversy over whether a deterministic or a stochastic system is needed to cause the irreversibility of macroscopic processes is alleviated – chaos theory has established itself as a powerful mathematical intermediary. Poincaré was one of the pioneers in this field – but nevertheless, Boltzmann was aware as well that the dynamic properties of a thermodynamic system depend crucially on the initial state of the system, and prediction becomes impossible.[43]

What has all this to do with finance? A great deal – because it is well known that Einstein's mathematical treatment of Brownian motion was pioneered by Bachelier. The surprising fact is, however, that Bachelier wrote his thesis under the supervision of Henri Poincaré, whose sympathy with the probabilistic modelling of dynamic systems was, as discussed before, limited. It is in fact amazing how strong Bachelier's belief was in the power of probability theory – Delbean and Schachermayer (2001) even call it 'mystic'. This is best reflected in the concluding statement of his thesis:

> Si, à l'égard de plusieurs questions traitées dans cette étude, j'ai comparé les résultats de l'observation à ceux de la théorie, ce n'était pas pour vérifier des formules établies par les méthodes mathématiques, mais pour montrer seulement que le marché, é son insu, obéit à une loi qui le domine: la loi de la probabilité. (If, in regard to several questions dealt with in this study, I have compared the results of observation with those of theory, it wasn't to verify established formulae by mathematical methods, but only to show that the market, unconsciously, obeyed a law that ruled it: the law of probability.) (Bachelier 1900, p. 86)

Maybe his exuberant commitment to probability was not too beneficial for the overall evaluation of the thesis by his adviser, Poincaré! After all, 'it must be said that Poincaré was very doubtful that probability could be applied to anything in real life ... ' (Taqqu 2001, p. 9) which was fundamentally different from Bachelier's view and ambition.

In any case, Bachelier's approach would have emerged more naturally from Boltzmann's statistical mechanics. The similarity of the theoretical reasoning is most evident if one compares the first page of Bachelier's thesis, where he describes the motivation and adequacy of probability theory for characterizing stock price movements, with the set-up of Boltzmann's (1877) kinetic gas theory. The uncountable determinants of stock prices, their interaction and expectation seem to have a similar (or the same?) role with respect to the unpredictability (or maximum chaos) of the system as the collision of innumerable small molecules and the second Law of Thermodynamics.

Was thermodynamics ever applied to economic modelling? While not in a probabilistic setting, Vilfredo Pareto (1900) made an analogy with the second Law in discussing the redistribution of wealth between individuals by changing the conditions of free competition. He claims that this process necessarily leads to a corrosion of wealth – and attributes to this 'theorem' the same (or 'analogous') role as the second Law in physics. But we are not aware of entropy-based foundations of economic systems or financial markets around the turn of the century. Was there a probabilistic revolution in economics at all?[44]

Unfortunately, Bronzin, being an admiring student of Boltzmann, did not use any element of statistical mechanics for modelling price processes or their distribution – which is a surprising fact indeed. Rather, his approach was more in the probabilistic tradition of actuarial science.

7.2 Probability in actuarial science and the treating of market risks

Much has been written about the long tradition of probabilistic modelling in actuarial science, and there is no need to replicate the history here. Also needless to say that actuarial science played a pivotal role in the expansion of the insurance sector as the driving force behind the economic growth and industrialization in the nineteenth century.[45] From reading actuarial textbooks and monographs published in German, towards the end of the nineteenth century, three (related) features become apparent.

First, we observe a more rigorous probabilistic treatment of the key concepts of insurance mathematics – the emergence of elements of a formal 'risk theory'. A good example is an encyclopaedia article on 'insurance mathematics' by Georg Bohlmann (1900) containing an axiomatic treatment of probability with many elements of Kolmogorov's famous treatment 33 years later. This resulted from the insight that the insurance business needed a more solid, *scientific basis* for calculating risks, covering potential losses and determining adequate premiums.[46] Also, there was an increasing demand for a precise, probability-based terminology of the key actuarial terms.

A second observation is the increasing analogy between the nature of insurance contracts and 'games of chance' (*Zufallsspiele*). An early although non-mathematical characterization of this kind is Herrmann (1869), and a rigorous mathematical treatment is Hausdorff (1897); both authors characterize insurance contracts as special forms of games of chance.[47] Hausdorff's treatise is particularly revealing; he analyses different types of (what we would call nowadays) financial contracts, their expected loss and profit for various parties. He also analyses the impact of various amortization or redemption schedules on optimal call policies and bond prices (such as for callable bonds, lottery bonds and premium bonds).[48]

This directly leads to the third observation, namely the increasing – although still quite limited – perception of market risk – as opposed to the (traditional) actuarial risk.[49]

The growing perception of market risk was caused, among other things, by substantial and permanent deviations of market interest rates from their actuarial (fixed) level, as well as by the substantial losses insurance companies suffered during the stock market crash in the 1870s. Companies were forced to hold special reserves[50] (*Kursschwankungsreserven*). Although the analytical methods were quite advanced, the treatment and economic understanding of market risk was quite limited. Even Emanuel Czuber (1910a, b), a renowned professor at the Technische Hochschule in Vienna specializing in insurance mathematics, was pessimistic whether a formal 'risk theory' could be helpful for managing market risk.

In simple terms: risk theory is about computing value-at-risk-based reserves to cover the risks from inadequate actuarial assumptions (e.g. interest rates). But Czuber (1910a, p.411) claims that risk theory is not applicable to interest rate risk, i.e. interest rates do not behave randomly! Even if this were correct, what about other market risks? Indeed, the same author argues elsewhere (Czuber 1910b, p.233) that past asset returns (*Verzinsung*) behave so randomly (*unregelmässig*) that they cannot be used to predict future returns. Obviously, there was no consistent picture about market risks and their probabilistic (stochastic) modelling – which is quite representative of the actuarial literature at this time. Therefore, Bronzin's (1908) contribution constituted a substantial step forward. Armed with standard tools from probability theory, he took the challenge to price the specific type(s) of derivative contracts extensively discussed in the earlier sections of this chapter.

7.3 Bronzin's interests and academic work

Why was Bronzin interested in probability theory? Why was he interested in derivative (option) contracts? We have only partial answers, or hypotheses, to these questions.[51] In accordance with his son Andrea Bronzin, we suggest that Vinzenz Bronzin wrote his (1908) book for educational purposes. This seems to be true for all his earlier publications (e.g. 1904, 1906, 1908), which grew out of subjects of his lectures at the Accademia di Commercio e Nautico in Trieste, where he was a professor of 'political and commercial arithmetic'. Both fields were part of the mathematical curriculum and also included actuarial science and probability theory. *Political arithmetic* was strongly focused on the needs of the insurance companies. *Commercial arithmetic* was more suited to the needs of the banking industry and internationally oriented trading companies. At this time, it was a well-established tradition among professors to publish books about the topics they covered in their lectures.[52]

The first publication of Bronzin which is documented in his own curriculum is a short article entitled '*Arbitrage*' in a German journal for commercial education (Bronzin 1904).[53] The paper is about characterizing relative price ratios of goods across different currencies and associated trading (arbitrage) strategies. While interesting *per se*, it is unfortunately not directly related to the 'arbitrage valuation principle' of derivatives valuation – which Bronzin, ironically, uses in his option pricing booklet, however without using this term.

Bronzin's second publication (Bronzin 1906) is a monograph on political arithmetic (*Lehrbuch der politischen Arithmetik*); it was approved by the ministry of education as an official textbook to be used at the commercial schools and academies in the empire. Bronzin had not – in contrast to many of his collegues at the Accademia – published extensively. It is therefore more than surprising, if not strange, that he did not quote his (1908) option pricing piece in a publication (a *Festschrift*) released for the centenary of the school (subsequently quoted as Subak 1917)! Had it become such a 'queer' subject in the meantime? As shown in the last section, it was indeed unusual to apply probability theory to speculation and financial securities pricing in these times, but why should he suppress the major scientific contribution he had produced so far? Was the subject too complicated for the target audience, or did he get frustrating responses?

It is true that gambling, speculation, or trading with derivatives did not enjoy a major popularity around this time.[54] In the last decade of the nineteenth century, derivatives were increasingly blamed for causing exuberant market movements and being socially harmful. Furthermore, in 1901, a court of justice accepted the 'gambling' argument (*Spiel und Wette*) in a legal case in Vienna. Thereafter, forward trading declined and became less and less important.[55] At the rather small stock exchange of Trieste, premium contracts were not traded at all during these years.[56] But was this a sufficient reason for Bronzin to suppress this publication? After all, our overall impression is that Bronzin's interest in derivatives (and finance in general) was predominantly on the theoretical side.

Writing books must have been hard work for Bronzin anyway. Besides his academic position, Bronzin was nominated director of the Accademia in 1909, but he was not yet able to accept the nomination, because he was suffering from a strong nervousness, apparently caused by his efforts of writing the two books ('in forte nervosità' because of 'compilazione e pubblicazione di libri matematici').[57] One year later he was offered the same position again, and he then accepted. He resigned in 1937 at the age of 65. His major achievement as a director of the Accademia was seen in his ability to guide the school through a time of significant political turbulence before, during and after the First World War. He still had a great reputation as a mathematician. Moreover, at least during his study years in Vienna, he was reputed to be a successful gambler.[58] Combining mathematics with gambling seemed to have been perfect for writing his option pricing theory. Interestingly, no consulting activities are known or documented. He was asked several times to join insurance companies but preferred to stay in academia.[59]

BOX 11.1 BRONZIN: A FEW FACTS

Vincenz (later: Vincenzo) Bronzin was born in Rovigno (today: Rovinj), a small town on the peninsula of Istria (Croatia), on 4 May 1872, and died in Trieste on 20 December 1970 aged 98. He was the son of a Slovenian commandant of a sailing-ship. After completing the gymnasium (high school) in Capodistria, a town on Istria, he became a student in engineering at the University of Polytechnics in Vienna, where he passed his exams after two years's study. He then studied mathematics and paedagogics at the University of Vienna, and at the same time, he took courses for military officers in Graz.

In his obituary, his nephew Angelo Bronzin reports that he was a well-known gambler and a champion in fencing during his time in Vienna. In 1897 he became a teacher in mathematics at the Upper High School of Trieste ('Civica Scuola Reale Superiore di Trieste'). In 1900 he was appointed professor of commercial and political arithmetic at the I.R. Accademia di Commercio e Nautica. He was the director of this institution from 1910 to 1937. Apparently, his reputation was overwhelming. To celebrate him, he was euphorically called 'Eine Zierde der Menschheit!' ('a jewel of humanity') and 'a heroic scientist'.[60]

7.4 The Accademia in Trieste and the 'kaiserlich und königlich' educational system

The Accademia di Commercio e Nautica in Trieste was the oldest Accademia in the Habsburg–Hungarian empire, and was founded in 1817 by the Austrian administration, in order to develop Trieste as the empire's seaport. Later, international insurance companies such as Generali, Llyod Adriatico and Riunione Adriatica di Sicurta, corporations with a strong life-insurance branch and with assets exceeding those of the big banking corporations of Vienna, recruited their employees from the Accademia. In this process, the Accademia also started to include courses on money, banking, finance, probability, etc. in the curriculum for students, and to offer evening courses for practitioners.

Trieste was the main port of the Austria–Hungarian empire in the Mediterranean, and thus the main trading place for commodities – both physically and in terms of derivatives. Even though trading declined during the last quarter of the nineteenth century, a majority of the citizens of Trieste still believed in the strength of their town as a commercial, social and cultural melting-pot, and continued to attract an international clientele of businessmen, artists and scientists: Italians, Austrians, Slovenes, Germans. Business was key to amalgamating the different nations, and created a liberal, international atmosphere in the town. This contrasted sharply with the emerging perception of 'nationality'. In his book Il mio Carso, the Triestinian writer Scipio Slatapter took the perspective of a man who wanted to maintain his Italian nationality: 'Ogni cosa al commercio necessaria è violazione d'italianità; ciò che ne è vero aumento danneggia quello' ('Everything that helps to bring up commerce is necessarily a violation of *italianità* and thus adds to its damage') (p. 181).[61]

This was the political atmosphere which prevailed at the time when Bronzin started his career in Trieste. The economic situation was still flourishing in the empire; the central government in Vienna, particularly the k.u.k. Administration, closely governed and controlled the publicly owned institutions in the empire.

This was particularly true for the commercial education system. One of the driving forces behind this process was Eugenio Gelcich. He was the director of the Accademia in Trieste from 1899 to 1901, and thus was responsible for the appointment of Bronzin in 1900. One year later, he became the central inspector of 'commercial education' in the empire, which reflects the high standard and reputation the Accademia (and possibly other commercial schools) had in Trieste. He was a very involved person and visited by order of the Austrian government several European countries to study their commercial education system and wrote reports about his visits.[62] He regularly organized conferences in which the professors of all commercial academies and schools of the empire participated. In 1910 he even made Trieste the permanent centre of the international association for developing the commercial education (see Subak 1917, pp. 269 ff.). In 1903, a curriculum for all advanced commercial schools (*höhere Handelsschulen*) of the empire was developed under his guidance. This constituted the basis for establishing a (the first?) standardized curriculum in business finance, including topics such as

- introduction to probability theory;
- life annuities;
- exchange traded commodities and securities;
- the system of exchanges and contracts/instruments (commodities and securities; spot and forward; options).

This is a surprisingly modern course outline. Given Bronzin's strong educational efforts, we do not believe that he wanted to launch a new research programme with his option pricing booklet, but rather provide a solid educational tool for accomplishing the standards defined above. It may be that this interpretation understates his real ambition, but it is amazing what emerged.

8. Summing up: Bronzin's contribution to option pricing

When comparing Bronzin's contribution with Bachelier's thesis, it can be seen that Bachelier was not only earlier, but his analysis was more rigorous from a mathematical point of view. Bronzin cannot be credited with having developed a new mathematical field, as Bachelier did with his theory on diffusions. Bronzin did no stochastic modelling, applied no stochastic calculus, derived no differential equations (except in the context of our equation 7), he was not interested in stochastic processes, and hence his notion of volatility has no time dimension. But except this, every element of modern option pricing is there! His contribution can be assessed as follows:

1. He noticed the unpredictability of speculative prices, and the need to use probability laws to price derivatives.
2. He recognized the informational role of market prices for pricing derivatives, and developed a theory relying on the current forward price of securities to price options. No expected values show up in the pricing formulae. His probability densities can be easily re-interpreted as risk-neutral pricing densities.
3. He understood the key role of arbitrage, although he is not very explicit about it; derives the put–call parity condition, and uses a zero-profit condition to price forward contracts and options.
4. He develops a simplified procedure to find analytical solutions for option prices by exploiting a key relationship between their derivatives (with respect to their exercise prices) and the underlying pricing density. He also stresses the empirical advantages of this approach.
5. He extensively discusses how different distributional assumptions affect option prices. In particular, he shows how the normal law of error – which is the normal density function – can be used to price options, and how it is related to a binomial stock price distribution.
6. Besides pricing simple calls and puts, he develops formulae for chooser options and, more important, repeat options.

His preference-free valuation equation (43) is closer to the Black–Scholes formula than anything else published before Black, Scholes and Merton. All this is a remarkable achievement, and it is done with a minimum of analytics. There are a few things on the less elegant side: the discussion and the large systems of hedging conditions in the first part belongs here, and some numerical procedures to solve for the repeat-option premiums. But nevertheless, Bronzin's contribution is important, not only in historical retrospect. He definitely deserves his place in the history of option pricing, among others. This was pointed out in a survey article by Girlich (2002). His introduction concludes our chapter:

> In the case of Louis Bachelier and his area of activity the dominant French point of view is the most natural thing in the world and everybody is convinced by the results. The aim of the present paper is

to add a few tesseras from other countries to the picture which is known about the birth of mathematical finance and its probabilistic environment.

We are happy to have added another piece to this fascinating picture. Bachelier in his way was unique. But, more important, he was not the only one who was working successfully on option pricing at the beginning of the twentieth century. So the question remains: why did the results of Bachelier, Bronzin and possibly others yet to be rediscovered not get a broader acceptance? Why did their research not find immediate successors, academics to continue the way towards a practicable formula that made the pricing of options a subject of ongoing scientific research? Finding answers to these questions could help us to better understand the cultural background of financial mathematics, and would probably add an interesting chapter to the sociology of science. This would be a fascinating agenda for future research.

Notes

1. For example it was mentioned in a standard banking textbook from Friedrich Leitner (1920) and a book by Karl Meithner (1924). The most notable exception is a follow-up paper by the mathematician Gustav Flusser (1911) extending some of Bronzin's results. Moreover, the book got a short review in the famous *Monatshefte für Mathematik und Physik* in 1910 (Vol. 21).
2. Except a recent reference from our colleague Yvan Lengwiler (2004), we are aware of only one modern reference on Bronzin's book in a German textbook on option pricing (see Welcker et al. 1988). The authors do not comment on the significance of Bronzin's contribution in the light of modern option pricing theory. A short appreciation of Bronzin's book is also contained in a recent monograph of one of the authors of this chapter, Hafner (2002).
3. There is a paper on the French premium market by Courtadon (1982).
4. They are also briefly addressed by Bachelier; see (p. 53) on *double primes*.
5. The German word '*noch*' is uncommonly used as a noun here; in common language it is a pronoun and means 'another', i.e. an additional one of the same kind, one more.
6. Also these contracts are briefly analysed by Bachelier; see Section 6 for a direct comparison.
7. Except in the final numerical example on the penultimate page, where he refers to 'shares' (*Aktien*).
8. In this chapter, 'modern' option pricing always refers to the state of the theory after the Black–Scholes–Merton breakthrough.
9. Bronzin argues in terms of the 'number' of options, but obviously, he assumes equal dollar amounts and equal exposures (which is trivially the case since all options have the same exercise price, B, by assumption).
10. This specification is not made by Bronzin, but is obvious.
11. The same is also true for Bachelier; amazingly, Bronzin published a paper entitled 'Arbitrage' a few years earlier; Bronzin (1904).
12. An arbitrage profit is risk-free and does not require a positive amount of capital to be invested.
13. He notes that the tools required for this task are beyond elementary mathematics – only the application of probability and integral calculus is able to shed light on this important question (p. 39).
14. It is interesting to note that his focus is from the beginning on the variability (volatility) and the current state of the market (*Marktschwankungen*), not the trend.
15. On p. 56, the reasoning for this insight is justified by the fact that the call and put prices coincide if the exercise price is equal to the forward price.
16. The same is true for Bachelier's analysis. In contrast to Bronzin, he does not argue with the forward price, but he apparently assumes that the price at which a forward contract (*opération ferme*) is executed is equal to the current spot price (see his characterization on p. 26; note that his is the deviation of the stock price at expiration from the current value).
17. It is important to note that the statement, in the literal sense, is about expected, not current (riskless), profits. It is therefore not a no-arbitrage condition.
18. Many years ago, William Margrabe made one of the authors aware of this paper. Not many people seem to know this tiny piece; e.g. it is also missing in the Merton and Scholes *Journal of Finance* tribute after Fischer Black's death, where all his papers and publications are listed.
19. Interestingly, Bachelier (1900) on p. 51 also shows this expression, but without motivation, comments, or potential use.
20. For a discrete distribution of states, the state price (also called Arrow–Debreu price) is the current price of a claim, which entitles its owner to receive a dollar in one specific future state, and nothing otherwise.
21. This does not keep the standard deviation of the distribution the same, of course.
22. The (normal) law of error should not be confused with error *function*, which is an integral defined by

$$erf(x) = 2\int_0^x \frac{1}{\sqrt{\pi}} e^{-t^2} dt,$$

related to the cumulative standard normal N{·} by $erf(x) = 2[N\{x\sqrt{2}\}-0.5]$.

23. As a historical remark, the analytical characterization as well as the terminology related to the 'normal' distribution was very mixed until the end of the nineteenth century; while statisticians such as Galton, Lexis, Venn, Edgeworth and Pearson have occasionally used the expression in the late nineteenth century, it was adopted by the probabilistic community no earlier than in the 1920s. Stigler (1999), pp. 404–15, provides a detailed analysis of this subject.
24. Again, there is no reference to a time dimension in Bronzin's approach. In the Cox et al. (1979) setting, these would be interpreted as consecutive market movements. In the Bronzin setting, the binomial approach is just used to characterize the deviations from the expected (i.e. forward) price.
25. We are extremely grateful to Ernst Juerg Weber from the School of Economics and Commerce, University of Western Australia, who called our attention to this paper and made it available to us.
26. Gustav Flusser studied mathematics and physics, and was a professor at the German and Czech University of Prague. He was also a member of the social-democratic party in parliament. He starved in the concentration camp of Buchenwald in 1940.
27. We adopt the common terminology in using 'Black–Scholes' for the models developed by Black and Scholes (1973) and Merton (1973).
28. It can also be shown how Bronzin's explicit pricing formula based on the Error distribution, as displayed in Table 11.1, can be related to our equation (14). The equivalence of the integration boundaries, however, requires the following approximation:

$$\ln\frac{K}{B} + \frac{1}{2}\sigma^2 \approx \frac{K}{B} - 1.$$

Details can be found in Zimmermann and Hafner (2004), pp. 44–7.

29. See, e.g., James (2003), pp. 299–309.
30. Or to use Samuelson's own wording: 'Yes, I had the equation, but "they" got the formula…'; see Geman (2002).
31. To be precise, the notion of a 'near' riskless hedge strategy can also be found in the Samuelson and Samuelson and Merton papers. Samuelson (1965) analyses the relationship between the expected return on the option (warrant), β, and the underlying stock, α, and argued that the difference 'cannot become too large. If $\beta > \alpha$ … hedging will stand to yield a sure-thing positive net capital gain (commissions and interest charges on capital aside!)' (p. 31). Samuelson and Merton (1969) extend the earlier model and derive a 'probability-cum-utility' function Q (see p. 19), which serves as a new probability measure (in today's terminology) to compute option prices. They show that under this new measure (or utility function), all securities earn the riskless rate; they explicitly write $\alpha_Q = \beta_Q = r$ to stress this point (see p. 26, equations 20 and 21 and the subsequent comments). Although Merton and Samuelson recognized the possibility of a (near) riskless hedge and a risk-neutral valuation approach, they were not fully aware of the consequences of their findings.
32. Black (1988) gives proper credit to Robert Merton: 'Bob gave us that [arbitrage] argument. It should probably be called the Black–Merton–Scholes paper'.
33. Bernstein (1992) and Black (1989) provide interesting details about the birth of the Black–Scholes formula.
34. Eg. Leitner (1920), p. 624.
35. The argument is derived from a strange analogy: he considers the mean (or fair) value of an asset as the centre of a circle, and every point within the circle represents a possible future price. The radius describes the standard deviation. He then assumes that, as time elapses, the range of possible stock prices as represented by the area within the circle increases proportionally. This implies that the radius (i.e. the standard deviation) increases with the square root of time. A detailed analysis of Regnault's contribution is given in several papers by Jovanovic and Le Gall; see, e.g., Jovanovic and Le Gall (2001).
36. Poincaré was the main adviser for Bachelier's thesis; he writes in his report: 'Le sujet choisi par M. Bachelier s'éloigne un peu de ceux qui sont habituellement traités par nos candidats' ('The subject chosen by M. Bachelier is slightly different from those that are usually dealt with by our candidates'); Taqqu (2001), Appendix.
37. See Whelan (2002) for detailed references.
38. This term is borrowed from Krüger et al. (1987).
39. Based on our communication with his son, Andrea Bronzin, who also showed us testimonies signed by L. Boltzmann.
40. An excellent description of this topic can be found in chap. 14 (Vol. 2) of Krüger et al. (1987), contributed by Jan von Plato.
41. See Klein (1973), p. 73.

42. See Fischer (2000), p. 167.
43. This statement originates from a reply to one of Zermelo's criticisms; see Fischer (2000), p. 174.
44. See Krüger et al. (1987), Vol. 2, chap. 6, on this point.
45. It is interesting to see how nation-building and the development of the old-age-pension system paralleled each other. For example, Bismarck installed the state-sponsored old-age-pension system with the intention to create a conservative attitude by the workers. Loth (1996), p. 68, quotes Bismarck: the pension system was created '[um] in der grossen Masse der Besitzlosen die konservative Gesinnung (zu) erzeugen, welche das Gefühl der Pensionsberechtigung mit sich bringt' ('in order to raise the conservative ethos in the mass of the poor, which comes with the sense of being entitled to a public pension').
46. Assicurazioni Generali (in Trieste) was apparently very proud to publish the actuarial foundations of its life business in 1905, elaborated by Vitale Laudi and Wilhelm Lazarus over many years, as an opulent monograph. But ironically, in 1907, Generali changed their foundations of its life business and re-adopted the generally used formula of Gompertz-Makeham (see: Die Jahrhundertfeier der Assicurazioni Generali, Trieste 1931, p. 99).
47. The term 'games of chance' (Zufallsspiele) had already been used by the physiologist, logician, philosopher and mathematician Johannes Von Kries (1886), chaps 3 and 7, although not in a rigorous mathematical setting.
48. The treatise also contains a lucid discussion on the distinction between aggregate and average risk of games, i.e. the distinction between adding and subdividing risks. Samuelson (1963) is typically credited with this clarification.
49. The insignificant perception of market risk before the 1870s is, for instance, reflected in Herrmann's (1869) treatise on insurance companies, devoting four lines (!) to interest rate uncertainty, by stating that the problem can be handled simply by choosing a sufficiently low actuarial rate in the computation of premia.
50. Between 1878 and 1884, Assicurazioni Generali increased these newly created reserves ('Reserve für die Coursschwankungen der Werthpapiere') from 43 000 to 845 000 Kronen, or in relation to the book value of equity, from 1 per cent to 16 per cent; source: Jahresbericht der Generali-Versicherungsgesellschaft für 1884, Trieste 1885, p. 6.
51. Although we had the opportunity for extensive talks with his (92-year-old) son, Andrea Bronzin, many questions remain open because Andrea was born after the time period most relevant for our research (1900–10).
52. See Subak (1917), pp. 257ff., and Piccoli (1882).
53. We found only one reference to this paper, in Subak (1917), p. 274. The aim of the journal was to publish critical and original surveys on subjects relevant for educational purposes, contributed by the leading scholars in the field ('Die "Monatsschrift für Handels- und Sozialwissenschaft" berichtet über alle das Gebiet ... (des) Unterrichtswesen betreffenden Fragen in kritisch zusammengefassten Originalartikeln von ersten Fachleuten'); Source: *Monatsschrift für Handels- und Sozialwissenschaft*, **12** (15 December 1904), pp. 356–60.
54. See Stillich (1909), pp. 1–18, pp. 181–227, for a representative discussion of these issues at that time.
55. Schmitt (2003), p. 145.
56. Archivio dello stato di Trieste, atto 'Listino Ufficiale della Borsa di Trieste' from 1900 to 1910.
57. Archivio dello stato di Trieste, atto Accademia di commercio e nautica in Trieste, b 101 e regg 273, 1909, AA 345/09, from 31.07.1909. Also, in August 1909, one of his beloved daughters died.
58. Obituary of his nephew, Angelo Bronzin.
59. Letter of 30 December 2004 from Arcadio Ogrin, summarizing a conversation with Andrea Bronzin.
60. De Tuoni (1925).
61. Quoted from Ara and Magris (1987), p. 48.
62. He wrote reports on the commercial education system in Italy, France, Greece, Switzerland, Hungaria, Belgium and Austria; see Subak (1917), p. 271.

References

Ara, Angelo and Claudio Magris (1987), *Trieste – Un'identità di frontiera* (*Trieste – a frontier's identity*), Einaudi.

Bachelier, Louis (1900, 1964), *Théorie de la speculation*, Annales Scientifiques de l'Ecole Normale Supérieure, Paris, Ser. 3, 17, pp. 21–88. English translation in: *The random character of stock market prices* (ed. Paul Cootner), Cambridge, MA: MIT Press (1964), pp. 17–79.

Bernstein, Peter (1992), *Capital ideas*, The Free Press.

Black, Fischer (1974), 'The pricing of complex options and corporate liabilities', unpublished manuscript, University of Chicago.

Black, Fischer (1976), 'The pricing of commodity contracts', *Journal of Financial Economics*, **3**, pp. 167–79.

Black, Fischer (1988), 'On Robert C. Merton', *MIT Sloan Management Review* (Fall).

Black, Fischer (1989), 'How we came up with the option formula', *Journal of Portfolio Management*, **15** (Winter), pp. 4–8.

Black, Fischer and Myron Scholes (1973), 'The pricing of options and corporate liabilities', *Journal of Political Economy*, **81**, pp. 637–54.

Bohlmann, Georg (1900), 'Lebensversicherungs-Mathematik' ('Life insurance mathematics'), *Enzyklopädie der mathematischen Wissenschaften*, Vol. I/ Part II/ D4b, Teubner.

Boltzmann, Ludwig (1877) 'Über die Beziehung zwischen dem zweiten Hauptsatz der mechanischen Wärmetheorie und der Wahrscheinlichkeitsrechnung resp. den Sätzen über das Wärmegleichgewicht' ('On the relation between the second law of the mechanical theory of heat and the probability calculus with respect to the theorems on thermal equilibrium'), Wien. Ber. 76, pp. 373–435, reprinted in Boltzmann (2000).

Boltzmann, Ludwig (2000), *Entropie und Wahrscheinlichkeit* (*Entropy and Probability*), Harri Deutsch (Ostwalds Klassiker der exakten Wissenschaften, vol. 286).

Bouleau, Nicolas (2004), *Financial markets and martingales. Observations on science and speculation*, Springer (translated from French original edition, Odile Jacob Edition 1998).

Breeden, Douglas and Robert Litzenberger (1978), 'Prices of state-contingent claims implicit in option prices', *Journal of Business*, **51**, pp. 621–51.

Bronzin, Vinzenz (1904), 'Arbitrage', *Monatsschrift für Handels- und Sozialwissenschaft*, **12**, pp. 356–60.

Bronzin, Vinzenz (1906), *Lehrbuch der politischen Arithmetik* (*Textbook on political arithmetics*), Franz Deuticke.

Bronzin, Vinzenz (1908), *Theorie der Prämiengeschäfte* (*Theory of premium contracts*), Franz Deuticke.

Cootner, Paul (1964), *The random character of stock market prices*, Cambridge, MA: MIT Press.

Courtadon, Georges (1982), 'A note on the premium market of the Paris Stock Exchange', *Journal of Banking and Finance*, **6**, pp. 561–5.

Cox, John and Stephen Ross (1976), 'The valuation of options for alternative stochastic processes', *Journal of Financial Economics*, **3**, pp. 145–66.

Cox, John, Stephen Ross and Mark Rubinstein (1979), 'Option pricing: a simplified approach', *Journal of Financial Economics*, **7**, pp. 229–63.

Czuber, Emanuel (1910a), *Wahrscheinlichkeitsrechnung und ihre Anwendung auf Fehlerausgleichung, Statistik und Lebensversicherung* (*Probability theory and its applications to the modelling of errors, statistics and life insurance*), 2 vols, 2nd edn, Teubner.

Czuber, Emanuel (1910b), 'Der mathematische Unterricht an der Technischen Hochschule', in: *Bericht über den mathematischen Unterricht in Österreich* (*The teaching of mathematics at technical universities*), Wien.

Delbaen, Freddy and Walter Schachermayer (2001), 'Applications to mathematical finance', Working Paper, ETHZ.

De Tuoni, Dario (1925), *Il Regio Istituto Commerciale di Trieste* (*The regional institute of commerce in Trieste*), Saggio Storico.

Einstein, Albert (1905), 'Über die von der molekular-kinetischen Theorie der Wärme geforderte Bewegung von in ruhenden Flüssigkeiten suspendierten Teilchen' ('On the movement of smell particles suspended in stationary liquids required by the molecular-kinetic theory of heat'), *Annalen der Physik*, **17**, pp. 549–60.

Fischer, Peter (2000), 'Ordnung und Chaos. Physik in Wien an der Wende zum 19. Jahrhundert' ('Order and chaos. Physics in Vienna at the turn of the 19th century'), in: *Paradigmen der Moderne* (ed. by Helmut Bachmaier), John Benjamins Publishing Company.

Flusser, Gustav (1911), 'Über die Prämiengrösse bei den Prämien- und Stellagegeschäften' ('On the size of premiums of premium contracts and straddles'), *Jahresbericht der Prager Handelsakademie*, pp. 1–30.

Geman, Helyette (2002), 'Foreword', *Mathematical Finance – Bachelier Congress 2000*, ed. by H. Geman et al., Springer.

Girlich, Hans-Joachim (2002), 'Bachelier's predecessors', Working Paper, Universität Leipzig.

Hafner, Wolfgang (2002), *Im Schatten der Derivate* (*In the shadow of derivatives*), Eichborn.

Harrison, Michael and David Kreps (1979), 'Martingales and arbitrage in multiperiod securities markets', *Journal of Economic Theory*, **20**, pp. 381–408.

Hausdorff, Felix (1897), *Das Risico bei Zufallsspielen* (*The risk of games under uncertainty*), Berichte der mathematisch-physischen Classe der Königl. Sächs. Gesellschaft der Wissenschaften zu Leipzig 49 (Sitzung vom 13 November 1897), pp. 497–548.

Haw, Mark (2005), 'Einstein's random walk', *Physics World* (January), pp. 19–22.

Herrmann, Emanuel (1869), *Die Theorie der Versicherung vom wirthschaftlichen Standpunkte* (*The theory of insurance from an economic perspective*), 2nd edn, Graz.

James, Peter (2003), *Option theory*, Wiley.

Jeffreys, Harold (1939, 1961), *Theory of probability*, Oxford: Clarendon Press.

Johnson, Norman, Samuel Kotz and N. Balakrishnan (1994), *Continuous univariate distributions*, Vol. 1, 2nd edn, Wiley.

Jovanovic, Franck and Philippe Le Gall (2001), 'Does God pratice a random walk? The "financial physics" of a 19th Century forerunner, Jules Regnault', *European Journal for the History of Economic Thought*, **8**, pp. 332–62.

Klein, M.J. (1973), 'The development of Boltzmann's statistical ideas', in: *The Boltzmann Equation* (ed. by E.G.D. Cohen and W. Thirring), Springer-Verlag, pp. 53–106.

Krüger, Lorenz, Gerd Gigerenzer and Mary Morgan (eds) (1987), *The probabilistic revolution*, 2 vols, Cambridge, MA: MIT Press.

Kuhn, Thomas (1978), *Black-body theory and the quantum discontinuity 1894–1912*, Oxford: Oxford University Press.

Leitner, Friedrich (1920), *Das Bankgeschäft und seine Technik* (*Banking and its techniques*), Sauerländer (4th edn).

Lengwiler, Yvan (2004), *Microfoundations of financial economics*, Princeton, NJ: Princeton University Press.
Loth, Wilfried (1996), *Das Kaiserreich. Obrigkeitsstaat und politische Mobilisierung* (*The empire. The authoritarian state and political mobilisation*), Munich: Deutscher Taschenbuch Verlag.
Meithner, Karl (1924), *Abschluss und Abwicklung der Effektengeschäfte im Wiener Börsenverkehr* (*Settlement and execution in securities trading at the Vienna stock exchange*), Veröffentlichungen des Banktechnischen Institutes für Wissenschaft und Praxis an der Hochschule für Welthandel in Wien.
Merton, Robert C. (1973), 'Theory of rational option pricing', *Bell Journal of Economics and Management Science*, **4**, pp. 141–83.
Pareto, Vilfredo (1900). 'Anwendung der Mathematik auf Nationalökonomie' ('Application of mathematics on political economy'), in: *Encyklopädie der Mathematischen Wissenschaften*, Vol. 1, Part 2, Leipzig (1900–1904).
Piccoli, Giorgio (1882), *Elementi di Diritto sulle Borse e sulle operazioni di Borsa secondo la Legge Austriaca e le norme della Borsa Triestina, Lezione* (*Elements of a securities and stock exchange law, based on the legal system in Austria and the rules of the Trieste stock exchange*), Trieste: Editrice la Gazetta dei Tribunali.
Regnault, Jules (1863), *Calcul des chances et philosophie de la bourse* (*Mathematics of probability and philosophy of the stock exchange*), Paris: Mallet-Bachelier et Castel (an electronic version of the book is available online).
Ross, Stephen (1976), 'Options and efficiency', *Quarterly Journal of Economics*, **90**, pp. 75–89.
Roy, Aripta (2002), 'Black-body problematic: genesis and structure', *Theory and Science*, **3**.
Samuelson, Paul A. (1963), 'Risk and uncertainty: a fallacy of large numbers', *Scientia*, **98**, pp. 108–13.
Samuelson, Paul A. (1965), 'Rational theory of warrant pricing', *Industrial Management Review*, **6** (2), pp. 13–32.
Samuelson, Paul A. (1973), 'Mathematics of speculative price', *SIAM Review (Society of Industrial and Applied Mathematics)*, **15**, pp. 1–42.
Samuelson, Paul A. and Robert C. Merton (1969), 'A complete model of warrant pricing that maximizes utility', *Industrial Management Review*, **10**, pp. 17–46.
Schmitt, Johann (2003), *Die Geschichte der Wiener Börse – Ein Vierteljahrtausend Wertpapierhandel* (*The history of the Vienna stock exchange – a quarter-millenium of securities trading*), Wien Bibliophile Edition.
Smith, Clifford (1976), 'Option pricing. A review', *Journal of Financial Economics*, **3**, pp. 3–52.
Stigler, Stephen (1999), *Statistics on the table. The history of statistical concepts and methods*, Boston, MA: Harvard University Press.
Stillich, Oskar (1909), *Die Börse und ihre Geschäfte* (*The stock exchange and its operations*), Karl Curtius.
Stoll, Hans (1969), 'The relationship between call and put option prices', *Journal of Finance*, **23**, pp. 801–24.
Subak, Giulio (1917), *Cent'Anni d'Insegnamento Commerciale – La Sezione Commerciale della I.R. Accademia di Commercio e Nautica di Trieste* (*A century of commerical education – the commerce department at the I.R. Accademia di Commercio e Nautica di Trieste*), Presso la Sezione Commerciale dell 'I.R. Accademia di Commercio e Nautica, Trieste (Publisher).
Taqqu, Murad S. (2001), 'Bachelier and his times: a conversation with Bernard Bru', *Finance and Stochastics*, **5**, pp. 3–32.
Von Kries, Johannes (1886), *Die Principien der Wahrscheinlichkeitsrechnung* (*Principles of probability*), Akademische Verlagsbuchhandlung, Tübingen: J.C.B. Mohr.
Welcker, Johannes, Jörg Kloy, Klaus Schindler and Jörg Audörsch (1988), *Professionelles Optionsgeschäft* (*Professional options trading*), Verlag Moderne Industrie.
Whelan, Shane (2002), 'Actuaries' contributions', *The Actuary* (December), pp. 34–5.
Zimmermann, Heinz and Wolfgang Hafner (2004), 'Amazing discovery – Professor Bronzin's option pricing models (1908)', Manuscript, Universität Basel.

Index

Printed and bound by CPI Group (UK) Ltd, Croydon, CR0 4YY

25/04/2025

14662136-0001